THE
CRITICAL CALLING

THE
CRITICAL CALLING

Reflections

on

Moral Dilemmas

Since

Vatican II

RICHARD A. MCCORMICK, S.J.

Georgetown University Press

Washington, D.C.

Library of Congress Cataloging-in-Publication Data

McCormick, Richard A., 1922-
    The critical calling : reflections on moral dilemmas since Vatican
II / Richard A. McCormick.
      p.   cm.
    Includes index.
    ISBN 0-87840-463-5. — ISBN 0-87840-464-3 (pbk.)
    1. Christian ethics—Catholic authors.   2. Medical ethics.
I. Title.
BJ1249.M24   1989
241'.042'09045—dc20   89-7622
                                              CIP

For Nancy

CONTENTS

PREFACE

Vatican II and the two and a half decades which followed represent the best of times or the worst of times, depending on what you read, where you sit, on your expectations, aspirations, psychological mind-set and a host of other factors. I should make it clear from the outset that I believe the Council was a work of the Spirit—desperately needed, divinely inspired, devotedly and doggedly carried through. This is not an uncritical endorsement of everything the Council did and said. Far from it. There were inconsistencies and misfires. For instance, the documents on education and communications are embarrassments that deserve the quiet obsequies they have received.

On the other hand, there are the great charters of the future: The Pastoral Constitution on the Church in the Modern World; the Constitutions on the Church, on Divine Revelation, the Decree on Ecumenism; the Declaration on Religious Liberty; the Decrees on the Liturgy and the Laity. These will not, thank God, go away. They quite simply define the consciousness of many contemporary Catholics. I do not mean to deny abuses practiced in the name of the "spirit of the Council." That was to be expected and could surprise only those with short historical memories. Rather I mean that these documents forever reversed certain ways of thinking in and about the Church, its being and mission, its relation to the world and other Christians and non-Christians. These "certain ways of thinking" are the basis for the Church's being and action in the world—in short, for its moral life and that of individual Catholics.

This book is an attempt to see how some of these "certain ways of thinking" spell themselves out in the area of moral theology. In order to put this attempt into sharper focus, I want to make two introductory points. One concerns the author, the other the subjects selected for this volume.

As for the author, this volume coincides with the completion of thirty-four years in the field of moral theology. During those more than three decades it has been my privilege to be involved in thousands of difficult "cases," in many committees and advisory boards and in the lives of many

individuals and families. Such involvement has brought me into close contact with bishops, priests, physicians, politicians, educators, married couples, attorneys and business executives. Furthermore, as teacher I have
learned a great deal from my students. These have included Jesuits prepar-
ing for the priesthood (they put up with me for seventeen years), priests
around the country, religious women, bishops, medical personnel, and the
general public. Since 1965 I have composed "Notes on Moral Theology" for
Theological Studies, a task that has brought me both enlightenment, humility
(I hope) and the friendship of colleagues around the world.

All of this does not necessarily bring wisdom, not by a long shot. But it
does generate the desire to put together some enduring impressions. This is
especially the case since the last thirty-five years span three discernibly different eras: the pre-Vatican II period, Vatican II and the years following
(roughly until around 1980), and what I will call the era of reconstruction, a
period covered by the pontificate of John Paul II. Undoubtedly my own
analyses, emphases and even choice of subjects will bear marks from all
three eras, marks that I am probably incapable of recognizing.

That brings me to the choice of subjects. Clearly, the choice would
have been virtually endless in a field as open-ended as moral theology. For
instance, I could have detailed my own involvement in some of the following events: the 1971 *Ethical Directives for Catholic Health Care Facilities*; the
struggle with *Humanae Vitae*; discussions on various versions of *The
Challenge of Peace*; the alternate pastoral that five of us (Bryan Hehir, Francis Lally, James Burtchaell, Philip Murnion and I) developed in an attempt
to improve what the late Bishop James Rausch (then secretary of the
National Conference of Catholic Bishops) regarded as a weak and pale
document (*To Live in Christ Jesus*); the Catholic-Methodist dialogues of the
late sixties; the emergence of the Kennedy Institute of Ethics in 1971;
dealings with various bishops around the country on delicate moral questions; the ethics committee of the American Hospital Association and its
deliberations, of the American Fertility Society, of the National Hospice
Organization, etc. I have chosen none of these, interesting as they are in
themselves.

Rather than such themes, I have chosen the chapters presented here.
They fall into two groupings: general moral theology and special problems.
The first grouping includes chapters that cover some areas of controversy. I
have chosen these areas because I am convinced that a contemporary
"reconstructionism" is attempting to reverse emphases and processes laid
out in Vatican II. This explains, to some extent, the prominence of Cardinal
Joseph Ratzinger in several chapters. He has been both prolific and (shall
we say?) "active." Furthermore, he is *perceived* to be the vehicle of this
reconstruction. A single, subordinate individual would scarcely merit such
attention were he not both a respected theologian and, by reason of office, a

powerful one. Thus the chapters on the Chill Factor, on dissent and on Charles Curran represent reflections on the new centralization occurring in the Church. The chapter on public policy is an attempt to avoid a new Catholic sectarianism in the public forum, a tendency powerfully (but mistakenly, in my view) supported by theologians like Stanley Hauerwas. The chapter on moral argument takes aim at what I perceive as a renewed authoritarianism in moral theology. The chapter on fundamental option represents resistance to a simplistic, one-sidedly objectivist anthropology in Catholic moral theology. The essays dealing with pluralism will obviously give little comfort to those who see reality and authentic Church teaching in rather black and white, fundamentalistic ways. I believe that the perspectives of Vatican II would slam the door firmly against the resurgent paternalism involved in such "clarities."

Something similar needs to be said about the more particular themes. Obviously, I selected these themes because I am familiar with the problems and because they are of contemporary concern. But above all, I chose them because they have carry-over value. That is, they allow for the emergence of more general themes. For instance, the chapters on homosexuality and the consistent ethic of life underline the limits of normative statements. The chapter on divorce points up the inherent limits of ecclesiastical policies and processes. The chapter on *in vitro* technology raises the issue of doctrinal development and the limits of past authentic teaching. The essay on nutrition-hydration is an attempt to force us to identify the substance of Catholic concerns as we face new technology. The chapter on the physician and teenage sexuality is much less about a case than it is about self- and vocational definition as central to the moral life. The few pages on the artificial heart are meant to operate as a symbol of the emergence of macroethical considerations (e.g., socioeconomic) in discussions of medical ethics. Such considerations increasingly frame the questions and limit the available responses.

Two things should be highlighted here. First, I take seriously the suggestion made in chapter 7—that theologians should be ready, willing and able to admit mistakes. In that spirit it goes without saying that I would welcome criticism and correction. Second, if even expression of the papal judgment (*sententia*) does not always foreclose discussion or debate—as I argue in chapter 9—this is a fortiori true of any judgment or analysis in this volume. I go out of my way to underscore what should be obvious because of the fear in some places that theologians are usurping the teaching prerogatives of the hierarchy by presenting their writings as practical, pastoral moral guidelines. The essays in this volume represent *theological explorations*. Either they make Christian sense or they do not. Whether they do or do not—and, therefore, whether they can eventually be the basis for conduct or policy—is not ultimately in the hands of the explorer alone, but in those of the larger believing community under its God-given leadership. But I remain convinced that if our "God-given leadership" is isolated from or ignores theological explorations founded not only in historical research but in contemporary life and reflection upon it, it assaults its own credibility.

In conclusion, then, my concern throughout this book has been methodological. Parts of some of the essays published here have appeared elsewhere, but in most cases I have done three things: (1) attempted to update; (2) attempted to interrelate; (3) made substantial additions.

As I look over this material, I believe it suggests—even if it does not always incarnate—the qualities we should expect of Catholic moral theology of the future: *open* (the Church is a world-church); *ecumenical* (takes seriously the activity of the Spirit in other Christian and non-Christian churches); *insight-oriented* (rather than one-sidedly moralistic); *collegial* (drawing upon the experience and reflection of all those with a true competence); *honest* (not rigged to justify pretaken positions); *centered on Christ* (an acknowledgment of the value but limits of moral philosophy); *scientifically informed* (this speaks for itself); *adult* (theology that takes personal responsibility seriously, both in developing moral convictions and applying them); *realistic* (that acknowledges the limits of human conceptual and verbal tools); *Catholic and catholic* (proud enough of and loyal enough to its heritage to be critical of it in ways that make it more challenging to and meaningful for the non-Catholic world and prevent it from becoming comfortably and/or defensively sectarian).

That is a tall order. If the essays in this book point up these qualities— even if by their absence—they will have achieved their modest purpose.

Richard A. McCormick, S.J.

Notre Dame, Indiana
August, 1988

PART I

Fundamental Moral Theology

Chapter 1

Moral Theology since Vatican II: Clarity or Chaos?

It has been nearly twenty-five years since the close (December 8, 1965) of Vatican II. That great Council opened October 11, 1962, in St. Peter's Basilica, with the opening address of John XXIII.[1] In that address Pope John stated clearly his hopes and dreams for the Council. It was not to be a Council that discussed "one article or another of the fundamental doctrine of the Church."[2] The pontiff took that for granted. As he put it, "for this a Council was not necessary." Rather Pope John expected a new "doctrinal penetration" and a fresh "formation of consciousness" in the Church. He referred to this as "bringing herself up to date where required."[3] John realized clearly that "the substance of the ancient doctrine of the deposit of faith is one thing, and the way in which it is presented is another."[4] It is this latter that should occupy the Council and make of its exercise of the magisterium one that is "predominantly pastoral in character."[5] This renovated "presentation" of the Church's riches should take place in accordance with "the signs of the times," a phrase John used in *Humanae salutis*, December 25, 1961 when he officially convoked the twenty-first ecumenical Council.[6]

John was a light-hearted, optimistic man whose optimism was rooted in a simple but profound faith. He was also a shrewd observer of the human scene. He seemed to sense in advance that his vision for the Council could die a slow and tortuous death at the hands of bureaucratic "stand-patters." So in a burst of remarkable candor, he told the assembled conciliar fathers:

> In the daily exercise of our pastoral office, we sometimes have to listen, much to our regret, to voices of persons who, though burning with zeal,

are not endowed with too much sense of discretion or measure. In these modern times they can see nothing but prevarication and ruin. They say that our era, in comparison with past eras, is getting worse, and they behave as though they had learned nothing from history, which is, none the less, the teacher of life. They behave as though at the time of former Councils everything was a full triumph for the Christian idea and life and for proper religious liberty.

We feel we must disagree with those prophets of gloom, who are always forecasting disaster, as though the end of the world were at hand.[7]

Pope John's words were not only a warning for the deliberations of 1962. They were prescient of things to come, as we shall see. Between October 11, 1962 and December 8, 1965, Vatican II elaborated and issued sixteen documents that required no less than 103,014 collegial words exclusive of footnotes. Such an explosion was bound to have an enormous influence on moral theology both within and without the Catholic community. It did.

In the theological community, one of the most significant offshoots of the Council was a more intense, and even in a sense new, ecumenism of methodology. Catholic and non-Catholic scholars worked together cooperatively as never before. It was at this time that Catholic moral theologians began joining the Society of Christian Ethics, a group that had been exclusively Protestant before that. Speaking personally, my own friendship with such outstanding Protestant theologians as James Gustafson, Paul Ramsey, Arthur Dyck, James Childress and others dates to this very period.

This interesting ecumenism of procedure brought together two currents that might otherwise have passed in the night. First, there was a growing practical rigor in non-Catholic circles—a kind of "new casuistry" in dealing with the many personal and social moral problems of the contemporary world. I associate this above all with the needling and prodding administered to his colleagues by Paul Ramsey. But the needling and prodding worked and began to surface in the work of Alan Geyer, Ralph Potter, John Swomley, Edward Leroy Long and others, especially (not exclusively) in their analyses of America's involvement in Vietnam.

On the Catholic side, there was a move away from what had been an all-too-often onesided preoccupation with such casuistry. This move involved a reexamination of some of the traditional and hallowed analyses that structured such casuistry. Indeed, the Council encouraged and even enjoined this. After noting that other theological disciplines should be renewed by livelier contact with the mystery of Christ and the history of salvation, the Council stated bluntly: "Special attention needs to be given to the development of moral theology."[8] This could hardly be taken as a compliment for those of us treading these choppy waters. Actually, that single sentence is a quite massive indictment of the so-called "manualist tradition" in moral theology. The indictment took dead aim not at the particular analyses and pastoral applications of the manuals—which were, respectively, often shrewd and compassionate—but at the very concept of the moral life that they symbolized and the corresponding emphases that they projected and inculcated.

During the past twenty-five years, moral theology has experienced this special attention so unremittingly, some would say, that the Christianity has been crushed right out of it. When reform is in human hands, the result will inevitably bear the imprint of human handling. Thus there have been oversimplifications and even caricatures, resulting in some confusion and malaise. But these things are inseparable from growth. Those who think otherwise have yet to raise a child.

When this discussion first got underway, it was crammed with fetish phrases such as "authentic," "responsible," "mature," "relational," "provisional," "contextual"—what Robert E. Fitch once referred to as "the flourishing of shibboleths . . . We look up for the water of life, but are drowned under a cascade of cliches."[9] After one has used such neon words, all the problems remain basically untouched. "Mature" in what sense? "Responsible" to whom? "Relational" in what identifiable contexts? Unless such weasel words are made carefully precise, we get increasingly mired in a method by incantation.

Thus, for example, in some of Joseph Fletcher's writings we read: "Love is the only absolute." "Study the situation and do the loving thing." "Anything is good if it is done from love." Besides confusing the good and the right, these usages remain gapingly open to Gustafson's devastating remark that "'love' like 'situation' is a word that runs through Fletcher's book (*Situation Ethics*) like a greased pig . . . It refers to anything he wants it to refer to."[10]

The Catholic community has not escaped this type of thing, and especially the polarizations that set in and are symptomatized by ad hominem putdowns and repeated exhortations to return to the securities of neoorthodoxy. Some years ago, the late bishop of Steubenville (Ohio) referred in a pastoral letter to a committee of the Catholic Theological Society of America (that had authored the book *Human Sexuality*) as "free-wheeling people who in intellectual conceit strive to twist the Word of God."[11] They are "destroyers" and "self-excommunicates." As everyone knows, the archconservative and near-libelous *The Wanderer* abounds in this type of thing. Gregory Baum and Daniel Maguire (among others) are always referred to as "ex-priests." Bryan Hehir is the "establishment liberal." Certain prelates who do not share *The Wanderer*'s venomous, nonhistorical orthodoxy are "Jadot bishops." And on and on endlessly.

My colleague and good friend Charles Curran was once described by a columnist in a Catholic diocesan newspaper as "that aging '*enfant terrible*' who issues outrageous moral pronouncements." (I cannot recall the paper. It is perhaps not an unmitigated tragedy that some diocesan weeklies are not library-preserved.) In a column in the *National Catholic Register* I was described as "one of the most dangerous men in America."[12] I hereby publicly decline the honor. *Domine non sum dignus.* Such accolades should be reserved for those who merit them: those who have no questions or doubts.

Two things become clear amid such imprecation. First, very little is enlightened. Second, among the highest and most urgent qualities required of theologians in our time is a relatively impenetrable epidermis and a sharp sense of the ridiculous. If others are taking theologians far too seriously, they at least must not take themselves too seriously. And I emphasize that for the reflections in this book. If theologians are taken too seriously, they tend to lose, besides their humility, their freedom—to probe, question, hypothesize, reformulate. On the other hand, if they are not taken seriously enough, there is serious danger of rigor mortis within the corpus of the believing community.

I noted that Pope John's reference to "prophets of gloom" was prescient of things to come. The most serious contender for that prophetic role is Joseph Cardinal Ratzinger. There is no question as to how Ratzinger would answer the questions posed in the title of this chapter. In a recent book, *The Ratzinger Report*[13]—a summary of some August 1984 interviews held in the south Tyrolean town of Bressanone—Ratzinger sees *après-concile* developments as a "progressive process of decadence." Though he discusses many areas of ecclesiastical life, it is fair to say that moral theology is high on his suspect-list. For he believes that "today the area of moral theology has become the principal locus of tension between the magisterium and theologians." He mentions several areas where this appears: premarital sexual relations, masturbation ("presented as a normal phenomenon of adolescent growth"), admission of the divorced and remarried to the sacraments, radical feminism, homosexuality.

What is the root problem? Ratzinger identifies it as "consequentialism" and "proportionalism" and sees it as infecting especially American moral theologians. According to consequentialism, as the cardinal sees it, "nothing is good or bad in itself. The goodness of an act depends only on its end and on its foreseeable and calculable consequences."[14] The diagnosis continues by revealing that this view is prevalent "in the United States where it is elaborated and diffused more than anywhere else. Some moralists have tried to soften 'consequentialism by proportionalism': the morality of an act depends only on its end and on the evaluation and comparison made by man among the goods which are at stake. Once again, it is an individual calculation, this time of the 'proportion' between good and evil."

When the interviewer, Vittorio Messori, correctly pointed out that traditional theology evaluated and compared the goods at stake in our actions, Ratzinger replied: "Certainly. The error consists in constructing a system on what was only an aspect of traditional moral theology, which ultimately, certainly did not depend on the personal evaluation of the individual. Rather, it depended on the revelation of God, on 'instructions for use' inscribed by Him in an objective and indelible way in His creation. Therefore nature, therefore man himself insofar as he is part of created nature, contain in themselves their own morality."[15]

Denial of all this leads to devastating consequences. Ratzinger sees this proportionalist methodology at the root of some liberation theologies. Thus "'the absolute good' (and that is the building of a just society, a socialist one) becomes the moral norm that justifies all the rest, including if necessary, violence, homicide, lying."[16] Ratzinger refers several times to an individual calculus, "the 'reason' of each individual" to highlight the subjectivism that seems to be his main concern in this "system."

Where did all of this originate? According to Ratzinger, it began shortly after Vatican II with the discussion on the specifically Christian character of moral norms. Some theologians concluded that there are none. "From this false starting point one arrives inevitably at the idea that morality is to be constructed uniquely on the basis of reason and that this autonomy of reason is valid even for believers."[17] Ratzinger reads this to mean that the "decalogue upon which the Church has built its objective morality" is viewed as only a "cultural product" which need not apply to us. Since the decalogue no longer provides a firm basis, these moralists have turned to a "morality of goals" or consequences. Thus "the moral theologians of the West end up confronted with an alternative: it seems necessary to them to choose between dissent from contemporary society or dissent from the magisterium."[18] No small number have chosen this latter route and, as a result, search for theories or systems that admit compromise between Catholicism and cultural currents.

In summary, Ratzinger sees postconciliar moral theology in terms of an organic development from the denial of specifically Christian moral norms. This denial means: the abandonment of revealed morality (the decalogue); the enthronement of reason; the development of a morality of goals by reason (consequentialism or proportionalism); the necessary contamination of objective morality by subjectivism (an individualist reading of proportion, etc.). This subjectivism ends up in a face-off with the magisterium. The result of this development: chaos.

I have serious problems with Ratzinger's "organic development" reading of postconciliar moral theology and with his interpretation of nearly every phase of that development. But more of that in another chapter. Before outlining my own impressions of the emphases and themes prompted, occasioned or induced by Vatican II, it is important to point out that Ratzinger's view of moral theology is but a logical unpacking of his overall approach to the postconciliar Church.

What is that approach or view? Let me say at the outset that my intent here is not polemical, but merely reportorial. "Polemics," if that term is read as connoting a confrontational testiness, gets us nowhere because it is beside the point. Nicholas Lash, in disagreeing with Ratzinger's "unqualified bleakness," writes: "It is not Catholicism that is 'decomposing' or 'collapsing,' but that particular citadel which we once erected."[19] That "citadel" was the disengagement for several centuries from the forces shaping the modern world. This disengagement spawned the "classicist mentality," to use Bernard Lonergan's phrase, which conceives culture normatively and abstractly.

> The worlds of meaning and value have, as it were, an identifiable "center" from which discrepancy and distance can readily be measured. Accordingly, to the classicist, dissent is tantamount to unfaithfulness, significant disagreement is suspect of sedition and genuine pluralism appears to be the mask of anarchy.[20]

Such a classicist mentality is the interpretative framework of Ratzinger's assessment of our predicament and of moral theology specifically. That framework, as Lash notes, *is* collapsing. Theology, the conscious reflection upon the message of the gospel, occurs in quite specific situations. Our situations are diverse, confusing, conflictual and can no longer be confined within the normative grammar of Ratzinger's classicist view.

The classicist mentality is capable of being—as, indeed, I suppose we all are—remarkably sweeping. John Mahoney, S.J., has adverted to this in Ratzinger's assessment of moral theology.[21] The cardinal, he says, sets up a confrontation between the magisterium and society and sees moral theologians as forced to choose between them. This ignores the mediating role of moral theology between gospel values and modern culture. It also identifies the moral experience and reflection of the Church with the magisterium in a way that would be unrecognizable to Vatican II. Moreover, it totally overlooks the critical function of moral theology (to aid in correcting and purifying the magisterium's teaching) and, more generally, its mediating function between the hierarchical magisterium and the faithful.

Eamon Duffy points out that the classicist mentality is also the source of easy and misleading dualisms.[22] For instance, there is the world-Church dualism in Ratzinger's thought. The world is the residence of the demonic, poisoned by the "'liberal-radical ideology of individualistic, rationalistic, hedonistic' tertiary educated bourgeoisie." At the other end of the stark polarity is an altogether idealized Church (truth, beauty, incorruptibility, stability, a superhuman reality with a "core" in dogma). *Fuga saeculi* is suggested.

In his idealized account of the Church, Ratzinger sees the theological task as defense of an unadulterated deposit. Duffy regards this as unreal, as "an attempt to bypass the messiness of reality and of engagement with the puzzle and pain of being human." Certainly it conveys no flavor of Pope John's "doctrinal penetration" and "formation of consciousness."

It is, therefore, out of a classicist mentality that Ratzinger has constructed his indictment of moral theology since the Council. Furthermore, he has elevated this indictment into a systematic, organic development toward chaos. Of course, he does not attribute this to the Council itself, but to hazy and formless appeals to the "spirit of the Council." My reading of things is remarkably different.

So what has happened since Vatican II in moral theology? It has become commonplace to say that the Council reinserted the Church into history, the wider context of Christianity and the world. It is also commonplace to interpret this as meaning the abandonment of a classical consciousness for a renewed historical consciousness. To me "historical consciousness" means taking our culture seriously as soil for the "signs of the times," as framer of our self-awareness. That means a fresh look at how Christian perspectives ought to be read in the modern world so that our practices are the best possible mediation of gospel values in the contemporary world. Fresh looks often lead to new emphases and a modification of more ancient formulations—formulations and emphases appropriate to one point in history but not necessarily to all. This is deeply resisted and especially in moral thought—probably because our own personal investments in morality are precisely very *personal*. Here I want to do nothing more than list some of the areas of major reexamination and shifting in the past twenty-five years. When these emphases are shaken and mixed, they do not mean that the Catholic Church has abandoned its hallowed tenets for contemporary fads. This is not really a "new morality" at all but the invigorating rediscovery of a very old one.

1. *The rejection of legalism.* Legalism is a point of view and a corresponding emotional response that gives priority to a human structure over the gospel purposes it serves. Practically, as Daniel Maguire has observed, it is a gimmick whereby we get all wrapped up in lesser laws and get frightfully serious about them. We convince ourselves that we are good because of their observance. This is the constant temptation of people of faith—to derive their religious security from a structure, to lean upon it. St. Paul attacked it vigorously in his letter to the Galatians. Faith, however, is something we must recover and deepen daily.

The Pharisees were familiar with this phenomenon. They gave tithes and felt justified. They would not untie knots or put out lamps on the Sabbath. The Protestant community has been stamped by it in its attitudes toward Sunday dancing, drinking and smoking, though in these latter two cases they may have been on to something we are only now realizing. Catholics, of course, showed legalistic leanings in their observance of Friday abstinence, the Eucharistic fast, Sunday Mass, servile work and in some areas of sexual morality. I recall my early days of teaching when a whole literature had developed around the distinction between sewing and knitting as forbidden Sunday work. I also recall people removing ham bits from split-pea soup on Friday thinking they were doing something profoundly important. I think we can also say that some of our structures were interpreted in this way. For instance, the rubrics for the liturgy, the procedures for our marriage tribunals, the requirements of priestly prayer.

The fearsome thing about this attitude is that it equivalently circles certain things that I *must* do. This has two implications: (1) other things do not much matter; (2) these things get me in and keep me in good standing.

The new emphases today do not, or at least should not, involve a rejection of law. As a believing community, we need good laws. They are corrective of our inconstancy and instructive of our ignorance. They function as symbols of our coherence as a visible community. But if they are to function properly for us, we must focus on the value that underlies and generates them. As Anglo-Saxons, we have often missed this. For many Catholics, Friday abstinence meant a shift from prime rib to Maine rock lobster. The penance had gone out of it. We were taking up our crosses and relaxing.

For this and other reasons Pope Paul VI, in his *motu proprio* "Paenitemini," totally reorganized the Church's discipline on penance. Attention, he said, needs to be focused on the need and value of penance in our lives. In St. Paul, concrete ethical directives are an aid to understanding something deeper—the call to sanctification. Thus, by revising penitential discipline, Pope Paul was putting the question squarely to us as individuals: "What is good penance for me, and am I doing it?"

This shift in the area of institutional penitential practices was just a symbol of a more general shift in the types of concerns we ought to have. Instead of asking "Is this a holy day of obligation?" we now are invited to ask: "What does it mean to be a Christian in a sensate culture?" "How does one grow as a Christian in a four-day-a-week culture?" "What is the Christianly constructive use of leisure, money in my life?" "How can we, as a married couple, be a sacrament to the world, revealing in our lives a little of what God is like?"

The moral theological questions we consider important are tied more to values and life-style than they are to rules and acts. One can overreact here, of course. In this sense I agree with Hans Küng that people who no longer worship with the community on Sundays should stop calling themselves Catholics. The new emphasis simply reminds us that we can observe all the details of laws and rules and end up spiritual pigmies.

2. The depth of the moral life. In our ordinary way of thinking and acting, we identify the moral-spiritual life with the thing done or omitted. Certain things are mortal sins, others venial, and so on. The attention is heavily focused on discrete actions and omissions, especially of an external kind. Actually, in and beyond such symptomatic manifestations there is something much deeper. Morality is above all a matter of a profound personal response, the acceptance and deepening of God's enabling love into my being, or, by contrast, the ratification of sin in the unfolding of my life. Thus the moral act is primarily a profound personal self-disposition, self-actualization, the yes of faith flowering into love. Sin is a change in this basic orientation; conversion is a restabilizing of this fundamental posture. Thus, Fuchs points out that it is more Johannine to say "qui tollit peccatum mundi" than "peccata mundi."[23]

The love that the Holy Spirit is working within us cannot be identified with this or that action, sacrifice, observance or failure. It is primarily and much more the use of our fundamental freedom, what theologians refer to as the fundamental option. When the moral spiritual life is viewed in this way, it is much more a growth process, a deepening of the biblical *adherere Deo*, a radicalizing of our fundamental position or option.

An image can help. Marriage is a thousand and one things a week (strains, difficulties, frustrations, sacrifices, celebrations), but beneath them all, two are becoming one in a symbiosis that remains mysterious and only dimly perceived as it is being lived. The same is true of our friendship with God.

The notion of fundamental freedom (and of a fundamental option) entered systematic theological reflection largely through the anthropology of Karl Rahner. Rahner viewed freedom not simply as the power to perform this or that action, but as the transcendent power to decide about and actualize ourselves. Thus the human person is a "many-layered being . . . constructed as it were in layers starting at an interior core and becoming more and more external."[24] On this basis Rahner distinguishes core (or transcendental) freedom and freedom of choice (categorical freedom). As Ronald Modras summarizes it:

Here we find the basis in Rahner's anthropology for distinguishing between ordinary free decisions and those which constitute a fundamental
option. It is out of the inmost core of our beings that we make those basic
decisions of transcendental freedom (fundamental options) which lead to
or away from God.[25]

The notion of fundamental or core freedom has enormous implications for
moral theology. For instance, it affects our notion of sin and conversion.
Modras puts it neatly:

Formerly, it was generally presumed that every conscious and free commission of a seriously wrong act involved a mortal sin, and that one could
sin and repent in a succession virtually approaching the proverbial seven
times a day. The theology of fundamental option along with modern psychology rejects this presumption by recognizing that such acts can be free
and yet not so totally involving as to constitute a negative fundamental
option, synonymous with mortal sin.[26]

Furthermore, the notion will clearly affect our concept and practice of sacramental confession, our notions of what is objectively serious matter, our
attitudes toward temptation, prayer, Church laws and a whole host of
things. The notion of fundamental freedom is taken for granted in most
theological circles—so much so that even the Congregation for the Doctrine of the Faith used the concept in its controversial "Declaration on Certain Sexual Questions." In some recent literature the idea of a fundamental
option has come under some fire. But more of that in chapter 10. Here I
simply want to indicate that it is one of the themes or perspectives that entered moral theology systematically about the time of the Council.

3. *The social character of the moral life.* It is true to say, I believe, that the Catholic community has had a veritable flow of outstanding
social statements from the time of *Rerum Novarum* through *Pacem in Terris*,
Octogesima Adveniens, *Laborem Exercens* to *Sollicitudo Rei Socialis*. Yet it is
also true to say that corporately we are possessed of a dormant social conscience. Far too many think of morality and the moral-spiritual life in
domestic terms—and this in spite of the words of Paul VI (in *Octogesima Adveniens*) that "these are questions that because of their urgency, extent and
complexity, must, in the years to come, take first place among the preoc-
cupations of Christians . . ."[27]

One of the emphases in contemporary moral theology is, therefore, an
emphasis on the fact that our radical acceptance of God is tied to love of the
neighbor—a love that secures rights, relieves suffering, promotes growth.
God is speaking to us in history and we are not free to be uninvolved. This
means not simply individual one-on-one action for those we generally avoid

(the mentally ill, the starving, the sick, criminals, poor minorities, etc.); it means organizing the corporate power of the community in such a way that so-called "sinful structures" are changed. The structures and institutions which oppress people, alienate them, deprive them of rights, are embodiments of our sinful condition. The sins and selfishness of one generation become the inhibiting conditions of the next. The impoverishment of the exploited embodies the selfishness of the exploiter.

Contemporary moral theology has come to realize in a fresh and new way that just as Christ's liberation is twofold (from sin and its expressions in our structures and institutions), so the Church, the believing community, is simply a continuation of Christ's liberating presence, and *thus*, a sacrament to the world. The conclusion of the study document of the Inter-American Bishops' meeting (Mexico City, 1971) put it this way: "If the Church's message and mission are redemptive, it must denounce and attack sin wherever it reigns, whether over an individual's selfish heart or throughout an unjust social order."[28] In summary then: if personal sin embodies itself in unjust and enslaving structures, if Christ is the liberator supreme (in the words of Paul VI), if the Church is the continuance of his liberating presence—then clearly the Church's main task is liberation, and this means from all enslavement, both its roots in sin and its appearance in unjust structures. Just as there is a continuity between sin and social enslavement, so there is a continuity between personal liberation by grace and concrete social action.

I emphasize this because it is so easily overlooked or forgotten. There are still millions of people who externalize their Samaritanism or their social concern with statements such as "Some of my best friends are black." This only thinly disguises a radical noninvolvement, and it makes the Church simply incredible. If persons are truly what we say they *are* (redeemed in Christ and sharers of His unspeakable sonship), if we are *really* this and not merely imprisoned spirits who will be this in the hereafter if we behave, then preaching this (evangelization) means doing all those things that remind persons of their true dignity. For if the person *is* someone of dignity, he/she must be treated as such. To deny human rights or to tolerate their deprivations is to tell people in a practical way that they are not worth these rights, that they are not dignified.

We are reminded of our true worth and dignity by being treated in accordance with this dignity. It is axiomatic that we expand and become capable of love by being loved. Hence the Church's proclamation is necessarily action. She does not civilize in order to evangelize (a kind of *removens prohibens*). She civilizes because that is an essential aspect of evangelizing. It is the most concrete and effective, indeed, indispensable way of communicating to human beings their real worth—that is, the good news. Proclamation of the gospel is by inner necessity concern for those to whom the gospel is proclaimed.

4. The centrality of the person in moral thought. This is a technical emphasis in moral theology but one with enormous implications. Perhaps it could be summarized as follows. Moral norms are generalizations about the significance or meaning of our conduct. If concrete actions promote a value, they are prescribable. If they generally attack a value, they are generally proscribed. If they always attack a value, they are always proscribed. Now, whether an action attacks a value or not, whether it is loving or not, is determined by its relation to the order of persons.

In an earlier period, significance was often drawn from an analysis of faculties and finalities. Thus the faculty of speech was given to us for the purpose of communicating true information. To use it in a way contradictory of this purpose (*locutio contra mentem*) was morally wrong. If, however, we view speech in broader perspective and see it not simply as an informative power, but as an endowment meant to promote the overall good of persons in community, we have altered the basis for our definition of a lie.

This emphasis was explicitly introduced by Vatican II. *Gaudium et Spes* asserted that "the moral aspect of any procedure . . . must be determined by objective standards which are based on the nature of the person and the person's acts."[29] The official commentary on this wording noted two things: (1) The expression formulates a general principle that applies to all human actions, not just to marriage and sexuality where the phrase occurs. (2) The choice of this expression means that "human activity must be judged insofar as it refers to the human person integrally and adequately considered."[30]

Clearly, this is of basic importance to moral methodology. But what does it mean to use as a criterion "the human person integrally and adequately considered"? The best explanation I have seen comes from Louis Janssens.[31] "Integrally and adequately" refers to the human person in all her/his essential aspects. Janssens lists eight such aspects. The human person is (1) a subject (normally called to consciousness, to act according to conscience, in freedom and in a responsible way); (2) a subject embodied; (3) an embodied subject that is part of the material world. (4) Persons are essentially directed to one another (only in relation to a Thou do we become I). (5) Persons need to live in social groups, with structures and institutions worthy of persons. (6) The human person is called to know and worship God. (7) The human person is a historical being, with successive life stages and continuing new possibilities. (8) All persons are utterly original but fundamentally equal.

Janssens then formulates from these characteristics a general criterion of the rightness or wrongness of human actions. An act is morally right if, according to reason enlightened by faith, it is beneficial to the human person "adequately considered in himself (nos. 1 and 2) and in his relations (nos. 3, 4, 5, 6)." He refers to this as an "ethic of responsibility on a personalistic foundation."

This becomes particularly delicate and controversial in the area of sexual ethics. In impoverishing summary, what many are saying is that the significance—morally speaking—of our conduct must be derived from its relationship to the overall good of persons. Thus, for example, where contraception or sterilization is concerned, the appropriate question is: does contraception or sterilization promise to help or hinder the total relationship that is marriage? Faculties and powers are for persons, not vice versa. Or as Bernard Häring once put it to me: the tubes are for the woman, not the woman for the tubes. Andreas Laun worded it as follows: actions are morally right "not because they correspond to the nature of the agent, but because they respond properly to the ethical importance of the object."[32] Whether some procedure or form of conduct is for the overall good of the person is not always an easy assessment. We are always liable to self-interested judgments and insensitivity to the call of basic values.

Furthermore, because of our limitations our actions are often characterized by ambiguity. That is, they are at times simultaneously both detrimental and beneficial to the human person, containing both values and disvalues. Thus, an amputation can be indicated to save one's life (value) but necessarily involves a burden for the person (disvalue). The key moral question for Janssens is: When is there a *ratio proportionata* "to perform an activity in a morally responsible manner which simultaneously results in values and disvalues?" Janssens insists that the answer must consider the action as a whole (exterior action, intention, situation or circumstances, consequences); what, in a recent study, Anthony J. Blasi calls "the emergent ensemble."[33] Janssens insists that only about this *whole* can it be said whether or not an action is worthy of man or appropriate for the human person. He contrasts this with an approach he calls "Roman theology," which believes it possible to pass a judgment on the "external act alone." I shall expand the implications of this in chapter 7.

What has happened in the past is, I believe, that we have attached an almost mechanical significance to the *inclinationes naturales*. Thus we saw divine providential wisdom at work in these natural purposes. *Deus* (natura) *nihil facit inane* (God does nothing in vain). When natural ends, by appeal to God's creative wisdom, are viewed as inviolable, the significance gets set and the norm becomes absolute. Thus, no contraception, no matter what. However, many contemporary theologians argue that the extent to which these "natural ends" must be respected in individual cases depends on whether they must deserve the preference when in relationship with concurring personal values. To decide that is the natural end of the power of human judgment. In other words, to say that procreation is the highest end served by sexual intercourse is not to say that such an end must always be served, or that its frustration is necessarily wrong.

In the *Questiones quodlibetales*, St. Thomas laid the foundation for this type of assessment. He wrote: "There are some actions which, absolutely considered, involve a definite deformity or disorder, but which are made right by reason of particular circumstances, as the killing of a man . . . involves a disorder in itself, but, if it be added that the man is an evildoer killed for the sake of justice . . . it is not sinful, rather it is virtuous."[34] Here something which is a "deformity" is "made right by reason of particular circumstances." Contemporary moral theology would say "Amen" to that and would add that the Thomistic phrase "by reason of particular circumstances" can be translated "by reason of the good of the person or persons."

It is interesting to note that St. Thomas once wrote that "we do not wrong God unless we wrong our own good."[35] His "our own good" is identical with the "person adequately considered." This matter is of major methodological importance, because there are still some theologians who acknowledge this in theory but whose analyses and conclusions reveal different perspectives at work. For this reason discussions of these matters quickly become discussions about authority, that is, that notwithstanding the inner reasonableness of an analysis or argument, official teachers have taken an authoritative position and that settles the matter.

5. *The tentativeness of moral formulations.* This is an aspect of historical consciousness that is upsetting to many people. Deep within us is a hankering that our clarities be sempiternally valid. It is simply more comfortable that way, especially when the authority of the institutional Church stands behind a particular formulation. Yet two influences have combined to lead us to a renewed awareness of the necessary tentativeness of our formulations: the complexity and changeability of reality and a knowledge of the cultural influences that went into past formulations. This suggests powerfully to us that our grasp of significance is at any time limited, rooting as it does in limited self-awareness and imperfect formulations.

This tentativeness was explicitly recognized by the Vatican Council. Following John XXIII, it states: "The deposit of faith or revealed truths are one thing; the manner in which they are formulated without violence to their meaning and significance is another."[36] Here we have a clear distinction made between the substance of a teaching and its formulation. This distinction has led Karl Rahner to assert that concrete moral statements (behavioral norms) are inherently provisional and simply incapable of being dogmas of the Church.[37]

Moral theologians are more aware than ever of the validity of this distinction—and, I must add, of the difficulty of applying it. There is, therefore, a new willingness to reexamine past formulations. We know that at a given time our formulations—being the product of limited persons, with limited insight, and with imperfect philosophical and linguistic tools— are only more or less adequate to the substance of our convictions. It is the task of theology constantly to question and challenge these formulations in an effort to reduce their inadequacy. This is not an attack on value or on authority, though unfortunately it is perceived as such by some elements in the Church.

The assertion of the Council in distinguishing formulation and substance must be properly understood. Otherwise theology could easily be reduced to word shuffling. If there is a distinction between substance and formulation, there is also an extremely close, indeed inseparable, connection. One might say they are related as are body and soul. The connection is so intimate that it is difficult to know just what the substance is amid variation of formulation. Indeed, it is so intimate that improving a formulation may involve, at times, altering a conclusion.

I want to take two sensitive instances of this from the area of applied moral theology. The first concerns life, and specifically abortion. We know down our pulses as human beings (and with powerful supportive warrants from our belief that all persons are unique and equal before our heavenly Father) that human life is sacred, that no person may play God with regard to another. Yet we also know from experience that there are tragic instances of conflict, instances where we must kill to maintain our grasp on the very values to which we adhere. Across our history we have attempted to provide for these instances as well as contain them by reversing the conflicted conditions that lead to them. "No *direct* killing of an *innocent* person" is the rule we have developed to state the exceptions and to contain them.

Applying this to the abortion situation, several popes have stated that direct abortion is never permissible, even to save the life of the mother. Thus in the classic if rare case where the options are two (do nothing and both mother and nonviable child die; abort and save the only life that can be salvaged), it was concluded: better two deaths than one murder. Almost no one would hold that conclusion today. Some would argue that in such a case the abortion is indirect. Others would say that it is direct but morally permissible as the only life-saving, life-serving alternative available. The Belgian hierarchy, in its pastoral on abortion, summarized the matter as follows: "The moral principle which ought to govern the intervention can be formulated as follows: Since two lives are at stake, one will, while doing everything possible to save both, attempt to save one rather than to allow two to perish."[38] This is not identical with "no direct taking of innocent human life."

In summary, "no *direct* taking of *innocent* human life" seems to be a concrete rule teleologically narrowed to its present form rather than a principle. I shall return to this point in chapters 6 and 12. If such rules are viewed as absolutely final and all-encompassing, both their origin and their nature are obscured. Furthermore, we run several risks in the process. First, we risk missing the teleological character of exception-making. Second, in the process of such oversight, we lose the dynamic of the movement away from taking more life. In other words, we risk hardening and perpetuating our allowances (exceptions to the presumption against taking life) when in changing times they are no longer justifiable. Thus, overemphasis on the absoluteness of the rule "no *direct* taking of *innocent* life" might comfort people in their very aggressive notions of war and their sometimes vindictive sentiments about capital punishment. That these can work against a healthy ethic of life seems clear.

The only point I am making here is that our formulations of behavioral norms are only more or less adequate, and for this reason are inherently revisable. The fact that some theological formulations have been thought useful by the magisterium of the Church does not change this state of affairs. Historical consciousness has made us freshly aware of the fact that it is our onerous theological task to continue to explore theological formulations, even some very hallowed ones. If we do not, we become imprisoned by words and commit the ever fresh *magnalia Dei* to unwarranted risks.

Let another example be in the area of sexuality. For centuries the Church has been concerned to preserve the integrity and viability of sexual intimacy and language. This has led her to view sexuality as the language of covenanted friendship, marriage. She has equivalently been saying that sex and eros are fleeting, fickle and frustrative unless they live in and are supported by *philia*, the friendship of two people who take public responsibility for each other in a bold venture of family-making. In formulating this value judgment, she has, of course, condemned premarital sexual intimacy. Of such conduct she has at one time or other said the following:

1. It is morally wrong—that is, something is always missing in such conduct.
2. It is wrong because it is *contra bonum prolis*, violative of the procreative atmosphere which is inseparably associated with sexual intimacy.
3. It is intrinsically evil—that is, *ex objecto* and regardless of circumstances.
4. It is seriously wrong in each act.
5. There is a presumption of serious guilt on the part of those involved.

I would suggest that the Church's substantial teaching is contained in the first statement. The last four statements variously involve cultural, philosophical and empirical data that are subject to modification and reformulation. This point is very effectively illustrated in Lisa Sowle Cahill's recent book on sexuality.[39] As Congar puts it: "The encyclicals of Leo XIII and Pius XII are theological. They are not purely the expression of apostolic witness according to the needs of the times, but a *doctrine* of the 'cathedrae magistralis' incorporating data from the natural law, human wisdom and classical theology."[40] Certain elements in the Church—especially archconservative elements—identify changeable formulations with the doctrine of the Church. The next step is to accuse of disloyalty theologians who are attempting to purify these formulations. In my jugdment this is responsible for much of the current polarization in the Church. Notwithstanding the certainties of nay-sayers, a sense of tentativeness is inseparable from historical consciousness.

6. The nature of the moral magisterium. Closely connected with the foregoing point is the change that has been occurring in our conception of the magisterium. This traces, of course, to subtle but profound changes in the very notion of the Church, the *ecclesia*, and of effective teaching in our time. For the magisterium is nothing more or less than the *Church teaching*.

It has been pointed out by Yves Congar, Avery Dulles and others that the contemporary understanding of the magisterium is relatively recent, dating to the 1830s. It reached its pinnacle in the encyclical *Humani Generis* under Pius XII. This model treats teaching in a highly juridical way. The focus that went into its making—about which I will have more to say in a subsequent chapter—produced a notion of magisterium with the following three characteristics: (1) an undue distinction between the teaching and learning function in the Church, with a consequent unique emphasis on the right to teach—and relatively little on the duty to learn and the sources of learning in the Church; (2) an undue identification of the teaching function with a single group in the Church, the hierarchy; (3) an undue isolation of a single aspect of teaching, the judgmental, the decisive, the "final word." Thus it was taken for granted by many that on any moral problem, however complex, *Roma locuta causa finita*. The term "magisterium" came to mean the hierarchical issuance of authoritative decrees.

Within this theological perspective—altogether understandable within the context of the factors that gave rise to it—the appropriate response of the loyal Catholic to authentic teaching was said to be obedience. Some still speak of the "obligation to assent." The teaching was as correct as the authority was legitimate. Thus Congar notes that *Humani Generis* brought these developments to a high point in two ways: "(1) The ordinary magisterium of the pope demands a total obedience—'he who hears you hears me.' (2) The (or one) role of theologians is to justify the pronouncements of the magisterium."[41]

The factors that gave rise to and supported this notion of magisterium have altered in the past fifteen to twenty years, as I indicate in chapter 5. Gradually—and even against resistance in some quarters—a fresh notion of the teaching function of the Church has unfolded in our midst. It is a notion with the following three characteristics: (1) the learning process is seen as essential to the teaching process; (2) teaching is a multidimensional function, of which the judgmental or decisive is only one aspect; (3) the teaching function involves the charisms of many persons. Thus we are freshly aware of the old distinction between *magisterium cathedrae magistralis* and *magisterium cathedrae pastoralis*. Bishop Butler has put this in less barbaric language when he says that we all are at times genuine *magistri* in the Church.[42]

Within these perspectives much more attention is given to evidence and analyses in evaluating authentic teaching. Only persuasive reasons command assent. The appropriate response to authentic noninfallible teaching is no longer seen as unquestioning acceptance and obedience. Rather, it is a docile personal attempt to assimilate and appropriate the teaching—a process that can end in failure or dissent.

No one has put this better than Bishop B.C. Butler. "To require," he says, "the same adhesion for doctrines that are indeed taught by officials with authority but to which the church has not irrevocably committed herself is to abuse authority." After referring to the "respect that is due to the considered actions and utterances of those in positions of legitimate and official authority," Butler states the proper response: "the mood of the devout believer will be . . . a welcoming gratitude that goes along with the keen alertness of a critical mind, and with a good will concerned to play its part both in the purification and the development of the Church's understanding of her inheritance . . . "[43]

When we realize that we must bring "the keen alertness of a critical mind" to official teachings if we are to contribute to them—as we must if we are to stay loyal to the truth—we realize also that dissent is a distinct and nonthreatening possibility. I say "nonthreatening possibility" because Bishop Juan Arzube (Los Angeles) is correct when he says: "There must . . . be room for legitimate criticism and dissent from the ordinary teaching of the Church, given the very real possibility of the development of the doctrine by way of correction and change of such teaching. To think otherwise is to sink our heads in the sand and hinder the work of the Spirit."[44] For some, to hear a bishop speak of the need for "correction and change" in official teaching will sound "offensive to pious ears," as we say, and even disloyal. For a renewed historical consciousness, however, it will be a welcome breath of fresh air, possibly even of that wind we know as the Spirit. For it is clearer now than ever that moral formulations do call for change and that this is a developmental process, a process I like to call the teaching-learning function of the Church. We would not have *Dignitatis Humanae* (on religious liberty) had not John Courtney Murray conducted a long, uphill, dissenting, and personally painful critique of the teaching of *Mirari Vos* and the Syllabus of Errors. It is especially disturbing that a Church whose trust in the Spirit is second to none should feel threatened by such necessary critiques.

7. *Rejection of paternalism in moral pedagogy for a pedagogy of personal responsibility.* It is easy, of course, to caricature here. But what I have in mind is an approach toward conscience formation which was too onesidedly paternalistic—a refusal by the individual to share in the discovery of moral truth. Too often in the past an individual would approach a priest, usually in confession, as one prepared to give the answers. The person would detail the facts; the confessor would apply them with a *licet* or *non licet*.

We realize now better than ever that the articulated wisdom of the community—the teaching of the magisterium—*enlightens* conscience; it does not *replace* it. As *Gaudium et Spes* puts it:

> Let the layman not imagine that his pastors are always such experts that to every problem which arises, however complicated, they can readily give him a concrete solution, or even that such is their mission. Rather, enlightened by Christian wisdom and giving close attention to the teaching authority of the Church, let the layman take on his own distinctive role.[45]

That is, I think, downright revolutionary. It is a final goodbye to the dependency instinct in all of us. But let us be clear about what that statement does not say. It does not say that we abandon consultation in the formation of conscience. It does not say we decide by ourselves what is right and wrong. We are members of a community and we form our consciences in a community, a community of experience, reflection and memory. One who thinks he is simply autonomous in the formation of conscience is roughly analogous to the patient who makes his own diagnosis. That is a path to the intensive care room and eventually the morgue. It can be no less so in the spiritual life.

What the Council was saying here was quite different. It was saying two things. First, it was reminding lay people—and really all of us—that we have certain competences and therefore certain responsibilities. We are expected to make ourselves knowledgeable about the Christian and moral dimensions of these competences—and bring this knowledge to the Church. Thus, doctors, just by being M.D.s, do not have thereby an insight into the Christian dimensions of the healing profession. The Church is urging them to develop this. The same could be said of married persons, lawyers, teachers, business persons.

Second, this very pregnant statement is saying that there are applications of the well-formed conscience that cannot be preprogrammed. They remain the individual's responsibility. This is so because of the very individual, complex and changing character of the choices which must be discerned by the well-formed conscience. Is anyone, for example, in prior possession of the truth, and very detailed moral truth, where the ethics of recombinant DNA research is involved? I think not.

These are but some of the emphases which cluster about our new historical consciousness in moral theology. There are many others: a more dynamic, less aprioristic notion of natural law; collegiality by the teaching office of the Church in the discovery of moral truth; respect for the religious liberty of others in implementing our convictions in the public forum; a fresh look at our pastoral policies and practices where certain irregularities are involved (e.g., the divorced and remarried); a new awareness of the conflict model of decision-making, and of the sinfulness of the world in which we must pattern our lives and grow in Christlikeness; a more positive and pastoral pedagogy in the communication of moral values.

Are there dangers in some of these emphases? Most certainly. History shows our penchant to fluctuate between theological extremes, a kind of "teetertotter" syndrome. Because we have been legalists in our past, our escape involves the danger of antinomianism. We have been overauthoritarian; our escape involves the danger of anarchism. We have been "supernaturalists"; our escape runs the danger of secular paganism, a kind of baptism of the status quo. We have been individualists; our correction of this risks a suffocating collectivism. Overreactions incorporate the very weaknesses of that against which they react.

I see the dangers of the moral currents that have flowed freely since Vatican II as especially the following: a neospiritualism which ignores the concrete character of sin and virtue; a selective responsibility which collapses responsibility in one sphere to emphasize it in another; a narrow consequentialism which ignores the fact that the neighbor is Everyman—or Everyperson; a rationalistic secularism which ignores the deep influences of Christian realities on our moral sensitivities and imaginations.

Some—those Pope John XXIII referred to as "prophets of gloom"—will see these dangers as a cause for corporate ecclesiastical panic. I can read *The Ratzinger Report* in no other way. In the words of Fergus Kerr, O.P., it is "pervaded with images of entropy." It sees the Church "infected by some degenerative malady," "drowning under hostile seas," plagued with "alarming symptoms of almost terminal disease."[46] I do not see things this way at all. I hope that in the following chapters I can—largely implicitly, I suppose—explain why. To the question "Do we have clarity or chaos?" I would say: a little bit of both. But it is always so in human affairs. It can be no less so in the *ecclesia semper reformanda*. Even a minimum residual trust in the Spirit—the Holy Spirit—can inspire the hope, even the conviction that we moral theologians, in our honest if stumbling efforts to recover the freshness of a very old morality, will not, indeed *cannot* scuttle the Bark of Peter. For if the Council taught us one thing, it is this: it is more than theologians who man the oars.

Notes

1. *Documents of Vatican II*, ed. Walter M. Abbott, S.J. (New York: America Press, 1966), 710-19. Hereafter cited simply as *Documents*.
2. *Documents*, 715.
3. *Documents*, 712.
4. *Documents*, 715.
5. *Documents*, 715.
6. *Documents*, 706.
7. *Documents*, 712.
8. *Documents*, 452.
9. Robert E. Fitch, *Religion in Life* 35 (1966):186.
10. James M. Gustafson, "How Does Love Reign?" *Christian Century* 83 (1966):654.
11. *Steubenville Register*, 7 July 1977.
12. Patrick Riley, "Fr. Richard McCormick: Theologian as Ethicist," *National Catholic Register*. The date has faded on my copy; but I believe the year was 1978.
13. Joseph Ratzinger, *The Ratzinger Report* (San Francisco: Ignatius Press, 1985). Hereafter cited simply as *Report*.
14. *Report*, 90.
15. *Report*, 91.
16. *Report*, 91.
17. *Report*, 89.
18. *Report*, 86.
19. Nicholas Lash, "Catholic Theology and the Crisis of Classicism," *New Blackfriars* 66 (1985):179-87.
20. Loc. cit., 282.
21. John Mahoney, S.J., "On the Other Hand . . . ," *New Blackfriars* 66 (1985):288-98.
22. Eamon Duffy, "Urbi, but not Orbi," *New Blackfriars* 66 (1985):272-78.
23. Joseph Fuchs, S.J., *Theologia Moralis Generalis*, pars altera (Rome: Gregorian University, 1967-68), 110.
24. Karl Rahner, "Some Thoughts on a Good Intention," *Theological Investigations* 3 (Baltimore: Helicon, 1967), 113. Cf. also 16, passim.
25. Ronald Modras, "The Implications of Rahner's Anthropology for Fundamental Moral Theology," *Horizons* 12 (1985):70-90, at 74.
26. Loc. cit., 86.

27. Paul VI, *Octogesima Adveniens*, *Catholic Mind* 69 (1971):37-58, at no. 7.

28. This study document was prepared by William F. Ryan, S.J., and Joseph Komonchak. It may be found in *Catholic Mind* 64 (1971):13-28. Similar concepts are found throughout the synodal document "Justice in the World." Cf. *Catholic Mind* 70 (1972):52-64. The notion of "sinful structures" received powerful reinforcement in John Paul II's *Sollicitudo Rei Socialis* (1988). He noted: "If the present situation can be attributed to difficulties of various kinds, it is not out of place to speak of 'structures of sin'." The pontiff continued: "'Sin' and 'structures of sin' are categories which are seldom applied to the situation of the contemporary world. However, one cannot easily gain a profound understanding of the reality that confronts us unless we give a name to the root of the evils which afflict us." *New York Times*, 20 February 1988.

29. *Documents*, 256.

30. *Schema constitutionis pastoralis de ecclesia in mundo huius temporis: Expensio modorum partis secundae* (Vatican Press, 1965), 37-38.

31. Louis Janssens, "Artificial Insemination: Ethical Reflections," *Louvain Studies* 8 (1980):3-29.

32. Andreas Laun, "'Natur'—Quelle von sittliche Normen," *Die neue Ordnung* 31 (1977):97-111.

33. Anthony J. Blasi, *Moral Conflict and Christian Religion* (New York: Peter Lang, 1988).

34. *Quaestiones quodlibetales* 9, q.7, a.15.

35. *Summa contra gentiles* 3, 122.

36. *Documents*, 268-69.

37. Karl Rahner, "Basic Observations on the Subject of Changeable and Unchangeable Factors in the Church," *Theological Investigations* 14 (New York: Seabury, 1976):3-23, at 14.

38. "Déclaration des évêques belges sur l'avortement," *Documentation catholique* 70 (1973):432-38.

39. Lisa Sowle Cahill, *Between the Sexes: Foundations for a Christian Ethics of Sexuality* (Mahwah, N.J.: Paulist, 1985).

40. Yves Congar, O.P., "A Brief History of the Forms of the Magisterium," *Readings in Moral Theology No. 3*, ed. Charles E. Curran and Richard A. McCormick, S.J. (Mahwah, N.J.: Paulist, 1982): 320-21.

41. Congar, loc. cit., 325.

42. Christopher Butler, O.S.B., "Authority and the Christian Conscience," in *Readings No. 3* (cf. note 40):182.

43. Christopher Butler, loc. cit., 186.

44. Juan Arzube, "When Is Dissent Legitimate?" *Catholic Journalist* (June 1978):5.

45. *Documents*, 244.

46. Fergus Kerr, O.P., "The Cardinal and Post-Conciliar Britain," *New Blackfriars* 66 (1985):299-308.

Chapter 2

Dissent in the Church: Loyalty or Liability?

The years immediately ahead promise to be interesting for those who navigate the choppy waters of moral theology. The reflections in chapter 1 already foreshadowed this. Just five years ago, Cardinal Edouard Gagnon, head of the Vatican's Pontifical Council for the Family, suggested that ninety percent of American moral theologians should seek employment elsewhere ("change 90 percent of the teachers of moral theology and stop them from teaching" was the cited elegance).[1] A similar "final solution" was proposed recently by John Kippley. In answer to a questionnaire about what the Extraordinary Synod of Bishops of 1985 should do, Kippley gave as one of his answers: "Declare Curran, McCormick, McBrien, Kosnik, Keane etc. as 'not a Catholic theologian' and get them out of their prestigious positions of power."[2] That little "etc." looks innocent enough. Actually, it is daunting. It constitutes a huge net with a potentially enormous haul.

Kippley's concerns are quite narrowly focused (birth control). He is the founder of the Couple to Couple League which exists to promote and instruct in natural family planning. His remarks appeared in a newsletter of a group whose membership litmus test is acceptance of the *Hauptthese* of *Humanae Vitae*.

But I believe it fair to say that there are pockets of Kippleys in the contemporary American Church whose concerns include but are not limited to birth control. According to press reports, Cardinal Bernard Law complained in the 1985 Synod about theological dissent in the American Church. Exegete Raymond Brown, S.S., is regularly picketed, as is Charles Curran. Hosts of theologians are pilloried in the conservative press. The list is impressive. It includes Avery Dulles, S.J., Richard McBrien, Gregory

Baum, Margaret Farley, Walter Burghardt, S.J., Joseph Fuchs, S.J., Daniel Maguire, Bruno Schüller, S.J., Bryan Hehir, David Tracy, Anthony Kosnik, Philip Keane and a host of others. I have even been so honored at times. Some of these people are routinely excluded from certain dioceses. Theresa Kane, the Mercy sister who, in the presence of John Paul II, requested fullness of ministry for women, is pictured as the paradigm of defiant antipapalism. Nor are bishops spared. Some who have received their stripes are Peter L. Gerety (Newark), Raymond G. Hunthausen (Seattle), Rembert Weakland (Milwaukee), James V. Casey (Denver), Joseph Bernardin (Chicago), Joseph L. Hogan (formerly of Rochester), Thomas Gumbleton (Detroit), Kenneth Untener (Saginaw), Francis J. Mugavero (Brooklyn), Raymond A. Lucker (New Ulm), Walter Sullivan (Richmond), etc., and perhaps above all Jean Jadot, former apostolic delegate to the United States. If such bishops are not dissenters themselves, then they are scored for "harboring" dissenters, favoring them, being soft on them, being silent about them and, in general, for conducting themselves in a thoroughly Christian way.

But this matter should be brought closer to home. I want to detail several personal incidents that reveal the depth and feeling that surround the issue of dissent. In late July, 1968, Pope Paul VI issued his encyclical *Humanae Vitae*. I had been studying the problem intensely for years. Charles Curran phoned me at 11 P.M. the night before the encyclical appeared in *The New York Times* and asked if I was ready to sign a dissenting statement. I said no. I wanted to study the encyclical first and formulate my own response for the December (1968) issue of *Theological Studies*. I did so. After anguishing over the matter hundreds of hours, I finally formulated my response. It read in part as follows.

> In the light of these reflections it is the opinion of the compositor of these notes that the intrinsic immorality of every contraceptive act remains a teaching subject to solid and positive doubt. This is not to say that this teaching of *Humanae Vitae* is certainly erroneous. It is only to say that there are very strong objections that can be urged against it and very little evidence that will sustain it. One draws this conclusion reluctantly and with no small measure of personal anguish . . .
>
> If other theologians, after meticulous research and sober reflection, share this opinion in sufficient numbers, if bishops and competent married couples would arrive at the same conclusion, it is difficult to see how the teaching would not lose the presumption of certainty ordinarily enjoyed by authoritative utterances.[3]

When this quite temperate (I still believe) conclusion appeared, I received a good deal of supportive mail. However, one letter from a fellow Jesuit, who shall remain nameless , read as follows:

Re: Your article in *Theological Studies*

Coming from one who finds little of the "peace of Christ" in his heart partially because of your own writings, I still do not feel hypocritical but I do think that my own impulse is such that I do think something of the spirit of God has to be behind it for me, a priest of God whom God in His providence has entrusted with reaching and influencing the moral judgments of millions of Catholics and non-Catholics, to say to you that I am convinced that you have suffered something of shipwreck in faith, and that you are essentially no longer Catholic because of your refusal to admit papal teaching. Your attempts at this and that distinction are admirable; but *the one common theme is:* NON SERVIAM. The unspeakable tragedy of our age is the wholesale treason to the principles of thinking with the Church. Certain of our provincials and bishops have gone along with their priests and laity. I, with millions of others, feel the hopelessness of fighting the multimillion-dollar "popular-liberal" treason which you represent; all I can do is to tell you.

Another incident was the visit of John Paul II to the United States in 1979. During that visit the pope repeated traditional Catholic teaching on birth regulation. I was contacted by *U.S. News and World Report* and was cited as follows: "The pontiff's statements against birth control are 'simple answers to complex questions'."[4]

That elicited the following letter from a fellow Jesuit (once again I withhold the name because identification is irrelevant to my point).

Dear Enemy of the Holy Father:

You have made yourself a theologian against the Church, not of and for the Church. You are engaged in the project of breaking down the reverence for life, for marriage, for human and divine love. Now, your impudence in challenging the Holy Father publicly, immediately during his pastoral and teaching visit, makes one wonder whether you have not left the priesthood and the Church but are not willing to admit the fact. Has the Holy Father or you the backing of the Holy Spirit? It certainly cannot be both of you. I do wish that our Father General would have the courage and integrity to dismiss you from the Society. You have already totally separated yourself from the Society and the priesthood and the Holy See in spirit.

In sum, dissent was then and still is a quite emotional and deeply divisive matter in the Church.

When I began to teach moral theology in 1957, dissent was virtually unknown in theological circles in the United States, at least in those areas (e.g., sexuality) where the Holy See views dissent as most threatening. True, some of the finest theologians of the time were silenced (Chenu, de Lubac, Murray, and partially Rahner). But in general, the attitudes of

Humani Generis (a disputed question authoritatively settled by the pope is no longer a matter of free theological discussion) dominated the atmosphere. Theology was to defend, mediate and interpret ordinary (noninfallible) papal teaching, not qualify it or depart from it. These latter practices would have threatened professorial longevity.

In the mid-sixties things began to change. At that time the late John Cardinal Heenan (Westminster) noted that "the decline of the magisterium is one of the most significant developments in the postconciliar Church."[5] It would be tempting—but far too facilely simplistic—to write off this decline as a transient share by the Church in the antirationalism and spirit of rebellion that infected the culture of the times. If that is one's analysis, dissent in the Church is only and straightforwardly disloyalty, a basic departure from and assault upon the Catholic idea. This is the attitude revealed in the letters cited above.

We might unravel this matter a bit by asking the following question: why has dissent occurred in the Church and what does it mean? There are two remarkably different answers given to this question. The first may be exemplified by James Hitchcock, professor of history at St. Louis University. If there is an analogue to Cardinal Ratzinger's "grim and doleful rhetoric" in the United States, it is Hitchcock, who begins his analysis of dissent as follows:

> The truth of the matter is that, at least in the United States, it would be difficult to find a major institution more internally disorganized, more ideologically divided and less effective in its governing structures than is the Catholic Church.[6]

There are references to "present disarray," "the unraveling of the Catholic system of authority," "the subversion of authority," "the spectacle of a great institution apparently coming apart," "all the teachings of the Church . . . in jeopardy," "the gradual erosion of faith." For Hitchcock, dissent is no longer the province of courageous outsiders. Like a cancer, "it challenges the Church not from the margins but through the Church's own central organs. Indeed, it is the official institutions of the Church which are now used to propagate dissent and, often enough, to repress orthodoxy."[7] Church bureaucrats learn their dissent from academics, especially theologians. It has become "the working orthodoxy of most of the theological profession."[8]

In the face of all this, bishops remain irresponsibly silent or show active sympathy with dissenting opinions. Many show endless sensitivity to "liberal anguish" while "similar manifestations of anguish from the 'right' are mere hysteria." Thus dissent has become organized and entrenched. What explains all of this? Hitchcock continues:

Explanations as to why this is allowed to happen could range from simple confusion and timidity on the part of some Church leaders, through the mistaken idea that the flames should be allowed to burn themselves out, to undeniable active sympathy with dissenting positions on the part of an increasing number of bishops.[9]

What is the effect of all this? The erosion of faith. In Hitchcock's words:

Many American Catholics regularly experience, from official sources, direct attacks on their faith. Even those who do not, have now experienced, for nearly two decades, the gradual erosion of that faith, as a rock is eroded by small but relentless drops of falling water. A tone of voice, a passing comment, a strategically situated smirk, a raised eyebrow are means by which those charged with upholding official teaching in fact contrive to undermine it.[10]

And what are the key issues around which dissent (and recall, a dissent that erodes *faith*) occurs? Celibacy of the clergy, ordination of women, divorce and contraception. However, Hitchcock sees in such dissenters people who "instinctively oppose any reaffirmation of teaching authority, in no matter what area."[11] Thus eventually "all of the teachings of the Church are in jeopardy."

In summary, then, Hitchcock sees dissent as opposed to orthodoxy, as disloyalty and "infidelity," as a denial of authority, as the cause of confusion and an attack on faith, as catering to fads and ecclesiastical careerism, as reflecting timidity in high places, as a cave-in to lobbyists, as inevitably involving the destructive notion of a dual magisterium in the Church. One can see all of this in the Catholic press: *Commonweal, U.S. Catholic, America, New Catholic World, Theological Studies* ("the chief organ for advancing dissenting opinion on the scholarly level"). For all practical purposes, there no longer exists "an official Catholic press in the sense of publications which faithfully convey only official positions."

There is another approach to the question "Why has dissent occurred?" Hitchcock wonders whether the phenomenon of dissent occurred *because of* or *in spite of* Vatican II. He opted for the latter. Indeed, he argues that one of the many failures of leadership over the past twenty-five years has been the failure to articulate what the Council really said and did. One thing it did not do, according to Hitchcock, is provide the basis for the kind of dissent he laments.

I disagree with that judgment. I will list here twelve factors (more could be enumerated) that I believe encouraged a new critical awareness in the Church and helped explain the emergence of dissent in the postconciliar Church.

1. *Changing times.* The Council was sharply aware of the rapidity of change in the modern world. It went so far as to characterize our times as "a new stage of its history."

> Today, the human race is passing through a new stage of its history. Profound and rapid changes are spreading by degrees around the whole world. Triggered by the intelligence and creative energies of man, these changes recoil upon him, upon his decision and desires, both individual and collective, and upon his manner of thinking and acting with respect to things and to people. Hence we can already speak of a true social and cultural transformation, one which has repercussions on man's religious life as well.[12]

2. *Newness of problems.* Speaking of the harmony between Christian teaching and culture, the Council noted the difficulty of this harmony because changing times raise new questions. It stated:

> Recent studies and findings of science, history and philosophy raise new questions which influence life and demand new theological investigations.[13]

Donald R. Campion, S.J., in his commentary on this sentence, rightly notes that it "reveals the council's own conviction that the notion of a theological 'aggiornamento' means more than a rephrasing of conventional theological teaching in contemporary terminology."[14]

3. *The variety of competence in the Church.* Once again noting the rapidity of change in the world and the desirability of an exchange between the Church and diverse cultures, the Council acknowledged that "the Church requires special help." That is,

> She must rely on those who live in the world, are versed in different institutions and specialties, and grasp their innermost significance in the eyes of both believers and unbelievers.[15]

And even more explicitly, the form of that reliance is specified in the paragraph already cited (in chapter 1) that urges laypersons to take on their own distinctive role.

4. *Openness to the sciences.* Speaking of pastoral care, the Council fathers insisted that

> appropriate use must be made not only of theological principles, but also of the findings of the secular sciences, especially of psychology and soci-

ology. Thus the faithful can be brought to live the faith in a more thorough and mature way.[17]

The Council then went on to urge the faithful to "live in very close union with the men of their time."

> Let them blend modern science and its theories and the understanding of the most recent discoveries with Christian morality and doctrine. Thus their religious practice and morality can keep pace with their scientific knowledge and with an ever-advancing technology.[18]

5. Freedom of theological inquiry and speech. At the end of chapter 2 of *Gaudium et Spes* (on the proper development of culture), the Council expressed the hope that laypersons would be well formed in the sacred sciences. It continued:

> In order that such persons may fulfill their proper function, let it be recognized that all of the faithful, clerical and lay, possess a lawful freedom of inquiry and of thought, and the freedom to express their minds humbly and courageously about those matters in which they enjoy competence.[19]

6. The Church's modesty about its own competence. Sometimes in the past, the teaching competence of the Church was presented in a way that was all-encompassing and triumphalistic. The Council fathers noted simply:

> The Church guards the heritage of God's Word and draws from it religious and moral principles, without always having at hand the solution to particular problems.[20]

7. The independence of the sciences. The Council insisted on the autonomy of "earthly affairs" in the sense that created things and societies have their own laws and values that must be deciphered and respected. It then applied this explicitly to the sciences.

> Consequently, we cannot but deplore certain habits of mind, sometimes found too among Christians, which do not sufficiently attend to the rightful independence of science.[21]

That little phrase "sometimes found too among Christians" is officially annotated with a reference to a two-volume study of the works of Galileo Galilei.

8. The fact of doctrinal development. This matter was treated by the Council in the *Dogmatic Constitution on Divine Revelation*. There we read:

> This tradition which comes from the apostles, develops in the Church with the help of the Holy Spirit. For there is a growth in the understanding of the realities and the words which have been handed down. This happens through the contemplation and study made by believers (cf.Lk. 2:19, 51), through the intimate understanding of spiritual things they experience and through the preaching of those who have received through episcopal succession the sure gift of truth.[22]

The Constitution then speaks of the constant movement of the Church "forward toward the fullness of divine truth." Several things should be noted here. First, movement forward "toward the fullness of divine truth" implies an incomplete possession of such truth at given points in history. Second, if this is true of the "words which have been handed down," it would be a fortiori true of the solutions to certain moral problems that have not been "handed down." Third, the first medium of this development is the contemplation and reflection of the faithful. Finally, the *Declaration on Religious Freedom* was the key conciliar example of doctrinal development. As John Courtney Murray, S.J., stated: "It was, of course, the most controversial document of the whole Council, largely because it raised with sharp emphasis the issue that lay continually below the surface of all the conciliar debates—the issue of the development of doctrine . . . The Council formally sanctioned [in this document] the validity of the development itself."[23]

9. Adaptation of practices. In its *Decree on Eastern Catholic Churches*, the Council modified its sacramental discipline with regard to the churches of the East. Specifically, in permitting access to the sacraments of penance, the Eucharist, and anointing of the sick, Vatican II stated:

> In view of special circumstances of time, place, and personage, the Catholic Church has often adopted and now adopts a milder policy, offering to all the means of salvation and an example of charity among Christians through participation in the sacraments.[24]

10. Acknowledgement of legitimate pluralism. After calling attention to the key role of laypersons in the elaboration of moral doctrine and practice, the Council stated:

> Often enough the Christian view of things will itself suggest some specific solution in certain circumstances. Yet it happens rather frequently, and

legitimately so, that with equal sincerity some of the faithful will disagree with others on a given matter.[25]

11. Conciliar admission of errors and deficiencies. As might be expected, this remains largely implicit. But, as Avery Dulles, S.J., has pointed out, Vatican II has implicitly admitted Church error and injustice by rehabilitating, as it were, and using the insights of theologians previously silenced. As Dulles puts it:

> Most importantly for our purposes, Vatican II quietly reversed the earlier positions of the Roman magisterium on a number of important issues. The obvious examples are well known. In biblical studies, for instance, the *Constitution on Divine Revelation* accepted a critical approach to the Bible, thus supporting the previous initiatives of Pius XII and delivering the Church once and for all from the incubus of the earlier decrees of the Biblical Commission. In the *Decree on Ecumenism*, the Council cordially greeted the ecumenical movement and involved the Catholic Church in the larger quest for Christian unity, thus putting an end to the hostility enshrined in Pius XII's *Mortalium animos*. In Church-State relations, the *Declaration on Religious Freedom* accepted the religiously neutral state, thus reversing the previously approved view that the state should formally propose the truth of Catholicism. In the theology of secular realities, the *Pastoral Constitution on the Church in the Modern World* adopted an evolutionary view of history and a modified optimism regarding secular systems of thought, thus terminating more than a century of vehement denunciations of modern civilization. As a result of these and other revisions, the Council rehabilitated many theologians who had suffered under severe restrictions with regard to their ability to teach and publish. The names of John Courtney Murray, Pierre Teilhard de Chardin, Henri de Lubac, and Yves Congar, all under a cloud of suspicion in the 1950's, suddenly became surrounded with a bright halo of enthusiasm. By its actual practice of revision, the Council implicitly taught the legitimacy and even the value of dissent. In effect the Council said that the ordinary magisterium of the Roman Pontiff had fallen into error and had unjustly harmed the careers of loyal and able scholars.[26]

Moreover, even more explicitly, in its *Decree on Ecumenism*, after noting the need of "continual reformation," the Council adds:

> Therefore, if the influence of events or of the times has led to deficiencies in conduct, in Church discipline, or *even in the formulation of doctrine* (which must be carefully distinguished from the deposit itself of faith), these should be appropriately rectified at the proper moment.[27]

In commenting on the words I have italicized, Walter M. Abbott, S.J., states: "It is remarkable, indeed, for an Ecumenical Council to admit the possible deficiency of previous doctrinal formulations."[28] Remarkable indeed!

12. The new task of theology. It is clear that Christians want to profess and apply their faith in the times and cultures in which they live. This powerfully suggests the need of a new language, new formulations. The Council explicitly acknowledged this need in its distinction between the substance and formulation of the faith. This means that theology must move from a mere repetition of past formulas to a search for fresh and more appropriate ones, to much more innovation than was envisaged in the past.

It would be immodest to belabor the obvious. But what do we have here? We have Vatican II underlining the rapidly changing times, the novelty of the problems cast up by these changes, the many competences needed to face them adequately, the independence of the sciences and the openness to them required to face our problems, the freedom of inquiry and expression necessary, the incompleteness of the Church's competence, deficiencies in past efforts to grapple with problems, the fact and need of development, the legitimacy of differences of opinion among believers, the fact of variation in Church discipline. If such considerations do not explain, and even foster and validate the notion of dissent in the Church, then I should like to know why not. It is playing the ostrich to say that dissent emerged in the Church in the mid-sixties *in spite of* the Council, not *because of* it. There may have been other factors involved, but anyone who reads the conciliar texts dispassionately will, I think, agree that Vatican II authorized a new critical spirit in the Church, a spirit that lifted the notion of dissent from a suspect gloss in theological textbooks into the mainstream of Catholic life and polity. One may, of course, regret this, may squirm under its untidiness; but that is a matter of one's psychological posture and of one's intellectual tolerance for the tentative and the unresolved. It is not a question of what Vatican II did or did not say. *That* I think is clear.

The title of this chapter speaks of dissent *in the Church*. As a moral theologian I am concerned above all about moral teaching and understanding. The phrase "in the Church" is meant to highlight the fact already stated in chapter 1: as Catholics, we form our consciences in community, not in splendid isolation. The major, but not the only, vehicle of the community's moral knowledge is the authentic magisterium. We believe that the ordinary sources of error are better excluded when Catholics form their consciences in tune with the magisterium of the Church. I say "better excluded," for the ordinary magisterium does not absolutely exclude error unless we are lost in a haze of historical amnesia. Thus we speak of the presumption of truth, not absolute certainty.

The authoritative teaching office cannot be mythologized, that is, exempted from the ordinary and mandatory procedures associated with human understanding, as Karl Rahner so frequently insists. This is especially true in moral matters, where it has been a centuries-old conviction that concrete moral obligations are not inherently mysterious, but are in principle available to human insight and reasoning. We are neither Athens nor Jerusalem. Jerusalem, it is said, tells stories, but has no theology to speak of. Athens reasons and rationalizes in lofty precision from any story. Catholics reason about their story.

If there is one thing that is clear about human understanding, it is that it is a process—subject to the limitations of partial insight, historical change, limited philosophical concepts and language, and the intransigence and unpredictability of concrete reality. Thus, with John XXIII and Vatican II, we properly distinguish between the substance and the formulation of a truth, the implication being that our formulations are at best imperfect and in constant need of revision and purification. Part of the process of revision and purification is necessarily a distancing from, a rejection of an older or even more current formulation. This we may call dissent.

We saw this phenomenon in the development of *The Declaration on Religious Freedom* in Vatican II. Since the Syllabus of Errors, circumstances had gradually changed by 1965 and "the American experience" had been reflected upon sufficiently to generate efforts at a new formulation of the Church's concerns. In moral matters, this should surprise no one, for even dogmas are historically conditioned. The Congregation for the Doctrine of the Faith (*Mysterium Ecclesiae*, 1973) acknowledged a fourfold historical conditioning. Statements of faith are affected by the presuppositions, the concerns ("the intention of solving certain questions"), the thought categories ("the changeable conceptions of a given epoch") and the available vocabulary of the times.[29]

So, departure from past formulations—in this sense, dissent—is a normal part of the human scene. It is this aspect of Christian ethics and the Christian moral life that I wish to focus on further in this chapter, because it is becoming a major obstacle and distraction.

Let me begin by noting that everywhere I go throughout the country moral problems quickly degenerate—and I use that word deliberately—into authority problems. Symbols of this abound and they can get nasty.

A former professor of moral theology on the west coast (Joseph Farraher, S.J.) was asked why bishops tolerate dissent from official teaching in Catholic universities and seminaries. He stated that if theology professors persist in their dissent after fraternal or sororal warnings, "all efforts" should be made to remove them.[30] In a similar spirit, the Jesuit editor of the *Homiletic and Pastoral Review* (Kenneth Baker, S.J.) asserts that theologians and intellectuals who "refuse to submit to the magisterium of the Church" should be excommunicated.[31]

That is one attitude toward dissent. And I am sure that many share it. Clearly, James Hitchcock does. I do not. I am much closer to Bernard Häring's view. Häring speaks of dissent as a prophetic ministry within the Church, one required to prevent "ossification of doctrines" and "temptations of ideologies." "Common dedication to truth," he writes, "is possible only if there is freedom of inquiry and freedom to speak out even in dissent from official documents."[32] Failure to do so has resulted in unfortunate errors. We must leave room for the privilege of growth. Doubt and questioning is peculiarly the onerous task of the theologian, a task assigned him/her by the Church. As Walter Burghardt, S.J., puts it:

> A critical facet of that function is to subject any earthbound affirmation of Christian truth to the test of Christian truth: Does it square with, correspond to, adequately represent the Word of God? In doing so, we are not setting ourselves above Pope or bishop; we are collaborating with them in a joint effort to understand what God says to us and what God wants of us. The paradox, a humbling paradox, is that at times our very loyalty demands that we dissent.[33]

Thus, as we have seen, there are two radically different identifiable attitudes toward dissent in the contemporary Church. Using Henry Higgins to summarize them, we may identify them as: "throw the baggage out," "I've grown accustomed to her face." Behind these different attitudes toward dissent lie some basic differences in some very fundamental concepts. There are different concepts of revelation—a thoroughly given *depositum*, interpreted propositionally versus a skeletal one that operates symbolically as it reveals its meaning in ever fresh daily appropriations. There are different concepts of the function of theology—repetition of traditional formulations versus exploration, the descending model versus the ascending model. There are different notions of the function of theologians in an academic setting—extension of the magisterium versus personal enquirer. There are different notions of authoritative teaching and the response due to it—obedience versus critical assimilation. There are different notions of the processes required in implementing the so-called hierarchical charism of truth. There are different ideas about what unity in the Church means. There are different notions or models of the Church. In our time there is the reemergence of the institutional or juridical model, the pyramid of the old manuals.

All of these notions certainly play a role in our attitudes toward dissent. But the key notion, I believe, is the notion of the Church. How ministry—theological or other—is conceived traces back to one's notion of the Church. It is the notion of the Church that separates a Hitchcock from a Häring, a Grisez from a Curran.

Let me illustrate this by appeal to the notion of *sensus fidelium* in doctrinal and moral matters. How should the experience and reflection, the instinct, of the faithful relate to authoritative teaching? I know there are problems here. There is the problem of reducing this sense to polls and statistics. However, granted these problems, I believe that there are two schools of thought, clearly distinguishable, that root in distinct notions of the Church.

The first approach asserts that the experience and reflection of the faithful (and I include in that term all of us—lay people, theologians, priests and even bishops, for bishops surely must be numbered among the *fideles*) ought to be listened to, but it is ultimately the responsibility of authoritative teachers to determine the truth. For example, if huge segments of the Church believe that the ordination of women is compatible with the gospel and doctrinal development, yet the Congregation for the Doctrine of Faith determines otherwise, then the CDF is right because authoritative.

The second view is that the *sensus fidelium* is absolutely essential to a certain and binding proclamation of the truth. Concretely, if large segments of the community do not see the analyses and conclusions of an authoritative teacher, it is a sign that (a) either the matter is not sufficiently clear, sufficiently mature for closure, or (b) that it is badly formulated or (c) that it is wrong.

Now notice. Bishops of the first view see their task as telling people what is right. Bishops of the second view see their task as discovering with us what is morally or Christianly right. Bishops of the first view see moral and doctrinal truth in terms of authoritative formulations. Bishops of the second view are much more aware of doctrinal development and the changing nature of our concrete personhood. Bishops of the first view see the magisterium in terms of clarity and certainty. Bishops of the second view are much more likely to hesitate, question and doubt. Bishops of the first view see dissent, and even openness, as disloyalty. Bishops of the second view regard dissent as a necessary condition for doctrinal and moral advance.

My contention—and it is far from novel or idiosyncratic—is that these diverging perspectives spring from and foster a certain notion of Church. It is the notion of Church that lies behind two competing perspectives or attitudes in the contemporary Church, the fundamentalist and, for lack of a better word, the collegial. Gabriel Daly, an Irish Augustinian, has described fundamentalism or ultramontanism as consisting "in the rooting of one's entire faith in the pronouncements of authority."[34] It is a kind of fideism, "the kind of religious faith which does not regard itself as in any way accountable to reason."

Daly observes that during the century preceding Vatican II there were three major attempts to open the Church to its critical responsibilities (Liberal Catholicism, Modernism, the "New Theology" of the 1940s). All were literally wiped out (*Tuas Libenter* [1863], *Pascendi* [1907] and *Humani Generis* [1950]) by an alliance between fundamentalist attitudes and juridically centralized authority. These condemnations enshrined two constant features: (1) neoscholastic supremacy over all other systems; (2) the use of papal power to impose Scholasticism and Thomism in particular. These were the integral props of the ultramontane program whose essence is "the wish for *total* conformity with papal ideas and ideals in *all* things." This is the ultimate form of Roman Catholic fundamentalism. It becomes tyranny whenever it creates an atmosphere "in which open inquiry and honest dissent are arbitrarily construed as disloyalty or worse." Daly concludes his vigorous analysis by noting that "orthodoxy is meaningless and possibly immoral if it is not the answer to a genuine search for truth."

In marked contrast to such an attitude is that which I have called collegial. Its characteristics are well known. It is *broadly consultative, questioning, critical, open, appropriately tentative*. The best recent symbols of this mentality in action are the American episcopal pastorals, *The Challenge of Peace* and *Justice for All*.

As I noted, these two mentalities are vying for dominance in the contemporary Church. But most importantly, they are transparent of a notion of Church, what it means to be Church. How one views dissent will point to these deeper theological undercurrents. In what follows, I want to present two scenarios of the magisterium—which is, after all, the *Church* teaching. Some of these reflections could apply, mutatis mutandis, to civil society and dissent within it. There is a difference between a "law and order society" and "a just and sustainable society." These two scenarios are generated by two sets of cultural variables that affect the notion of teaching and of Church, and therefore of the meaning of dissent.

Let the first scenario be called the "preconciliar model." It covers the period from Trent to Vatican II. Some years ago, with the infallibility that attaches to younger years, I identified these variables as the following:[35]

1. The self-definition of the Church. For years the juridical model prevailed, the pyramidal model of the manuals with truth and authority descending from above, from Rome. In this model the very term "Church" (as in "the Church has always taught") referred to a small group in authority in the Church.

2. Mass media. For years the information flow in the Church and world was slow, restricted. This allowed opinions to be formed without the richness of the contribution of varying traditions. Furthermore, authentic formulations were received less critically and retained a formative influence sometimes disproportionate to their value.

3. Complexity of issues. For many decades Catholic education was defensive. Our seminaries were isolated sanctuaries. These are but symbols of the fact that ecclesial attitudes could take shape without full exposure to contemporary sciences and disciplines, and therefore at times without an existential awareness of the complexity of issues.

4. Exercise of authority. Authority was highly centralized, consultation was quite limited. Oswald von Nell-Breuning, S.J., composed *Quadragesimo Anno* all alone, without consultors or critics.[36] The official version of *Casti Connubii* was altered in *Acta Apostolicae Sedis* because the Vatican latinist misrepresented the mind of Franciscus Hürth on punitive sterilization. After the definition of papal infallibility it was—and still is—in some circles unthinkable to question papal statements, a development that reached its pinnacle in *Humani Generis*, as Congar has noted.[37]

5. Educational status of lay people and clergy. For many centuries the clergy were the best educated persons in the Church, not least because they had access to higher education. In such a situation it is understandable that the clergy would assume responsibilities that might be differently dispersed in other eras.

6. Ecclesial groups existed in an atmosphere of polite warfare. Protestants, all Protestants were *adversarii* of our doctrinal and moral theses. Their doctrinal and moral writings were forbidden reading. We did not turn to these as sources of wisdom. Their very separation from the one true Church was a presumption against their orthodoxy.

7. Educational styles. The "master concept" dominated seminary and university teaching, the "hand-down" notion of teaching where the professor dictated from his notes, often yellow with age. This was rendered viable and possible by uniformity of philosophy and language in the Church.

Now, if we take these variables, shake and mix them, I want to argue that they generated a notion of teaching in the Church with the characteristics I noted in chapter 1 (cf. p. 19). *Roma locuta causa finita.* For many people, the magisterium meant the "hierarchical issuance of authoritative decrees."

Our theology supported these notions. We laid a heavy stress on the authority of the teacher. The conclusion was as sound as the authority was legitimate. The response to these teachings was heavily obediential. We were to "submit." We had an "obligation to assent." The theologian's task was to defend the teaching of the hierarchy, in the words of Pius XII.

Of these developments Yves Congar, O.P., asks: "Is this consonant with what nineteen centuries of the Church's life tell us about the function of 'didascale' or doctor?" His answer: "No, not exactly."[38] Yet this concept reappeared in Vatican II (*Lumen Gentium* 25) under the term "religious submission of will and mind" owed to the Holy Father. The term was further elaborated: "The judgments made by him are sincerely adhered to, according to his manifest mind and will." These statements are often used as a club to invalidate *any* kind of disagreement with authoritative papal pronouncements.

Yet, they need not be, nor should they be. Karl Rahner, for example, regards these statements of Vatican II as an inadequate portrayal of the appropriate theological response. "If, for example, the statements of *Lumen Gentium* on this matter were valid without qualification, then the worldwide dissent of Catholic moral theologians against *Humanae Vitae* would be a massive and global assault on the authority of the magisterium. But the fact that the magisterium tolerates this assault shows that the norm of *Lumen Gentium* (and many other similar assertions of the past one hundred years) does not express in sufficiently nuanced form a legitimate praxis of the relationship between the magisterium and theologians."[39] Similar points have been made recently by Avery Dulles, S.J., Francis Sullivan, S.J., and André Naud.[40] They underscore the point highlighted by the distinguished Roman theologian, Josef Fuchs, S.J., that the unity we seek in the Church is not mere uniformity, but unity *in the truth*.[41]

Now let me turn quickly to what I will call a postconciliar scenario. The variables have all changed.

1. The Church now defines herself as the People of God, a *communio*. The model is concentric. It is the people who are the repository of wisdom. As Cardinal Suenens put it, "the pyramid of the old manuals was reversed."[42]

2. Where the media are concerned, we live in the age of instancy, instant communication. Canon Louis Janssens writes an obscure probe in *Ephemerides Theologicae Lovanienses* and it is reported in *Newsweek* a few weeks later.[43] An even more obscure theologian, then from the Kennedy Institute of Ethics at Georgetown, writes a rather conservative essay on neonatal intensive care in *Journal of the American Medical Association* and is banned in Melbourne a week later.[44] Rapid communication suggests that the laity is better informed than ever—if not always wiser than ever.

3. In our day Catholics are profoundly immersed in the social and intellectual world about them. They are exposed to many modes of thought. Our seminaries are cheek-by-jowl with the great universities in the country. In sum, we exist in an atmosphere highlighting the genuine complexity of moral and doctrinal issues.

4. Authority. Collegiality prevails, and theoretically at all levels—papal, episcopal, parochial. The Church mimics in her internal life and organization the currents of the secular world in which she lives. It is no accident that collegiality emerged in the Church at the very time secular institutions were captivated by democratic processes and shared decision-making.

5. Lay and clergy education. There is now intense specialization and widespread availability of higher education. Lay persons are often capable of relating their experience and expertise to doctrinal matters in a most enlightening way. Vatican II recognized this when it urged the layperson to "take on his/her own distinctive role." This urging is, as I noted, a final farewell to the "dependency syndrome" in Catholic moral and pastoral formation and practice.

6. Ecclesial groups now exist in an ecumenical sunshine. Those who were *adversarii* are now separated brothers and sisters. Vatican II recognized this when it stated: "In fidelity to conscience, Christians are joined with the rest of men in the search for truth and for the genuine solution to the numerous problems which arise in the life of individuals and from social relationships."[45]

7. In education, we have student involvement, experiment, creativity. We have discussion, seminars, cross-disciplinary dialogue. Philosophical uniformity has long disappeared from the scene.

These remarkable and rather massive sea changes have generated—or perhaps more accurately, should generate—a modified notion of teaching in the Church, the magisterium. This modified notion has the characteristics I noted in chapter 1 (cf. pp. 21 ff.).

Theology itself reflects these changes in its emphases and language. There is more attention to evidence and analysis. As Avery Dulles has noted, sound teaching must persuade, not merely command. The proper response is not obedience (we do not obey teachers *qua* teachers). It is rather a docile personal attempt to assimilate—which is my private rendition of *obsequium religiosum*. This was discussed in chapter 1, where I reported Bishop Christopher Butler's analysis. What Butler is more than suggesting is that "the keen alertness of a critical mind" is an essential part of what I like to call the teaching-learning *process* of the Church. Without that essential part, the process will be enfeebled, as I believe it has been through short-circuiting of this process. Butler's phrase reflects Rahner's notion of person as *ein kritisches Wesen.*[46] Rahner puts it this way: "All the energies of a living Christianity can be implemented only in a process which must inevitably have a critical component."

It is within this understanding of Church and magisterium that an assessment of dissent should occur. Concretely, if I dissent, it is the *end* of a process, a docile attempt to assimilate. The process must be prayerful, arduous, reflective. Otherwise there is no *learning*. My point is: Responsible dissent is not only a temporary *end* to a search. It is and must be seen as a new beginning, a beginning of new evidence in the Church. Concretely, if large segments of competent and demonstrably loyal Catholics disagree with certain formulations of *Humanae Vitae*, this must be seen as the beginning of a new reflection. The very same thing is true of a document like *The*

Challenge of Peace. One of the interesting offshoots of this pastoral letter is that more conservative Catholics—who strongly reject elements of it—are learning that dissent does not necessarily involve disloyalty or disrespect. Otherwise, we have ruled personal reflection out of order in the learning process of the Church—and that is intolerable.

In this perspective, the magisterial function in the Church is much more a matter of a teaching-learning *process*, in which dissent should play a positive, nonthreatening role. It is part of the ordinary way of progress in human growth in understanding. I must insist on this: *we must learn to institutionalize dissent and profit from it.*

I say this with considerable confidence born of backing from a well-known continental thinker. He wrote: "The structure of a human community is correct only if it admits not just the presence of a justified opposition, but also that effectiveness of opposition which is required by the common good and the right of participation."[47] These words of Karol Wojtyla in *The Acting Person* are no less true of the Church than any community.

Let me summarize. What I am pleading for—and, I think, into the teeth of some strong counterwinds—is a continued move from *classical* consciousness to *historical* consciousness after Vatican II. "Counterwinds," I say, because in the Catholic community truth can easily be the victim of the soothing blandishments of subjective certainty. We have seen this in the past. Those who forget history are doomed to repeat it. The move to an historical consciousness means a change in outlook on the Church as teacher, and in two ways.

1. *The context has changed.*
   (a) There is the loss of the homogeneous culture (as Rahner has called it).
   (b) There is the emergence of awareness about the historical relativity of authoritative statements (scriptural, traditional, magisterial).
   (c) There is a new awareness that the authoritative tradition is no longer mediated exclusively by the ecclesiastical magisterium—but also by autonomous principles, criteria, historical investigation.
   (d) There is a collapse of the unitary method and language in theology.
   (e) There is the collapse of the theologian as the "universal person."
2. *Specific points have been modified.*
   (a) There is criticism of a purely juridical description of theologians and the magisterium, whereby theologians speak only as extensions, delegates of the pope and bishops.
   (b) There is a newly recovered conviction about the subordination of

the magisterium to Scripture and tradition—a kind of qualification of the idea of magisterium as the *regula fidei proxima*.

(c) There is a new awareness of the inadequacy of "formal" or "official" authority. Authority must vindicate itself.

(d) There is pervasive conviction that the "assistance of the Spirit" must refer to the whole Church.

(e) There is fresh awareness of the intrinsic need of theological reasoning in communal Church discernment.

(f) There is a new sense of the variety of modes in which the magisterium is exercised. Baseball is not to be identified with the Chicago Cubs of 1918. Neither is the magisterium to be identified with its exercise under Pius IX. There is the realistic sense of the possibility of failure, or inadequacy in official formulations.

In summary, I believe it is accurate to say that we are viewing teaching in the Church from the perspective of different cultural variables and a correspondingly altered consciousness. In our time dissent is viewed as a contribution to a process of growth, not as a challenge to a superior. If the Church is conceived in juridical terms within a classical consciousness, dissent is viewed with alarm, as disturbing unity, as challenging superiors. The standard vocabulary to convey this is "disturbing the faithful," "confusion of the faithful." But, as Raymond Brown once observed, when Jesus Christ confronts us we ought to be disturbed. He challenges everything we stand for. Growth demands wrestling and uprooting.

The American bishops recently debated the question of nuclear arms. The distance between a Hannan and a Hunthausen on what the gospel asks of us was and is immense. Impishly, I like to remind bishops that these differences on this greatest moral problem of our times are "disturbing theologians."

In a more serious vein, I think it is a very healthy sign. It is a sign of a growing reshaping of the teaching office, especially a move from ultramontanism. This is indispensable. The value of the magisterium will be preserved only if we see it as both a privilege and a responsibility, something we receive but also something to which we contribute. If we are to continue to enjoy the privilege, we must incur the responsibility. Our responsibilities are those of docile, loyal yet critical Catholics who have both the humility and the courage to be led. I say "courage" because in our time to be properly led means to share the burdens of the leader, even if we are hurt in the process, even if we are wrong.

Perspectives such as these were recently submitted to a kind of Catholic "trial-by-visit" by John Paul II in 1987. The Holy Father was expected by many to encounter dissent and by a relatively small minority to quash it. Encounter he did, quash he did not—at least as I read his remarks.

In Los Angeles, John Paul II addressed the American Catholic bishops. He referred to the "inacceptability of dissent and confrontation *as a policy and method* in the area of Church teaching."[48] He did not spell this out. But in combination the two words ("policy and method") describe the posture of one who *regularly* and *on principle* ("policy") dissents as a *way of approaching* (method) Church teaching. That is, indeed, totally unacceptable because it quite simply empties authentic teaching of any presumption of truth. But I know of no one who does this. When one qualifies this or that teaching (almost always an application of a more general principle) because he/she cannot find sound reasons to support it and proposes weighty reasons against it, this is not dissent "as a policy and method." Obviously, then, the pope is not rejecting any theological dissent, but only a certain kind—and, I would think, a relatively rare kind.

John Paul II referred to the bishops' "role as authentic teachers of the faith when opinions at variance with the Church's teaching are proposed *as a basis for pastoral practice*."[49] This clearly points to a distinction between "opinions at variance with the Church's teaching" and such opinions "proposed as a basis for pastoral practice." Only these latter are rejected by the pope. I adverted to this in the preface to this volume. What the Holy Father did not adequately address is what authentic teachers do about respectful disagreement with Church teaching. Is it simply to be ignored? Or does it invite official leadership to a new reflection? If one opts for the "ignore-alternative"—and much of this volume targets that option as inadmissible theologically—then the key theological issue embedded in dissent has not been faced.

Again, the pope stated: "Dissent from Church doctrine remains what it is, dissent; as such it may not be proposed or received on an equal footing with the Church's authentic teaching."[50] This more than obviously suggests that John Paul II is not concerned with theological dissent as such, but with its presentation or acceptance "on an equal footing." That is, it is presented or received as if the Church had no authentic teaching or as if such teaching did not matter. One wishes—vainly, I suppose—that some of the pope's cantankerous loyalists were as nuanced as the Holy Father.

Is dissent a form of loyalty or a liability? It can be the latter (when irresponsible in form) but it should be the former. From my perspective it is an outcome, not a first-foot forward, aggressive starting-point. It is a normal outcome—even if infrequent—of an attempt to assimilate in a pilgrim and imperfect Church, which realizes that just as it is *in via* and can only imperfectly symbolize the coming reality of the Kingdom, so too its formulations of its convictions are always *in via*.

Christ did not promise us that as individuals we would always be right when deliberating about the practical implications of "being in Christ." He did not promise that the ultimate official teaching would always be right.

He did say, *in the fact of our being a community of believers*, that there is no better way of walking a narrow path than to walk it together—with the combined eyes and strength and experience of the entire people, all supporting each other's charisms and gifts.

Is that risky? Yes. Is the risk avoidable? No. Is that sufficient for us? It is what God, through His Incarnate Word, has left us. It is sufficient—for in God we trust.

Notes

1. *Wanderer*, 29 September 1983.
2. *Fellowship of Catholic Scholars Newsletter* 8 (September 1985):9.
3. *Theological Studies* 29 (1968):737-38.
4. *U.S.News and World Report* 87 (22 October 1979):41.
5. John Cardinal Heenan, "The Authority of the Church," *London Tablet* 222 (1968):488-90.
6. James Hitchcock, *The Dissenting Church* (New York: National Committee of Catholic Laymen, 1983), 3.
7. Hitchcock, loc. cit., 5.
8. Loc. cit., 26.
9. Loc. cit., 55.
10. Loc. cit., 53.
11. Loc. cit., 54.
12. *Documents*, 202.
13. *Documents*, 268.
14. *Documents*, 268, footnote 200.
15. *Documents*, 246.
16. *Documents*, 244.
17. *Documents*, 269.
18. *Documents*, 269.
19. *Documents*, 270.
20. *Documents*, 232.
21. *Documents*, 234.
22. *Documents*, 116.
23. *Documents*, 673.
24. *Documents*, 384.
25. *Documents*, 244.
26. Avery Dulles, S.J., "The Theologian and the Magisterium," *Proceedings of the Catholic Theological Society of America* 31 (1976):235-46, at 240.
27. *Documents*, 350.
28. *Documents*, 350, footnote 33.
29. *Catholic Mind* 71 (October 1973):58-60.
30. Joseph Farraher, S.J., "Why Don't Bishops Take Action against Dissenters?" *Homiletic and Pastoral Review* 79, n. 7 (1979):64-66.
31. Kenneth Baker, S.J., "Magisterium and Theologians," *Homiletic and Pastoral Review* (as in note 30):14-23.

32. B. Häring, *Free and Faithful in Christ I* (New York: Seabury, 1978), 280-81.

33. Walter J. Burghardt, S.J., "Stone the Theologians: The Role of Theology in Today's Church," *Catholic Mind* 75, n. 1315 (September 1977): 42-50, at 50.

34. Gabriel Daly, "Conflicting Mentalities," *Tablet* 235 (1981):361-62; "The Ultramontane Influence," ibid., 391-92; "The Pluriform Church," ibid., 446-47.

35. Richard A. McCormick, S.J., "The Teaching of the Magisterium and Theologians," *Proceedings of the Catholic Theological Society of America* 24 (1969), 239-54.

36. Cf. Oswald von Nell-Breuning, S.J., "The Drafting of Quadragesimo Anno" in *Readings in Moral Theology No. 5*, ed. Charles E. Curran and Richard A. McCormick, S.J. (Mahwah, N.J.: Paulist, 1986), 60-68.

37. Yves Congar, O.P., "A Brief History of the Forms of the Magisterium and Its Relations with Scholars," in *Readings in Moral Theology No. 3*, 314-31.

38. Loc. cit., 325.

39. Karl Rahner, "Theologie und Lehramt," *Stimmen der Zeit* 198 (1980):353-75, at 373.

40. Cf. "Notes on Moral Theology," *Theological Studies* 42 (1981):115-19, and 45 (1984):114. Cf. also and especially André Naud, *Le magistère incertain* (Québec: Editions Fides, 1987).

41. Joseph Fuchs, S.J., "Bischöfe and Moraltheologen: Eine innerkirchliche Spannung," *Stimmen der Zeit* 201 (1983):601-19. An English version may be found in *Christian Ethics in a Secular Arena* (Washington: Georgetown University Press, 1984):131-53.

42. *National Catholic Reporter*, 28 May 1969, 6. That these perspectives are not universally shared is clear from remarks made by Nicholas T. Elko, retired auxiliary bishop of Cincinnati. He referred to the Church as "a spiritual monarchy" that "operates from the top down" (*Catholic Chronicle*, April 1988).

43. Louis Janssens, "Morale conjugale et progestogènes," *Ephemerides theologicae Lovanienses* 39 (1963):787-826.

44. Richard A. McCormick, S.J., "To Save or Let Die," *Journal of the American Medical Association* 229 (1974):172-76. Also in *America* 130 (1974):6-10.

45. *Documents*, 214.

46. Karl Rahner, as in *Theological Investigations* 17, 135, footnote.

47. Karol Wojtyla, *The Acting Person* (Boston: D. Reidel, 1979), 343.

48. *John Paul II in America* (Boston: Daughters of St. Paul, 1987), 196.

49. Ibid., 196.

50. Ibid., 195.

Chapter 3

Moral Argument in Christian Ethics

In the encyclical *Humanae Vitae*, Pope Paul VI made reference to the type of response he expected to his teaching.

> That obedience, as you well know, obliges not only because of the reasons adduced, but rather because of the light of the Holy Spirit, which is given in a particular way to the pastors of the Church in order that they may illustrate the truth.[1]

That statement raises the issue of moral argument in Christian ethics; it does not solve it. For surely, the pope does not mean that concrete moral prescriptions are totally independent of the arguments that can be marshalled to support them. That would be a new fideism in the area of morals that is ill at ease with centuries of Catholic tradition, as we shall see, and is unintelligible to the modern mind.

Bernard Häring, writing shortly after the appearance of the encyclical, spoke of the possibility of a reformulation of the matter and said there was little hope for this "unless the reaction of the whole Church immediately makes him [Paul VI] realize that he has chosen the wrong advisors and that the arguments which these men have recommended as highly suitable for modern thought are simply unacceptable."[2] Häring then went on to relate moral argument to the special light of the Spirit as follows:

> If the Holy Spirit gives a very special grace in the composition and promulgation of this document, then one may legitimately expect that this grace will manifest itself in the way the question itself is handled. That means in the solid presentation of proofs from human experience and with good arguments. In my opinion that is not true in the present instance.[3]

Dissent is really a generic term. It includes any kind of disagreement regardless of quality, tone or argument. In chapter 2, I referred to dissent as possibly irresponsible. The obvious implication is that dissent can be either responsible or irresponsible. The difference is not primarily or chiefly in the quality of the argument used. It is in the dispositions and conduct of the dissenter. The proper response to authentic noninfallible teaching is, as I noted, a docile personal attempt to assimilate the teaching. This docility will translate practically into four dimensions: (1) a respect for the teacher and his office; (2) a readiness to reassess one's own opinion and therefore a shedding of obstinacy; (3) a reluctance to conclude prematurely to error because one realizes (or presumes) that the wisdom of the entire Church has gone into the teaching; (4) a public behavior that fosters respect for the authentic magisterium.

If these are the practical accomplishments of docility, it seems clear that it is possible to violate them either by excess or defect. One would violate docility by defect through disrespect of the person or office of the teacher, through close-minded obstinacy, through unconsidered and hasty opposition, through careless and cavalier public expression. Some of this we have certainly seen in the past twenty-five years.

What is often and easily overlooked, however, is violation of docility by excess. Here I include excessive dependence, a no-thought and uncritical compliance, a nonhistorical mythologizing and glorification of the magisterium. We have seen far more of this recently than is generally acknowledged and in those very circles that pride themselves on their loyalty. The appropriate docility must be critical, since we are, after all, involved in a learning process in which all of us have a part to play. ("Having a part to play" translates into democracy only for those with a retarded sense of nuance or with certifiable ill will.) Docility means responding to the objective value of the authentic magisterium. Such fitting response does not guarantee good arguments. Far from it. But it does remove one source of bad ones. It is, so to speak, the right foot forward.

By saying that docility must be critical, I am implying that there is some relationship between the conclusions drawn and the arguments used. This is exactly what Häring meant when he said that we may legitimately expect that the grace of the Spirit granted to authentic teachers will manifest itself in "good arguments." In this sense, it would be a "wrong foot forward" (a violation of critical docility) to dissociate completely moral conclusions from moral argumentation. This has happened. For instance, on April 14, 1975, the deservedly admired Joseph L. Bernardin, then president of the United States Conference of Catholic Bishops, wrote a letter to the American bishops communicating the contents of a response of the Congregation for the Doctrine of the Faith on sterilization in Catholic hospitals. The letter asserted:

> I am writing to give assurance that the 1971 guidelines [of the Ethical and Religious Directives for Catholic Hospitals] stand as written, and that direct sterilization is not to be considered as justified by the common good, the principle of totality, the existence of contrary opinion, *or any other argument.*[4]

That "or any other argument" effectively removes the moral conclusion from any kind of critical scrutiny. It is itself a bad moral argument since neither history nor sound moral methodology will support such a sweeping conclusion. But it is above all a wrong *approach* to concrete moral objections. It is this approach that I wish to address in this chapter under the title of "Moral Argument in Christian Ethics."

The subject I have chosen is, of course, huge, even unmanageable in a brief chapter. Let me delimit the subject from the outset. There are several things that I have no intention of doing, or even attempting to do. I have no intention of rehearsing and refereeing the philosophical discussions on cognitivism, noncognitivism, emotivism and so on, informative even necessary, as these might be to a fully adequate treatise on moral arguments in ethics. Second, I have no intention of displaying at length and abstractly the pros and cons of the age-old tiresome discussion between deontologists and teleologists. I am increasingly convinced of two things: (1) the terms are direction-indicators rather than informative categories; (2) very few contemporary ethicians and moral theologians fit either generic term without rather severe qualifications, at least as these terms are elegantly elaborated by C.D. Broad.[5]

I want to attempt something much more modest, but I hope not trivial. I propose to examine and speak out of my own Catholic tradition of normative ethics and use it as the basis for some scattered remarks about the nature of moral argument in Christian ethics. These scattered remarks will organize around two general assertions or theses: (1) cultural factors or variables have a great deal to do with how we understand the nature and function of moral argument; (2) in contemporary moral discourse there is a great deal of patently bad moral argument going on.

As for the first point, Vatican II explicitly acknowledged it in several places. For instance, in the passage I cited in chapter 2, it stated:

> Today, the human race is passing through a new stage of its history. Profound and rapid changes are spreading by degrees around the whole world. Triggered by the intelligence and creative energies of man, these changes recoil upon him, upon his decisions and desires, both individual and collective, and upon his manner of thinking and acting with respect to things and people.[6]

Clearly, changes that affect our way of "thinking and acting" will affect the notion of moral argument, since moral argument is precisely an attempt to render intelligible, consistent, and persuasive the ways we believe we ought to think and act. As regards the second assertion, there may seem to be no connection between it and the first; but I believe there is. Specifically, though the connection will not be elaborated, it could be argued that the root of at least some, perhaps many, of the bad arguments, is the unconscious assumption and use in moral analysis of a set of cultural variables that no longer obtain, or are at least highly suspect.

Before approaching these two points, it is necessary to state what I take to be the substance of Catholic tradition on moral argumentation and analysis. The reason for this is found in the two convictions that summarize the substance of this tradition on the nature of moral argument. First, the concrete moral implications of our being-in-Christ can per se be known by human insight and reasoning. In other words, those concrete or behavioral norms (commands and prohibitions) regarded as applying to all persons precisely as human persons,[7] are not radically mysterious. Thus the traditional concept of a natural law (one based in the very being of persons) knowable by insight and reason. Over a period of many centuries, therefore, the criterion of right and wrong action was said to be *recta ratio*.[8]

Second, the tradition has viewed man as redeemed but still affected by the *reliquiae peccati*. In the words of the scholastics, man is *totus conversus sed non totaliter* (a total convert but not totally). This means that notwithstanding the transforming gift of God's enabling grace, we remain vulnerable to self-love and self-deception (sin) and that these noxious influences affect our evaluative and judgmental processes (*"primi hominis culpa obtenebrata"* "obscured by the fault of the first human being").[9] For this reason, Vatican Council I stated that revelation is morally necessary that we may know expeditiously, firmly, and without error *"quae in rebus divinis humanae rationi per se impervia non sunt"* ("those things that in divine matters are not *per se* impervious to human reason.")[10]

The balancing of these twin currents of Catholic tradition is often summarized in the lapidary phrase, "reason informed by faith." The balance is tricky and fragile and has not always been successfully realized. At times the word "informed" has been practically understood as "without" and Catholic moral consciousness has slipped into rationalism. At other times "informed" has been understood as "replaced by" and moral consciousness has been infected by a type of procedural gnosticism. When I say "I speak out of my own Catholic tradition," I mean to suggest the *ideal* mix of these two currents, that which very few of us probably achieve, try as we may. One of the reasons for this is that the "enlightened" (as in "reason enlightened by faith") still cries out for penetrating and systematic study, as some contemporary debates indicate.[11]

Cultural Factors Affecting the Understanding of Moral Argument in Catholic Tradition

Moral analyses often reflect basic assumptions and cultural variables that operate behind them. Karl Rahner, in discussing moral argument, refers to such assumptions as "global prescientific convictions."[12] These are "prejudgments" that stand behind moral arguments and take explicit form in them. As Rahner puts it:

> There are also *false* (historically time-conditioned, global, instinctively operating) convictions which then seek objective expression in explicit conceptual "proofs," so that to anyone who shares these convictions the proofs are very obvious and they are put forward and defended with the absoluteness with which people cling to such a prescientific global conviction, even though the latter is false or at least questionable.[13]

These "prescientific global convictions" are responsible for the impression we have that certain "proofs" in moral theology assume from the outset the conclusion they purport to establish. In this fashion the conclusions are, in Rahner's words, "smuggled into the premises of the argument." I believe we could find several "prescientific global convictions" at work in the nineteenth century analysis in the Church of religious freedom (e.g., certain convictions about the state as ideally Christian). The same could be said of the notions of "natural" and "unnatural" as they weave themselves in and out of discussions of, for example, reproductive technology and genetic engineering. Something similar may be said of the Church's prohibition of lending money at interest. Money came to be viewed as a productive good, not merely a consumptible one.

Rahner concludes by noting that:

> The actual development and history of moral theology in the Church has to do largely, not only with the destruction of incorrect or uncertain theological arguments purely as such, but with the demolition of such prescientific instinctive convictions which are false or unproved, but hitherto make the explicit arguments seem "obvious."[14]

Thus the task of the moral theologian is "not only to expose as such what is unproved in the course of the argument [the faulty, inconsistent argument], but also to work to break down the preconceptions behind it." Because these preconceptions are present not only in textbook theology but also in the pronouncements of the magisterium, "the courage to take risks, to face opposition and criticism, is therefore among the virtues of the moral theologians."[15]

In what follows, I will list nine variables that could deeply influence our notion of moral argument and its function in Christian ethics. Sometimes this "influence" will be on the very place and importance we give to moral argument. At other times (e.g., the very notion of God, no. 2 below) the "influence" will be in the form of a "prescientific instinctive conviction" that affects the very substance and outcome of the argument.

1. *Educational status of clergy and laypeople in the Church.* As briefly noted in chapter 2, for many understandable historical reasons Christianity spread and matured through many centuries in societies composed of the educated and uneducated. Often enough the only ones with access to education, especially "higher" education, were the clergy. Since one of the tasks of the clergy was moral education—therefore the education by an educated elite of an illiterate and uneducated faithful—it is understandable that moral education would take the form of simple inviolable rules rather than broad principles requiring discernment when they are to be applied. It is simply easier to teach people to obey rules; it is much more difficult to teach them to use their judgment according to the circumstances. Thus organizational Christianity could well have reinforced a notion of moral teaching and learning that dispensed with moral argument and analysis on the part of the vast majority of its adherents, and underemphasized the possibility and need of exception-making and the type of moral argument required to support and control it.

Clearly, things have changed in our day with the broad availability of higher education and the remarkable ability of so many in the Church to relate their own expertise in an enlightening way to moral and religious matters. This will certainly have an impact on the way moral argument is viewed in the Church. Yet when all is said and done, I still observe a more or less profound anti-intellectualism in certain segments of society. For instance, many physicians are notorious for their impatience with careful analysis. "I am on the firing line. I need answers." The same kind of resistance to analysis is operative in the kind of "magisteriolatry" I identified as sinning against docility by excess. This will certainly have an impact on the way moral argument is viewed in the Church.

2. *The notion of God and his providential wisdom.* James Gustafson has pointed out the importance in moral argument of the very notion one has of God.[16] God is, Gustafson argues, not only the creator and preserver of order; he is the enabler of our possibilities. "God not only acts to sustain and preserve life, but his power creates the conditions in which new possibilities for well-being occur, and in which different actions are required to preserve the well-being of the whole of creation."[17] According to the scholastic theology of the seventeenth to the nineteenth century, and the modern moral manuals, the principles of our well-being were viewed as "fixed and immutable," in Gustafson's wording. Gustafson notes that this view led to moral arguments and conclusions in medical ethics that were very conservative, "formidable dikes against morally heedless actions." He further states that the "crucial theological difference between Ramsey and me is in the emphasis that I give to God as the power that creates new possibilities for well-being in events of nature and history. . . . "[18] He explicitly notes that this emphasis opens possibilities for alteration of traditional principles and the ordering of traditional values.

I think two things are clear. First, Gustafson is correct in his contention that our notion of God will affect profoundly the shape of our moral arguments. Second, earlier theologians had a much more creator-preserver perspective than some contemporary theologians do.

3. *Cultural liberalism.* In the past centuries moral consciousness was heavily stamped by conformity to rule and community policy as the source of moral rightfulness. By way of contrast, the contemporary liberal assumptions of Western society tend to overemphasize, as a source of rightfulness, the sheer fact that the decision is the individual's. For example, we often hear: "It is not my concern what another does." "Each person must decide for him or herself." "Who am I to determine another's morals?" Or again, "I do not myself accept abortion, but I do not want to impose my morality on others." We see similar sayings frequently in many areas of moral concern. This is, of course, not an objective moral *argument* of any kind. Or perhaps better, it is an implicit moral analysis that identifies moral rightness and wrongness with self-determination. Americans are notoriously people who want to get along well with others and hence tend to leave others alone as one good way of doing this. But as a libertarian emphasis that effectively renounces moral argument, or refuses to state and discuss it, this perspective will have a great deal to say about how moral argument is viewed and accepted in a particular culture. It can easily lead to an attitude of apathy or even disdain toward careful discourse.

4. *Prevalent concept of authority in the Church.* Where teaching authority is claimed within a religious community and where this authority is associated by divine design with officeholders (the hierarchy), there is the tendency that such authoritative teaching will become self-validating, that is, it will be regarded as correct simply because it is proposed by authorities. This is probably especially true where authority is highly centralized, either at the Roman or diocesan level.

Such perspectives have a devaluating effect on the importance of moral argument and analysis, and the processes that nourish them. Moral positions will be regarded as correct regardless of the arguments or analysis used to support them. When moral analysis is devalued and replaced by authoritative assertions in the public consciousness, there is the grave danger that it will become careless and undisciplined. The nonfunctional easily becomes the neglected. That this can happen is evident in the types of moral argument sometimes made by manualist theologians to uphold ecclesiastical positions.

However, we are in a situation now—after and largely because of Vatican II—of decentralization of authority, though it is all too easy to detect in our times the reemergence of an older ecclesiastical imperialism. Collegiality at all levels is accepted in principle even if not always implemented. The French bishops summarized this as follows: "We have reached a point of no return. From now on the exercise of authority demands dialogue and a certain measure of responsibility for everyone. The authority needed for the life of any society can only be strengthened as a result."[19]

The decentralization of authority in the Church—always, of course, within proper measure—suggests that moral argument will again resume its proper role in the Church's ethical enterprise.

5. The notion of Church. The very self-definition of the Church can be tremendously influential in determining the nature and function of moral argument. For instance, if the prevalent notion is highly juridical, drawn up according to the pyramidal model noted in chapter 2, then this easily leads to a notion of unity intolerant of differences in moral analysis and conclusions. Arguments are viewed as wrong or unimportant because they lead to a difference of opinion at a very detailed and concrete level. In a juridical model of the Church, this is viewed as divisive and intolerable, and the analysis that led to it as somehow mistaken. This is the unspoken assumption of the "Questions and Answers" column in *The Homiletic and Pastoral Review*. The term "approved authors" appears there repeatedly. It is all but synonymous with "those who agree with the present formulations of the magisterium."

With a somewhat different view of the Church, a rather different approach to moral argument becomes possible. I refer to the view which sees the Church as a *communio*, the People of God. The model is concentric, not pyramidal. It is possible, of course, to understand *communio* in such a verticalized and rarified way that all is ultimately shrouded in mystery. When this happens, the notion of "church as *communio*" becomes exempt from human appeals, human analysis and human criticism, and in the process becomes so utterly otherworldly that it is literally unreal. But this is not inseparable from the notion of *communio*. The people are the repository of Christian wisdom and truth. As I noted in chapter 2, Cardinal Suenens wrote:

The Church seen from the starting point of baptism rather than that of the hierarchy, thus appeared from the first as a sacramental and mystical reality first and foremost, rather than—which it also is—a juridical society. It rested on its base, the People of God, rather than on its summit, the hierarchy. The pyramid of the old manuals was reversed.[20]

If this is the pervasive theological view, clearly moral argument will be deeply affected. For one thing, a key test of its validity will not be organizational or institutional conformity. Furthermore, purely deductive approaches will be seen as inadequate. Experience and reflection upon it will be proportionately more important in building and assessing moral analysis.[21]

6. Attitudes toward morality and public policy. It is the temptation of the Anglo-American tradition to identify these two. We are a pragmatic and litigious people for whom law is the answer to all problems, the only answer and a fully adequate answer. Thus many people confuse morality and public policy. If something is removed from the penal code, it is viewed as morally right and permissible. And if an act is seen as morally wrong, many want it made illegal. Behold the "there ought to be a law" syndrome.

When these two spheres, interrelated as they are, get confusedly identified, then the moral arguments establishing the one or the other get confusedly identified. Since public policy must be sensitive to a whole host of pragmatic considerations (e.g., enforceability, pluralism of conviction, social costs, social priorities) gatherable under the term "feasibility," it is possible for moral argument to be affected—indeed, corrupted—by such considerations. Furthermore, it is possible that the tactics used so often to move public policy can come to be regarded as "moral arguments." An example of these can be drawn from the late sixties and early seventies, when "gut feelings," confrontation, symbolic acts of protest, and other forms of nondiscursive exchanges prevailed over analytic discourse and were frequently regarded as adequate warrants for *moral* stances. The prophet was confused with the philosopher. That such conditions will have repercussions on the way Christian ethics is set forth, I have no doubt.

7. Cultural attitudes toward individualism and social insertion. This is similar to but distinguishable from the concerns mentioned previously in no. 3. The attitudes I refer to will affect above all the substantial emphasis in a person's moral reasoning, and even the topics one considers it worthwhile arguing about. For instance, James Gustafson, once again adverting to some differences in approach between himself and Paul Ramsey, notes that Ramsey's views on medical ethics are deeply stamped by his notion of *agape* and covenant fidelity between persons.[22]

Gustafson is more comfortable with a broader canvas. He writes:

> God wills the well-being of the creation. Just as there are historical oc-
> casions on which human physical life is not only risked but sacrificed for
> what is judged to be a human common good, for example, in the defense
> of a nation against unjust attack, so also there are occasions in which new
> possibilities for the well-being of individual persons, the human com-
> munity, and the whole of creation require action that risks harm, indeed
> irreversible harm, to individuals.[23]

Different times and different cultures will reflect either Ramsey's emphasis
on covenant between individuals or Gustafson's concern also with future
benefits for the community. I believe that a culture or nation where individual human rights are grossly violated is one where individual rights will
be highly emphasized, possibly even to the point of individualism. Thus,
the years immediately following World War II (Nuremberg trials) were
much more likely to reflect Ramsey's emphasis. It may be questioned
whether the same is true today. Be that as it may, such cultural variations
will certainly affect the kind of moral argument one constructs.

8. *Unity and pluralism of philosophical systems and language.*
In times of unity in philosophical systems and language, moral arguments
will tend to be more uniform, to share more basic anthropological
assumptions, and to recommend themselves to a much broader constituency. Where such unity does not exist, just the opposite will be the
case. Not only will there be diversity of emphasis, language, and conclusions, but the very moral arguments used will appear to the diverging
point of view to be not simply different, but erroneous.

An interesting example of this is the document of the Congregation for
the Doctrine of the Faith, *Declaration on Certain Questions Concerning Sexual
Ethics*.[24] Issued in 1976, the document deservedly met with a veritable
avalanche of severe criticism. One of the reasons for this was stated by Bernard Häring. He notes that the natural-law perspectives of the contemporary consultors to the Congregation are "represented as *the* constant
tradition and the teaching of the Church."[25] He argues that "there speaks in
the document not *the* preconciliar theology, but a very distinct preconciliar
theology," the type rejected by the Council in its rejection of several preliminary drafts for *Gaudium et Spes*.

We exist in an age of profound philosophical pluralism. It is clear that
this will affect moral argument in Christian ethics, its notion, function
and acceptability.

9. Relevance of experience and cognate empirical disciplines. It seems clear that a culture which is not scientifically oriented, especially if it be one where there is a clear chasm between the few educated and the masses of uneducated, will not be terribly sensitive to the importance of empirical sciences and human experience in the construction and evaluation of moral argument. Certainly in our time the enormous sensitivity to lived experience and the relevance of the cognate disciplines make moral argument much more complicated.

These are but a few of the cultural variables that can influence moral argument in Christian ethics. What is one to make of these influences? It is very dangerous to generalize, especially when some of these currents seem to be moving in opposite directions. But I would suggest the following three rather innocuous implications. First, moral argument is more important than ever in our time to the preservation of the substance of our value judgments. Why? Because many of the variables listed suggest that we are transitional between one form of argument (deductive, abstract, individualist, authoritarian, etc.) to another (inductive, community and benefits oriented, scientifically informed, less authoritarian, etc.). However, as in most cultural transitions, there will be segments that will resist the transition (even at times with some legitimacy) and there will be segments that will promote it. In such cases moral argument tends to collapse into the rhetoric of resistance and/or of promotion. In such a situation the danger is that the very relevance of moral argument will be questioned or lost. For resistance and promotion are not careful analytical arguments. They are postures of theological preference resembling political agenda. We all know that such postures are terribly vulnerable to short-cuts and frequently issue in poor moral arguments.

Second, moral argument is more difficult than ever to make and to make persuasive in the public forum, precisely because so much more must be attended to in constructing a good argument.

Third, poor arguments are often due to a failure to take these variables seriously enough, or to a too simplistic acceptance of them. I would hasten to add that this failure is not unique to a single school of thought.

Poor Moral Arguments in Contemporary Discourse

It may seem that there is little gain to be derived from identifying poor arguments; for the crucial question remains: What are the constitutive ingredients of a good argument? However, I believe that though the gain may be modest it is nevertheless not trivial. For poor arguments that are accepted not only establish nothing, they leave the resultant conclusions entrenched. Both of these considerations are formidable obstacles to the progress of Christian ethics. Identifying them is, therefore, a necessary step (*removens prohibens*) in the development of a sound ethic. Most of the analyses that deserve the title "poor" or "invalid" fit into either of two categories: *petitio principii* (begging the question), or *ignorantia elenchi* (missing the point). Clearly, these failures very frequently overlap and interpenetrate each other. That is, one who begs the question misses the point; and one who misses the point frequently begs the question. Furthermore, as is clear, there are many ways in which one can be said to "miss the point." For instance, as Rahner notes,[26] there can be appeal to a historically conditioned state of human beings that is taken for granted but is no longer valid or accurate. In what follows I shall simply list and exemplify a series of contemporary failings in moral discourse without attempting to classify them under either major fallacy.

1. *Confusion of parenetic discourse with normative discourse.* Parenesis is a form of discourse used to exhort to a form of conduct or to pass judgment upon it. It does not treat the pros and cons, the validity of a certain precept or prohibition. It takes it for granted. Normative ethics deals with the pros and cons of a prohibition, what is to count as unjust conduct and why.

A clear example of parenesis is 1 Corinthians 13:4-7 ("Love is patient; love is kind. Love is not jealous, it does not put on airs, it is not snobbish," etc.). Such salutary exhortations leave totally untouched what is to count as jealousy, snobbery, self-seeking, or forbearance. Similarly, the Johannine pericope on the woman taken in adultery is parenetic in character. The question is not whether adultery is right or wrong; all agree it is wrong. The only question is whether the woman has committed it and what should be done.

Confusion of these two forms of discourse is probably the most common error in contemporary Christian ethics. It results in both of the aforementioned logical fallacies (*petitio principii, ignorantia elenchi*). Let me list just a few examples.

Item. Paul Quay argues that some contemporary moral theologians are trying to "'relativize' so-called 'absolute prohibitions' against defrauding laborers, adultery, abortion, and the like."[27] Of course, adultery and defrauding laborers are always wrong. So is cruelty to children. But the normative question is: What forms of conduct are to count as adultery, cruelty, etc., and why? We have here a failure to distinguish fact-description (*Tatsachenbegriff*) from value-description (*Wertbegriff*). Certain actions (killing) are presented in terms of an already concluded value-description (murder) when the normative question is whether this or that killing truly is *unjust* killing, murder. Value-descriptions pertain to the area of parenetic discourse.

Item. Donald McCarthy, in describing certain recent developments in moral theology (what he calls "proportionalism") writes: "Other extenuating circumstances or good intentions as adultery for the good of marriage . . . can never make these actions good."[28] Furthermore, he notes several categories of nonsexual actions described by Vatican II as "criminal" (genocide, slavery, abortion, euthanasia) and then adds: "it seems clear that the Church cannot open these actions to the kind of circumstantial justification that the ethical principle of proportionalism might allow. . . . "

When something is described as "adultery" or "genocide," nothing can justify it, for the very terms are morally qualifying terms meaning unjustified killing. That is, they are tautological. The normative question is: What (in descriptive terms) is to count as genocide?

Item. Gustave Martelet compares the evil of contraception with the use of violence and a lie.[29] These latter, it should be noted, are two remarkably different terms. The first is descriptive and presents a premoral disvalue (since violence is occasionally justifiable). The second is a morally qualifying term. Confusion of the two results in *ignorantia elenchi*. Many more examples of this could be adduced. For instance, I have frequently heard "We are baptized in the Spirit, set apart" proposed as normative warrant for the rejection of direct sterilization as intrinsically evil. As Stephen Toulmin remarks: "To show that you ought to choose certain actions is one thing; to make you *want to do* what you ought to do is another, and not a philosopher's task."[30]

Somewhat similarly, authors like J. Ratzinger, Hans Urs von Balthasar, H. Schürmann constantly assert that "Christ is the concrete categorical imperative," that his word is "the ultimate decisive moral norm."[31] These statements are, of course, true. But with such statements one does not raise the issue of *how* one originally knows God's will, "whether through faith alone as a distinct manner of knowing or through human reason. Jesus' word is the 'ultimate decisive norm' even when one accepts the fact that Christ by his authority newly confirmed these (natural) precepts and added to them greater binding force."[32]

2. Rhetoric as normative argument. This is simply another example of the point made in no. 1; yet it is so frequent that it deserves to be highlighted. For instance, in the ethical debates on in vitro fertilization with embryo transfer, we frequently hear the following: "Who are we to play God?" "We must not tamper with nature." These are blatant examples of the confusion of parenesis with normative discourse ending in *ignorantia elenchi*.

In ecclesial circles we often hear responses to ethical analysis couched in the following words: "Theologians are causing confusion." "The faithful have a right not to be disturbed." Into this category also fit appeals for unity, for respect for authority, etc. Little more need be said about such "arguments" except to add, in all fairness, that "this is in violation of academic freedom" pertains to the same category. Procedural purity is confused with argumentative purity.

3. The straightforward petitio principii. Many forms of moral argument imply a begging of the question. Others are undisguised examples of it.

Item. The Congregation for the Doctrine of the Faith issued in 1975 a document reaffirming the condemnation of all direct sterilization.[33] It argues that the principle of totality may not be invoked, because sterility intended as such (*in se*) is not directed to the integral good of the person because it is an assault on (*nocet*) the ethical good (*bono ethico*) of the person. Why does it do this? The Congregation responds: Because it deliberately (*ex proposito*) deprives "foreseen and freely chosen sexual activity of an essential element" (the potential to procreate).

No one would quibble with the assertion that an intervention which harms the *moral* good of the person (*quod est supremum*) cannot be justified by the principle of totality. That is clear from the very meaning of that principle. What is not clear, however, is that the power to procreate is an element so essential to sexual intimacy that to deprive freely chosen intimacy of this power is in every instance to assault the ethical good of the person. That is precisely the point to be established. Until it has been, mere reassertion of the prohibition begs the question.

Donald McCarthy, in comparing the new procedure of low tubal ovum transfer (LTOT), where the ovum is transferred to the uterus to be fertilized by natural intercourse, with in vitro fertilization (IVF), contends that it "differs radically and essentially" from the latter.[34] In IVF there is "no personal involvement of the parents with each other." They simply supply their gametes. Second, in IVF there is no expression of the marriage covenant and the child is produced by technology. Thus he approves LTOT but rejects IVF.

I think we must grant these differences. But what is their ethical significance? To accept one technology (LTOT) and reject the other (IVF), the meaning of McCarthy's descriptive differences must be: (1) The parents must be personally involved through sexual union in the procreation of new life. (2) In the conception of new life the marriage covenant must be expressed through sexual union. But these assertions are, of course, the very things to be established if IVF is to be totally rejected. *Why* must the parents be personally involved in all, even exceptional and last-resort, cases of generation of new life? Merely to describe differences and then give them ethical weight is what Schüller refers to as "persuasive description." It nearly always contains a *petitio principii*.

Item. In attempting to justify the moral significance of the distinction between direct and indirect voluntariety, Paul Ramsey rejects the notion of proportionate reason as sufficient because it involves the weighing of incommensurables. He writes: "There is, of course, measurable meaning in some judgments of proportion, that is, in cases in which one takes (indirectly) one life to save the only one that can be saved (rather than lose two) in abortion cases."[35] He then states that "obviously one should choose the lesser of these commensurate evils," but adds that such body counts "are the only instances I can think of in which there is clear commensurate meaning in the final judgment of proportion under the rule of twofold effect."[36]

Notice what we have here. (1) Ramsey argues that it is precisely incommensurability of goods that demands indirectness of intent. (2) He admits that there is in the case clear commensurability of the goods and evils involved. (3) Yet he asserts in such abortion decisions the notion and need for indirectness.

If evils are commensurable and one should "obviously . . . choose the lesser of these commensurate evils," then what does indirectness have to do with it? This is a clear *petitio principii*, the smuggling in of a notion as necessary whose very necessity is the issue.

4. Doubling the middle term. This is a well-known logical fallacy that corrupts moral analysis. What is not known is that it is a frequently used and unrecognized form of argument in contemporary discourse. Let me take an example in the form of the following syllogism:

> Every action contrary to nature is morally evil. But falsehood and contraception are contrary to nature. Therefore they are morally evil.

In the major of the syllogism, "contrary to nature" must mean unreasonable. Yet in the minor, "contrary to nature" can only mean "relative disvalue," even though the argument intends it to mean more. Therefore the argument is invalid because it equivalently says that "to cause a disvalue is unreasonable."[37] But such a conclusion is false and its falsehood is made apparent when we realize that all innerworldly goods are relative. This is clear when we consider the most urgent of basic goods, life itself. There are times when it may reasonably, even if tragically, be taken.[38] Clearly, therefore, norms that impose realization of a relative value (or avoidance of a relative disvalue) always include a built-in exception clause. That is, they have binding force unless the value they impose competes in the situation with a value to be preferred. (For example, one must keep the entrusted secret unless the only way to prevent greater evil is to reveal it.) When we act in this way, we act "according to nature," because we act reasonably.

5. Confusing authority for argument. One of the tasks of the moral theologian is to aid in purification of the conceptual models and formulations wherein we concretize our substantial moral concerns. Formulations (and conclusions) are only more or less adequate to the abiding substance. But the magisterium has frequently taught concrete morals in an authoritative way, using the formulations available at a particular time in history. This means that theologians can sometimes suggest formulations and conclusions at variance with official ones.

In some circles this mere variation is taken to be sufficient evidence of a failed moral argument. Thus the argumentative phrases: "These are mere theological *speculations*." "Who is to be followed, the pope or theologians?" "The theologian issues personal opinions, the pope issues authentic teaching." "Once the hierarchy has spoken, the obligation is to assent and obey." Etc. (*Roma locuta, causa finita*).

Without wishing to forfeit the kernel of truth in these statements, one can still insist that as used they tend to replace moral argument with merely juridical assertions. Authoritative assertions can never replace moral argument. That is why moral positions asserted authoritatively against a prevailing consensus of moral analysis become simply incredible. But when "loyalty to the Holy See" becomes the test of the legitimacy of a moral argument, then things are upside down. Truth becomes subordinate to institutional purposes and the instruments of its search. Stephen Toulmin remarked in a slightly different context that if we are never to be allowed to question the pronouncements of those who administer a moral code, then we are no longer dealing with morality but with authority.[39]

6. Various forms of the "genetic fallacy." By this I refer to the "argument" which identifies (labels) the arguer (the source), and thereby thinks to have discredited the argument or to have clinched it. For instance, some Catholic theologians are identified as "deviants" or "dissenters" and that is taken to be an adequate refutation of what they say. This is a blatant *ignorantia elenchi*. But the shoe fits the other foot too. It simply misses the point to respond to an argument that it is "conservative."

A more subtle form of this type of thing is seen in M. Zalba's recent statement made of Charles Curran: "The ecclesiastical magisterium cannot be accused of physicalism without grave injustice, since it is stated without any demonstration or possibility thereof, that the magisterium 'identifies' the human and moral act with the physical structure of the conjugal act."[40] Whether there is injustice or not depends entirely on the correctness of the conclusion that *every act* must always remain open to the possibility of procreation if it is to avoid being intrinsically evil. It would have been more helpful and enlightening had Zalba discussed the arguments for the traditional conclusion rather than justice-injustice. These latter categories suppose that the argument is clear and the conclusion correct. Thus the genetic fallacy leading to *ignorantia elenchi*. One's position is "argued" in terms of unjust accusations.

Some of the most mischievous forms of the genetic fallacy are involved with the terms consequentialism, utilitarianism and deontology. In some circles it is considered a sufficient dismissal of an argument or analysis to say that it is "teleological"—or, if better mileage is desired from the stereotype, "utilitarian."

Actually, these terms are so diversely understood that they have become all but useless. For instance, some identify teleological and utilitarian; others do not. Some talk of "mixed deontologists," others do not. In other words, the terms are often used as if they are clear when they are not.

For the record, let me say that I believe there are at least three theories about rightness and wrongness of actions. (1) Actions are right or wrong depending solely on the consequences. (2) Some actions are right or wrong regardless of the consequences. (3) Consequences play a determining but not the only role in rightness or wrongness.

There is, of course, an enormous ambiguity about the meaning of the term "consequence." (For example, is the death of an aggressor a consequence of my act, or part of the very definition of the act?) Even after this ambiguity has been clarified, I am convinced that most contemporary Catholic moral theologians fit the third category, a grouping best named "moderate teleologists" or "mixed deontologists," if a name is considered essential. In this group I would include Josef Fuchs, Franz Böckle, Bernard Häring, Bruno Schüller, Charles Curran, Alfons Auer, Louis Janssens, Franz Scholz, and most Catholic moral theologians writing today.

This is not surprising. Anyone familiar with the centuries-old tradition of Catholic moral theology would have to agree with Schüller "that the normative ethics of Catholic tradition . . . is overwhelmingly teleological."[41] Similarly, James Gustafson rightly notes that "the teleological framework of Catholic theology and ethics has always set the concern for consequences in a central place in moral theology."[42] Even the deontologically understood rules that did develop had a teleological basis. Thus, as Gustafson notes, adultery not only violates a covenant but the rule against it has validity because adultery is harmful to the parties involved.

One can see that teleology at work in the process of restrictive interpretation given over the centuries to the commandment "Thou shalt not kill." If we adhere to the prohibition literally, we find that our hands are tied against unjust aggressors who disdain the rule. The result is that more lives are lost than if we had not adopted the rule. Therefore we qualify the rule, interpreting it as forbidding the taking of *innocent* human life. Then there are cases (birth room conflicts) that are not covered by the exceptions comprised under "innocent." So we refine the rule further, distinguishing between direct and indirect killing, the latter being at times permissible. The rule is, in a sense, as acceptable as it is capable of being restricted to accommodate our sense of right and wrong, and our firm commitment to save more lives than we lose in situations of conflict.

Another form of what we call the "genetic fallacy" is a confusion between Christian ethics in the normative sense and Christian ethics in the genetic-historical sense. The traditional thesis for centuries has been that the moral rules incumbent on a Christian are materially identical with the precepts or prohibitions of the so-called natural law (*recta ratio*). Joseph Ratzinger denies this and one of his reasons is that faith is reliable but reason is not.[43]

Here we must distinguish between the truth value or internal validity of moral judgments, and the genetic explanation of true and false judgments. Thus we may distinguish between two types of Christian ethics: (1) Christian ethics in the normative (truth value) sense—what Christ said and did, as expressed in the words of the New Testament. In this sense the ethic is absolutely true. (2) Christian ethics in the genetic-historical sense— e.g., St. Thomas' interpretation of what Christ said and did. In this second sense it remains questionable whether the ethic is truly Christian.[44]

Similarly, one can distinguish (1) philosophical ethics in the normative sense, that is, the law of reason, and (2) philosophical ethics in the genetic-historical sense, that is, Kant's understanding of this.

In saying that faith is more reliable than reason, Ratzinger confuses these two levels. Reason is more reliable than faith if philosophical ethics is taken in the normative sense and Christian ethics in the genetic-historical sense. However, faith seems more reliable if taken in the normative sense and philosophical ethics in the genetic-historical sense. The traditional teaching on norms (revelation does not add anything concretely to them) concerns only the epistemological status of norms, not the sociological, historical, or psychological conditions that may hinder reason from arriving at true value judgments. This is overlooked by Ratzinger.

7. Misplaced or misnamed pairs. Here two examples will suffice. Theologian Norbert Rigali contrasts abstract with historical. Thus, "while the preacher can discuss morality in an abstract way, the confessor, if he is performing his duty in an even minimally adequate way, must become historically involved with morality; the confessor is involved with an individual in his or her personal life."[45] Here we have abstract contrasted with historical and then historical defined in terms of individual or personal life.

Two remarks. First, this identifies and confuses normative ethics with pastoral understanding and compassion, and raises this latter to the status of the former. The proper contrast is abstract and concrete; for a norm can be at once abstract and historical. Second, this identification, if pushed, does away with the possibility of generalization in ethics, which means it does away with ethics as a science. In other words, unless I misunderstand him, Rigali has so described historical consciousness that it wipes out the pair right-wrong to concentrate on the pair good-bad, and at the level of individual discernment.

A second instance is contained in the excellent study by Robert Weir, *Selective Nontreatment of Handicapped Newborns.*[46] Weir mentions several ethical options or approaches, among them the best-interests criterion and a quality-of-life approach. He rejects the latter for the former. This is a misnamed pair because it is impossible to determine the best interests of a handicapped newborn without reference to the *kind of life* he or she would experience as a result of treatment or its withholding. Weir makes this clear repeatedly. For instance, "the central question in the best interests position is this one: given the possibility that a handicapped infant will not have a meaningful life by normal standards, is that life likely to represent a fate worse than death or a life worth experiencing even with the handicaps." A "life likely to represent a fate worse than death" is, in my judgment, a straightforward quality-of-life assessment.

8. *Post hoc ergo propter hoc.* There is a fairly heavy body of Roman Catholic literature that groups together contraception-sterilization-abortion. Furthermore, such literature frequently blames the frequency of abortion in this country on the acceptance of contraception.

I have no doubt that there are those who view contraception and abortion along a psychological continuity. That is, they are prepared to do anything to avoid having a child. Thus if contraception fails or is not used, they are ready for abortion. However, contraception and abortion are entirely different procedures. To use the prevalence of abortion as a form of argument to reject every contraceptive act as intrinsically evil is to use a nonargument. Furthermore, it is inconsistent with a tradition which holds that not every killing need be murder, not every falsehood is a lie, not every violation of a promise is infidelity, not every taking of another's property is theft, etc.

9. *Attributing and attacking positions no one holds.* This is transparently bad argument and a case of *ignorantia elenchi*. But in a polarized church it is unfortunately increasingly frequent. For instance, William May criticizes the work of those theologians who base their exception-making on what has been called for decades in Catholic tradition "proportionate reason." While he concedes that estimating proportions in conflict is not solely the prerogative of the individual and therefore is not necessarily subjectivistic, he does believe that this structure of moral reasoning is relativistic. That is, an act is not wrong "simply because the community deems that it is." To think so is "cultural relativism."[47]

May seems to believe that certain Catholic revisionists hold an act to be objectively wrong "*because* the community deems that it is." Of course, that is untenable. But, to be blunt, no one says this nor is anyone who recommends communal discernment vulnerable to such accusations. We are a believing community; hence we learn within a community and form our consciences within a community. This does not imply that the community is always right. It says only that a realistic individual will understand the dangers of trying to discover moral truth alone. Pilgrims are imperfect even when they join hands and minds. But none of these reflections leads to the conclusion that an act is objectively wrong *because* the community thinks so.

Another example of this type of thing is found in the writings of Gustav Ermecke. Ermecke has been among the gloomiest commentators on recent trends in moral theology. He rejects a teleological understanding of moral norms outright. One of his reasons: a value measure or scale must be based in Christian ontology and anthropology. Of course it must. Furthermore, he argues, the use of prudence must conform to an objective value scale. Of course it must. But what does *that* have to do with a rejection of teleology, except to attribute imprudence and an un-Christian anthropology to those whose teleology he rejects?[48]

I believe this listing has gone far enough, even though it could be prolonged much further by pointing up the following errors: biblical literalism; appeal to experience alone as if it were a sufficient moral warrant; mistaking givenness or facticity for the normative (a mistake that runs wild in discussions of birth regulation); accepting mere descriptions as "proofs" (this too in re birth regulation); confusing ideal statements (e.g., "No more war, never") with their application in conflict situations, etc.

I have pointed out in some detail the bad arguments that others have made. In doing so, it is quite possible that I have left the impression that bad arguments are invariably those "of the others." Quite the contrary. I blush at some of the "prescientific instinctive convictions" that I have uncritically accepted and foisted on my students. I blush at my introduction of parenesis at the precise moment when the argument is weakest. And even a beginner with the foolishness to peruse some of my past writings would find in them, I am sure, begged questions and non sequiturs in sufficient numbers to bring a smile to even the most dour of logicians.

But that is not the point. We all see only darkly. We all seek refuge in still harbors. Etc. The point is the importance of recognizing and exposing faulty argument wherever it occurs because "this is a difficult task for which the Church's magisterium with its conservative attitude (understandable but perhaps also unjustified) generally shows little gratitude."[49] Moreover, he who fails to recognize faulty arguments will be doubly disadvantaged in constructing good ones.

Moral analysis—the struggle to arrive ever closer to a genuine convergence of probabilities in our value judgments, a convergence that is based in human reality as the Christian sees it and that is consistent—will always retain a central place in Christian ethics because, I submit, this ethics takes its Christology seriously. An ethics that takes the Incarnation seriously will be the very last to abandon moral reasoning and argument; for the Incarnation, no matter what the depth of its mystery, was, as Vatican II repeatedly noted, an affirmation of the human and its goodness. And this "human," however nondiscursive it may be in our future life, is one that presently builds its moral norms, understands exceptions to them, and communicates them through a difficult discursive process known as moral analysis.

Notes

1. Paul VI, *Humanae Vitae* ("On the Regulation of Birth") (Washington: U.S. Catholic Conference, 1968), n. 28.

2. Bernard Häring, "The Encyclical Crisis," *Commonweal* 88 (1968):588-94.

3. Ibid.

4. Joseph Bernardin, *Linacre Quarterly* 42(1975):220.

5. C.D. Broad, *Five Types of Ethical Theory* (London: 1930).

6. *Documents*, 202.

7. Norbert J. Rigali, S.J., "On Christian Ethics," *Chicago Studies* 10 (1971):227-47. Rigali distinguishes four levels of the term "Ethics": essential, existential, essential Christian, and existential Christian, the first alone comprising those actions that apply to persons as persons without further qualifiers.

8. That there have been distortions of this *recta ratio* is easily seen in John Courtney Murray's enumeration of them in *We Hold These Truths* (New York: Sheed and Ward, 1960).

9. Denziger-Schonmetzer, *Enchiridion Symbolorum* (Barcelona: Herder, 1963), no. 2853 (1670).

10. Ibid., no. 3005 (1786).

11. Cf. Richard A. McCormick, S.J., *Notes on Moral Theology 1965-1980* (Lanham, Md.: University Press of America, 1981), 626 ff.

12. Karl Rahner, "Über schlechte Argumentation in der Moral-theologie," in *In Libertatem Vocati Estis*, ed. H. Boelaars and R. Tremblay (Rome: M. Pisani, 1977), 245-57. This is also found in *Theological Investigations*, vol. 18 (New York: Crossroad, 1983).

13. Rahner, *Theological Investigations* (as in note 12), 78.

14. Loc. cit., 78.

15. Loc. cit., 81.

16. James M. Gustafson, *The Contributions of Theology to Medical Ethics* (Milwaukee: Marquette University, 1975).

17. Loc. cit., 38.

18. Loc. cit., 44.

19. *National Catholic Reporter*, 28 May 1969.

20. *National Catholic Reporter*, 28 May 1969.

21. Cf. Bruno Schüller, S.J., "Die Bedeutung der Erfahrung für die Rechtfertigung sitttlicher Verhaltensregeln," in *Christlich Glauben und Handeln* (Düsseldorf: Patmos, 1977).

22. Gustafson, as in note 16 at 44.

23. Loc. cit., 45-46.

24. Cf. *Catholic Mind* 74 (no. 1302, 1976), 52-65.

25. B. Häring, "Reflexionen zur Erklärung der Glaubenskongregation über einige Fragen der Sexualethik," *Theologisch-Praktische Quartalschrift* 124 (1976):115-26.

26. As in note 13, 84.

27. Paul Quay, S.J., "Morality by Calculation of Values," *Theology Digest* 23 (1975):347-64.

28. As cited in McCormick (cf. note 11), at 732-34.

29. G. Martelet, S.J., *L'Existence humaine et l'amour: Pour mieux comprendre l'encyclique Humanae vitae* (Paris: Desclée, 1969), at 140 and 149.

30. S. Toulmin, *Reason in Ethics* (Cambridge: Cambridge University Press, 1950), 163.

31. Cf. Joseph Ratzinger, *Principien Christlicher Moral* (Einsiedeln: Johannes Verlag, 1975).

32. Bruno Schüller, S.J., "Zur Diskussion über das Proprium einer Christlichen Ethik," *Theologie und Philosophie* 51(1976):321-43.

33. *Origins* 6 (10 June 1976):33-35.

34. *Medical-Moral Newsletter* 20 (1983):30-31.

35. Paul Ramsey, "Incommensurability and Indeterminancy in Moral Choice," in *Doing Evil to Achieve Good*, ed. R.A. McCormick, S.J., and Paul Ramsey (Chicago: Loyola, 1978).

36. Ibid., 71.

37. Cf. B. Schüller, S.J., "Typen Ethischer Argumentation in der Katholischen Moraltheologie," *Theologie und Philosophie* 45 (1970):526-50.

38. Gustafson, cf. note 16, at 45.

39. Toulmin as in note 30, at 101.

40. M.Zalba, S.J., "Ex personae ejusdemque actuum natura," *Periodica* 68 (1979):201-32, at 232.

41. B. Schüller, S.J., "Types of Grounding for Ethical Norms," in *Readings in Moral Theology No. 1*, ed. Charles E. Curran and Richard A. McCormick, S.J. (Mahwah, N.J.: Paulist, 1979), 188.

42. James Gustafson, *Protestant and Roman Catholic Ethics* (Chicago: University of Chicago Press, 1978), 49.

43. Cf. note 31.

44. Cf. note 32.

45. Norbert Rigali, S.J., "Morality and Historical Consciousness," *Chicago Studies* 18 (1979):161-68.

46. Robert Weir, *Selective Nontreatment of Handicapped Newborns* (Oxford: Oxford University Press, 1984).

47. William May, "Modern Catholic Ethics: The New Situationism," *Faith and Reason* 4 (1978):21-38. Cf. also May, "The Moral Meaning of Human Acts," *Homiletic and Pastoral Review* 79 (October 1978):10-21.

48. As in McCormick (cf. note 11), 689-91 and 530-32.

49. Rahner, *Theological Investigations* (vol. 18, as in note 12), 81.

Chapter 4

The Chill Factor in Contemporary Moral Theology

At the end of chapter 3, Karl Rahner was cited as saying that the magisterium of the Church "generally shows little gratitude" for the performance of theology's critical tasks. This is a typical Rahnerian understatement. For instance, the Congregation for the Doctrine of the Faith hardly exulted when I accused them of a begged question.[1] Nor could that same Congregation have been overjoyed with John R. Donahue's fine treatment of *Inter insigniores*.[2] In that declaration, which rejected the ordination of women, the Congregation had cited St. Thomas as rejecting such ordination. The citation read:

> For since a sacrament is a sign, there is required in the things that are done in the sacraments not only the "res" but the signification of the "res."[3]

Donahue simply shows that the declaration breaks off the citation in midsentence. It continues:

> . . . as was stated above, that in extreme unction, it is necessary to have someone sick in order to signify healing. Since, therefore, it is not possible in the female sex that any eminence of degree be signified, for a woman is in the state of subjection, she cannot receive the sacrament of orders.

In other words, according to Thomas, it is not a lack of natural representation, but the presence of natural subjection that is the undergirding reason against the ordination of women. Yet the text is cited to show that women cannot signify the male Christ. Thomas' argument (the inferiority of women) was rooted in what above was called a "prescientific global conviction." Today, it would be identified as a colossal cultural bias and would be thoroughly disowned. Donahue was not, he tells me, deluged with congregational gratitude for doing what was simply his critical theological task.

If gratitude and encouragement is not the ordinary Roman response, what is it? In a general way, I believe it is accurate to designate it as "defensive negativity." That is, of course, a sprawling term that can include everything from a verbal frown to a wrist slap to a silencing. Whatever form it takes, the important point is that such negativity includes, indeed embodies, a theology.

Let me provide an example here. On October 18, 1980, bioethicist Corrine Bayley and I published an article questioning the absoluteness of the Church's prohibition of direct sterilization.[4] The occasion was the issuance of a document by the National Conference of Catholic Bishops (July 3, 1980) repeating this traditional prohibition. Anyone familiar with the discussion will realize two things. First, the traditional formulation is a matter of theological dispute. Many reputable theologians are convinced that direct sterilization can occasionally be justified. Second, insistence on the traditional teaching is creating enormous problems for Catholic health care facilities. Indeed, *Commonweal* argued that the sterilization edict "promises to reduce rather than increase respect for traditional teaching." It continued: "It will create bureaucratic problems for Catholic hospitals, but for most Catholics it will only add to the Church's unfortunate loss of credibility in all matters of sexual morals."[5]

Bayley and I had no solution to the practical institutional problem. All we urged was that "the conversation must continue." We concluded: "When a question is the object of a genuine dispute in the Church, the very worst thing to do is to close the conversation, decree a solution and select as consultants only those who will support it."

This was a quite modest and unthreatening conclusion. Yet it occasioned a written response by (then) Archbishop Jerome Hamer, second in command at the Congregation for the Doctrine of the Faith. Hamer objected to the fact that we "cast doubt upon the directives of the competent ecclesiastical authorities in this matter." He stated that our public dissent makes dialogue difficult and asked that the local ordinary, James Hickey, discuss the matter with me.

On December 15, 1980, I responded in part as follows.

Dear Archbishop Hamer:

Your letter (Prot. 168/75) reached me through the kindness of Archbishop James Hickey. Archbishop Hickey and I discussed the content of your letter in a very warm and cordial evening together at his residence. I am sure we did not agree on all points and I trust that the Archbishop will be in touch with you on this matter. I told Archbishop Hickey that I would write to you on this matter and he thought it a good idea.

Your letter mentioned that our article ("Sterilization: the Dilemma of Catholic Hospitals," *America*, Oct. 18, 1980) makes dialogue with the magisterium difficult. I am frankly at a loss to explain why you should con- clude that. Undoubtedly behind such a conclusion there are ecclesiological assumptions about how theologians ought to conduct themselves vis-a-vis the hierarchical magisterium. Archbishop Hickey and I found ourselves in disagreement on some of these points, especially on whether or not dissenting views ought to be restricted to professional theological journals. I suspect that the CDF and I would have similar disagreements. Hence I wish to communicate to you my convictions (and those of a majority of the theological community) on this subject.

1. *Theology as public enterprise.* In the modern world the day is simply passed when theological opinion can be buried in and restricted to theological journals. Your Excellency may recall, as an example, the modest probe made by Louis Janssens in *Ephemerides Theologicae Lovanienses* ("Morale conjugale et progestogènes," 1963, 787-826). A short time later a summary appeared in *Newsweek*. My own response to the Congregation's March 13 (1975) letter on sterilization (*Theological Studies*, 1976, 471- 477) was picked up by the *New York Times*. That happens over and over and is simply unavoidable in the modern world. As you know, important documents of the Holy See are frequently published *in toto* in outlets such as the *New York Times*. It is but a part of realism to expect that reactions to these documents will be published in accompanying stories.

It is simply unreal to think that theological opinion can be restricted to professional journals. I am contacted on an almost daily basis by the news media. So are many others. We consider it a responsibility to contribute to the free flow of ideas in the Church and the world. If this free flow of ideas makes dialogue with the magisterium difficult, then that should not be attributed to public dissent as such, but to the persistence of outdated ideas about the function of the theologian, the response due to the authentic teaching of the magisterium, and the free flow of ideas in the Church. Surely it is not the case that before dialogue can occur there must be agreement on all subjects.

In this respect I should like to call your attention to the fact that Archbishop Jean Jadot sent me a copy of the CDF's "Declaration on Euthanasia" several days before its release. He knew I would be approached by the news media. He also knew that the document was a good one. When the document was released, I was contacted by the *Washington Post, New York Times, NC News, Newsday, U.S. News and World Report* and several radio stations. I was able to say that the document is excellent, to summarize it, and to support the magisterium in this way. This is the way things should work out.

When they do not work out this way, we ought to identify the true source of the problem. It is not publicity as such. The true source of the problem is rather a poorly argued and poorly articulated document. If the Church expects to have a document like the "Declaration on Euthanasia" publicly supported and praised—as it should be—then it must, in the modern world, expect a similar critical honesty where documents do not achieve excellence.

2. *The quality of the NCCB statement on tubal ligation.* The document asserts "the objective immorality of direct sterilization" and that such sterilization cannot be justified by the principle of totality. That assertion will not win theological support. In a conversation with Archbishop John Quinn (the then president of the NCCB) prior to the issuance of the statement on tubal ligation, I told him that. I further told him that I would be obliged in conscience to say so. I knew exactly what would happen: the media would call. One must be honest. I could do nothing but criticize the document, because it was poor. One cannot honestly agree with a document that he—with many others—judges to be unnuanced or wrong. Nor can one with good conscience remain silent.

Frankly, Your Excellency, we shall always be in trouble when members of the hierarchy, or the CDF, or even the Holy Father reassert conclusions as *certain and binding* when such conclusions do not have theological support. But let us be accurate on the source of that trouble and confusion. It is not primarily public criticism by theologians. It is first of all and at root a problem of the use of authority. I would call Your Excellency's attention to the splendid article by Bishop B.C. Butler ("Authority and the Christian Conscience," *Clergy Review* 1975, 3-17). Of authentic noninfallible teaching he states that to "require the same adhesion for doctrines that are indeed taught by officials with authority but to which the Church has not irrevocably committed itself is to abuse authority." More specifically, he describes the proper response as "a welcoming gratitude that goes along with the keen alertness of a critical mind, and with a good will concerned to play its part both in the purification and the development of her inheritance." In this respect, I believe Archbishop Quinn's intervention in the recent [1980] Synod was outstanding. Speaking of contraception and the division in the Church, he noted: "And so in the normal and foreseeable course of events, this problem is not going to be solved or reduced merely by a simple reiteration of past formulations or by ignoring the fact of dissent."

Here I should like to call Your Excellency's attention to an article by the eminent Karl Rahner ("Theologie and Lehramt, *Stimmen der Zeit*, 1980, 363-375). He states: "What are contemporary moral theologians to make of Roman declarations on sexual morality that they regard as too unnuanced? Are they to remain silent, or is it their task to dissent, to give a more nuanced interpretation? Rahner is unhesitating in his response. "I believe that the theologian, after mature reflection, has the right and many times the duty, to speak out against (*'widersprechen'*) a teaching of the magisterium and to support his dissent."

3. *The status of "intrinsece inhonestum" in the Church.* As Your Excellency is surely aware, there is not a *major* theologian that I can locate who will support that formulation. E. Chiavacci noted this in 1978 (*Rivista di Teologia Morale*, 519-527). Indeed, it may be of interest to you to know that an esteemed American bishop said to me this November (about the article on sterilization in *America*): "I can name a hundred bishops who agree with you, but not one who will say so publicly." Several bishops thanked me for the article and told me that they agreed with it.

That seems to be the source of many of our problems. It is a known fact that bishops do not feel free to speak their true minds. When they do so, great pressures are brought to bear on them. In this respect I should like to call Your Excellency's attention to an article by André Naud ("Les voix de l'église dans les questions morales," *Science et esprit*, 1980, 161-176). Naud insists that much of our problem (sc., that of the magisterium) is due to the fact that bishops do not speak their true minds both before and after Roman interventions. If this continues, the magisterium is going to be paralyzed and suffer continuing credibility problems. I am one who believes that the magisterium is a great gift. But to be effective it must operate in ways effective in the modern world.

4. *The right of the faithful to information in the Church.* The faithful have a right to know of the status of theological opinion in the Church, especially when it affects their own personal lives. In an address at Holy Cross Abbey, Bernard Häring stated: "Those who are doubtful whether they can accept it (*Humanae vitae*) have to study it thoroughly, have to read it with good will, but they also have to accept other information in the Church. They cannot dissociate the pope from the whole of the Church." (*Commonweal*, 1980, 493-497). That reflects the conviction of many of us in these difficult matters. And if the faithful have a right to such "other information," what can possibly be wrong with publishing it in a magazine like *America?* . . .

Let me conclude this long letter by noting that the *America* article did no more publicly than Archbishop Quinn did publicly—that is, call for continuing conversation. I find it difficult to understand how that can be a threat to anyone or anything. My devotion and loyalty to the magisterium remains firm, as it always has been. But I find that that very loyalty demands that I voice my opinion, even on controversial matters, clearly and publicly. Any other alternative I find incompatible with loyalty to the Church and the magisterium.

With cordial regards for you personally, I remain

Sincerely yours in Christ,
Richard A. McCormick, S.J.

In a kind letter dated January 22, 1981, Archbishop Hamer stated that there was indeed a disagreement between my views and the CDF's on theological responsibility. He noted that if a theologian disagrees with the magisterium then that person should make such disagreement known to magisterial authorities rather than "to call this teaching into question through an appeal to public opinion."

On March 18, 1981, I responded as follows.

Dear Archbishop Hamer:

In your letter of Jan. 22, 1981, you stated: "In this case, the theologian's responsibility is to make whatever difficulty he may have with the authentic teaching in question known to the magisterial authority rather than to exercise a presumed right to call this teaching into question through an appeal to public opinion."

Your Excellency, with all due respect, I feel compelled to note two things. First, the theology behind "make . . . known to the magisterial authority" is simply outmoded. It presupposes a notion of the Church according to which the faithful are "outsiders" with no responsibility for or competence in the Church's teaching. I know of no reputable theologian who would endorse such a notion.

Second, and far more serious, is your phrase "through an appeal to public opinion." I must protest this in the strongest language possible. That language supposes that when theologians discuss controverted matters they are attempting to enroll the public *against* the magisterium. Several things are wrong with that. First, it improperly ascribes motives. Second, it misconceives the nature of theological discussion in the Church. Theology is a public enterprise. This is especially true of those matters that touch the daily lives of the faithful. The faithful assuredly have the right to know what is the authentic teaching of the Church. They also have the right to know of the theological response to such authentic formulations. If such responses, presented humbly and respectfully in a magazine such as *America,* are seen as a threat to the good of the Church, then that indicates an unsupportable preoccupation with authority (rather than the issue at stake) and a corresponding distrust of the free flow of ideas in the Church.

As a theologian deeply concerned with the truth and the pastoral good of the Church, I cannot accept such notions. Nor can my colleagues. It is in a spirit of profound loyalty to the Church and of respect for Your Excellency that I convey these concerns to you.

Sincerely in Christ,
Richard A. McCormick, S.J.

Once again Archbishop Hamer took the time to respond to my concerns. On May 7, 1981 he simply called my attention to the statement of Pius XII in *Humani Generis*. "But if the Supreme Pontiffs in their official documents purposely pass judgment on a matter up to that time under dispute, it is obvious that the matter, according to the mind and will of the same Pontiffs, cannot be any longer considered a matter of open debate."

On July 27, 1981 I responded in this way.

Dear Archbishop Hamer:
. . . In your letter of May 7, you mentioned to me (in re "controverted matter") that the teaching of *Humani generis* remains in force: "Quodsi Summi Pontifices in actis suis de re hactenus controversa data opera sententiam ferunt, omnibus patet rem illam, secundum mentem ac voluntatem eorumdem Pontificum, questionem liberae inter theologos disceptationis jam haberi non posse."

I want to call Your Excellency's attention to the fact that this judgment of Pius XII is no longer supported by most reputable ecclesiologists. It represents a very unnuanced and culturally conditioned attitude toward the authentic magisterium of the Church, a point repeatedly made by Yves Congar, O.P. and Karl Rahner, S.J., among many others.

It has become clear that doctrinal development is possible only if the response of theologians to Roman interventions is both docile *and critical*. One thinks of the long dissenting processes that led ultimately, not without considerable Roman resistance, to *Dignitatis humanae*. Similarly, the huge worldwide theological reaction to *Humanae vitae* by demonstrably loyal and competent theologians is an indication that we have gone beyond the quite narrow formulations of Pius XII in *Humani generis*. The absoluteness of Pius XII's assertion is defensible only if the authentic magisterium never erred in its pronouncements, a tenet which sound historical studies will not support. The critical aspect of theological response to Roman interventions is an inseparable part of doctrinal purification and is an absolutely indispensable aspect of a theologian's loyalty to the Holy See.

Your Excellency, these perspectives are taken for granted in competent theological circles.

With all best personal wishes to you, I am

Sincerely in Christ,
Richard A. McCormick, S.J.

This exchange looks to be and is relatively harmless in itself. That is, no heads rolled. As far as I know, the matter was dropped there. But it represents the "defensive negativity" I mentioned. Such negativity only thinly disguises a difference in theology and world view that could, and I believe does, contain the seeds of things far more ominous.

What are these "things far more ominous"? Simply put, the phrase points to the results of the way the official Church seems ready to face the almost unavoidable conflicts that occur between theology and the magisterium. This must be spelled out a bit more. Merely to leave it at that (the acknowledgement of conflict) would lead many to view the matter in the uneven terms of superior-subject, official-unofficial and eventually ruly-unruly. Within the confines of these pairs, how such conflicts should be resolved is clear from the outset. One side has, as it were, larger muscles.

But the matter is not as simple as comparing jurisdictional muscle. No one has discussed the magisterium-theology conflict more honestly and thoroughly than Archbishop Robert Coffy (Albi).[6] Coffy analyzes the conflict in terms of two complexes of causes, one associated with theology, the other with the magisterium.

Where theology is concerned, Coffy identifies three causes. The first is the difficulty of theology today. Contemporary people live in specific cultural contexts. They no longer live in the cultural worlds that witnessed "the development of the existing propositions of faith and of the major theological systems." They look for a new faith-language and turn to their pastors and theologians for help. Development of a new faith-language takes time and freedom, the freedom to make honest mistakes. Furthermore, and therefore, theology is acutely aware of the need to be immersed in concrete pastoral situations before theologizing and developing working hypotheses. Christians who do not live in such situations do not face the same problems and often reject the theological working hypotheses. They then ask the bishops to intervene. If the bishops do so, "they are seen as total strangers to the problems."

Second, there was a time when humanity enjoyed a religious culture. During such a time there was little problem vindicating theology as a science. Theology was accepted as the queen of the sciences. But this is not the case today. Theologians must justify theological investigation. They will see themselves as credible only to the extent that they submit to rigorous verification, the type of vertification not necessarily the expertise of the magisterium.

Finally, there is theological pluralism. This pluralism is qualitatively different than in earlier eras. Furthermore, theology must take account of other sciences as never before, of other cultures and manners of thought. Given this diversity and complexity, how can the magisterium intervene? Does it select one theology to the detriment or even condemnation of another? I adverted to these developments in chapter 2.

Then there is the situation of the magisterium. It is faced with theologians who insist that it exercise its ministry in new ways suited to the times. Concretely, it limps under the burden of earlier interventions that were "clumsy and excessive." One thinks of the Syllabus of Errors, *Pascendi* and *Humani Generis*. Furthermore, it deals with a theological world conscious that faith can be expressed legitimately in different theologies. It realizes that theologians will demand that "it make explicit its theological options and abstain from presenting them as the only possible way of expressing the faith."[7]

A final difficulty the magisterium faces is the shift in the relationship between revelation and magisterium. Since the eighteenth century, the relationship was shaped by the defensive apologetic of the times. There was a felt need to establish the fact of revelation "scientifically," by appeal to miracles and prophesy-fulfillment. As Coffy puts it:

> And so apologetics created a kind of separation between the very fact of revelation and its meaning. The truth of revelation was not justified on its own merits but through something different from it . . . As a normal and—we can really say it—necessary consequence of this manner of demonstrating the credibility of the faith, people began to focus on demonstrating the need of the divine magisterium of the Catholic Church. It was from this magisterium that the credibility of the teaching of the Church was seen to derive directly.[8]

And so the magisterium came to be viewed as the only basis for the credibility of the faith. As it did so, theology took on the structure of comment on the definitions and propositions of the magisterium. And this helps to explain why magisterial interventions were so frequent. The drafter of propositions supposedly knows more about them than anyone else. Advantage magisterium.

But Coffy insists that times have changed. We have moved from apologetics to fundamental theology. "The truth of revelation has no other justification but its very content."[9] The contemporary effort is not just to guarantee the *fact* of revelation, but to illumine its inner riches. Appeals to formal authority are no longer sufficient. In this setting the magisterium must justify its interventions by the cogency of its presentation. For Coffy this means "new styles of intervention."

I mentioned above that the theology and world view revealed in the Hamer correspondence contained the seeds of "things far more ominous," specifically the way the official Church is going to face conflicts between theology and the magisterium. If it does not face such conflicts out of a realistic and up-to-date grasp of the changes—theological, cultural, ecclesial—that have occurred in the past twenty-five years or so, we could be in for much more serious problems. There could be a simple standoff of theologies and world views that would leave the magisterium isolated and stripped of respect by and influence in a world that had passed it by.

I believe that this has already happened in some areas of contemporary life. In the sexual sphere, it is no exaggeration to assert that the Church's teaching is viewed, if it is considered at all, as an irrelevant relic. For instance, *Persona Humana* simply did not speak the language of our times. It was the product of three curial consultors whose perspectives are entirely deductive.[10] In spite of its occasional nod to contemporary psychological studies, the document could have been written in 1876. This is sad; for if there is any area where modern society is adrift and floundering, and needs a healing, prophetic voice, it is the area of sexuality.

What will happen and why? I am far from sure. But there are reasons for concern. Nearly everyone is aware of innate Roman conservatism and of its dominant concern for authority. These have provided the background in the last few years for what has been called "the chill factor," a phrase coined by the *National Catholic Reporter*. In the rest of this chapter I will treat three points: (1) the Church chill and its counterproductivity, (2) a new model for guarding the faith, (3) the resistance to this model.

The Chill Factor

"The chill factor" encompasses a variety of things. The immediate reference is to the Congregation for the Doctrine of the Faith's (CDF) mandate to Archbishop Peter Gerety of Newark to withdraw the imprimatur from *Christ Among Us*, a popular catechetical introduction to the Catholic faith authored by Anthony Wilhelm. Furthermore, the Paulist Press was told to discontinue issuing the book because "even a corrected version would not be suitable as a catechetical text." The immediate reference is also to the same congregation's mandate to Archbishop Raymond Hunthausen of Seattle to withdraw the imprimatur from Philip Keane's *Sexual Morality*. Then there was the notice about the inquiry into *Human Growth and Development Guidelines*, used in the diocese of Toledo for sex education. Add to these the ominous early references by Cardinal Joseph Ratzinger to the works of liberation theologians Jon Sobrino and

Gustavo Gutierrez, the silencing of Leonardo Boff, the threat of dismissal made to the priests and (especially) religious women who signed the *New York Times* "abortion ad," the visitation of two bishop ordinaries by Roman appointees, etc.

Let me concentrate on the imprimatur removals. What is going on? Are these isolated instances of post-Vatican II dustups that merit the attention bestowed on television commercials? Or are they symbols that point to more profound and disturbing realities that should be unpacked and critically assessed? The first option is the easier. The second is, I believe, the more accurate. For this reason the National Conference of Diocesan Directors of Religious Education, meeting in 1984 in Kansas City, expressed "serious concern" about the actions of the Roman congregation.[11] That concern is justified, and the far-reaching implications should be spelled out.

A news item can serve as the backdrop for these implications. Betty Smith (Sandusky, Ohio), a member of Catholics United for the Faith (CUF), a self- appointed vigilante group, reported that she and her husband met recently with Cardinal Silvio Oddi. They gave him a copy of *Christ Among Us.* "He was unbelievably kind. He showed the book to his secretary and demanded to know why he had not seen it before. We know we did something on that trip and hope we can do a whole lot more." In other words, the archconservative CUF is claiming credit for doing in the Paulist publication and is determined to do more.[12] Raymond Brown, S.S., as well as Avery Dulles, once referred to such people as "the third magisterium."[13]

This should come as no surprise. Archconservative elements in the American church have for years been campaigning against those they consider "dissenting," "dissident," "deviant," "unorthodox," as if these words were all synonyms for one another. The most frequent form of the campaign is accusatory mail. Thus the near-calumnious *Wanderer,* well known for its attacks on centrists in the church, has repeatedly urged readers to write to the Congregation for the Doctrine of the Faith in an attempt to remove Charles Curran from Catholic University.

This type of thing could be dismissed as the tired nostalgia of the marginalized right. That is a fundamentally sound response. The trouble is, this tiny minority seems to have found ears in Rome. As the distinguished historian John Tracy Ellis noted: "I have the impression that certain curia officials are listening too much to one side—and that side is usually the far right."[14] A similar point was made by Archbishop John Roach, the then president of the National Conference of Catholic Bishops, in his opening remarks to the NCCB.[15] With this in mind, Archbishop John L. May of St. Louis spoke only half the truth when he stated to a group of religious: "It's people here that don't understand us and disagree with us and have very strong opposition to us, and they are the ones who write [to the Vatican]."[16] Point granted. But someone at the Vatican reads this mail and takes it seriously.

How seriously has become all too clear. In late November 1985, a fundamentalist group from Newport News (Virginia) composed a thick dossier entitled ponderously "Report on the Teachings of Fr. Richard A. McCormick, S.J., on Certain Medical Ethic [sic] Issues." Copies were sent to Archbishop Pio Laghi (Apostolic Delegate to the United States) with two extra copies intended for Cardinals Joseph Ratzinger and Silvio Oddi. Copies were also sent to Bishop Walter Sullivan and Archbishop James Hickey. If these episcopal worthies suffer from intractable insomnia, they now have at hand its sure cure. Even dull fiction has its uses.

This "listening too much to one side" seems to be taking the form of unilateral Roman actions that violate nearly all the canons of due process worked out by canonists and theologians in conjunction with the American bishops. Authors are not consulted, reasons are not given, consultations are shrouded in secrecy.

At the beginning of the tenure of Cardinal Franjo Seper as head of the CDF, a meeting of some twelve bishops and their periti (experts) was convened by the Cardinal. I accompanied the late Bishop Alexander Zaleski (then chairman of the NCCB's Committee on Doctrine) to this meeting. Bishop Zaleski made a blunt and even impassioned plea that scholars be treated fairly and above board in church processes, not secretly and without adequate protections and guarantees. It must be remembered that in one of the most dramatic moments of Vatican II, Cardinal Joseph Frings confronted Cardinal Alfredo Ottaviani (then head of the Holy Office) and referred to the Holy Office "whose methods and behavior do not conform to the modern era and are a source of scandal to the world." It was against such a historical backdrop that Bishop Zaleski made his plea. Cardinal Seper promised that his congregation would fully comply with Bishop Zaleski's points.

But it is not due process that I wish to emphasize here. Violations of this are bad enough in themselves. But they have been duly identified and recorded by others. Rather it is the long-term counterproductive character of such interventions that should be underlined. The recent interventions by the CDF can easily reinforce a series of confusions detrimental to the vitality and maturity of Catholic life. Here I will briefly develop but ten such confusions.

1. *Confusion between the ordinary and extraordinary magisterium.* When an imprimatur is ordered removed, there is the implication that something in the book is somehow at odds with Catholic doctrine and potentially harmful to Catholic belief. But the term "doctrine" includes many gradations of teaching, not all of the same value or binding force. Some very

few are things "to be definitively held," others are more provisional and reformable. Unexplained withdrawal of the imprimatur tends to lump these together and confuse the two, and therefore to conflate and confuse the ordinary and extraordinary magisterium.

There is already enough confusion in this area. Many Catholics—and non-Catholics, for that matter—erroneously believe that all authoritative utterances of the pope deserve the same kind of unqualified response. This is often referred to as "creeping infallibility" or "magisterial maximalism." Yves Congar, O.P., as I pointed out earlier, has noted that under recent popes "this [ordinary] magisterium has assumed preponderant importance and, in light of an intense 'devotion to the Pope,' has been almost assimilated, in current opinion, to the prerogatives of the extraordinary magisterium."[17] This development reached its zenith under Pius XII (*Humani Generis,* 1950), who required total obedience to his ordinary magisterium.

Yet Bishop B.C. Butler rightly distinguishes between the irrevocable and the provisional in Church teaching and sees the identification of the two as an abuse of authority,[18] as I noted in my letter to Archbishop Hamer.

2. Confusion about the formulation and substance of Catholic teaching. Very close to the point just made is the distinction between the formulation and substance of Catholic teaching, a matter touched on earlier in chapter 1. Vatican II, following John XXIII, explicitly made this distinction.[19] This applies all the more in the area of concrete moral statements that do not pertain to the deposit of faith and are rooted in contingent realities. To fail to make such a distinction is to freeze the Church's expression of her faith and convictions in the language and conceptual tools of a particular historical era. Obviously, this cripples the Church's teaching function because it forces the Church to speak to people in a language they do not understand or find meaningless.

Fundamentalist Catholics frequently forget this. They measure the acceptability of an analysis by its conformity to a past formulation. However, it remains true—to cite but a single example—that it would be a disservice to both the People of God and the magisterium to insist that Pius XII spoke the final word on the ethics of procreative technologies (e.g., artificial insemination by husband, in vitro fertilization). To regard his statements as unalterable "Catholic teaching" and to condemn any attempts to reformulate the matter is to confuse and identify formulation and substance, and in the process to disallow in principle any doctrinal development.

That is why singling out Philip Keane's *Sexual Morality* is quite troubling. One may disagree with this or that statement. But Keane's approach is well within the mainstream of Catholic thought and in line with the Church's substantial concerns. To single it out for an imprimatur removal smacks of a form of literalism that confuses changeable formulation and abiding substance.

3. *Confusion between principles and their application.* The Challenge of Peace, the American bishops' 1983 pastoral letter on war and peace, distinguished clearly between universally binding moral principles and their concrete applications to specific cases. Of this latter category, it noted that "prudential judgments are involved, based on specific circumstances" and that "the church expects a certain diversity of views even though all hold the same moral principles." Application of moral principle to specific cases involves mixed or synthetic judgments—judgments mixed with empirical data, data that can be and often are variously assessed by different people.

Past official formulations have often been precisely of this mixed variety involving concrete and historically conditioned assumptions and data. For instance, as I noted above, in the past the Church excluded common worship with those not in union with Rome as involving the danger of indifferentism and inseparable from scandal. Vatican II offically modified this application.[20] Such a modification stems from an altered understanding of the factual underpinnings of the earlier application.

To measure attempts to apply basic principles to a contemporary setting merely by reference to past formulations obscures the difference between a basic principle and its application. Such a confusion overcommits the magisterium in a harmful and ultimately embarrassing way. More of this in chapter 8.

4. *Confusion between authority and competence.* The distinguished German theologian Josef Fuchs, S.J., has recently noted the difference between these notions.[21] If one is to pass judgment on the moral rightness or wrongness of concrete human conduct, clearly one must have the competence to understand and judge the many factual dimensions involved in such problems. If this judgment is to be issued to the Christian community, one must have authority. But authority is not competence.

Where competence is concerned, it is the same for bishops, moral theologians and others. For instance, anyone wishing to determine the rights and wrongs of genetic interventions must be competent in the field. Episcopal authority does not coincide with such competence.

An overexpansive notion of the Church's competence obscures this difference. What is the morally right or wrong way of acting in concrete areas is determined by human experience, human evaluation, human judgment. As Fuchs words its: "Catholic lay people as Catholics, priests as priests, bishops and the Pope as such do not have a specific Christian or ecclesiastical competence in regard to these matters."[22] This does not mean that pastors of the Church should not offer guidance on right-wrong activity. It merely suggests two things. First, they simply must consult those who are competent. Second, even after such consultation they must show appropriate caution and modesty. For horizontal activity in this world does not belong to the Church's competence in the same way the deposit of faith does. In this sense the Church enjoys the assistance of the Spirit in offering concrete moral guidance, but this assistance is not the specific assistance that according to Vatican I and II guarantees infallibility under certain conditions.

There are grounds to fear that unexplained, unilateral Roman actions will confirm an imprecise notion of the Church's competence and hence buttress the confusion between competence and authority.

5. *Confusion on the role of lay persons.* Closely related to the point just made is that touching the role of lay people in the elaboration of the Church's moral judgments. Lay status as such does not confer competence. But there are competent lay persons in abundance. Vatican II noted that "the church guards the heritage of God's word and draws from it religious and moral principles, without always having at hand the solution to particular problems."[23] As I have noted several times, it further reminded lay persons not to shirk their own distinctive responsibilities.[24]

Concrete moral judgments are not simply deduced from universal principles, as a past theological practice and some present attitudes imply. They demand experience and reflection, hence expertise from a variety of sources. Bernard Cooke stated this well: "What is needed—and has been needed for many years—is open and careful discussion that includes all the responsible voices in the church."[25] Cooke rightly argues that we need structures that allow bishops' collegial witness to apostolic tradition to interact openly with the reflection and research of scholars and both to be challenged by the life experience of devoted Catholics. Why so? Because although the bishops, together with the bishop of Rome, possess and pass on the truth upon which Christianity is grounded (Jesus' death and Resurrection), still "where we move beyond this core reality to which the papacy and episcopacy witness, when we move to questions about the meaning and applicability of Christs's death and resurrection, other kinds of knowledge and experience enter the picture."

Here one may note the difference in quality and reception of two documents of the SCDF, the "Declaration on Certain Questions Concerning Sexual Ethics" (poor) and the "Declaration on Euthanasia" (excellent). This latter document explicitly insists on the broad consultation that formed it. The former obviously lacked it, limited it or was unsuccessful in incorporating it. One can only speculate what the document would have been had lay expertise been incorporated.

6. *Confusion about the response due ordinary teaching.* This matter was touched on in no.1, and in earlier chapters, but it needs to be lifted out for special attention. In a church with a doctrine of infallibility, there is the

constant danger of overstating the meaning of ordinary teaching. Many Catholics have the inaccurate notion that such teaching demands uncritical and unqualified obedience and excludes any possibility of dissent. Archconservative elements in the Church perpetuate these ideas by viewing dissent on a particular point as deviancy, lack of loyalty and ultimately unorthodoxy. But faithfulness is not fundamentalism. Nor is it uncritical obedience. I fear that the recent Roman interventions only support such confusion.

It must be recalled that three bishops introduced an emendation (modus) to no. 25 of Vatican II's *Dogmatic Constitution on the Church.* It concerned the case of "an educated person [who], confronted with a teaching proposed noninfallibly, cannot, for solid reasons, give his internal assent." The doctrinal commission rejected the suggested addition and stated: "For this case approved theological explanations should be consulted."[26] Traditional theological manuals had for years justified dissent.

Furthermore, the *Declaration on Religious Freedom* states (no. 14): "In the formation of their consciences, the Christian faithful ought carefully to attend to the sacred and certain doctrine of the church." An emendation was proposed for "ought carefully to attend to." It read: "ought to form their consciences according to." The Theological Commission rejected this: "The proposed formula seems excessively restrictive. The obligation binding on the faithful is sufficiently expressed in the text as it stands."[27]

This "obligation binding on the faithful" does not, then, involve uncritical obedience. Rather, as Francis Sullivan, S.J., shows in his fine book *Magisterium: Teaching Authority in the Church,* it involves renunciation of attitudes of obstinacy and adoption of those of docility.[28] It involves "an honest and sustained effort to overcome any contrary opinion I might have, and to achieve a sincere assent of my mind."[29] This does not exclude dissent. Until we learn that lesson, the critical reflection of Catholics will, to our lasting regret, play little part in the ongoing enrichment of our heritage.

7. *Confusion about the unity-task of bishops.* One aspect of the episcopal task is unity of the faithful. But this must not be overstated. Unity in faith is not to be confused with uniformity on moral teaching. Vatican II admitted that believing Christians could at times come to different conclusions about important moral problems. *The Challenge of Peace* reaffirmed this, as I have noted. The point should be obvious. Yet it is unity on such moral judgments that seems to preoccupy too many authorities, some theologians and many Catholics. For instance, there are still bishops who exclude from their diocese scholars who dissent on relatively marginal points of the moral life, especially in the area of sexuality. This is jurisdictional overkill that has the effect of confusing unity in the faith and truth with mere uniformity. It often roots in a preoccupation with certainty and authority rather than truth and can easily lead to what no less an authority than Cardinal Rat-

zinger once referred to as an "ever more pronounced positivism of magisterial thinking that embraces and regulates this [abstract natural-law] ethical system."[30]

It is easy to see how certain Roman interventions can reinforce a confused notion of the unity-task of bishops.

8. *Confusion about other aspects of the episcopal role.* The public record gives no indication that specific reasons were provided against *Christ Among Us* and *Sexual Morality.* If a bishop has given his imprimatur and it is ordered withdrawn from above, he has both the right and responsibility to demand specific reasons for such action. And if the reasons are not given or are not persuasive, he should stand his ground. Otherwise, the bishop's true teaching and leadership responsibilities are being collapsed, and he is reduced to a functional go-between. This violates the very thoroughly Catholic idea of subsidiarity. When the process bypasses national episcopal conferences, it also undermines the fact and spirit of episcopal collegiality.

There are those, of course, who would welcome such a development. But it is not the ecclesial vision of Vatican II. Gabriel Daly, O.S.A., felt compelled to refer to a new ultramontanism in the Church ("the wish for *total* conformity with papal ideas and ideals in *all* things"). Of this mentality he stated: "The collegial ideal which might have been the queen of Vatican II's achievements is now a sleeping princess. Some day her prince will come; but on present showing he will need to be a man of unusual qualities, not indeed in order to awaken her . . . but to occupy the fortress where she has been placed in suspended animation."[31]

9. *Confusion about the nature of theology.* When believers begin to reflect on their faith, theology comes into being. Such reflection is a continuous wrestling to reappropriate God's great deeds in Christ in different times and cultures. Such reflection can be reduced to repetition of past formulations only at the cost of theological paralysis. Certain forms of doctrinal centralization tend to do just this.

The distinction is sometimes made between "official teaching" and "theological speculation." Surely, there is a legitimate basis for such a distinction. There is theological speculation that the Church has not incorporated (or is not ready to incorporate) into its ordinary thought-patterns. But the tone and meaning of "theological speculation" is often *mere* speculation, as if contemporary reflection could be totally relegated to a kind of irrelevant outer-space status and deprived of all formative influence. This again is a form of fundamentalism at odds with history and contemporary consciousness. Certain conclusions are not correct simply because Vatican officials approve them. Vatican officials can approve them only because they are seen as correct. And that is a process in which theological reflection has an indispensable role.

10. *Confusion about the meaning and function of an imprimatur.* Certainly, the CDF has the right to interpret the meaning of an imprimatur. But what is that meaning? In the past, authors writing within the Catholic tradition who dissented on a particular point but did so respectfully and with a clear statement of the official formulation could receive an imprimatur, an official declaration that the work was free of doctrinal and moral error. Indeed, these were the grounds on which Archbishop Hunthausen stated that he granted Keane's book an imprimatur. In other words, a respectful dissenting opinion was not considered to contain doctrinal or moral error.

The CDF has apparently given the imprimatur a more restrictive interpretation. The book must contain no departure in any way from official teaching. If this is the new understanding of the imprimatur, then, first, the CDF ought to say so clearly. After all, reputations of individuals are at stake. As things now vaguely stand, the removal of the imprimatur unavoidably leaves the misleading impression that the author is not an acceptable Catholic theologian.

Second, if the CDF has indeed given the imprimatur this more restrictive meaning, then the implications of this should be noted. The new code requires an imprimatur only for books intended as catechetical tools, and indeed for certain age groups. But it encourages all authors who write on doctrinal or moral questions to seek the imprimatur. But remember: if there is a new interpretation, the imprimatur can be given only if there is no departure—however tentative and respectful—from official teaching. That means that books that dissent in any way from Catholic teaching apparently cannot be published with Church approval. The clear implication is that any dissent is unacceptable. And that means that the Church cannot officially encourage theologians to do their job—what Rahner referred to above as their critical "duty."

In a 1984 talk to American bishops, Cardinal Ratzinger stated that dissent cannot extend to officially stated moral norms. Bishop Butler felt compelled to assert that "I think some clarifications are needed."[32] He once again distinguished between infallible teaching and the response to it (assent of faith) and ordinary teaching that calls for "respect motivated by religious considerations." Of this latter in the sphere of morals he notes: "It is surely difficult to exaggerate such respect to the level of a 'norm' that short-circuits theological investigation." The only remaining question: Must the faithful be shielded from such investigation? If so, why?

If this restriction of the meaning of the imprimatur is indeed the case, and if the restriction and subsequent Roman interventions are based heavily on archconservative complaints, then that will spell the trivialization of the imprimatur. There is clearly place for doctrinal oversight and vigilance in the Church. But if such vigilance gets identified with or is heavily influenced by archconservative elements, the imprimatur will be reduced to what Catholics United for the Faith is willing to approve. That would trivialize it quite as much as would an imprimatur that recklessly endorsed every liberal fad or conviction.

These are but ten of the confusions I see potentially reinforced by doctrinal interventions that are unexplained, unjustified, unilateral, ill-timed, or all of these. It is an unpleasant task to say these things and, I suspect, even a risky one in the present atmosphere. But Catholics deserve to have them said, not least of all to protect them against the old accusation of monolithic simplicity. They also deserve to have their bishops weigh these things carefully and respond appropriately. However, if bishops do not always "talk back," that is quite understandable. There are many more important episcopal tasks than trying to win battles already decided.

A New Model for Guarding the Faith

Borrowing from *Christus Dominus,* Archbishop Coffy states that the mission of the magisterium "in the current situation" must be described by the two words "promoter" and "guardian." By "in the current situation" he means to highlight many of the changes noted at the end of chapter 2 (loss of homogeneous culture, collapse of unitary method and language in theology, awareness of historical relativity of past authoritative statements, the inadequacy of purely formal authority, etc.). Coffy then makes an extremely interesting observation:

> The best way to guard is to promote, because fidelity to the testimony of the apostles doubtlessly consists in finding new formulations of the faith, as well as finding new ways of living and celebrating it.[33]

By "guarding" Coffy means watching, so that the faith taught is that which comes to us from the apostles. By "promoting" he means the positive role of proposing the faith to peoples of all cultures in a way adapted to their needs. It is in this sense that the best way to guard is to promote. Thus fidelity to the ancient faith demands, for its survival and integrity, innovation ("finding new formulations of the faith, new ways of living and celebrating it").

Coffy's perspectives ("guarding by promoting") strike me as being absolutely correct, as well as thoroughly foreign to the way the task of the magisterium is conceived in Rome today. Interventions are by and large negative. Departures from verbal conformity result in the removal of the imprimatur. Dissent is at best suspect. One need only peruse *The Ratzinger Report* to verify this spirit.

During a press conference in Rome (May 30, 1985), Ratzinger stated that the views expressed in the *Report* were "completely personal" and "in no way implicate the institutions of the Holy See."[34] The fact that the head of the Congregation for the Doctrine of the Faith expresses such personal and negative opinions (what Nicholas Lash refers to as "nightmares of the negative") about postconciliar developments is loaded with theological concerns. For instance, to what extent are his opinions accurate, especially about theology's role in what Ratzinger blackens as a "progressive process of decadence"? What are the criteria of judgment? What are the sources of information? What do such negative judgments imply about the movements of the Holy Spirit in the Church? About the task of theology? About the responsibility and actual performance of bishops? What concept of church undergirds Ratzinger's views? What concept of magisterium is at work?

One question deserves underlining here. Do the "completely personal" opinions of the *Report* represent the theological assumptions and attitudes theologians will encounter as they deal with the Congregation? If so, and if these assumptions and attitudes are one-sided, and even inaccurate (as I believe they are), what is the possibility of anything approaching an objective hearing at the Congregation for the Doctrine of the Faith? Very little in the proceedings of the present Congregation inspires confidence here.

Furthermore, and no less importantly, if the assumptions and attitudes of the *Report* provide the theological climate of the Congregation, to what extent is orthodoxy being confused with a particularist ("classicist") theology, and therefore being compromised, and that at the very time it is being authoritatively imposed? Has not "guarding" been totally isolated from "promoting" and therefore been severely weakened? To say, as Ratzinger does, that the views expressed in the *Report* are "completely personal" sounds innocent enough. Actually, it raises theological concerns—really worries—of the first magnitude. Cardinal Ratzinger is telling us that his own personal theological views have nothing to do with the way he judges the theology of others. Is that not roughly similar to saying that one's political views have nothing to do with the way one votes? It would require a rather remarkable epistemology to sustain such a separation.

Closely related to this concern is the fact that the way the Congregation is proceeding inspires nothing but fear. This is a distraction. That is, as theologians spend far too much time and energy looking over their shoulders, they are distracted from the enormous issues that face contemporary society. In the meantime, leadership quietly passes beyond the Church to voices not deeply influenced by religious faith as the Church preoccupies itself with its own authority. This is the sad heritage of ecclesiastical narcissism. It is commonly admitted now and commonly regretted that there are few moral theologians left with the stomach to write on sexual ethics. The "official mentality" is that no reexamination or reformulation is required here. All is simple and clear.

"Guarding by promoting" is, therefore, a very *positive* function of the Church's teaching office. In my judgment, it should include the following: (1) the provision of a kind of clearing-house where the best Catholic thought is recognized, discussed, supported, and disseminated; (2) the establishment of policies that institutionalize and protect freedom of inquiry; (3) promotion and stimulation of intercultural exchange; (4) notice, criticism and correction of repressive violations; (5) provision of structures that identify and admit past errors; (6) stimulation and guidance of the Church's ongoing challenge to reformulate its inheritance.

Here we must ask whether the Congregation for the Doctrine of the Faith is an appropriate body to fulfill these functions. I think it is not, and for several reasons. It is dominantly Western in conceptual outlook, irretrievably conservative, situated within an ecclesiastical authority structure to which it is subordinate and sensitive, almost exclusively negative in the way it conceives its guardian function. Thus it tends to "manage" theology. The faith committed to us from the apostles would in no way be threatened were the Congregation for the Doctrine of the Faith abolished and the guardian function of the Church's teaching office absorbed by others.

The pastoral implications and ramifications of theological work could easily be absorbed by other congregations and/or episcopal conferences. The task of "guarding by promoting" could be entrusted to an International Theological Commission. As things now stand, the magisterium is crippled by its own instruments.

Resistance to This Teaching Model

It takes no crystal ball to discern the depth and extent of resistance to the task of the magisterium as conceived by Archbishop Coffy. Many Catholics have been nurtured and supported in a classicist mentality. This is especially true in practical moral matters.

Let the idea of a universal catechism be the symbol here. At the Extraordinary Synod of Bishops (1985), such a catechism was proposed and supported by Cardinal Bernard Law and others. In their final report, the synodal bishops stated:

Very many have expressed the desire that a catechism or compendium of all Catholic doctrine regarding both faith and morals be composed, that it might be, as it were, a point of reference for the catechisms or compendiums that are prepared in the various regions.[36]

That seems innocent enough. But several things should be noted. First, what does "a point of reference" mean? Cardinal Oddi revealed (December 16, 1985) that the Congregation for the Clergy, which he heads, had practically completed this catechism. He stated: "This will be a directory of the truth, followed by a directory that proves the Church has always followed that particular doctrine."[37] A "directory of truth" in moral theology will be interesting to see. Presumably, if it purports to be just that, any diverging view will be subject to its judgment.

Then we must consider the kind of reception the idea of a universal catechism received. Frank Morris welcomed the idea with unrestrained glee.

> This would shut the door to the invasion of Catholics' integrity and heritage of the faith by ideologues and religious speculators. It would help end the game whereby the so-called progressives produce "catechisms" and then use them to clone themselves religiously and intellectually.[38]

And who will produce this catechism?

> It is to be hoped that scholars like Bishop-elect Donald Wuerl, Fr. William Smith, Fr. Michael Wren, Fr. John Hardon, Msgr. Eugene Kevane, Fr. William Most, Msgr. George Kelly, Fr. Richard Gilsdorf, Fr. Robert Bradley and others of their orthodoxy will be utilized in producing this catechism.

Enough said. The "chill factor" in moral theology is still blowing in the wind.

Well, almost enough. It is time, indeed way beyond time, for the American bishops, religious superiors (*et alii*) to stand up to the intimidating nonsense that I have called the "chill factor." If they do, *they* will suffer. If they do not, we all will.

Notes

1. Richard A. McCormick, S.J., "Sterilization and Theological Method," *Theological Studies* 37 (1976): 471-77.

2. John R. Donahue, S.J., "Women, Priesthood and the Vatican," *America* 136 (1977): 285-89.

3. Note 18 on IV Sent., dist. 25, q. 2, a. 1.

4. Corrine Bayley, C.S.J., and Richard A. McCormick, S.J., "Sterilization: The Dilemma of Catholic Hospitals," *America* 143 (1980): 222-25.

5. "Edges of Life," *Commonweal* 107 (1980): 420-21.

6. Robert Coffy, "The Magisterium and Theology," in *Readings in Moral Theology No. 3,* ed. Charles E. Curran and Richard A. McCormick, S.J. (Mahwah, N.J.: Paulist, 1982), 206-22.

7. Coffy, 212.

8. Coffy, 213.

9. Coffy, 214.

10. J. McManus, Sean O'Riordan and Henry Stratton, "The 'Declaration on Certain Questions Concerning Sexual Ethics': A Discussion," *Clergy Review* 61 (1976): 231-37.

11. From NC releases.

12. From NC releases.

13. Raymond E. Brown, S.S., "The Magisterium vs. Theologians: Debunking Some Fictions," in *Readings in Moral Theology No. 3*, 277-96, at 285.

14. *Catholic Review*, 18 November 1983. In an interview in New York (30 January 1988), Cardinal Ratzinger stated: "Oh yes, I get many letters from the United States, not only from bishops but from Catholic lay people as well." When asked what kinds of American Catholics take the time to write, Ratzinger stated that many letters come from those in "deep loyalty" to the Holy See. Then— astonishingly—the Cardinal added: "I think the letters provide us with a reflection of *typical Catholics* (my emphasis). They are people who are preoccupied with the thought that the Catholic Church should remain the Catholic Church" (*Florida Catholic*, 5 February 1988). Anyone with even an elementary knowledge of church affairs knows the source of these letters and the kinds of people who write them. Yet here is one of the highest officials of the Roman Curia asserting that they are "typical Catholics."

In a not unrelated event, the pope told (March 1988) visiting Midwestern bishops that he had been misled about the condition of the American Church. In other words, he admitted to mistaken judgments. As one bishop stated: "I have to wonder whether or not the same people that are telling the pope that everything is going to hell in a basket over here are not the same people who are reading the *Wanderer*. Because it certainly didn't come from the bishops. He was evidently buying it, or at least had some anxiety about it, but then he came here and found it to be a lot of baloney" (*National Catholic Reporter*, 18 March 1988). Further comment would be redundant—except to note two things: (1) where actions or interventions have been based on misleading information, rescission of some kind is in order; (2) the sources of misleading information should be corrected and remain in the future appropriately suspect.

15. From NC releases.

16. *Catholic Review*, 25 May 1984.

17. Yves Congar, O.P., "A Brief History of the Forms of the Magisterium and Its Relations with Scholars," in *Readings in Moral Theology No. 3*, 325.

18. *Readings in Moral Theology No. 3*, 185.

19. *Documents*, 268-69.

20. *Documents*, 384.

21. Josef Fuchs, S.J., *Christian Ethics in a Secular Arena* (Washington: Georgetown University Press, 1984), 48-67. Also in *Readings in Moral Theology No. 6*, 330-53.

22. Loc. cit., 57-58.

23. *Documents*, 232.

24. *Documents*, 244.

25. Bernard Cooke, "The Responsibility of Theologians," *Commonweal* 107 (1980): 39-42.

26. *Acta Synodalia Sacrosancti Concilii Vaticani II*, vol. III, pars VIII, 88.

27. Cf. note 26, vol. IV, pars VI, 769.

28. Francis Sullivan, S.J., *Magisterium: Teaching Authority in the Church* (Mahwah, N.J.: Paulist, 1983).

29. Karl Rahner, S.J., "Theologie und Lehramt," *Stimmen der Zeit* 198 (1980): 363-75, at 374.

30. Cited in J. Fuchs, S.J., "Teaching Morality: The Tension between Bishops and Theologians within the Church," in *Readings in Moral Theology No. 6* (Mahwah, N.J.: Paulist, 1988), 352, footnote 4.

31. Gabriel Daly, "The Ultramontane Influence," *Tablet* 235 (1981): 391.

32. *Tablet* 238 (1984): 467.

33. Coffy as in note 6, 219.

34. From NC releases and in *National Catholic Reporter,* 6 September 1985.

35. *Tablet* 239 (1985): 298.

36. *Wanderer,* 19 December 1985.

37. *National Catholic Register,* 27 December 1985.

38. *Wanderer,* 2 January 1986.

Chapter 5

Bishops as Teachers, Scholars as Listeners

The changes and shifts detailed in chapter 1 could be expected to influence many aspects of ecclesial life. They did. Here I want to explore just one, the relationship of the episcopal teaching office to scholarship, especially theological scholarship.

The rather obvious stimulus to my title is the new method of episcopal teaching we are seeing in the American Church. We have always had documents and pastoral letters, tons of them. By "new method" I refer to the open and revisionary process that has taken place in the pastorals on nuclear war and peace, and on the economy. I agree with Theodore Hesburgh when he notes of *The Challenge of Peace* that "that process was almost as important, for bishops and laity, as the document produced."[1] Indeed, more important. The major problem now is how to keep these pastorals alive once they are born. Respirators can take them just so far. Whatever the case, the letters' theological and pastoral implications are enormous and highly relevant to the notion of bishops as teachers and scholars as listeners. I want to explore that issue briefly in this chapter and will do so under six points.

1. Teaching competence of episcopal conferences. During the preparation of *The Challenge of Peace*, there was a conference convened in Rome (18-19 January 1983) on peace and disarmament. It was organized by an apparently nervous Vatican in conjunction with the American pastoral letter and presided over by Cardinal Casaroli. During the proceedings, Cardinal Joseph Ratzinger stated that bishops' conferences do not have a *mandatum docendi* (a mandate to teach). That belongs only to the individual bishop in his diocese or to the college with the pope. Ratzinger has repeated the statement since then and the point was of major concern at the 1985 extraordinary synod. I think I know what is going on here. It looks suspiciously like an attempt to lay a theological foundation for the centralizing efforts of the present pontificate. This has been brilliantly displayed and documented in a recent and somewhat frightening article by the respected Italian journalist, Giancarlo Zizola, entitled "The Counter Reformation of John Paul II."[2] The implication of denying a *mandatum docendi* to national conferences is that their doctrinal utterances are bereft of any genuine doctrinal significance.

But attempts to monarchize and pyramidize the teaching function in the Church just will not withstand theological scrutiny, though I realize that much more needs to be said about episcopal conferences and that the matter is presently under study. First off, they collide with canon 753 of the new code. Far be it from me to canonize canons. But in this case canon 753 has cornered a piece of reality. It reads: "Bishops who are in communion with the head and members of the college, either individually or gathered together, whether in episcopal conferences or particular councils, although they do not have infallibility in teaching, are authentic teachers and masters of the faith for the Christians committed to their care . . . "

Furthermore, as Avery Dulles has noted, Ratzinger argued in 1965 that national conferences are genuine, though partial, realizations of collegiality.[3] In this capacity, they can exercise their teaching function. A reflection of this is the repeated reference to the differing levels of authority in the episcopal pastorals. Such references are hardly in place if national conferences have no authority. John Paul II, in his address to the American bishops October 5, 1979, congratulated the bishops on their exercise of the ministry of truth in their collective statements. Congratulations are hardly in order for those who have exceeded their mandate.

So recent denials to episcopal conferences of a *mandatum docendi*, besides appearing to me to be transparently political in purpose, have a quaintly juridical tinge to them. Collective statements are factually and practically the way bishops do much of their teaching in our time, as witness Medellin (1968) and Puebla (1979) as well as *To Live in Christ Jesus* (1976) and many other documents. But merely identifying and validating episcopal conferences as having authentic doctrinal or teaching prerogatives does not tell us much about how bishops ought to teach or how scholars ought to listen. That brings me to my second point.

2. Doctrinal status of moral statements. As background, let me cite the famous no. 25 of *Lumen Gentium*.

> In matters of faith and morals, the bishops speak in the name of Christ and the faithful are to accept their teaching and adhere to it with a religious assent of soul.[4]

Although the individual bishops do not enjoy the prerogative of infallibility, they can nevertheless proclaim Christ's doctrine infallibly. This is so, even when they are dispersed around the world, provided that while maintaining the bond of unity among themselves and with Peter's successor, and while teaching authentically on a matter of faith or morals, they concur in a single viewpoint as the one which must be held conclusively.[5]

Here we have the oft-cited phrase "in matters of faith and morals." This is a very tricky phrase. It was used at Trent but clearly did not mean there what it is taken to mean now. Recent studies of Levada and Riedl[6] show that the exact meaning of "in questions of morals" was never established in Vatican I. The same must be said of Vatican II.

The problem can be put as follows. *On the one hand,* the magisterium claims competence with regard to questions of the natural moral law. It is clear that this competence refers not only to revealed morality and very general principles, but to concrete moral questions.

For instance, Pius X wrote in *Singulari Quadam:*

Whatever a Christian man may do, even in affairs of this world, he may not ignore the supernatural, nay he must direct all to the highest good as to his last end, in accordance with the dictates of Christian wisdom; but all his actions, in so far as they are morally good or evil, that is, agree with, or are in opposition to, divine and natural law, are subject to the judgment and authority of the Church . . . [7]

Similar statements can be found in Pius XI,[8] Pius XII,[9] John XXIII[10] and Paul VI,[11] a matter I will flesh out in chapter 8. Perhaps the clearest and most all-encompassing statement is found in Pius XII's *Magnificate Dominum.*

The power of the Church is not bound by the limits of "matters strictly religious," as they say, but the whole matter of the natural law, its foundation, its interpretation, its application, so far as their moral aspect extends, are within the Church's power. For the keeping of the natural law, by God's appointment, has reference to the road by which man has to approach his supernatural end. But on this road the Church is man's guide and guardian in what concerns his supreme end. The apostles observed this in times past, and afterward from the earliest centuries the Church has kept to this manner of acting, and keeps to it today, not indeed like some private guide or adviser, but by virtue of the Lord's command and authority . . .

Many and serious are the problems in the social field . . . they pertain to the moral order, are of concern to conscience and the salvation of men . . . Such are: the purpose and limits of temporal authority; the relations between the individual and society; the so-called "totalitarian

State," the "complete laicization of the State" and of public life; the complete laicization of the schools; war, its morality, liceity or non-liceity when waged as it is today, and whether a conscientious person may give or withhold his cooperation in it; the moral relationships which bind and rule the various nations.

Common sense, and truth as well, are contradicted by whoever asserts that these and like problems are outside the field of morals and hence are, or at least can be, beyond the influence of that authority established by God to see to a just order and to direct the consciences and actions of men along the path to their true and final destiny.[12]

On the other hand, Vatican II states that the charism of infallibility is coextensive with the "treasure of divine revelation" (what Vatican I called the *depositum fidei*).[13] This would exclude from infallibility those moral questions that are not revealed. "Competence," therefore, is a very analogous concept. One can be competent without being infallibly competent. As we shall see, that is the case in concrete moral questions. The sense in which the bishops are competent will be profoundly important in specifying our response to their moral teaching.

There are those who try to avoid this problem by use of the phrase "truths of salvation." Thus the German theologian and apologist Gustave Ermecke regards the central thesis of *Humanae Vitae* as "a truth of salvation that obliges under sin."[14] Similarly, Marcelino Zalba, S.J., John Ford, S.J., Jan Visser and others argue that concrete moral norms can be taught infallibly because they belong to man's way to his supernatural end, to his sanctification. The argument here is: whatever affects our salvation is an object of infallibility; for that is the very purpose of the charism.

Here a very important distinction must be made, the distinction between moral goodness and moral rightness. Moral goodness refers to the person as such, to the person's being open to and decided for the self-giving love of God. It is the vertical dimension of our being. It is salvation. Therefore what we can say about the moral goodness of the person is a "truth of salvation."

Another level is the horizontal. This refers to the proper disposition of the realities of this world, the realization in concrete behavior of what is promotive for human persons. We refer to this as the rightness (or wrongness) of human conduct. We sometimes call this innerworldly activity "moral" rightness or wrongness. But it is moral only in an analogous sense. That is, moral goodness contains an inclination, an intention, a goodwill, a readiness to do what is right. It is because of this relationship between personal moral goodness and material rightness that this rightness is called "moral." But this rightness is not *directly* and *in itself* concerned with personal moral goodness. Salvation (as in "truths of salvation"), therefore, does not have a *direct* relationship to right behavior, but to personal goodness. Concrete moral norms, therefore, are truths of salvation only in an analogous sense.[15]

It is the failure to distinguish the pairs good-bad, right-wrong that leads to an uncritical notion that the Church is *equally* competent on all moral questions, a notion that does not make a great deal of sense in our time.

What is the right way of acting in different areas of human life is determined by human experience, human evaluation, human judgment. As I noted in chapter 1, St. Thomas says: "We do not offend God unless we harm our own good."[16] What is harmful to us is a human determination. In chapter 4 I cited Josef Fuchs: "The Catholic lay people as Catholics, the priests as priests, the bishops and the pope as such do not have a specific Christian or ecclesiastical competence in regard to these matters."[17]

Earlier, Karl Rahner, approaching this matter from the point of view of infallible teaching, stated:

> Apart from wholly universal moral norms of an abstract kind, and apart from a radical orientation of human life towards God as the outcome of a supernatural and grace-given self-commitment, there are hardly any particular or individual norms of Christian morality which could be proclaimed by the ordinary or extraordinary teaching authorities of the Church in such a way that they could be unequivocally and certainly declared to have the force of dogmas.[18]

What Rahner is saying is that "particular or individual norms" (about rightness or wrongness) are not "truths of salvation" as this phrase is understood by certain "infallibilists."

These statements of Rahner, Fuchs and others do not mean that the pastors of the Church should not offer guidance on right-wrong activity such as peace, economics, sexuality, abortion, etc. It merely suggests appropriate caution and tentativeness; for horizontal activity in this world does not belong to the Church's competence in the same way as the *depositum fidei*. In this sense we may say that the Church enjoys the assistance of the Spirit in offering concrete moral guidance, "but this assistance does not necessarily mean the specific assistance that, according to Vatican I and Vatican II, is promised to her and guarantees infallibility under certain conditions."[19]

I believe that a discerning reader might easily detect a difference between the rather sweeping statements of, for example, Pius XII in *Magnificate Dominum* and those of Vatican II. There is a certain modesty in Vatican II on natural law. The Council applies the notion to universal principles. Only very egregious actions are listed and it is stated that the human conscience gives voice to these principles. I shall return to this point in chapter 8.

The point I am making—and in doing so I am following the lead of Rahner and Fuchs—leads to the conclusion that the term "competence" when applied to the teaching office of the Church is an analogous term—which means that it must be understood differently when applied to different realities, specifically the deposit of faith and the concrete applications of this. The Church has a definite mission to provide concrete moral guidance; for "faith throws a new light on everything, manifests God's design for man's total vocation, and thus directs the mind to solutions which are fully human."[20] But this mission with regard to concrete moral guidance (rightness-wrongness) is not precisely and *directly* concerned with "truths of salvation" and hence is not buttressed by the certainty and stability such truths can rightly claim. This is clear from the history of moral teaching in the Church. We cannot be accused of washing dirty linen in public when we candidly acknowledge that our tradition is not free of moral distortion and error.

It is also clear from the Pauline corpus. For instance, in Galatians Paul refers to the good news that he has directly from the Lord. It is not "human knowledge." There are other matters that are indeed human knowledge (e.g., in 1 Cor 7, whether to live in virginity or not). The moral rightness-wrongness of concrete actions is in this latter category. And so are matters like capital punishment, abortion, business ethics, social ethics, contraception and sexual ethics in general.

I mention this here because there is still a deep-seated hankering in the Church to "infallibilize" the ordinary activity of the magisterium, as Yves Congar has often noted. For instance, K.D. Whitehead, writing in the *New Oxford Review*, stated of past controversies: "what was better understood in the past, however, that is not so well understood today, is that where the teaching authority of the Church stepped into these controversies to *decide* some aspect of them, any further 'dissent' from the points decided meant that one was henceforth placing oneself in the ranks of the heretics."[21] To this the proper response is: What is better understood today is that Whitehead has fallen into serious theological error by lumping any dissent from a decision of Church authority with heresy. Such expansiveness only heaps ridicule on the teaching office of the Church. What is also better understood today is that the solution to complex moral questions cannot simply be "decided" by Church authority—if "decided" means resolved independently of evidence about the personally promotive or destructive character of the actions in question.

3. The importance of nonepiscopal competence. The modifications on episcopal competence recognized by recent historical and theological studies can be seen from another point of view, by flipping the coin to see the other side, to examine the acknowledged competence of others than bishops. I have already cited two statements of Vatican II to the effect that (1) the Church does "not always have at hand the solution to particular problems" and (2) that laypersons have "their own distinctive role" in discovering them. The admission of such competence contains a staggering implication and admission: that the Church is a learning institution and that it cannot learn—*and ergo teach*—without the contributions of many competences. That is not a reactionary modesty in the face of a previous triumphalism. It is plain common sense.

Let me illustrate this from the world of business. In their interesting and best-selling book *In Search of Excellence: Lessons from America's Best Run Companies* (which I would urge all to read for its ecclesiological provocativeness), Thomas Peters and Robert Waterman cite Dana Corporation's Rene McPherson:

> Until we believe that the expert in any particular job is most often the person performing it, we shall forever limit the potential of that person, in terms of both his own contributions to the organization and his own personal development . . . We had better start admitting that the most important people in an organization are those who actually provide a service or make and add value to products, not those who administer the activity . . . That is, when I am in your 25 square feet of space, I'd better listen to you.[22]

When the Church says that it does not have the answers to all concrete problems and that laypersons have a distinctive role to play in discovering them, it is saying that when it is dealing with *their* twenty-five square feet of space (translate: concrete questions of moral right and wrong), it had better listen. A symbol of this sea-change of attitude is Patty Crowley, a member of the birth control commission in the mid-sixties. "We hung back," she said. "We didn't know what the Church wanted. It wasn't until later that we realized 'the Church' didn't know any more than we did. We were the Church."[23]

This was clearly acknowledged by Paul VI, both in the composition of the so-called "Birth Control Commission" and in his explicit statements. Speaking to the College of Cardinals on 23 June 1964, he noted:

> The Church recognizes manifold aspects of the problem [of birth control], that is to say, the manifold areas of competence, among which is certainly preeminent that of the spouses themselves, that of their liberty, of their conscience, of their love, of their duty. But the Church must also affirm hers, that is to say that of the law of God, which she interprets, teaches, promotes and defends; and the Church will have to proclaim this law of God in the light of scientific, social, psychological truths which have lately had new and very extensive studies and documentation.[24]

4. Distinction of levels. My fourth point centers around the different levels of authority in episcopal statements. In their pastoral *The Challenge of Peace,* the American bishops distinguish three levels or types of episcopal statements: (1) universally binding moral principles; (2) statements of recent popes and of Vatican II repeated by the bishops; (3) application of moral principles to concrete cases. With regard to this latter category (application), they explicitly note that "prudential judgments are involved based on specific circumstances which can change or which can be interpreted differently by people of good will." The bishops add that such applications call for "serious attention and consideration by Catholics" but do not oblige in conscience. I believe it is helpful to recall that some of the most hotly debated moral questions fall into this category, e.g., public policy on abortion. I will pursue this matter in greater detail in chapter 8. When officials in the Church use their office to impose positions at this level, they abuse authority and bring the teaching office into disrepute. In my opinion this happened in the case of Agnes Mary Mansour.

So far we have seen: (1) that episcopal conferences can exercise a true teaching function; (2) that in understanding episcopal competence we must distinguish the morally good-bad from the morally right-wrong (only the former being strictly "truths of salvation"); (3) that other competences are utterly essential to determine the morally right-wrong in human action; (4) that there are several levels to be distinguished in discussing the morally right and wrong in human action. That brings me to a fifth point, our response to the contemporary teaching of the American bishops.

5. The proper response to episcopal teaching. Clearly, if there are different levels of teaching on the morally right-wrong, there are different levels of response. I will take this for granted—for instance, I will take for granted that we are free to disagree on applications of moral principle, e.g., no first use of nuclear weapons. There is, of course, the question about what is a principle, what an application. For example, is the central conclusion of *Humanae Vitae* a principle or an application of a more general principle? I examine this in detail in chapter 8.

When the bishops appeal to universally binding moral principles, it is probably unnecessary to specify an appropriate response. Such principles should be evident to all if they are truly universal binding principles. For instance, the principle of a presumption against taking human life gains nothing in clarity or certainty by episcopal proposal. It is clear of itself and stands on its own.

The problem area is the response to episcopal proposals that simply repeat statements of the papal magisterium. The problem is not different than that of the response to the authentic teaching of the pope. It is the problem of *obsequium religiosum,* translated (even though it is untranslatable) as "religious submission of will and mind." The phrase is general enough to accommodate a range of interpretations, from the rigidity of *Humani Generis* to something incompatible with it. I have discussed the proper response to such teaching in chapters 1 and 2, and will only advert to two points here.

First, in the last chapter I cited two proposed emendations at Vatican II. These two texts, if it is thought that we need texts to establish the point, show conclusively that *obsequium religiosum* cannot exclude dissent.

Second, let me refer to a fanciful but utterly serious little article Karl Rahner composed in 1980.[25] Rahner dreams futuristically that he is present at a meeting in 1985 (of all things!) where the pope is addressing leading representatives of the Christian churches from all over the world. The pope is attempting to put papal teaching authority in a more understandable context to still non-Catholic fears and misgivings. Rahner's pope has several interesting observations. One is that since the pope is, in his ex-cathedra decisions, defining the faith of the Church, "the pope must necessarily have recourse to the sense of the faith of the whole Church." An explicit recourse to the episcopate is "absolutely morally necessary," and a "moral obligation." An analogous "moral obligation" would seem to be the case in the situation of practical moral matters where other competences are essential to discovering the truth.

But what is of more interest is the statement of Rahner's pope on noninfallible teaching. He states: "Even the Second Vatican Council did not speak clearly enough about such authentic but reformable Roman doctrinal decisions." The pope then adds: "Roman procedures after the council left something to be desired by way of straightforward clarity and modesty."

It is a well-known fact that Rahner refused to believe that no. 25 of *Lumen Gentium* (where the response to ordinary papal teaching is discussed) is the last word on authentic noninfallible papal pronouncements. The matter is mentioned here for the record, so to speak. There are still theologians whose theology has no room for respectful disagreement or dissent. This overlooks the fact observed by Rahner's pope: "The ordinary magisterium of the pope in authentic doctrinal decisions at least in the past and up to very recent times was often involved in error and, on the other hand, Rome was accustomed to put forward and insist on such decisions as if there could be no doubt about their ultimate correctness and as if any further discussion of them was unbecoming for a Catholic theologian."

In the past twenty-five years, we have been experiencing, I believe, a kind of mini-development of doctrine of the understanding of the authentic noninfallible magisterium. It is a known and acknowledged fact that the documents of Vatican II contain perspectives and statements that are ill at ease with each other. That is true, I believe, of the obediential overtones of no. 25 of *Lumen Gentium.*

In summary, the effort to articulate our faith and its behavioral implications in our time is clearly a dialogical and processive one. This point was specifically highlighted by Bernard Häring. He noted: "There is no doubt that for her own exercise of her pastoral magisterium, the Church needs an atmosphere of freedom to examine the enduring validity of traditional norms, and the right of a sincere conscience humbly to doubt about norms which, in many or even most of the cases, are not accepted by sincere Christians."[26]

In conclusion, then, I want to suggest that a theologian's (or competent person in general) "listening" to episcopal moral teaching is an *active* listening, a personal reflection that must itself contribute to the formulation of the teaching. To say anything else would be to deny the responsibility implied in the gift of a scholar's experience and expertise.

6. Rules for dealing with bishops. Because a scholar's experience, education and expertise means that his/her listening is *active, contributory*, I want to conclude with "McCormick's Ten Rules for Dealing with Bishops." These rules should facilitate the exercise of the episcopal magisterium in our time.

1. *Be respectful.* I mean, of course, primarily of the *office*. It remains necessary—even if at times, strenuously difficult—to distinguish the office from the officeholder. For example, when then Archbishop Hamer writes me, as detailed in chapter 4, and says that Pius XII's ruling still holds (once a pope has authoritatively intervened, the matter is no longer a matter for free theological discussion), the officeholder's datedness tempts me to demean the office. Briefly, no competent theologian holds that anymore in its unqualified sense. When an American archbishop gives as an example of loyalty to the pope his willingness to jump off the Ambassador Bridge, he tests my loyalty to the episcopal office. Our own mistakes should chasten us into maintaining respect for this office even as we recognize the gaffes of some officeholders.

2. *Be honest.* There can be a heavy price for this. But in the long run it is the only form of service worthy of the name.

Let me give a personal example. In 1984 I wrote an article for *America* entitled "The Chill Factor: Recent Roman Interventions."[27] It is given substantially in chapter 4. I happen to know that many bishops were furious about the procedures and actions of the Congregation for the Doctrine of the Faith. But they really could not say so, or at least they felt that way. In a sense, they needed a spokesperson. Several told me subsequently that they were grateful. That is a task scholars can continue to perform.

3. *Be supportive.* I mean that far too often good episcopal actions go unnoticed and unremarked. There are many letters of complaint, but few compliments. We are all familiar with this. Scholars, with their "protected

status," should be the first to call attention to the good things bishops do.

4. *Be realistic.* I have already touched on the point I want to make here in chapter 4. But I want to emphasize it again. Authority is not competence. For instance, anyone wishing to determine the rights and wrongs of genetic interventions must be competent in the field. Episcopal authority does not coincide with such competence. Respect for the episcopal office can easily trap us into an overexpansive notion of episcopal competence.

The distinction between competence and authority must be played out a bit more. Cardinal John O'Connor has stated on abortion that he is merely reiterating "the formal, official teaching of the Catholic Church." He added: "So Geraldine Ferraro doesn't have a problem with me. If she has a problem, it's with the Pope."

In a perceptive article, James Burtchaell has rejected this notion of "teaching."[28] For moral tutelage to be effective, the learner must look out over his own experience and have his eyes opened and see a truth he could not see before but which he now sees. Burtchaell gives the following example:

> An alcoholic in the back row at the A.A. meeting does not go home to his wife and quote the speaker as an authority. Instead, he might say that, with the speaker's help, his eyes have finally been opened and now he can see a truth about himself that everyone else had long seen. This truth is something he can now vouch for himself. He is grateful to the man who pressed home the truth for him, but he would never think of his acceptance of that truth as an act of loyalty or allegiance or submission.

True teaching means opening peoples' eyes and minds. Simply to say "this is Catholic teaching" *teaches* no one. As Burtchaell summarizes:

> If a bishop wishes to teach within this tradition, he must first enter it thoughtfully enough to learn from it. Then he can begin to vouch for it, and to speak with moral authority. It is not adequate for a bishop, or for any teacher, simply to state that a given action is right or wrong. If he lacks the true moral authority to enlighten people, and invokes his office instead, then he is authoritarian. He is obliged to portray the issue so that all might see it clearly enough to vouch for it themselves.

And finally:

> If all he can do is invoke "official doctrine," then he has failed as a teacher. If he has to cite the Pope to make his point that abortion deals in death, then the Pope is ill-served, and so are we, and so is the issue itself.

True moral authority is not simply the authority that comes with office. If it is truly to teach, to persuade, it must be the authority of an eyewitness, of an eye-opener. That demands competence. Otherwise, bishops will look like house whips, calling for a closing of ranks around a sectarian house rule. This is not authentically Catholic, especially because it involves the mutilation of moral discourse in our community.

5. *Be competent.* If bishops are not competent in concrete moral questions ex officio, they must rely on others. Bishops have told me repeatedly that their best support is the competence of their advisors. The matter is so obvious that it needs no elaboration. *The Challenge of Peace* would not exist without Bryan Hehir. *Dignitatis Humanae* would not exist without John Courtney Murray and Pietro Pavan. As Cardinal Basil Hume put it some years ago:

> The Church is so riddled with tensions and problems at the moment that any man who says he can give final answers to these problems is deluding himself. I really hope to be able to call on the best minds to guide me in forming attitudes and statements that I should be expected to make. I don't see myself as a great person. I see myself far more as a member of a team.[29]

6. *Be patient.* Some bishops have rather primitive and unsophisticated theological backgrounds. They see their episcopal responsibilities through the prism of a seminary theology that is running on empty. The feisty Karl Rahner adverted to this repeatedly. For instance, in 1980 in *Stimmen der Zeit,* after criticizing the secrecy of the procedures of the Congregation for the Doctrine of the Faith, Rahner stated that the final procedure before ten cardinals is outmoded, or, as Rahner puts it, "salva omni reverentia . . . nichts von Theologie verstehen" ("With all due reverence . . . they understand nothing of theology").[30] Examples abound. While testifying before a congressional committee, the late Cardinal Humberto Madeiros asserted that the Catholic Church prohibits all abortions, *all,* absolutely, even to save the life of the mother. In a stunning non sequitur Cardinal Luigi Ciappi asserted that the absolution of a priest who publicly disagrees with *Humanae Vitae* is invalid.[31] I could go on. The point is clear. Patience.

I want to raise another point here. During the deliberations on birth control in the mid-sixties, Cardinal Suenens intervened in an attempt to help some members of the Commission to understand how the Church could change. He stated:

> We have heard arguments based on "what the bishops all taught for decades." Well, the bishops did defend the classical position. But it was

one imposed on them by authority. The bishops didn't study the pros and cons. They received directives, they bowed to them, and they tried to explain them to their congregations.[32]

I think we must say the same today, and even more so. Given the current atmosphere or ecclesiastical climate, the bishops are simply not free—at least with regard to certain moral questions. If they take a position different from the official one, they know what will happen. This is regrettable, not least of all because it means that apparent unanimity is doctrinally meaningless.

7. *Be daring.* I do not mean wild. I mean that theologians and scholars ought to dare to dream new and imaginative ideas. Episcopal teaching is not different from any other to the extent that it is going to be influential and persuasive. Some years ago, Avery Dulles suggested that it might not be a bad idea if bishops issued statements co-signed by theologians.[33] That sounds like a daring idea. In terms of past practice, it is. But it makes a lot of sense. While the hierarchy does not learn the Christian message from theologians, still the appropriate restatement of this faith does depend on scholarly work. Why not make this explicit? Episcopal statements combine the scientific and the pastoral, the *magisterium cathedrae pastoralis* and the *magisterium cathedrae magistralis*, to use Thomas' language. Is there anything wrong with a bishop who offers a pastoral on business ethics co-signing it with business leaders in his area? I think not. I had a chance to see Bishop Roger Mahony's pastoral on peace and war before publication. It contained many references Mahony could not be expected to know thoroughly. I suggested that he add a final footnote listing his collaborators. He did. His statement lost nothing in credibility.

8. *Be prudent.* This caution may appear to be in the "motherhood" category. In some senses it is. But people with genuinely good causes and motives can get swamped by them to the point of a counterproductivity that weakens their overall ability to deal effectively with bishops.

9. *Be prayerful.* Dialogue within the Church must be the product of love. And genuine love—especially in delicate, controversial matters where we may have strong opinions—cannot survive without prayer.

10. *Be docile.* I do not refer here to docility toward bishops. That I take for granted. Rather, I refer to the scholar's need to allow his/her moral and pastoral judgments to be shaped by open listening to the faithful. Otherwise, scholarly service to the episcopate risks being either heavily ideological or a sterile rationality.

Such docility is not easy, especially because the Catholic faithful—and others too—are unfamiliar with theological language and conceptual tools. Nonetheless, if they have their own distinctive role, theologians must support them and encourage them in implementing it, and learn from their insights.

"Bishops as teachers and scholars as listeners"? It is not as simple as that. All of us must first be listeners. Then all of us, regardless of our office, can and should be teachers—if by that term we mean those who share in the ongoing process of moral discourse in the community. Only if that occurs can the Church fulfill its moral teaching task to the world—which is aptly described as "corrective vision."

Notes

1. Theodore M. Hesburgh, "Foreword" in *Catholics and Nuclear War* (New York: Crossroad, 1983), ix.
2. Giancarlo Zizola, "The Counter Reformation of John Paul II," *Magill* 7 (1985): 9-22. Cf. also Zizola, *La restaurazione di papa Wojtyla* (Rome: Laterza, 1985).
3. Avery Dulles, S.J., "Bishops' Conference Documents: What Doctrinal Authority?" *Origins* 14 (no. 32, 24 January 1985): 528-34; "The Teaching Authority of Bishops' Conferences," *America* 148 (no. 23, 11 June 1983): 453-55.
4. *Documents*, 48.
5. Ibid., 48.
6. W. Levada, *Infallible Church Magisterium and the Natural Law*, excerpt from dissertation (Rome: Gregorian University, 1971); A. Riedl, *Die kirchliche Lehrautorität in Fragen der Moral nach der ersten Vatikanishchen Konzils* (Freiburg, 1971). Cf. also John Mahoney, S.J., *The Making of Moral Theology* (Oxford: Clarendon Press, 1987).
7. *AAS* 4 (1912), 658-59.
8. *AAS* 23 (1931), 190.
9. *AAS* 42 (1950), 561-62.
10. *AAS* 53 (1961), 453; *AAS* 55 (1963), 300-01.
11. *AAS* 56 (1964), 626-27.
12. *AAS* 46 (1954), 671-73.
13. Cf. Josef Fuchs, S.J., "Moral Truths—Truth of Salvation?" in *Christian Ethics in a Secular Arena* (Washington: Georgetown University Press, 1984), 48-67.
14. Gustave Ermecke, "Die Bedeutung von 'Humanwissenschaften' für die Moraltheologie," *Münchener Theologische Zeitschrift* 26 (1975): 126-40.
15. Cf. note 13 for this analysis.
16. "Non enim Deus a nobis offenditur nisi ex eo quod contra nostrum bonum agimus," *Summa contra gentiles*, 3, 122.
17. Cf. note 13, at 57-58.
18. Karl Rahner, "Basic Observations on the Subject of Changeable and Unchangeable Factors in the Church," *Theological Investigations* 14 (New York: Seabury, 1976): 3-23, at 14.
19. Cf. note 13, at 61.
20. *Documents*, 209.
21. Cf. Richard A. McCormick, S.J., *Notes on Moral Theology, 1981 through 1984* (Lanham, Md.: University Press of America, 1984), 108.

22. Thomas J. Peters and Robert H. Waterman, Jr., *In Search of Excellence* (New York: Harper & Row, 1982), 250.

23. Robert Blair Kaiser, *The Politics of Sex and Religion* (Kansas City: Leaven Press, 1985), 83.

24. Paul VI, June 23, 1964. English version available in *Pope and Pill,* ed. Leo Pyle (Baltimore: Helicon, 1968), 5.

25. Karl Rahner, "Dream of the Church," *Tablet* 180 (1981): 52-55.

26. Cf. Richard A. McCormick, S.J., *Notes on Moral Theology 1965-1980* (Lanham, Md.: University Press of America, 1981), 579, note 16.

27. *America* 150 (1984): 475-81.

28. James Burtchaell, "The Sources of Conscience," *Notre Dame Magazine* (Winter, 1984-85): 20-23.

29. Cited in A.L. Descamps, "Théologie et magistère," *Ephemerides Theologicae Lovanienses* 52 (1976): 82-133, at 103.

30. Karl Rahner, "Theologie und Lehramt," *Stimmen der Zeit* 103.

31. Cf. *National Catholic Register,* 26 September 1982.

32. Robert Blair Kaiser, *The Politics of Sex and Religion* (Kansas City, Mo.: Leaven Press, 1985), 170.

33. Avery Dulles, S.J., "What Is Magisterium?" *Origins* 6 (1976), 81-87.

Chapter 6

L'Affaire Curran

I have already laid out some general perspectives on dissent in the Church in chapter 2. The matter cannot be left there if the overall good of the Church is to be served. On November 15, 1968, the American Catholic bishops issued a document entitled *Human Life in Our Day*. After listing the conditions that govern private dissent, the document turned to public dissent. It stated:

> Since our age is characterized by popular interest in theological debate and given the realities of modern mass media, the ways in which theological dissent may be effectively expressed, in a manner consistent with pastoral solicitude, should become the object of fruitful dialogue between bishops and theologians.[1]

As three outstanding Franciscan theologians (Regis A. Duffy, William E. McConville, Kenneth R. Himes) point out, fruitful dialogue "is exactly what has not taken place" between Father Charles Curran and the Congregation for the Doctrine of the Faith.[2] That brings us to the "Curran Affair."

The March 12, 1986 issue of *The New York Times* headlined a front-page article "Vatican Orders a Theologian to Retract Teachings on Sex." Clearly, the headline editor knew what she/he was doing. Every word is a grabber. "Vatican" and "Sex" jump at you. Then add to that "Orders" and "Retract" and the looming donnybrook takes even clearer shape. The scenario is given final touches with "Theologian" and "Teachings." It is not just analyzing, examining, proffering opinions, but "teaching." Similar reports, without such telltale headlines, were read across the country, from Shreveport (where I was) to Toledo, from Sacramento to Boston.

What is going on here? The Rev. Charles E. Curran, revered and reviled professor of moral theology at The Catholic University of America, had been in correspondence with the Congregation for the Doctrine of the Faith (CDF) since 1979 concerning certain of his writings. On March 8, 1986, there was a personal interview with Cardinal Joseph Ratzinger in Rome. The writings in question concern contraception, sterilization, indissolubility of marriage, abortion and euthanasia, homosexuality and masturbation. They could have concerned—but only by a vigorous stretch of the imagination—other issues, such as nuclear war, revolution, poverty, racial justice and economics. But, in a sense, the issues are not the issue. Beneath this bill of particulars is the tender nerve, dissent—and more precisely, as I shall make clear, public dissent.

What did Father Curran actually write about some of the subjects mentioned above? A few examples will suffice. In *Moral Theology: A Continuing Journey*, he states: "Human beings do have the power and responsibility to interfere with the sexual faculty and act. The official Catholic teaching is often accused of a physicalism or biologism because the biological or physical structure of the act is made normative and cannot be interfered with. I take this dissenting position."[3]

With regard to the indissolubility of marriage he writes: "In light of these and other reasons, I propose that indissolubility remains a goal and ideal for Christian marriage; but Christians, sometimes without any personal fault, are not always able to live up to that ideal. Thus the Roman Catholic Church should change its teaching on divorce."[4]

Finally, with regard to homosexuality, he summarizes his position, expressed previously, in this way: "My position affirms that for an irreversible, constitutional or genuine homosexual, homosexual acts in the context of a loving relationship striving for permanency are objectively morally good."[5]

Similar proposals could be adduced about sterilization, masturbation, abortion and premarital sexual relations. One thing should be absolutely clear: These conclusions do represent dissenting views. There should be no fudging on that.

But where do such views put Father Curran in the theological world? Is he the radical and notorious *enfant terrible* that *The Wanderer* describes and urges its readers to denounce to the Holy See? He has repeatedly argued that his positions, while departing from official formulations, fall within the mainstream of substantial Catholic concerns. He points to the fact that other theologians throughout the world have written similar things.

For instance, in his book *Medical Ethics*, Bernard Häring justifies direct sterilization in certain instances. Hundreds of theologians have dissented from the central thesis of *Humanae Vitae* (that every contraceptive act is intrinsically immoral). Any number of theologians have proposed "pastoral solutions" to the dilemma of homosexuality that do not always reflect the Congregation for the Doctrine of the Faith's 1975 "Declaration on Certain Questions Concerning Sexual Ethics." For instance, the conservative Roman theologian Jan Visser, one of the collaborators on this declaration, has admitted that it is sometimes the lesser of two evils for homosexuals to live in stable unions rather than in promiscuous relationships.[6]

So far as the indissolubility of marriage is concerned, Catholic exegetes and theologians have been struggling for some years to read the implications of Jesus' words for our time. Thus the late George MacRae, S.J., once wrote: "We must discern the process by which the teaching of Jesus was remembered, communicated, interpreted, adapted and enshrined in the practice of the early Christian communities. That process, we have seen, is one of accommodation in circumstances that were not the context of the preaching of Jesus Himself."[7]

Similarly, the distinguished exegete Joseph Fitzmyer, S.J., wrote in *Theological Studies:*

> If Matthew under inspiration could have been moved to add an exceptive phrase to the saying of Jesus about divorce that he found in an absolute form in either his Marcan source or in "Q," or if Paul likewise under inspiration could introduce into his writing an exception on his own authority, then why cannot the Spirit-guided institutional church of a later generation make a similar exception in view of problems confronting Christian married life of its day, or so-called broken marriages (not really envisaged in the New Testament), as it has done in some situations?[8]

None of these proposals—and many more could be adduced—is made in a spirit of defiance, with the authors claiming to be an official voice or competitive magisterium. Their intent as well as their tone is one of searching and questioning, of public theological wrestling proposed to scholars and the broader church community for careful consideration. The same can be said of Father Curran's writings, even though he proposes them under the rubrics of "position," "teaching," "dissent." He has a strong point, then, when he argues that in neither substance nor purpose do his writings constitute an extreme "left" position.

Why, then, is Charles Curran singled out for special scrutiny and threat? The answer to that question must remain speculative. Was it because he organized the public dissent against *Humanae Vitae* in 1968? It is no secret that some Roman institutions have elephantine memories. Was it because archconservative groups such as Catholics United for the Faith flooded the Congregation with mail against him? Was it because Rome feels that now is the time to make an example of someone so that others will take note? As I say, "speculative."

When the Congregation for the Doctrine of the Faith first broached this matter with Father Curran, it listed some of the subjects of concern noted above. At first, he did not respond to the individual subjects of concern, but instead presented his view about the legitimacy of public dissent in the Church. He stated that this was the key issue and that, before he could enter into dialogue with the Congregation, he would have to know its view on public dissent.

On June 21, 1982, he responded in detail to the Congregation's specific concerns with a twenty-three-page letter.[9] The Congregation was not satisfied with that reply and told him so in a letter dated February 10, 1983.

On May 10, 1983, the Congregation again wrote Father Curran, spelling out its problems. It listed issues where he was in clear dissent from the magisterium and some "issues that remain unclear," but stated that the "right to dissent publicly is at the basis of the C.D.F.'s difficulties with Father Curran." The Congregation implicitly admitted the right of *private* dissent but noted that "to further dissent publicly and to encourage dissent in others runs the risk of causing scandal to the faithful." It viewed such dissent as "setting up one's own theological opinion in contradiction to the position taken by the church." Curran was asked to reply within a working month.

On August 10, 1983, he wrote the Congregation, addressing only the first of its concerns (public dissent). He felt that the individual subjects of dissent could not be fruitfully addressed until the Congregation wrote him again about the incompleteness of his reply ("We still await your complete reply").

Because the Congregation's letters were sent through Washington's Archbishop James A. Hickey, Father Curran wrote to Archbishop Hickey on February 28, 1984, of his "growing frustration." He stated: "My reaction is one of growing frustration. I mentioned this to you in earlier correspondence and have said the same in my most recent detailed response to the Congregation itself."

"From my very first response in Oct. 1979, I have tried to determine as exactly as possible the differences between the Congregation and myself on the question of dissent. I formulated five questions at that time, but the Congregation has been unwilling to respond to them. I ended my response of Aug. 1983, with the request that the Congregation state what are the norms that should govern dissent . . . Why has the Congregation been unwilling to answer that question? Why are they stalling?" Curran was obviously referring to public, theological dissent, since private dissent is not the issue.

The Congregation wrote to Father Curran once more on April 13,

1984, asking for a reply by September 1 on its specific points. On August 22, he replied to those specific inquiries, but this reply was undoubtedly seen as unsatisfactory by the Congregation.

On September 17, 1985, Father Curran received a letter from the Congregation stating that its inquiry had been completed and that the results "were presented to the Sovereign Pontiff in an audience granted to the undersigned Cardinal Prefect [Joseph Ratzinger] on June 28, 1985, and were confirmed by him." The letter called attention to the fact that "Catholic theologians, hence those teaching in ecclesiastical faculties, do not teach on their own authority but by virtue of the mission they have received from the church." The letter then continued with an explanation of this "mission":

> In order to guarantee this teaching, the church claims the freedom to maintain her own academic institutions in which her doctrine is reflected upon, taught and interpreted in complete fidelity. This freedom of the church to teach her doctrine is in full accord with the students' corresponding right to know what that teaching is and have it properly explained to them. This freedom of the church likewise implies the right to choose for her theological faculties those and only those professors who, in complete intellectual honesty and integrity, recognize themselves to be capable of meeting these requirements.

The letter then details the issues concerning which Father Curran dissents (contraception, abortion and euthanasia, masturbation, homosexuality, premarital intercourse and indissolubility of marriage). It concludes:

> In light of the indispensable requirements for authentic theological instruction, described by the council and by the public law of the Catholic Church, the Congregation now invites you to reconsider and to retract those positions which violate the conditions necessary for a professor to be called a Catholic theologian. It must be recognized that the authorities of the church cannot allow the present situation to continue in which the inherent contradiction is prolonged that one who is to teach in the name of the church in fact denies her teaching.

The language in this letter is clear, and clearly ominous. "Indispensable requirements," "cannot allow the present situation to continue," leave little room for doubt or compromise. The inescapable message: Unless Father Curran retracts, he will be stripped of his mandate to teach as a "Catholic theologian." (That would mean practically that Father Curran could not teach theology at Catholic University, nor realistically at any Catholic university.) The only question remaining: When would the other shoe drop?

When I first saw the Congregation's letter, I wrote (November 15, 1985) to Archbishop Hickey, noting that it would be tragic if the letter (the Congregation's) were made public. My letter continued:

> I use the term "tragic" deliberately and thoughtfully. The reason: the theology of the letter is, in my judgment, at variance with Catholic tradition and, as such, open to serious criticism. When such a letter becomes public, it will quite properly be read as the official Roman attitude toward theological inquiry. Such an attitude represents a self-inflicted blow on the credibility of the magisterium.
>
> Why? Because the letter explicitly states that agreement with the ordinary magisterium on every authoritatively proposed moral formulation is required if one is to be called a Catholic theologian. After detailing four areas where Curran's opinions are at variance with official formulations, Cardinal Ratzinger refers to "those positions which violate the conditions necessary for a professor to be called a Catholic theologian." This contention—which undergirds the entire letter—disallows dissent from noninfallibly proposed teaching in principle. Such a point of view cannot survive historical and theological scrutiny.
>
> If Cardinal Ratzinger's letter were to be applied to theologians throughout the world, it is clear that the vast majority would not qualify as Catholic theologians; for, as a matter of record, most theologians have found it impossible to agree with the central formulation of *Humanae Vitae* (see, for example, *Sittliche Normen*, where this point is repeatedly made).[10] Indeed, if Cardinal Ratzinger's letter represented an acceptable ecclesiology, we would not have the Decree on Religious Liberty as an official church document. Only because John Courtney Murray, S.J., conducted a long uphill battle, and a dissenting one, could Vatican II arrive at the Decree on Religious Liberty. Briefly, dissent in the church must be viewed much more realistically and positively—as the ordinary way to growth and development. Even quite traditional ecclesiologists now view the matter in this way.[11]

When the Congregation would drop the other shoe and declare Father Curran no longer a Catholic theologian was not clear. *That* it would do so seemed unavoidable from the logic of its approach. It did so in a letter dated July 25, 1986, informing Curran that he would "no longer be considered suitable nor eligible to exercise the function of a Professor of Catholic Theology." Even after such a judgment, it remains important to unpack some of the issues that surround this matter.

Nonissues. Before listing the issues, it would be useful to clarify things by explicitly eliminating nonissues. I see five.

Agreement with Father Curran. One need not agree with all or any of Curran's analyses and positions in rejecting the Congregation's action. I have disagreed with Curran and he with me. Others have disagreed with both of us. That is neither here nor there, for discussion and disagreement are the very lifeblood of the academic and theological enterprise. We all learn and grow in the process, and it is a public process. Without such theological exchange and the implied freedom to make an honest mistake, the magisterium itself would be paralyzed by the sycophancy of theologians.

Dissent. Dissent as such is not the key issue. The Congregation admits as much when it states that personal dissent demands certainty that a teaching is erroneous—a statement whose rigor is open to serious challenge. The Church does not and cannot expect assent to moral formulations that one judges to be erroneous. The mind can assent to what it perceives to be true in itself or it can assent because of trust in the teacher. Neither can occur when there are contrary reasons utterly persuasive to an individual. This is quite traditional teaching. The issue is rather *public* dissent.

Infallibility. There is no question here of dissent from infallible teaching. Infallibility is not the issue it was in the case of Father Hans Küng. It is generally admitted by theologians that the Church's authentic teaching on concrete moral behavior does not, indeed cannot, fall into the category of definable doctrine. There is a recent tiny pocket of resistance to this, but even the Congregation for the Doctrine of the Faith makes no claim that Father Curran dissents from infallibly proposed teachings. In a press statement Bishop James W. Malone, president of the National Conference of Catholic Bishops, left the matter a bit murky. He referred to "the teaching of the church's magisterium on crucial points."[12] What does "crucial" mean? Is everything taught authoritatively, especially if frequently repeated, crucial? Crucial to what? And are crucial teachings removed from the possibility of dissent? Why?

Authority of the Church to teach. In dissenting from this or that authoritative formulation, one does not automatically deny the authority of the Church to teach in the area of morals. Indeed, the very anguish, ardor and prayerfulness of one's dissent assert the opposite. If one denied such authority, strenuous efforts, anguish and prayerfulness would be out of place. One simply would not care. Father Curran has repeatedly asserted the Church's moral teaching authority. Such authority is a nonissue in this case.

The right and duty to safeguard teaching. All theologians would, I think, admit that the Church has such a right and duty, and even that it could take the disciplinary form of removing one's mandate to teach as a Catholic theologian. That is not an issue. The issue is when and under what circumstances this form of safeguarding should be used. Only for outright heresy? For any dissent from any "crucial" teaching? I say "under what circumstances" because clearly Pope John XXIII acknowledged the Church's "right and duty to safeguard teaching" (Bishop Malone's phrase), yet he rejected the punitive measures associated with Cardinal Alfredo Ottaviani's Holy Office. "Nowadays," he said, "the Spouse of Christ prefers to make use of the medicine of mercy rather than that of severity. She considers that she meets the needs of the present day by demonstrating the validity of her teaching rather than by condemnations."[13]

Issues. If the above are nonissues, what are the true issues we ought to think about? There is but a single issue, but one with many ramifications. That single issue is public dissent. If one judges a teaching authoritatively proposed to be one-sided, incomplete, partially inaccurate or even erroneous, what is one to do?

There are two possible answers to this question. One is the Congregation's. Simply put, it is: Keep silence. For if one writes of one's disagreement, the Congregation sees an "inherent contradiction." It states it as follows: "One who is to teach in the name of the church in fact denies her teaching." For the Congregation this is intolerable ("the authorities of the church cannot allow . . . "). It "runs the risk of causing scandal."

A second possible answer is that presented by the late Karl Rahner, S.J., and cited in chapter 4. Recall that, writing in *Stimmen der Zeit,* Father Rahner asked: "What are contemporary moral theologians to make of Roman declarations on sexual morality that they regard as too unnuanced? Are they to remain silent, or is it their task to dissent, to give a more nuanced interpretation?" Rahner was unhesitating in his response: "I believe that the theologian, after mature reflection, has the right, and many times the duty, to speak out against a teaching of the magisterium and support his dissent."[14] In sum, where Rahner sees the right and duty to speak out, the Congregation sees scandal.

A view similar to Rahner's was expressed by noted ecclesiologist Francis A. Sullivan, S.J.[15] He stated: "The idea that Catholic theologians, at any level of education, can only teach the official position, and present only those positions in their writings, is new and disturbing." What is new and "quite extraordinary," according to Sullivan, is the implication "that infallible and non-infallible Church teachings are equally beyond criticism." What is disturbing is the threat to the critical role of theologians. In Sullivan's words: "If theologians cannot discuss and present the reasons they think a position can be changed, they cannot even communicate with their colleagues. When you do that, you shut off the whole theological enterprise." Sullivan specified this as follows: "If it were just a question of condemning some of Father Curran's views, that is one thing. Some would be disturbed, but not all that much. But the question being raised about the limit on the right to be critical affects everybody."

Most theologians would, I believe, share the Rahner-Sullivan view. A group of such theologians (all past presidents of the Catholic Theological Society of America and the College Theology Society) issued a statement on March 12 manifesting this and putting the following questions to the Congregation about the threat to Father Curran: "1) Which noninfallible teachings are serious enough to provoke such a result, and how are those teachings determined? 2) How many noninfallible teachings would one have to disagree with before this result would follow, and how is that number determined? 3) If disagreement with any noninfallible teaching of the Church is sufficient to provoke this result, on what theological, doctrinal or historical basis is that principle deduced?"[16]

These are serious questions, and we as a community of believers deserve clear answers to them. If such answers are not forthcoming or are unsatisfactory, and if the threat against Father Curran is carried out, it will be hard to avoid the conclusion that we are dealing with an abuse of authority.

The letter of the theologians noted one more important point: "If Father Curran's views on the various issues mentioned in the letter [of the Congregation] are so incompatible with Catholic teaching that he must be declared no longer a Catholic theologian, justice and fairness would dictate that other Catholic theologians who hold similar views should be treated in exactly the same fashion. Indeed, the credibility of any action on the part of the Congregation would be seriously undermined by a failure to identify and act upon other such cases. The problem is, of course, that there are very many Catholic theologians who do dissent from noninfallible teachings."

The implications of the Congregation's approach should not be overlooked. The first is that, to be regarded as a Catholic theologian, one may not dissent from *any* authoritatively proposed teaching. The second is that "authentic theological instruction" means presenting Church teaching, and never disagreeing with it, even with respect and reverence. Third, and correlatively, sound theological education means accepting, un-critically if necessary, official Catholic teaching. The impact of such asser-tions on the notion of a university, of Catholic higher education, of theology and of good teaching is mind-boggling. All too easily, answers replace ques-tions and conformism replaces teaching as "theology" is reduced to Kohlberg's preconventional level of reasoning (obey or be punished).

One has to wonder about the notion of church that undergirds all of this, the notion of magisterium, the notion of teaching and learning, the no-tion of the autonomy of earthly realities proclaimed by Vatican II,[17] the no-tion of collegiality and the notion of lay competence. Vatican II discarded much of the cultural and theological baggage that produced *Roma locuta, causa finita* (Rome has spoken, the matter is closed). The Congregation's ap-proach to theology and theological education reintroduces much of it. The invalidation of dissent discredits personal reflection and freezes the

Church's learning process within the last available official formulation. There is simplicity and security in this—but also the stillness of the mausoleum.

Let teaching be an example here. Teaching means helping others to understand, to see what they did not see. It is the exhilarating experience of seeing eyes opened to dimensions of reality formerly hidden. In practical moral matters, the very last thing one arrives at is a moral norm. A moral norm is a generalization about the significance of our actions. It is a conclusion drafted from understanding that significance. When it is up front as the dominant preoccupation, it hinders teaching and learning by bypassing the struggles that lead to understanding. We call this moralism.

Yet I dare say, if many educated Catholics were asked, "What is the Church's teaching on contraception, homosexual acts, masturbation?" the answer would be that they are intrinsically evil actions. One would not get an insightful view of the gift and challenge of sexuality as our capacity for human relatedness. One would get a conclusion, and a negative one. "Authentic Church teaching" has come to mean a set of conclusions. In this perspective, "learning" degenerates into accepting such conclusions. Understanding the significance on which they are based is almost beside the point. This is a caricature of both teaching and learning, yet it is a caricature powerfully supported by the rejection of dissent *in principle* from Catholic theology. Dissent is not an end-product; it is a way of getting at things, a part of the human process of growth in understanding. When it is viewed as having such enormous importance in itself (as it is when the title "Catholic theologian" is denied to one who dissents on noninfallibly proposed teaching), it is a sure sign that "authentic teaching" is being conceived in a highly moralistic way. The Church has paid and will continue to pay a heavy price for this type of short-cutting.

The Congregation's chief concern seems to be scandal. In its May 10, 1983 letter to Father Curran, it said of public dissent that it "runs the risk of causing scandal to the faithful." In the Curran dossier, that is the only peek we get at the Congregation's rationale. The introduction of the notion of scandal raises several interesting questions.

Scandal, it must be remembered, is not surprise or shock at the discovery of a skeleton in someone's closet. It has a technical theological sense, and the Congregation is using it in that sense. It refers to an action or omission that provides another or others with the occasion of sin. We must ask, therefore, what sin is occasioned by dissent from noninfallible teaching on sexual questions?

The first possible answer is that it occasions or facilitates those actions condemned by official teaching but approved by the dissenter. But that begs the whole question. It assumes that the actions condemned by official teaching are, indeed, morally wrong. Such an assumption would invalidate dissent in principle by elevating the teaching to the status of the unquestionably true. The Church does not make such claims for her concrete moral teaching.

Another possible answer is that dissent is the occasion of others' neglect of, and disrespect for, the teaching office of the Church. This seems to be the Congregation's view. For it uses the phrase "encourage dissent in others" and ties this to scandal. That will not work, either. Whether or not "encouraging dissent in others" is morally wrong depends on what the dissent is aimed at. If it is aimed at a teaching that is incomplete or inaccurate, it is quite appropriate, even obligatory. And that, of course, is precisely what the dissenter is saying. It is simply no response to object that dissent "encourages dissent in others," for if the teaching is inaccurate, that is what dissent should do.

But these are close arguments, and I would not expect everyone to appreciate them. There remain more general concerns stimulated by the term "scandal." Who are these "faithful" who are scandalized? Why are they scandalized? What is their notion of church, of theology? What is their notion of the magisterium? What is their notion of collegiality and the Church's accountability to reason for its moral teachings? What is their attitude toward the commercialism of ideas in the university setting? What is their attitude toward tradition (learning from the past or embalming it)? Is tradition, to borrow from Jaroslav Pelikan, the dead faith of the living, or, as it should be, the living faith of the dead?[18] Finally, and most tellingly, is not such intolerance of any dissent—in itself—a greater cause of scandal? Does it not lead many to believe that Rome is more interested in the authority of the teacher than in what is taught by the authority?

The Most Rev. Matthew H. Clark, Bishop of Rochester, N.Y. (Father Curran's bishop), issued a magnificent statement on March 12. After adverting to Curran's personal qualities as a priest and scholar, he stated:

> It is, I believe, commonly accepted in the Roman Catholic theological community that Father Curran is a moral theologian of notable competence whose work locates him very much at the center of that community and not at all on the fringe. I believe that perception is true. If Father Curran's status as a Roman Catholic theologian is brought into question, I fear a serious setback to Catholic education and pastoral life in this country. That could happen in two ways. Theologians may stop exploring the challenging questions of the day in a creative, healthy way because they fear actions which may prematurely end their teaching careers. Moreover, able theologians may abandon Catholic institutions altogether in order to avoid embarrassing confrontation with church authorities. Circumstances of this sort would seriously undermine the standing of Catholic scholarship in this nation, isolate our theological community and weaken our Catholic institutions of higher education.

In the same March 12 issue of *The New York Times* that reported the Curran affair, there appeared a report of the ethical aspects of certain sex-therapy techniques. The report cited the views of Moshe D. Tendler (Orthodox Jewish community) and Beverly Harrison (Protestant community). The article ended as follows: "Catholic tradition also forbids a practice like masturbation as violating the procreative purposes of sexuality. One Catholic ethicist, *who asked not to be identified* [my emphasis], said that an argument could be made for its use in therapy 'since it was designed to help people become sexually functioning and procreative.'"

Is such anonymity what we really want in the Church of our time?

The paragraphs above represent the substance of an article that appeared in *America* April 6, 1986. Not unexpectedly, it flushed out some predictable reactions. One Edward J. Capestany, for instance, sees the position presented as "Nullifying the Magisterium."[19] He begins as follows:

> In his recent article in *America*, April 5, McCormick places himself (along with the vast majority of theologians in the world) within the indictment of Ratzinger's letter. He has thrown the gauntlet, but, as we shall show, he has painted himself into a corner rendering the magisterium of the Church practically impossible in spite of the fact that he proclaims its existence. His attitude somehow reminds us of the position of the "pro-choicers" who proclaim that they are "personally opposed to, but." Indeed, McCormick says that there is a magisterium on moral matters but . . .

Capestany does not like such "buts." Indeed, he disowns any qualifications or conditions where the magisterium is concerned. Without pausing for breath or cracking a smile, he delivers this stunner:

> If we have decided that we must belong to the church because we have recognized her claim to be Christ's revelation to mankind and to be the pillar and ground of truth, then it follows that she must be incapable of error.

So much for history. Anything that follows is bound to be anticlimactic. But the Capestanys of this world are unfair targets. The jugular is far too exposed.

The same cannot be said of other commentators. Take John F. Harvey, O.S.F.S., for example. Harvey is an experienced and compassionate theologian. He makes several points on my Curran analysis that deserve comment.[20] First, Harvey argues that the issue is "the basic right of the magisterium . . . to bind the consciences of the faithful on concrete and individual moral actions." Because Church moral decisions are not infallibly proposed, "the conclusion drawn is that the church cannot bind the consciences of the faithful with regard to individual acts." For Harvey, this means that in practice "Catholics are free to choose the opinions of dissenting theologians to practice contraception in difficult circumstances," etc.

Here I believe Harvey has skipped a beat. The issue is not whether the magisterium can "bind the consciences of the faithful on concrete and individual moral actions." Of course it can, as theologians such as Karl Rahner have repeatedly insisted. The issue is the type of consultation that must occur before the magisterium makes binding proclamations. Can the magisterium issue such proclamations without consulting theological scholarship and the experience and reflection of the faithful? Do these sources count for nothing as the Church formulates her moral convictions? If one answers "yes" to such questions, is not the magisterium reduced to a merely juridical notion? In putting the matter this way, I do not mean to imply that any assertion or opinion of a theologian is self-validating or automatically "weighty." Far from it. I mean only to say that when theological work around the world raises certain doubts or begins to converge in a certain direction, it can be ignored only if one supposes that the magisterium is exempt from the ordinary processes and sources of human inquiry. If the Church is not a debating society, neither is it an arbitrary dictator of morals. It is, after all, the rightness of human conduct that is at stake here. The *charisma veritatis certum* (the certain charism of truth)[21] is not a substitute for consultation and deliberation in making this determination. It supposes it. If the pronouncements of the magisterium bypass these sources, they lose the presumption (of truth) we ordinarily associate with them.

Harvey next accuses me of misrepresenting the position of the Congregation for the Doctrine of the Faith when I say that "keep silence" is its response to one who disagrees with an authoritatively proposed teaching. As he puts it:

> Theologians and bishops have written to the congregation concerning the "Vatican Declaration on Sexual Ethics," offering suggestions concerning ways in which the same basic teaching could be supported by better arguments and expressed in language more understandable in our era.

In other words, when one disagrees with an official statement, one writes to the congregation (or bishop, or pope) that made the statement. One does *not* publish such disagreement or "offer suggestions" in a scholarly journal or a serious magazine of opinion like *America* or *Commonweal*. I call this "silence" if it is remembered that theology is a public enterprise. When Harvey restricts critical responses to private letters to congregations, he is offering us the traditional manualist directive— as well as the preconciliar ecclesiological assumptions behind it. Those assumptions have to do with the nature of the Church, of the magisterium, of theology, of lay competence, etc., and I have treated them elsewhere in this book.

One response to "L'Affaire Curran" needs to be lifted out. It was that of Patrick J. McGuire, who expressed disappointment in the article.[22] Why? "My personal inability to see the Ignatian commitment to the defense of the Holy Father." Most theologians would be surprised at this and their surprise is understandable. The theologian views his/her critical function as cut from the cloth of loyalty. Indeed, in a sense, it is the highest form of loyalty. Those who speak to us a painful truth do not love us less, but more.

Two recent events may be said to touch on the Curran affair, one indirectly, the other directly. Both involve Cardinal Joseph Ratzinger. The first was a speech delivered by Ratzinger at St. Michael's College, Toronto, on April 15, 1986.[23] Ratzinger had some beautiful things to say about conversion and the centrality of the Church for theology. I agree enthusiastically with them. Toward the end of his address he turned to the role of teacher in the Church. His remarks deserve full citation.

> When one teaches, not on his own authority, but in the name of the common subject, the church, the assumption is that he recognizes this fundamental rule and freely obliges himself to observe it. This is so because his opinions are given a weight which they could not possibly deserve on their own, precisely because he teaches on behalf of the church. Believers have confidence in the church's word and so naturally transfer that confidence to those who teach in her name.
>
> One hears a great deal today about the abuse of power within the church. Almost reflexively, there comes to mind the abuse committed by those in authority, and this is certainly possible. But little is said about another abuse of authority, namely the abuse of authority which the teacher has. This abuse is committed whenever that teacher exploits his students by using a position which the church gave him in the first place to encourage them to accept positions which are opposed to the teachings of the church. In this situation, it is also true that church authorities would abuse their authority if they were to serenely allow this paradoxical situation to continue, and thus lend their authority to support positions which the church has no authority, no revelation, no promise, no competence to maintain. The care of the faith of the "little ones" must always be more important than the fear of some conflict with the powerful.

There are two key phrases in Ratzinger's presentation of dissent: "exploits his students" and "encourage them to accept positions which are opposed to the teachings of the church." These phrases are heavy with rhetoric and cannot go unchallenged. If a teacher explains the teaching of the Church, provides the best available understanding for it and then offers a possible counterposition, is that "encouraging them to accept positions opposed to the teachings of the church"? What is a teacher supposed to do if a variant understanding recommends itself as more consistent, more defensible, more promotive of persons, more attuned to experience? Remain silent? Deny these things? Is the teacher to propose the official formulation as unquestionably certain and accurate when scholarly literature puts legitimate questions to such formulations? It should be noted that Ratzinger's understanding of a Catholic theologian denies dissent *in principle.* Even more generally, is teaching not primarily concerned with *understanding* human reality and human relationships? And has that understanding been set once and for all by magisterial formulations? Does not the ongoing reflection of teacher and student have something to offer to the magisterium? Instead of saying "encouraging them to accept positions opposed to the teachings of the church" as a description of theological reflection, why does Ratzinger not say "providing them with the most persuasive analysis"? The teacher does not exactly "encourage them to accept positions." The teacher attempts to provide understanding and it is this understanding that "encourages them to accept positions." Indeed, the teacher who would present the teachings of the Church as unquestionably accurate in all respects when he/she knew there were serious questions or doubts about it would be the one who "exploits his students."

I am afraid that behind Ratzinger's notion of teaching in the Church is a powerful juridicism wherein conformism achieves an independent and unassailable status. Packaging this as "care of the faith of the 'little ones'" only thinly disguises Ratzinger's denial of theology's critical role.

These points are raised once again in the second event I wish to note. It is an interview Ratzinger gave to the Milan-based magazine *30 Giorni* for its May (1986) issue. In the interview Ratzinger commented directly on the Curran case. Curran's position, he said, that one can legitimately dissent from noninfallible teachings "does not seem to me appropriate." He continued: "When it is affirmed that noninfallible doctrine, even when it is part of church teachings, can legitimately be contested, the end result is destroying the practice of a Christian way of life, reducing the faith to a collection of doctrines." Ratzinger concluded that for dissenting theologians "Christianity is not a force which gives life but a weight to be lifted as soon as possible." Dissenting moral theology in the United States is an "expression of middle-class Christianity."

Here is the chief officer of the Congregation for the Doctrine of the Faith (1) equating *any* dissent from noninfallible teaching with destruction of the Christian way of life; (2) accusing dissenters of regarding Christianity as a weight or burden; (3) describing their view scornfully as "middle-class Christianity."

Such statements have the gravest implications. (1) They disallow dissent in principle. (2) In doing so, they paralyze doctrinal development. (3) They blacken the personal integrity of the theologians involved by questioning, even denying their Christianity ("a weight to be lifted as soon as possible"). (4) They reveal the perspectives of the head of the CDF as being profoundly anti-American ("middle-class Christianity"). (5) In doing so, they compromise justice in ecclesial processes. I am saddened to see a high ecclesiastical official indulge in this type of theological Archie Bunkerism. The Cardinal Prefect needs to be set straight on who it is that is "reducing the faith to a collection of doctrines." To make my point, let me borrow from Cardinal Ratzinger's language. "When it is affirmed that noninfallible doctrine, even when it is part of Church teachings, *cannot* legitimately be contested, the end result is reducing the faith to a collection of doctrines." This latter sentence does make a good deal of sense. But it is not Ratzinger's. It is the exact opposite of his. The standard colloquialism to cover such unforeseen outcomes has to do with one's own petard.

I noted that "such statements have the gravest implications." The one that is of primary concern[24] is the politicization of theology, the adoption of one-sided perspectives (what Francis Sullivan, S.J., describes as "new and disturbing") as the basis for the judgment and practice of the universal Church. If theologians are to serve the long-term good of the Church, they must remain accountable for their writings and public statements. The same is assuredly true of public officials in the Church. It is in this spirit that I include these reflections. I am convinced that were the head of the CDF in closer contact with American theologians (not just a few with predictable perspectives), some of the statements I have noted would be reconsidered and modified.

If theology is to remain a vital and creative force in the Church, it cannot be politicized. And that is, I believe, what is happening. A symbol of this was a recent (April 7-12, 1986) International Congress on Moral Theology held in Rome. Only those considered—and who considered themselves—"orthodox" were welcome. The Congress was addressed not only by John Paul II, but by a list of notable prelates including Ugo Cardinal Poletti, Edouard Cardinal Gagnon, William Cardinal Baum, Alvaro Del Portillo (Prelate of Opus Dei). An anonymous participant reported on this Congress: "Orthodox moralists are organizing to meet the dissenters' challenge."[25] At one point, the report states of the participants: "They all knew that the Congress met at the time of the most blatant and defiant challenge to the moral magisterium of the church—the stand taken by Fr. Curran and his supporters, including, it seems, even bishops." The white hats and the black hats are firmly in place.

At another point, the anonymous author exults:

Considering the youthfulness of many of the participants, and the strong morale and sense of solidarity, those who favor dissenting schools of moral theology have everything to lose and much to fear from this determined resurgence of authentic Catholic moral theology, grounded in deep faith and in loyalty to the church.

Not really. If dissent were a game and the Church were composed of those who "favor dissenting schools of moral theology" and those who do not, then the notions of "lose" and "fear" might make sense. But that is not what respectful disagreement is all about. It is but the flip side of human limitedness and honesty that ought and does apply not only to theologians, but to the magisterium itself, as history so well documents. We are in grave danger of losing that realization when conformity exhaustively defines orthodoxy and when Roman institutions and personnel are marshalled politically to buttress that definition. That is why "the Curran affair" is far more important than its central subject. It is a reminder that when criticism is squelched and power enlists theology for its purposes, the entire Church suffers because theology has been politicized, i.e., corrupted. It is axiomatic that when parents welcome and encourage independent thought in their children, they liberate and empower not only the children, but themselves. Could it be that some in high places are fearful of their own self-liberation? But that takes us beyond the scope of this chapter.

I say that the entire church suffers. That should be spelled out. I see seven wounds, self-inflicted, by a coercive atmosphere.

1. *The weakening of the episcopal magisterium.* Here we should recall the theological force of episcopal agreement described in *Lumen Gentium*, no. 25. If the bishops around the world are united with the pope in their teaching, then that teaching can achieve a greater level of stability and certainty, and indeed achieve infallible status if the teaching is a proper object of infallibility and is presented as something to be held definitively. But the unity must be genuine and clear.

In a coercive atmosphere both the genuinity and clarity are put in serious doubt. First, the genuinity. In a coercive atmosphere people will repeat things because they are told to and threatened with punishment if they say anything else. Episcopal unity is revealed as enforced, not genuine.

As for clarity, the more likely scenario in a coercive atmosphere is that the bishops (some at least) will say nothing if they disagree. In such circumstances, to read episcopal silence as unanimity is self-deceptive.

When the genuinity and clarity of episcopal agreement have been cast into grave doubt by a coercive atmosphere, the episcopal magisterium itself has been undermined. The meaning of consensus has been eviscerated. The bishops should be the first ones to protest this diminishment of their magisterium, and the atmosphere that grounds it.

2. *The weakening of the papal magisterium.* This follows from the first point. If bishops are not speaking their true sentiments, then clearly the pope is not able to draw on the wisdom and reflection of the bishops in the exercise of his ordinary magisterium. When this happens, the presumption of truth in papal teaching is weakened, because such a presumption assumes that the ordinary sources of human understanding have been consulted, as the late Karl Rahner so repeatedly argues. That is why what is called the "enforcement of doctrine" is literally counterproductive. It weakens the very vehicle (papal magisterium) that proposes to be the agent of strength and certainty.

3. *The marginalization of theologians.* Coercive measures will almost certainly have the effect of quieting theologians, at least on certain issues. This further erodes both the episcopal and papal magisterium by silencing yet another source of understanding and growth. Many bishops, most recently James Malone, have noted the absolute necessity of theology for their work. In Malone's words, "As a bishop in an episcopal conference which had devoted substantial time and energy to the place of the Church in the world, I can testify to the irreplaceable role of the theological enterprise."[26] If reputable theologians are marginalized, the magisterium is proportionately weakened. And it is no response to exclude from the "reputable" category those with whom one disagrees. That begs the (or any) question.

4. *The demoralization of priests.* When juridical coercion (which is not altogether out of place) too easily dominates the Church's teaching-learning process, priests (and other ministers) become demoralized because they are expected to be the official spokespersons for positions they cannot always and in every detail support. Thus they become torn by their official loyalties and their better judgment and compassion. *Commonweal* referred to this as "occupational schizophrenia."[27] Archbishop John Quinn adverted to this in the Synod of 1980.[28]

5. *The reduction of the laity.* Coercive insistence on official formulations tells the laity in no uncertain terms that their experience and reflection make little difference—this in spite of Vatican II's contrary assertion about freedom of enquiry and expression.[29] If such humble and courageous expression counts for nothing, we experience yet another wound to the authority of the ordinary magisterium. The search for truth falls victim to ideology.

6. *The compromise of future ministry.* When a rigid orthodoxy is imposed on seminarians in the name of unity and order, the very ability of these future priests to minister to post-Vatican II Catholics is seriously jeopardized. I have seen this happen. Many thousands of Catholics have studied and struggled to assimilate the Council's perspectives. They do not understand and will not accept a new paternalism in moral pedagogy. This means frustration and crisis for the minister trained to practice such a pedagogy.

7. *The loss of the Catholic leaven.* Coercive insistence that the term "official teaching" is simply synonymous with right, certain, sound, and unchangeable (an identification powerfully supported by the suppression of any public dissent) will lead to the public perception that the role of Catholic scholars is an "intellectual form of 'public relations'," to borrow from Clifford Longley.[30] That means the serious loss of theological credibility in precisely those areas of modern development (e.g., science and technology) where the Church should desire to exercise a formative influence. The present pontiff wants both to unite the Church and to shape the world, both utterly laudable apostolic objectives. The means to the former could doom the latter.

"The Curran affair" brings to mind Karl Rahner's report of his audience with Paul VI.

> I said to him: "Look, Holy Father, ten years ago, the Holy Office forbade me to say anything on concelebration and today they themselves concelebrate." Then he laughed gently and said: "Est tempus flendi, est tempus ridendi" [There is a time for crying and a time for laughing]. What he meant in this context did not become altogether clear to me, but he probably wanted to say that it is the case in general and also in God's Church that the times and mentalities change; and there is nothing that can be done about it [und dagegen sei kein Kraut gewachsen].[31]

So they do.

Notes

1. *Human Life in Our Day* (Washington: United States Catholic Conference, 1968), 18.

2. Letters to the Editor, *America* 154 (1985): 363.

3. Charles E. Curran, *Moral Theology: A Continuing Journey* (Notre Dame: University of Notre Dame Press, 1982), 144.

4. Charles E. Curran, *Issues in Sexual and Medical Ethics* (Notre Dame: University of Notre Dame Press, 1978), 15-16.

5. Charles E. Curran, *Critical Concerns in Moral Theology* (Notre Dame: University of Notre Dame Press, 1984), 92-93.

6. J. McManus, Sean O'Riordan and Henry Stratton, "The 'Declaration on Certain Questions Concerning Sexual Ethics': A Discussion," *Clergy Review* 61 (1976): 231-37.

7. G. W. MacRae, S.J., "New Testament Perspective on Marriage and Divorce," *Divorce and Remarriage in the Catholic Church,* ed. L.G. Wrenn (New York: Newman, 1973), 1-15.

8. Joseph A. Fitzmyer, S.J., "The Matthean Divorce Texts and Some New Palestinian Evidence," *Theological Studies* 37 (1976): 197-226, at 224.

9. The complete documentation may be found in Charles E. Curran, *Faithful Dissent* (Kansas City: Sheed and Ward, 1986).

10. *Sittliche Normen,* ed. Walter Kerber, S.J. (Düsseldorf: Patmos Verlag, 1982). Of this volume Bernard Häring writes: "Very seldom have I read a collection with such full agreement as I have this rich book, to which proven and well-known moral theologians and the esteemed exegete Heinz Schürmann have contributed." Häring concludes: "If all those with magisterial authority, if theologians and pastors of souls would study this little book carefully and discuss it with each other, many misunderstandings would be dissipated and the pastoral peace of the Church would be well served . . . It would be a pity were this world-wide consensus of established authors not sufficiently noted" (*Theologie der Gegenwart* 26 [1983]: 66-67).

11. Francis A. Sullivan, S.J., *Magisterium: Teaching Authority in the Catholic Church* (Mahwah, N.J.: Paulist Press, 1983).

12. From NC releases.

13. *Documents,* 716.

14. Karl Rahner, "Theologie und Lehramt," *Stimmen der Zeit* 198 (1980): 374. A rather different criticism is leveled at Curran by Ronald Lawler. With a condescension that towers hugely over his own scholarly output, Lawler states of Curran that "he's just not very good at what he does" (*Our Sunday Visitor,* May 11, 1986).

15. From NC releases, May 6, 1986.

16. Cf. *Faithful Dissent,* 282-84.

17. *Documents,* 233.

18. Jaroslav Pelikan, *The Vindication of Tradition* (New Haven: Yale University Press, 1984), 66.

19. *Wanderer,* 1 May 1986.

20. *America* 154 (1986): 363-64.

21. *Documents,* 116.

22. Cf. note 20, at 366.

23. Joseph Ratzinger, "The Church and the Theologian," *Origins* 15 (1986), 762-70.

24. One of the most knowledgeable Church-watchers of our time, Msgr. George Higgins, stated at a symposium held at John Carroll University: "It is time for Ratzinger to go back to Germany and take a diocese" (*Catholic Universe Bulletin,* April 10, 1987).

25. *Wanderer,* 1 May 1986.

26. James Malone, "How Bishops and Theologians Relate," *Origins* 16 (1986), 169-74.

27. "The Curran Effect," *Commonweal* 113 (1986): 451-54.

28. John R. Quinn, "'New Context' for Contraception Teaching," *Origins* 10 (1980), 263-67.

29. *Documents,* 270.

30. Clifford Longley, "Cynicism and Sexual Morality," *Times* (London), 4 August 1986.

31. *Karl Rahner: Bilder eines Lebens,* ed. Paul Imhof and Hubert Biallowons (Freiburg im Breisgau: Herder, 1985), 72.

Chapter 7

Pluralism in Moral Theology

Let me begin with a citation from *Civiltà cattolica:*

> Catholic principles do not change either because of the passage of time,
> or because of different geographical contexts, or because of new dis-
> coveries, or for reasons of utility. They always remain the same, those
> that Christ proclaimed, that popes and councils defined, that the saints
> held and that the doctors defended. One has to take these as they are or
> leave them. Whoever accepts them in their fullness and strictness is
> Catholic; whoever wavers, drifts, adapts to the times or compromises can
> call himself whatever he likes, but before God and the Church he is a
> rebel and a traitor.[1]

These words were written in 1899 as an editorial commentary on the
condemnation of Americanism. They could well have appeared in last
week's *Wanderer* or *National Catholic Register;* for they are a symbol of the
Catholic integrist mentality. For such a mentality the very title of this
chapter does not represent a question; it represents an abominable error
and even a heresy.

I mention this at the very outset for two reasons. First, it is not the way
this discussion ought to be conducted. Second, it is unfortunately the way it
is frequently conducted. Daniel L. Donavon summarizes many of the discussions during the Modernist controversy as follows:

> The task of understanding was made more difficult by the use of
> stereotypes and generalizations. Recourse was constantly being had to
> "isms" of every kind. Blondel's *L'action,* for example, was condemned as
> Kantianism, psychologism and subjectivism. References to life and ex-

perience were rejected as fideism, false mysticism and pragmatism. Laberthonnière repudiated scholasticism under whatever form as intellectualism, and Tyrrell called the system that challenged him Vaticanism, Jesuitism and Medievalism. The atmosphere, in short, was not conducive to either understanding or discussion. The tendency to polarization was an important factor in all that happened.[2]

With a change of a few scarlet words, that paragraph could be written today about moral theology. The likely candidates for inclusion are: subjectivism, absolutism, situationism, dualism, dissentism, utilitarianism, biologism, consequentialism, deontologism, rationalism, etc. When theological issues get trapped in such language, they are usually suppressed and not faced squarely. When that happens, they return to haunt, harass and hurt us at a later date. If the Modernist crisis teaches us one thing, it is that. If we think we "solve" genuine theological issues with mere formal authority, the problem remains unsolved. For this reason, M. Petre has noted that "had it been feasible for the different sections of modernism to unite in the insistence on one point, which should be vital to all, that point would have been the character and limits of ecclesiastical authority."[3]

I want, therefore, to discuss pluralism in moral theology without surrounding the idea unduly with other "isms." I will proceed through five points: (1) areas where there is no disagreement; (2) areas of dispute; (3) how the issues get confused; (4) areas of pluralism in medical ethics; (5) some personal procedural suggestions on pluralism. Throughout I will use medical-moral problems as examples.

1. *Areas where there is no disagreement.* There are two areas here. First, all Catholic theologians would agree that there can be no pluralism at the level of universal principles and formal moral norms. By "universal principles" I mean generally stated moral norms that impose achievement of a value or proscribe a disvalue. An example would be: there is always a presumption against taking human life. Under the term "formal moral norms," we may include two types of statements. First, there are normative statements such as "our conduct must always be just." Second, there are normative statements that build around words that include their own value judgments. For example, "we must never commit murder" (murder=*unjustified* killing). Equivalent to this type of statement is one that exhaustively states the circumstances (e.g., it is morally wrong to kill a human being *merely to give pleasure to a third party*). People who advocate pluralism in these types of statements either do not understand them or have placed themselves beyond civil moral discourse.

The second area where there is agreement would be the area of acceptable pluralism. All Catholic theologians would accept pluralism in the following matters.

a. *The application of universal principles to contingent facts.* The American bishops in their pastoral *The Challenge of Peace* explicitly acknowledge the acceptability of pluralism here. Examples would be: the moral legitimacy of capital punishment, the morality of any (or first) use of nuclear weapons, whether a particular sterilization is direct or indirect.

b. *Emphases in issue areas.* Human beings are limited. Very few can be expert in a great many areas. That means that all of us must specialize, pick and choose our areas of concern according to our talent, competence and interests. Such specialization necessarily results in a kind of pluralism of focus and concern. No one questions the appropriateness of this pluralism within the Catholic idea.

c. *New problems.* In contemporary medicine, we experience almost daily the casting up of new and complicated questions. What is the most equitable approach to broaden access to health care? When is it morally justifiable to begin genetic therapy for single-gene defects? How should we analyze artificial nutrition-hydration for the permanently vegetative? When is joint-venturing likely to compromise the Catholic character of a health facility? Is the artificial heart, all things considered, a justifiable therapeutic modality? The list is endless. On many such questions—especially when they trace to new technology—there is little experience or reflection to draw upon. One expects pluralism in such areas.

d. *Disputed questions.* This is close to the third group but it does not perfectly overlap. I have in mind problems that have proven especially resistant to unanimous resolution within a believing community. A clear set of examples would touch on the best legal policy on divisive questions such as abortion, surrogate carriers, genetic screening, homosexual rights. Other examples would concern adolescents, their sex education and access to certain forms of health care. Such questions are often quite complicated and demand empirical knowledge from a variety of sources. We expect a genuine pluralism on questions like this and generally abide it rather well.

2. Pluralism: Areas of dispute. By "areas of dispute" I mean areas where some believe pluralism is acceptable, others that it is not. I can identify three general areas.

a. *Concrete moral norms.* The obvious examples here are some of the following. Every direct abortion is morally wrong. Artificial insemination by husband is always morally wrong. Masturbation, regardless of circumstances, is intrinsically evil. Every conjugal act must remain open to the possibility of procreation. Direct sterilization is always morally wrong.

The five examples of norms that I have given have all been proposed in authoritative fashion by the papal magisterium. Further examples could be cited. Furthermore, all of them have been contested in the moral theological literature of the past twenty-five years. Some find such contestation intolerable: it undermines authority, destroys unity, creates a theological paramagisterium, confuses the faithful and eviscerates morality into an adjustment to the comfortable.

Others take an entirely different point of view. Far from undermining authority, dissent on such issues, when well argued, is a high form of loyalty to the magisterium, by protecting it from the kind of self-preoccupation that subordinates truth to authority. As for unity, Catholic unity should not be staked on such details but on the true substantials of the faith. A paramagisterium is not created because it is of the very nature of theology to exercise a critical role. To negate this critical role is to conceive the magisterium in an utterly pyramidal, other-worldly, and magical way. If the faithful are confused by this, it is because they have been misled by past attitudes and practice into viewing the magisterium in simplistic and unrealistic ways. Correction of these attitudes, not denial of theology's critical role, is in place. This is the way the discussion has gone and I shall return to it below.

b. *Methodology of moral norms.* Within the past twenty-five years, many Catholic moral theologians have adopted a form of teleology in their understanding of moral norms. It is impossible in a brief space to give an adequate summary of this development or an adequate account of the differences that individual theologians bring to their analyses. However, common to all the analyses is the insistence that causing certain disvalues (ontic, nonmoral, premoral evils) in our conduct does not ipso facto make the action morally wrong. The action becomes morally wrong when, all things considered, there is no proportionate reason justifying it. Thus just as not every killing is murder, not every falsehood a lie, so not every artificial intervention preventing (or promoting) conception is necessarily an unchaste act. Not every termination of a pregnancy is necessarily an abortion in the moral sense. This has been called "proportionalism," especially by those who resist and reject the *Denkform.*

The point to be made here, however, is that those who resist this teleological analysis of moral statements do not only reject it. They regard it as incompatible with what they call "received teaching," even with revealed morality. Clearly, something incompatible with revealed morality is not a matter of free discussion—pluralism—in the Church.

Those who have proposed such a teleological foundation for the interpretation of moral norms obviously take a different point of view. They believe that such an interpretation is not only compatible with the abiding substance of Catholic teaching, but acutally better accommodates and explains it. For instance, they argue that only a form of teleology (what Bruno Schüller calls "restrictive interpretation") can adequately account for the formula "no *direct* killing of *innocent* human life." Depending on the subject matter, such a teleological structure for moral norms would lead to a rewording of certain past formulations, doctrinal development in some areas, dissent with regard to certain conclusions (e.g., the intrinsic moral evil of every contraceptive act), the abandonment of the rule of double effect as a critical analytic tool. All of these outcomes, however, are seen as quite compatible with, even demanded by an ethic that roots in the centrality of the person as the criterion of the morally right and wrong.[4] The New Testament, it is argued, did not present us with a fully developed ethical system. Therefore, the behavioral implications of our "being in Christ" could be systematized and detailed in a variety of ways—as indeed they have been over the centuries of Christian moral thought.

c. *Degree of authority in authentic teachings.* Once again, this is a matter of dispute. One school of thought—what I still regard as a minority view—contends that very detailed concrete norms (e.g., the prohibition of contraception) can be, and indeed are, proposed infallibly by the magisterium. This is the thesis of John C. Ford, S.J., and Germain Grisez.[5] They argue that what has been proposed unanimously by the magisterium (popes and bishops) over the centuries as a tenet to be held definitively is *infallibly* taught. It would be proposed, they argue, as a truth required to guard the deposit of faith as inviolable and to expound it with fidelity. At a meeting (April 7-12, 1986) of moral theologians held in Rome (described by Grisez as "a celebration of moral theology loyal to the Church's teaching authority"),[6] Grisez delivered a paper proposing as definable the following proposition: "The intentional killing of an innocent human being is always a grave matter." Clearly, then, authors like Grisez do not see the infallible proposal of concrete norms as an open question, one where pluralism might be appropriate.

Another school of thought—by far the vast majority of theologians—rejects this analysis on several grounds. First, it is one thing to teach something as involving a moral obligation. It is quite another to propose it as *to be held definitively* (sc., to give irrevocable consent). Second, there is little or no evidence that matters such as contraception are so necessarily connected with revelation that the magisterium could not safeguard and expound reveleation if it could not teach such matters infallibly. Third, there is the question of the significance of unanimous episcopal teaching in some areas. Recall here the statement of Cardinal Suenens[7] noted in chapter 5 (p. 106).

Finally, considerations such as these have led theologians like Karl Rahner to conclude that concrete moral norms are not the proper object of infallibility.[8]

So far, I have attempted to describe a factual situation as objectively and dispassionately as possible. My objective here has been accuracy, not precisely persuasion to this or that point of view. The same cannot be said for my third point.

3. Confusion of the issues. Under this title I will list factors that I believe confuse the issue of pluralism in Catholic moral theology. By "confuse the issue" I mean "make it more difficult to identify the level of tolerable pluralism." Usually, this "confusion of the issues" will take the form of an oversimplification in which pluralism will be presented as *being, involving, entailing, leading to* something that it need not be, involve, imply or lead to. I have in mind, therefore, a kind of guilt by association. It is clear that here my own perspectives begin to play a more prominent role in the analysis.

a. Fact and value words. When one intermingles these two indiscriminately as if there were no difference, then one whose analysis justifies a killing is seen as one who justifies *murder* (= unjust killing). If a *Denkform* does that, then clearly it represents an unacceptable pluralism of approach to the moral life.

Let me offer a few simple examples here. The literature of the past several decades overflows with accusations that certain Catholic revisionist theologians have adopted a system that justifies (or could justify) murder, adultery, cheating, etc. Clearly, there is confusion here between fact-description (*Tatsachenbegriff*) and value-description (*Wertbegriff*). Such confusion blackens pluralism of approach by associating it—inaccurately—with moral horrors we would all disown. This has happened so often in recent years, and even in high places, that the term "pluralism" itself has become suspect.

b. Teleology vs. deontology. At times, differences in moral theology in the Church have been formulated in terms of teleology and deontology. I do not believe that this has served well the cause of discovering an acceptable level of pluralism, and for many reasons. They are sprawling terms that are variously understood and as such allow people to talk past each other, making assumptions and attributing positions that are inaccurate or downright false. Thus, for instance, some Catholics who identify themselves as deontologists have accused others identified as teleologists of holding that "a good end justifies a morally evil means." No reflective theologian would or could hold such a thing; for if an action is said to be morally wrong, nothing will justify it. What has happened here is that certain actions that a Catholic deontologist sees as always morally evil (e.g., contraception), a teleologist does not. The discussion should center around why certain actions are morally wrong or not, and whether and why disagreement on such judgments is acceptable or unacceptable pluralism. If it escalates beyond this, it tends to take on the character of denunciation, rather than analysis. Thus Schüller notes:

> It is time, then, for the deontologists and teleologists finally to give up the business of discrediting each other with moral verdicts. Whether a

teleologist accuses a deontologist of "worshipping the law," or a deontologist slurs a teleologist by making him assert that a good end justifies every means, in both cases nothing has been produced that could contribute to an objective clarification of the controversy.[9]

When nothing is produced, the place of pluralism is not clarified. In this sense, teleology and deontology are about as revealing as "liberal" and "conservative."

c. *The pairs right-wrong, good-bad.* As already noted in chapter 5, this terminology is borrowed by some contemporary Catholic theologians from Anglo-American philosophy.

The discussion of moral pluralism in the Catholic community is concerned with the rightness-wrongness of human actions. For instance, is it unacceptably divisive for Catholics to disagree about the moral character (rightness-wrongness) of in vitro fertilization? And why? Failure even to make the distinction between right-wrong, good-bad means that the moral life can be absorbed into discussions of goodness-badness (involving intention, inclination, good will, the virtues, etc.). This is the key error in the work of Servais Pinckaers, O.P. It is responsible for his mistaken assertion that agape is not functional in so-called "proportionalist" thought.[10] Agape is simply not the issue under discussion. It is responsible for his misleading assertion that faith and the gospel must have first place in Christian morality. Of course they must; but that is not the issue. The question is: What do the faith and the gospel concretely demand of followers of Christ, and not merely in terms of sentiments and desires? The answer to that is a question of rightness and wrongness. Pinckaers fails to see this. The result is that he confuses the issue of pluralism by raising it in terms that have nothing to do with it. One does not clarify the nature and rules of baseball by emphasizing certain dimensions of football.

d. *Substance and formulation.* In contemporary moral writing this distinction has functioned far less that I think it should. As I pointed out in chapter 1, and several times thereafter, Vatican II, following John XXIII, stated it clearly.[11]

If there is a distinction between the deposit of faith and its formulation at a given time, this is a fortiori true of the behavioral implications of this deposit. For behavioral implications are even more dependent on the contingencies of time and place. To restate the Council's distinction in theological shorthand, we may and must distinguish between the substance of a moral teaching and its formulation.

If this distinction is not made, then certain kinds of disagreements among Catholics (pluralism) will be viewed as an attack on and corrosive of the substance of the Church's moral concerns and intolerably divisive. I believe that this happens frequently in the contemporary Church.

A few examples from bioethics can serve as illustrations. In 1986, the American Medical Association released its guidelines on treatment of the dying. The AMA statement accepted the moral acceptability of withholding or withdrawing artificial nutrition-hydration from those in a persistent vegetative state under certain conditions. Archbishop Philip Hannan (New Orleans) stated in his diocesan paper that "the Church strongly condemns this position."[12]

Whether such a position is "contrary to the Church's teaching" depends entirely on what one conceives to be the Church's teaching in this area. Pius XII, following the theology of his time, formulated that teaching in terms of the limits on the duty to preserve life. Furthermore, such limits were stated in terms of ordinary and extraordinary means. Pius XII acknowledged the great relativity (to time, place, circumstances, etc.) involved in fleshing out these notions in practice. What is ordinary care (and obligatory) for one time, place, patient might not be in altered circumstances.

So far so good. But when we range over a number of decades to see how these concepts were variously applied and lived out, we are faced with the question: "What is the Church's teaching?" The late and beloved John Connery, S.J., has answered this question as follows: The Church's teaching forces us to judge these matters in terms of the *quality of treatment* (its burden or benefit), not the *quality of the life* treated. Therefore, he concludes with Hannan, we may not withdraw artificial nutrition-hydration from the permanently comatose on the basis of their quality of life alone.[13]

I disagree with that analysis and I would argue that the Church's substantial teaching does not impose the hard-and-fast distinction between quality of treatment and quality of life that Connery posits. I would argue that the Church's teaching (its *substantial* concern) is as follows: *life is a basic good but not an absolute one and therefore there are limits on what we must do to preserve it.* That is the substantial judgment we must uphold and carry with us into a variety of changing circumstances and technological possibilities. Anything beyond that general judgment is changeable formulation. Thus, how we should formulate these limits (whether dominantly in terms of person or treatment), what we should call them, etc., do not pertain to the substance of Catholic teaching. I shall return to this matter in chapter 21. Whatever the case, failure to make the distinction between substance and formulation will confuse the issue of pluralism by locating unchangeable Catholic teaching at a level where it might actually be changeable.

Questions like this might be raised in a number of areas of medical ethics. For instance, the conclusion "direct sterilization is intrinsically evil" is not a *necessary* envelope for the Church's substantial concerns in this area. Until we acknowledge this, the discussion of pluralism will remain confused.

e. Situationism. I can be brief here. This sprawling term is often used to characterize the positions that provide for certain exceptions to otherwise binding normative statements. The term is used in a very pejorative way, presumably to underline the subjectivism and relativism its users reject in the positions they criticize. I have no doubt that there are certain metaethical positions that involve unacceptable components of relativism and subjectivism. But this should not be a pretext for use of a term to tar all approaches that provide for exceptions to normative statements sometimes regarded as absolutely binding. The reasons given for exceptions must be treated on their own merit. If they are not, certain forms of pluralism will be condemned before they have been examined. This only confuses the question.

f. The fonts of morality. Occasionally, the matter of pluralism is approached from the perspective of the fonts of morality. Thus some will assert that according to Catholic teaching, certain acts are morally wrong *ex objecto*. Denial of this is seen as unacceptable departure from Catholic teaching, as illegitimate pluralism.

Let me use John Paul II as an example here. In his apostolic exhortation *Reconciliation and Penance*, John Paul listed several influences that undermine the sense of sin in our time. One such influence he identified as a "system of ethics." He stated: "This may take the form of an ethical system which relativizes the moral norm, denying its absolute and unconditional value, and as a consequence denying that there can be intrinsically illicit acts, independent of the circumstances in which they are performed by the subject."[14] The Holy Father was, I believe, ill served by his theological advisors in framing the matter in this way.

Equivalently, the pope is saying that certain actions can be morally wrong *ex objecto* independently of the circumstances. But, as Bruno Schüller, S.J., has noted, that is analytically obvious *if the object is characterized in advance as morally wrong*.[15] No theologian would or could contest the papal statement understood in that sense. But that is not the issue. The problem is: What objects should be characterized as morally wrong and on what criteria? Of course, hidden in this question is the further one: What is to count as pertaining to the object? That is often decided by an independent ethical judgment about what one thinks is morally right or wrong in certain areas.

Let the term "lie" serve as an example here. The Augustinian-Kantian approach holds that every falsehood is a lie. Others would hold that falsehood is morally wrong (a lie) only when it is denial of the truth to one who has a right to know. In the first case the object of the act is said to be falsehood (= lie) and it is seen as *ex objecto* morally wrong. In the second case the object is "falsehood to protect an important secret" and is seen as *ex objecto* morally right (*ex objecto* because the very end must be viewed as pertaining to the object).

These differing judgments do not trace to disagreements about the fonts of morality (e.g., about the sentence "an act morally wrong *ex objecto* can never under any circumstance be morally right") but to different criteria and judgments about the use of human speech, and therefore about what ought to count as pertaining to the object. In this sense one could fully agree with the pope that there are "intrinsically illicit acts independent of the circumstances" and yet deny that this applies to the matters apparently of most concern to him (sterilization, contraception, masturbation).

In summary, then, if moral theological pluralism is discussed in terms of the fonts of morality, it is likely to be confused, not clarified.

g. Subjectivism. There are those who short-circuit the discussion of pluralism—thereby only confusing it—by describing departures from official formulations and the analyses that buttress them as "subjectivist." Let me refer once again to Joseph Cardinal Ratzinger as an example. In describing proportionalism, Ratzinger states: "the morality of an act depends on the evaluation and comparison made by man among the goods which are at stake. Once again, it is an individual calculation, this time of the 'proportion' between good and evil."[16] Ratzinger has nothing against a calculation of good and evil, as he makes explicitly clear. What bothers him is that he sees contemporary forms of this as rooted in "the 'reason' of each individual." He contrasts this with a morality based on revelation.

Two brief remarks are in place. First, Ratzinger implies that if a morality is revealed, no personal evaluation is necessary. That means that God's revelation, what Ratzinger calls His "instructions for use," is so utterly detailed that it covers all imaginable variations and conflicts and dispenses with human reflection. That is, of course, absurd and no one ever held it.

Second, if Ratzinger's real concern is the *individual* (hence potentially subjectivist) character of the discernment to be made, then the proper reply is twofold. First, evaluation by an individual does not mean individualistic evaluation. We form our consciences in community. Second, as Edward Vacek, S.J., has noted, being true to the relational character of reality is not being arbitrary and subjectivist.[17]

h. Complementary vs. contradictory pluralism. Some have attempted to enlighten the discussion by the use of this distinction. Let me use Thomas Dubay as an example.[18] Clearly, Dubay sees contradictory pluralism as inconsistent with scriptural insistence on unity, destructive of practical pastoral guidance and deadening to the Church's commission to speak out authoritatively on important moral matters.

But when is pluralism "contradictory"? Dubay's answer: when it touches "important moral and disciplinary matters." We must have unity based on "a secure knowledge of the moral implications of many acts."

Here I believe we must ask, what are these "*important* moral and disciplinary matters," what are these "*basic* matters or norms" confused by a contradictory pluralism? Are they rather detailed and concrete conclusions representing the application of more general norms? Or are they the more general norms themselves? Dubay's terminology ("basic matters or norms") suggests the latter, but I suspect he is really looking for unity and security at the level of application; for he speaks of "a secure knowlege of the moral implications *of many acts* . . . " So, how basic is basic?

The point I am making is that if discussions of pluralism are to be enlightened by the distinction between complementary (acceptable)-contradictory (unacceptable) pluralism, the implied criterion of *basic* must be spelled out. The same can be said of the usage "legitimate" pluralism (acceptable) and "radical" pluralism (unacceptable).

A personal reflection. A past tradition easily led us to believe that "basic" had to do with matters of self-stimulation for sperm-testing, removal of ectopic fetuses, actions that are *per se graviter excitantes* ("as a rule gravely stimulating") cooperation in contraception and a host of very concrete applications. We felt we ought to possess and did possess a kind of certainty and subsequent security in these matters, and that our certainty was founded on the natural law. These, I submit, are not "basic matters or norms," if by this term is meant material on which we must agree if our Christian unity is to remain integral. There is plenty of room for doubt, hesitation and change, even contradictory pluralism (dissent) at this level of moral discourse.

And yet, because the magisterium did get involved in such detailed practical applications in the past (e.g., allocutions of Pius XII, responses of the Holy Office), and in a way that was authoritative, it gave credence to the notion that our moral unity is or ought to be located at this level, and that disagreement or pluralism at this level is a threat to unity. In my view, that is an unrealistic view of both unity and the capacity of the human mind for certainty.

This is, of course, a key point, perhaps *the* key point, in discussing pluralism in Catholic moral theology. It must suffice here to note that my judgment is not altered by an escalation in the type of argument or analysis sometimes used to establish positions. For instance, Carlo Caffara has argued that contraceptive interventions contravene the rights of God and prevent God "from being God."[19] John Paul II has made similar statements. Such statements do not thereby show that the issue of contraception is so basic that pluralism on the matter is ruled out as destructive of Christian unity. For one thing, these are analytical theological arguments, and their validity is subject to rigorous theological critique. For another, nearly every moral conclusion can be cast in such broad theological terms that it seems to involve the assertion of divine governance, divine providence, trust in God, etc. This destroys the distinction between basic and nonbasic in principle. Furthermore, it offends common sense.

4. *Areas of pluralism in medical ethics.* When I speak of pluralism here, I mean it in a narrow and technical sense. In such a sense it comprises differences between *established and recognized theologians* (and philosophers). These differences fall into two categories: concrete and general.

a. Concrete. Issue areas where there is factual pluralism are the following:

—Contraception, sterilization.
—Reproductive technologies (artificial insemination, in vitro fertilization, masturbation).
—Abortion and the status of the pre-embryo.
—Life preservation (newborns; the nutrition-hydration questions).

b. General. The following points seem to cover the most disputed areas:

—Methodology (in the understanding of normative statements).
—Teaching authority (e.g., the significance of magisterial statements; the 1971 *Directives for Catholic Health Care Facilities*).
—Public policy (e.g., Medicaid and abortion).
—Hospital practice (e.g., cooperation; joint ventures).

5. *Personal procedural suggestions.* These final reflections root in a twofold conviction. First, it would be unwise to attempt to "solve" (i.e., do away with) the problem of pluralism by the use of authority. History (*Tuas Libenter, Pascendi, Humani Generis*) shows that while such interventions may achieve a short-term "peace of a kind,"[20] the long-term fallout is detrimental. This point has been underscored by Archbishop Rembert Weakland.[21] Weakland referred to the first decade of this century as a time of "theological suppression" and added that it resulted "in a total lack of theological creativity in the U.S.A. for half a century." Weakland referred to a "better way of proceeding" and cited John XXIII's opening speech at the Second Vatican Council, where the pope stated that the Church "prefers to make use of the medicine of mercy rather than that of severity." John XXIII added: "She considers that she meets the needs of the present day by demonstrating the validity of her teaching rather than by condemnations."

Second, it is impossible to give criteria, except of the most general (and therefore not very useful) kind for determining the limits of acceptable pluralism. For these reasons I want to offer some procedural suggestions for living and dealing with pluralism. These suggestions touch the magisterium, theologians (and scholars generally) and the Catholic public.

Magisterium. It might seem arrogant for a theologian to suggest to the magisterium how it ought to conduct itself. In reality, however, it is not. What the magisterium teaches, how it teaches, with what authority and consultative processes, are properly *theological* questions. Futhermore, teaching is never done in a vacuum. It is done in a historical moment and those taught live in particular and varying cultures. Theologians and other scholars who reside in those cultures should be presumed to have some idea of what effective teaching is in their particular cultures. With that in mind, I offer the following suggestions that touch the moral teaching of the magisterium.

—The magisterium should formulate its teaching in an *open, revisionary* teaching process. This means, among other things, that the consultative process is not narrowed to draw upon those only who agree with a foreordained position. That this is not presently the case needs no documentation.

—The magisterium must be *well informed* scientifically. Once again, this means broad consultation of all competences. One sees and praises this in the *Declaration on Euthanasia* but regrets its obvious absence in the *Declaration on Certain Sexual Questions.*

—The utterances of the magisterium should be appropriately *tentative.* Excessive claims, apart from their theological inaccuracy, are a source of future embarrassment to and confusion in the Church.

—Whenever feasible, the magisterium should be explicit about the *ecclesial status* of a teaching (what used to be known as the "theological note"). Karl Rahner argued for this for years and the American bishops followed the suggestion in their pastoral *The Challenge of Peace.*

—Moral teaching should be bolstered by *persuasive analysis.* It is counterproductive in our time to urge conclusions solely with the weight of formal authority. This is particularly true of condemnations. Practically, this means that the magisterium will not authoritatively propose conclusions against a strong theological counterposition.

—Persons in authority should be *realistic.* I mean to suggest under this rubric that the magisterium should not expect agreement with every official statement. So-called "official teaching" can be in various stages of development, as Ladislaus Orsy, S.J., has shown.[22] Furthermore, doctrinal development cannot be excluded, a point emphasized by Archbishop John Quinn in the synod of 1980.[23]

—Finally, if we are to live with pluralism in a joyful and mutually supportive spirit, it is essential that there be in place truly fair procedures for the implementation of fraternal correction. "Due process" must mean more than "what Rome thinks due." The Church can and should, without apology or embarrassment, learn a lesson from the Western democracies in this area. Until it does, we shall continue to hear even very legitimate interventions described in star-chamber language. We shall hear references to the fact that [in the Curran case] "Ratzinger was prosecutor, judge, jury and executioner."[24] Father Andrew Greeley concludes: "It doesn't work anymore. The leadership of the American Church knows it doesn't work, knows it is counterproductive, knows that burning of research data and star chamber trials are disgusting and terrifying phenomena to most American Catholics." We may fault the language and deplore the bile. But the substantial point survives such faulting and deploring: to the American Catholic, certain methods can be far more "confusing" than any pluralism in moral theology.

Theologians. Theologians must present their analyses and conclusions with *due modesty*. They should not claim practical probability for a position if there is no or little theological support for it. The claim to prophecy must be rare and relucant.

—Theologians must be *pastorally sensitive.* Specifically, they must realize that it is sometimes necessary for the magisterium to present an authoritative position, even if it is tentative and temporary.

—Theologians—at least some—must renew and fortify their resolve to present fairly (in the best light) positions with which they disagree. This means practically the avoidance of "isms," accusations of harm to the Church, *post hoc ergo propter hoc* allegations, etc.

—The traditional doctrine of the "presumption of truth" favoring the magisterium must play its appropriate role in theological discussion, notwithstanding the fact that it is *only* a presumption and that such a presumption can be undermined in practice by a short-circuiting of the deliberative process.

—Theologians must write, speak and act in a way that fosters respect for the magisterium. This is, to a Catholic, self-evident, even if at times some members of the magisterium make the task more arduous than it ought to be.

—Finally, it should go without saying but will not, that theologians and scholars should be ready, willing and able to admit mistakes—especially to each other. Without such readiness, differences degenerate into distance, and ultimately disorder.

Catholic public. The suggestions I make here are perhaps the most difficult to realize in practice. But that is not an excuse for not trying.

—The Catholic public must have a much more accurate notion of the place of the magisterium and scholarship in the Church. The gigantic character of the educational task becomes apparent when we recall that many priests have not achieved this accuracy. Far too frequently, even priests conceptualize the relationship competitively, in terms of the magisterium *or* scholars. Furthermore, the notion of infallibility is so badly misunderstood by the public that one nearly despairs of rectifying it.

—The public must be educated to understand that the Church does not have all the answers, or an immediate one to a new question. As I have pointed out several times in earlier chapters, Vatican II acknowledged this openly and realistically.[25]

—The Catholic public—and most especially, of course, competent professionals—must be educated to the responsibilities inseparable from their own competence. This was also clearly stated by the Council fathers.[26]

—The Catholic public must be educated more than they are to two facts: (a) priests do not always speak accurately and critically on moral issues; (b) moral theologians, in their public statements, do not always speak for the Church, or even for all moral theologians. On occasion, they present their own opinions, which can vary all the way from "strictly personal" to "Church teaching." Somehow or other we must find a way to clarify this and the burden of doing so is, I believe, largely on theologians and scholars.

—Finally, the Catholic public must be educated to the fact that the media thrive on confrontation. Many issues are not nearly as controversial as they are sometimes made to appear.

There will always be tension and conflict on moral questions in the Church. Where there is no pluralism in that sense, there probably is very little creative thought going on. And when that happens, problems much deeper than those associated with pluralism will begin to appear—sooner or later, soon at the latest. That is why the temptation of easy solutions is precisely that, a temptation.

Notes

1. Cited in Daniel L. Donavon, "Church and Theology in the Modernist Crisis," *Proceedings of the 40th Annual Convention* (CTSA), 40 (1985), 145-59.

2. Donavon, 155.

3. M. Petre, *Modernism: Its Failures and Its Fruits* (London: T.C. and E.C. Jack, 1918), 141.

4. *Schema constitutionis pastoralis de ecclesia in mundo huius temporis: Expensio modorum partis secundae* (Vatican Press, 1965), 37-38.

5. John C. Ford, S.J., and Germain Grisez, "Contraception and Infallibility," *Theological Studies* 39 (1978): 258-312.

6. *National Catholic Reporter*, 4 July 1986, 14.

7. Robert Blair Kaiser, *The Politics of Sex and Religion* (Kansas City: Leaven Press, 1985), 170.

8. Karl Rahner, "Basic Observations on the Subject of Changeable and Unchangeable Factors in the Church," *Theological Investigations* 14 (New York: Seabury, 1976), 14.

9. Bruno Schüller, S.J., *Wholly Human* (Washington: Georgetown University Press, 1986), 168.

10. Servais Pinckaers, O.P., "La question des actes intrinsèquement mauvais et le 'proportionalisme,'" *Revue thomiste* 82f (1982): 181-212.

11. *Documents*, 268.

12. *National Catholic Register*, 6 April 1986.

13. John R. Connery, S.J., "Quality of Life," *Linacre Quarterly* 53 (1986): 26-33.

14. *Reconciliation and Penance* (Washington, D.C.: U.S. Catholic Conference, no date (exhortation given 2 December 1984).

15. Bruno Schüller, S.J., "Die Quellen der Moralität," *Theologie und Philosophie* 59 (1984): 535-59.

16. Joseph Ratzinger, *The Ratzinger Report* (San Francisco: Ignatius, 1985), 90.

17. Edward Vacek, S.J., "Proportionalism: One View of the Debate," *Theological Studies* 46 (1985): 287-314, at 296.

18. Thomas Dubay, S.M., "The State of Moral Theology," *Theological Studies* 35 (1974): 482-506.

19. As cited in Josef Fuchs, S.J., "Das Gottesbild und die Moral inner-weltlichen Handelns," *Stimmen der Zeit* 202 (1984): 363-82.

20. *Documents*, 294.

21. *Catholic Herald*, 11 and 18 September 1986.

22. Ladislaus Orsy, S.J., "Reflections on the Text of a Canon," *America* 154 (1986): 396-99.

23. *Origins* 10 (1980), 263-67.

24. *Chicago Sun Times*, 14 September 1986.

25. *Documents*, 231-32.

26. *Documents*, 244.

Chapter 8

Catholic Moral Theology:
Is Pluralism Pathogenic?

In previous chapters I have examined the place of respectful disagreement (dissent) in the teaching-learning process of the Church, how it is being threatened by "the chill factor," and how this chill went below the freezing point in the case of Charles E. Curran. The acceptance of a certain amount of disagreement as we struggle to discern the will of the Lord implies the existence of pluralism in moral theology. In the previous chapter, I attempted to locate the areas of present pluralism. Some take such pluralism in stride as an expected state of affairs in a pilgrim Church that exists in a very baffling and complex world. Not so others. That is why I continue this exploration and raise the question: "Is pluralism pathogenic in Catholic moral theology?"

The answer to this question from every segment of the Catholic community would be: "It all depends." For instance, the magisterium itself quietly and peaceably departs from the perspectives of Leo XIII on Church and state. The Catholic Right rejects key aspects of *The Challenge of Peace* and *Economic Justice for All*. Many Catholics, along with large numbers of revisionist moral theologians, reject the absolutism of *Humanae Vitae* and some conclusions of the instruction on reproductive technology from the Congregation for the Doctrine of the Faith. And most recently, Catholic bishops publicly spar with each other on toleration of instruction in the use of condoms for the prevention of AIDS.

That these are examples of pluralism no one would doubt. Are they pathogenic to the believing community, a kind of devastation of its immune system against the diseases and ravages of a hostile viral world? As I said, it all depends. Above all, it depends on one's concept of the Church, what the believing community ought to be as it pilgrimages through history trying to witness to its Lord. Tell me your notion of church and I believe I can conclude to your attitudes toward moral pluralism. If you think of the Church as an army with a commander-in-chief or as a corporation with a CEO upon whom all responsibility weighs, you are likely to have predictable ideas about pluralism.

Important as this point is, it is not the one I want to make in this chapter. Rather I want to address pluralism from the point of view of the contingency of moral knowledge, and specifically from the distinction between a principle and its application.

In an interesting lecture ("Science and the Creation of Life") at the University of Chicago, Cardinal Joseph Bernardin noted that Catholic medical ethics leans heavily on the natural law tradition. He then continued:

> While extolling the strengths and longevity of this tradition, I also must point out its limits. Human experience is a mixed blessing. Contemporary philosophical and sociological developments have made us more aware of the contextual nature of all knowledge. What appears to be a proper understanding or application of an ethical principle in one age may be found wanting or even incorrect in another. It is also possible to confuse the *application* of a principle for the *principle itself*. Indeed, medieval scholars sought to distinguish between the unchanging primary principles of the natural law and other, less certain, knowledge.[1]

This citation makes two extremely interesting points that I want to emphasize and explore. The first is that the very understanding of an ethical principle may change. Bernardin refers to a "proper understanding or application of an ethical principle," a wording that seems to identify "application" of a principle with the very understanding of the principle itself. This identification is not a slip of the cardinalatial pen. The two notions are so closely related as to be virtually overlapping. When we make certain exceptions to a principle (applications)—or refuse to make them—we give greater precision to the terms of reference of the principle. We affect its understanding. Similarly, when we modify our understanding of the principle, this immediately entails a shift in the practical instances reached and touched by the principle. We affect its application. Thus we may refer to an "understanding or application of an ethical principle."

Let me illustrate this with an example. In several of his speeches Cardinal Bernardin has referred to " the traditional Catholic teaching that there should always be a *presumption* against taking human life, but in a limited world marked by the effects of sin there are some narrowly defined *exceptions* where life can be taken."[2] Bernardin then points out that in our time the presumption against taking human life has been strengthened. He gives two examples. First, Pius XII reduced the traditional threefold justification for going to war (defense, recovery of property, punishment) to the single "reason of defending the innocent and protecting those values required for decent human existence." Second, where capital punishment is concerned, the American bishops as well as several popes have argued against the exercise of the state's right.

The presumption against taking human life represents the principle. The failure to overcome this presumption in our time and culture in the cases mentioned represents its application. Interestingly, Bernardin refers to this application as a strengthening of the presumption; in other words, it is a shift in the very understanding of the principle. Thus the understanding of a principle and the subsumption or nonsubsumption of instances under its terms of reference may both be properly called applications.

For purposes of precision, then, I suggest that we keep in mind that the term "application" has two senses in this context. The first is the broad sense in which the very understanding of the principle shifts or is modified. The second refers to an assessment of contingent facts in relation to the principle's terms of reference. The point to be made is that applications of a principle in both senses can change.

The second interesting point made by Bernardin is that it is possible to "confuse the *application* of a principle for the *principle itself.*" Concretely, that means that it is possible to elevate to the status of principle what is really an application. Two questions occur at this point. What happens when this confusion occurs? The changeable is taken to be unchangeable, the contingent to be abiding, the formulation to be the substance. Revisions and modifications suggested by changing data, times and cultures are resisted as threats and sclerosis of the thinking body settles in. The past becomes exclusively normative and moral leadership quietly shifts into other hands, a victim of incredibility.

Second, why is such confusion possible? There are probably many reasons. For instance, certain practices representing applications of more general principles can become so identified with a historical religious community that they begin to be viewed as principles of a way of life. When they are challenged in any way, they are defended with conviction, passion, even vehemence because they seem inseparably part of a way of life.

In the Catholic community, one of the key reasons for the confusion of application and principle is the authoritative proposal, especially when it is repeated and insisted upon, of certain applications. One thinks, for example, of the rejection of every direct sterilization, the rejection of in vitro fertilization using the gametes of the husband and wife, and of every contraceptive act. Such applications—for that is what I think they are—are proposed in undifferentiated fashion as "Catholic teaching" and are often accompanied by supportive appeals to the special light of the Holy Spirit that is granted to the pastors of the Church as they acquit themselves of their teaching role. Furthermore, sanctions are often visited on those who modify such applications. I am not concerned here with the adequacy or accuracy of these teachings, but only with the fact that they are applications. Nor does saying this question the Church's competence or courage to be concrete. It simply asserts that competence is an analogous notion, as I have already noted. Authoritative imposition bestows on these applications a stability that makes them resemble principles.

The most obvious reason, however, for the confusion of principle and application is the close relationship of the two and the very malleability of the concepts. As a consequence, what some view as applications others see as principles. For instance, as noted above, Cardinal Bernardin refers to the presumption against taking human life as "the traditional Catholic teaching." In the same talk he refers to "the principle which prohibits the directly intended taking of human life." This latter he sees "at the heart of Catholic teaching on abortion." It also "yields the most stringent, binding and radical conclusion of the pastoral letter [*The Challenge of Peace*]: that directly intended attack on civilian centers is always wrong." Here we have two different statements (the presumption against taking human life, no direct killing of the innocent) referred to as "principle." I suggest that the presumption against taking human life is the substance or principle and "no direct taking of innocent human life" is a kind of formulation-application.

This was certainly the understanding of Aquinas. He distinguished between the first principles of natural law and secondary precepts that flow from them, that have the nature of conclusions.[3] These latter bind only *ut in pluribus* and are subject to change. This basic idea is also expressed by Aquinas when he states that underlying moral principles always make actions such as murder, theft and adultery unchangeably wrong, but that what can vary according to circumstances is whether individual situations satisfy the definition of what constitutes such actions.[4] Thomas would have regarded a rule such as "no direct killing of the innocent" as subject to variation and change. He would have seen it as a conclusion or application of a more general principle, as Franz Scholz has shown.[5]

John Mahoney, S.J., is certainly correct, therefore, when he states:

> On the whole it has been the fate of Aquinas' natural law teaching in moral theology that the logical appeal and coherence of his system has been stressed, while the provisionality and contingency of conclusions as they come closer to individual situations, features which he himself carefully built into his theory, have been either neglected or ignored.[6]

I suggest, therefore, that whatever is not a primary principle has the character and characteristics of an application, whether it be a derived middle axiom, a practical operating directive ("no direct killing of the innocent") or the strict application of these to political or pastoral situations. These characteristics are provisionality, flexibility and contingency—to a greater or lesser degree.

There are certain areas where applications frequently get confused with principles. Not surprisingly, many are associated with sexuality. I will mention six such areas: birth regulation, reproductive technologies, abortion, homosexuality, masturbation and divorce/remarriage. It is noteworthy that these are precisely the areas where pluralism is most controversial, where agreement with official formulations is applied as a litmus test of theological orthodoxy and suitability for episcopal office. In other words, they are the areas where pluralism is viewed as pathogenic. Yet concrete official formulations in these areas have the following three characteristics, as Charles Curran has noted: (1) They are remote from the core of the faith. (2) They are heavily dependent on support from human reason. (3) They are involved with such complexity and specificity that they suggest something more modest than absolute certitude.[7] In other words, they represent applications either in the broad or strict sense. Yet, unless I am mistaken, they are often presented with an insistence and strength that tends to confuse them with abiding principles.

Let me illustrate this by a few examples. In its *Instruction on Respect for Human Life in Its Origin and on the Dignity of Procreation*, the Congregation for the Doctrine of the Faith states:

> The Church's teaching on marriage and human procreation affirms the "inseparable connection, willed by God and unable to be broken by man on his own initiative, between the two meanings of the conjugal act: The unitive meaning and the procreative meaning."[8]

The quote within the quote is taken from *Humanae Vitae*. Both this encyclical and the CDF's instruction assert the inseparability of the unitive and procreative goods of marriage. They understand this inseparability as applying to each conjugal act. Thus, just as contraception separates the unitive and procreative dimensions of sexual expression, so also in an analogous way do technological interventions such as in vitro fertilization and artificial insemination by husband.

I do not wish to discuss the strengths and weaknesses of this understanding here. What is important to note is that it is an *understanding*—in this sense, an application—of a more general principle. Other Christian groups have supported a similar principle, but they have interpreted (that is, applied) it differently. They have asserted that the unitive and procreative dimensions should indeed be held together, that married love should be generously life giving, and that procreation should occur in the context of convenanted love. But they have viewed such inseparability as something to be realized in the relationship, not in the individual act. In his recent book *Life and Love*, Kevin T. Kelly summarizes this view.

> The Church of England and other Christian churches have agreed that, even when contraceptives are used, the procreational and relational "goods" of marriage are still held together in a loving marriage. That is because these two "goods" inspire the couple's whole relationship. They devote themselves to each other and to their children. Consequently, it is precisely within the couple's marriage relationship itself that these two "goods" are held together essentially. *Personal Origins* states: " . . . the important points are: that procreation should not occur entirely outside the loving relationship; and that the loving relationship should issue in the good of children, unless there are strong reasons to the contrary (like genetic defect of a grave kind.)"[9]

In summary, then, official Catholic formulations insist that the unitive and procreative be held together *in every act*—no contraception and, on the other hand, no in vitro fertilization. Others, asserting a similar inseparability, argue that the unitive and procreative should be held together *within the relationship*. Clearly, the difference here is one of application, not of the more general principle itself.

Very similar things can be said in the other areas mentioned above. For instance, virtually all of the Christian churches would view the heterosexual relationship of marriage as normative. By that they would mean that besides being biblically warranted, such a relationship offers us our best context for progressively humanizing our sexuality and therefore we *ought to attempt* (thus "normative") to structure its full expression within that relationship.

I believe there is broad agreement about the principle. Where divergences begin to appear is at the level of pastoral application of the principle. What does it mean for so-called "constitutional" homosexuals? Must they simply be continent? Or is a kind of pastoral of accommodation (stable and permanent relationship within the homosexual context) possible or tolerable? More about this later.

Or again, there is abortion. Beneath the many formulae that have developed over the centuries within the Catholic community, there remains an abiding substance: human life, as a basic human good, may be taken only when such taking is, all things considered, the only life-saving and life-serving option available. I believe that all Catholic moral theologians would accept that *principle* though they might haggle a bit, as moral theologians are wont to do, about whether it adequately catches the substance of Catholic concern. Where they might differ is over whether a particular abortion is, in the circumstances, the only life-saving and life-serving option available, or whether a particular termination (e.g., of an anencephalic fetus) should be called an abortion in the moral sense. In other words, they might disagree about the *application* of the principle.

Let marriage breakup be another example. One can hold tenaciously to the principle of the indissolubility of marriage (both intrinsic and extrinsic)—as I believe the Eastern Orthodox do—and yet disagree about the pastoral application of this principle. Are all those, for example, in a nonregularizable second marriage morally bound to live as brother and sister if they are to be regarded as properly disposed for the Eucharist, as John Paul II argues in *Familiaris Consortio*?[10] Is the decree of nullity issued by ecclesiastical tribunals the only possible and tenable way of pastorally implementing the principle of indissolubility? Whatever one's answers to such questions, it should not be overlooked that they are at a level of application of more general principles.

Is pluralism about such applications pathogenic? I noted above that "it all depends" on one's notion of church. More specifically, it depends on the level of our expectations. If the shape of Church teaching and life has led us to expect agreement and unity at the level of very concrete application, then pluralism is likely to be viewed and experienced as disruptive, dyspeptic, disharmonious, disloyal. If, on the other hand, we do not expect to find total agreement on such matters, then pluralism will be much more peacefully tolerated, indeed welcomed as a sign that rigor mortis has not yet overtaken the Church that must think in changing times.

It is the modest argument of this chapter that significant developments in the Church in the past twenty-five years (since Vatican II) should lead us to lower our expectations and view pluralism at this level as inescapably a dimension of being human (i.e., limited), committed, alert and honest. I shall mention but five such developments, aware of the fact that many more could be added.

1. The shift in magisterial awareness about its moral authority. The distinction between principle and application has, of course, been known for centuries. But in the quite immediate past, the implications of this distinction were not nearly so clear where magisterial (especially papal) teaching authority is concerned. Thus several popes spoke of their teaching competence in moral matters in quite sweeping and undifferentiated fashion, a matter I adverted to above in chapter 5. Let me cite a few examples.

Pius XI:

Indeed the Church believes that it would be wrong for her to interfere without just cause in such earthly concerns; but she never can relin-
quish her God-given task of interposing her authority, not indeed in
technical matters, for which she has neither the equipment nor the mission, but in all those that have a bearing on moral conduct. For the
deposit of truth entrusted to us by God, and Our weighty office of prop-
agating, interpreting and urging in season and out of season the entire
moral law, demand that both social and economic questions be brought
within Our supreme jurisdiction, in so far as they refer to moral
issues.[11]

Pius XII:

The power of the Church is not bound by the limits of "matters
strictly religious," as they say, but the whole matter of the natural law, its
foundation, its interpretation, its application, so far as their moral aspect
extends, are within the Church's power.[12] [The fuller citation is given in
chapter 5.]

John XXIII:

For it must not be forgotten that the Church has the right and the
duty to intervene authoritatively with her children in the temporal
sphere when there is question of judging the application of those principles [of the natural law] to concrete cases.[13]

John XXIII:

It is clear, however, that when the hierarchy has issued a precept or
decision on a point at issue, Catholics are bound to obey their directives.
The reason is that the Church has the right and the obligation, not
merely to guard the purity of ethical and religious principles, but also to
intervene authoritatively when there is question of judging the application of these principles to concrete cases.[14]

In such citations we witness a twofold assertion: (1) the authoritative
competence of the Church; (2) with regard to the entire moral law, applications included. There is no qualification expressed on the authoritative
character of the interventions where detailed applications are concerned.
One has only to examine the very detailed interventions of the Holy See (especially under Pius XII) in sexual and medical matters to see these assertions in action.

A rather remarkably different approach begins to appear with Vatican
II. The bishops provide guidelines for the interpretation of the *Pastoral Con-*

stitution on the Church in the Modern World. They state that "in Part II [where special urgent moral problems are treated] the subject matter which is viewed in the light of doctrinal principles is made up of diverse elements. Some elements have a permanent value; others, only a transitory one ... Interpreters must bear in mind—especially in Part II—the changeable circumstances which the subject matter, by its very nature, involves."[15]

The Council further stated, as I noted in chapter 2, that "it happens rather frequently, *and legitimately so*, that with equal sincerity some of the faithful will disagree with others on a given matter."[16] This legitimate pluralism is to be expected if even official teachers do not have all the answers, a point explicitly made by the Council when it stated:

> The Church, as guardian of the deposit of God's word, draws religious and moral principles from it, but it does not always have a ready answer to particular questions, wishing to combine the light of revelation with universal experiences so that illumination can be forthcoming on the direction which humanity has recently begun to take.[17]

This *nouvelle modestie* did not escape the notice of the American bishops. In *The Challenge of Peace*, they explicitly stress the difference between universal moral principles and their applications.

> We stress here at the beginning that not every statement in this letter has the same moral authority. At times we reassert universally binding moral principles (e.g., non-combatant immunity and proportionality). At still other times we reaffirm statements of recent popes and the teaching of Vatican II. Again, at other times we apply moral principles to specific cases.[18]

The bishops note that where applications are concerned, "prudential judgments are involved based on specific circumstances which can change or which can be interpreted differently by people of good will." They conclude that their judgments of application should be taken seriously but are "not binding in conscience." While the bishops understand "application" in its strict sense, what they say applies necessarily to the notion in its broad sense as well, that is, to the very understanding of the principles.

Since Cardinal Bernardin had a strong shaping hand in *The Challenge of Peace*, it is to be expected that this magisterial modesty would be repeated in his own corpus of writing. Speaking at Catholic University in 1985, he stated:

> In the pastoral letters—and in many other documents such as congressional testimonies, speeches and letters of individual bishops—we speak at the level of both moral principles and the applications of these

principles to particular policies. We regularly assert that we understand and want others to understand that the moral principles we present have a different authority than our particular conclusions. We invite debate and discussion of our policy conclusions.[19]

Archbishop John L. May stated after the November (1987) bishops' meeting that Church leaders believe that part of their role as teachers is to take positions on public as well as Church issues on moral grounds. He continued: "That doesn't mean that a Catholic, in good conscience, cannot disagree."[20]

Such nuanced statements are a far cry from the quite sweeping ones emanating from earlier popes. If many neurological issues in moral theology are matters of application, and if we are to expect a measure of diversity on such matters, then this pluralism is hardly a matter of pathogenesis. It is rather a realistic recovery of Aquinas' notion that the more one descends from the general to the particular the more difficult it is to achieve clarity and certainty. As moralist John Mahoney, S.J., notes, "this flexibility of conclusion and applications" is one "which later moral theology was not to accept in any wholehearted manner."[21]

2. The change in moral methodology. The move away from neoscholasticism that characterized so much of Vatican II brought with it many methodological shifts. For instance, Charles Curran has pointed out that the anthropological bases of Catholic social thought have shifted in our time.[22] We put great emphasis on freedom, equality, participation and historical consciousness. Such emphasis will unavoidably lead to nuancing of the practical application of general principles.

Here I want to highlight a single methodological shift: the criterion for judging moral wrongness in our actions and policies. It is the person "integrally and adequately considered."[24] I refer the reader to the discussion of this in chapter 1.

The importance of this criterion can scarcely be overstated. If "the person integrally and adequately considered" is the criterion for rectitude, it means that a different (from traditional) type of evidence is required for our assessment of human actions. For example, in the past the criteriological significance of sexual conduct was found in its procreativity. Deviations from this finality and significance were viewed as morally wrong and *the* decisive factor in judging conduct. One sees this emphasis on biological finality in the work of Franciscus Hürth, S.J., who was very influential in the pontificates of Pius XI and Pius XII. He saw in biological facticity "an almost unbelievable teleology." "The will of nature," he says, "was inscribed in the organs and their functions." He concluded: "Man only has disposal of the use of his organs and his faculties with respect to the end which the Creator, in His formation of them, has intended. This end for man, then, is both the biological law and the moral law, such that the latter obliges him to live according to the biological law."[25] The criterion at work here is certainly not the person adequately considered.

Once we have accepted the person as our objective criterion, we are committed to the relevance of the sciences and human experience in our discernment process. For, as Louis Janssens has noted, "from a personalist standpoint what must be examined is what the intervention as a whole means for the promotion of the human persons who are involved and for their relationships."[26] This is a more gradual, inductive, time-consuming, messy, uncertain and ultimately pluralistic process than the soothing certainties of a deductive method would allow us to believe.

3. The emergence of the lay voice in moral discernment. For many decades the Church was rather neatly—if artificially—subdivided into the teaching and learning Church. By and large the teaching Church was comprised of the hierarchy, the learning Church included the rest, most numerously and notably the laity. In any number of ways Vatican II shattered this easy compartmentalization. It insisted that "it is for God's people as a whole with the help of the Holy Spirit, and especially for pastors and theologians, to listen to the various voices of our day, discerning them and interpreting them, and to evaluate them in the light of the divine word, so that the revealed truth can be increasingly appropriated, better understood and more suitably expressed."[27] For this reason the Council fathers affirmed that all have freedom of inquiry and expression.[28]

Because every gift (i.e., competence) is a responsibility, Vatican II issued that remarkable summons to lay people that I cited in chapter 1.[29]

I confess that this is one of my favorite conciliar texts, not because it lightens the workload of moral theologians, but because it summarizes and symbolizes so many other things—theological things—the Council was striving to do. High on the list of these things was toppling the pyramidal notion of the Church wherein truth descends uniquely from above in a kind of mysterious paternalistic flow.

This gradual emergence of lay competence can be seen in the realm of social morality. In 1981, the Jesuit editors of *Civiltà cattolica*—a journal whose interest sometimes exceeds the merits of its offerings because it is censored by the Holy See—published a study that argued that the continuing relevance of *Rerum Novarum* consists in the method in which it approached social problems, not its conclusions.[30] In developing this thesis, they pointed out that the social teaching of the Church developed in stages. *Rerum Novarum* represents the first stage. It was dominated by "Christian philosophy" and a "rigidly deductive" method. This had two shortcomings. First, it left no room for the relevance of the sciences (political science, sociology, economics). Second, and a consequence, doctrinal elaboration was seen as an exclusively hierarchical task, lay persons being merely "faithful executors."

The second stage covers the pontificates of Pius XI and Pius XII and might be called the stage of "social doctrine." Indeed, *Quadragesimo Anno* used this term for the first time. It referred to an organic corpus of universal principles still rigidly deduced from social ethics that constituted a kind of third way between liberalism and socialism. However, there is greater emphasis on the historical moment and applications of principles to practice, hence the beginning of reevaluation of the place of lay persons vis-à-vis social teaching, a reevaluation completed by Vatican II. Lay persons do not simply apply the Church's social teaching; they must share in its very construction.

This analytic chronicle suggests a question: Has such a development occurred in the area of the Church's approach to familial, medical and sexual morality? The answer is rather clearly no. Perhaps the question were better worded as follows: Should not such a development occur in the approach to these other questions? If a clearly deductive method, one that left little room to the sciences and lay experience, prevailed in the elaboration of social teaching, it is reasonable to think that the same thing occurred in familial, medical and sexual morality. And if this method has evolved and changed during the pontificates of John XXIII and Paul VI with regard to social teaching, it is reasonable to think that the same thing ought to happen in all areas of Church teaching. Yet two things seem clear about the Church's teaching on these questions. First, earlier popes are invariably cited for their conclusions, not simply their systematic method. Second, the sciences and lay experience remain marginal factors in the continuing reflection of the Church on familial, medical and sexual matters. Such reflections suggest that we must learn to distinguish more than we have between loyalty to the magisterium and a certain clonal positivism or magisterial fundamentalism.

4. *The emergence of ecumenism.* Prior to Vatican II, serious ecumenism was in the rather lonely hands of a few theological pioneers on the continent. Official attitudes and practices were structured by the conviction that non-Catholic Christians were the *adversarii* of our central religious and moral tenets. A symbol of this was canon 1399, 4 of the 1918 code, which forbade the reading of books authored by Protestants that expressly treated of religious themes. Those were the days—and not that long ago—when attendance at non-Catholic weddings and funerals, involvement with the YMCA and common prayer were viewed as indifferentist threats to the one true faith. Believe it or not, they occupied large chunks of a moralist's time. We struggled mightily with the impulses of our common sense to cling to *extra ecclesiam nulla salus* and yet get Protestants into heaven. Their very separation from the one true Church was a presumption against the reliability of their religious and moral thought. The Lambeth Conference of 1930 that issued a hedged approval of contraception occasioned the swift retaliation of *Casti Connubii*. We did not turn to non-Catholics as a source of wisdom in moral matters. In brief, ecumenical warfare, sometimes latent and doily-polite, but always there.

Vatican II changed all that. The engaging persona of John XXIII was but a symbol of deeper theological stirrings. Instead of front-centering what separates, we began to see the vast area of common inheritance. The Council acknowledged the ecclesial reality of other Christian churches, the presence of the Spirit to their members and the grace-inspired character of their lives. It encouraged ecumenical dialogue and work, and relaxed its discipline on common worship. Pointedly, it stated:

> Nor should we forget that whatever is wrought by the grace of the Holy Spirit in the hearts of our separated brethren can contribute to our own edification.[31]

The Council took this very seriously and practically when it stated that Christians are joined in a common search for the solutions to moral problems.[32]

Now it is clear that non-Catholic Christians and other people of good will come from different—pluralistic, if you will—backgrounds and traditions. Such traditions may well yield differing perspectives, priorities and conclusions. The Council expected to be informed and enriched by these differences, not threatened. In an atmosphere of restoration, of course, these divergences are likely to be viewed as so many banana peels strewn across the path of conscience-formation. Thus an important document on reproductive technology is launched with nary an ecumenical reference or input.

5. The changing attitudes toward authority. Yves Congar, O.P., has pointed out that the ordinary magisterium of the Church—a term which originated in the nineteenth century—reached a kind of high watermark of one-sidedness in the pontificate of Pius XII, and specifically in *Humani Generis*.[33] In that encyclical, as was noted in chapter 1, the pope stated his position on two points. First, the ordinary magisterium of the pope requires total obedience. "He who listens to you listens to me." Second, the (or a) role of theologians is to justify the declarations of the magisterium. In this encyclical the pope stated that once he had expressed his *sententia* on a point previously controversial, "there can no longer be any question of free discussion among theologians." Congar ends his discussion of this point with the following cryptic and provocative remark: "Is this consonant with what nineteen centuries of the Church's life tell us about the function of 'didascale' or doctor? No, not exactly." Yet exactly this same expression was employed by John Paul II last summer in his comments on birth regulation. He stated: "What is taught by the Church on contraception does not belong to material freely debatable among theologians."[34] I will return to this question in chapter 9.

The effect of such remarks is a kind of disenfranchisement of pluralism on the point at issue, and by implication of any application so proposed. I cannot discuss the matter at length here but were I to do so, I would marshal the many reasons that lead one to believe that such statements reflect a neoscholastic notion of the magisterium. Of this notion, Congar states bluntly: "Its pretensions seem excessive and unreal." He then adds: "Today, theologians are going beyond the ecclesiastical work-category formulated for them by Pius XII and Paul VI; they are living according to a common standard of scholarly research."[35] The very same point was developed by Avery Dulles, S.J.:

> As a result of the experience of the Council and the growth of critical theology, the neo-scholastic theory of the magisterium is perceived as making insufficient allowance for distortion and possible error in the ordinary teaching of popes and bishops. Sophisticated Catholics of the 1970's are generally convinced that dissent and loyal opposition can play a positive role in the Church as well as in secular society. Any attempt by the hierarchy to settle disputed questions by unilateral decrees will inevitably be met by dissent or even protest on the part of some.[36]

The "positive role" that Dulles attributes to dissent is, of course, its contribution to the discovery of truth. Else it is not positive.

I would be remiss if I did not cite an even more formidable authority to bolster Dulles' claim of a "positive role." Writing in 1970, Joseph Ratzinger asserted:

> ... criticism of papal pronouncements is possible and necessary to the extent these pronouncements are not covered in Scripture and creed, especially by the faith of the entire Church. Where there is neither the consent of the whole Church, nor a clear witness from the sources, a binding declaration is not possible ... [37]

In summary, then, when the criterion for judging moral rightness and wrongness of actions has shifted, when lay competence in the discernment process has been admitted, when the reflections of our separated brothers and sisters in Christ are acknowledged as essential, when respectful disagreement (dissent) is granted a positive role in ecclesial discernment, when the bishops themselves acknowledge a different authority in their presentation of universal principles and applications, we see a convergence of factors that lead us to lower our expectations about clarity and certainty in the application of moral principles to human life. This conclusion is hardly a moral-theological sunburst. Indeed, to the extent that my reflections are accurate they constitute so many reasons why this chapter need never have been written. Thomas Aquinas got there first. Whatever the case, I believe that we have sustainable bases for saying that pluralism should not be a surprise.[38] And once we have grown accustomed to its face, it should not be pathogenic.

Notes

1. Cardinal Joseph Bernardin, "Science and the Creation of Life," *Health Progress* 68 (July-August, 1987):48-51.

2. Cardinal Joseph Bernardin, "Toward a Consistent Ethic of Life" (Fordham University, 6 December 1983), *Origins* 13 (1983-84), 491-94; "Enlarging the Dialogue on the Consistent Ethic of Life" (St. Louis University, 11 March 1984), *Origins* 13 (1983-84), 705, 707-9.

3. *Summa Theologica*, I-II, q. 94, a. 5. "Quantum ad prima principia legis naturae, lex naturae est omnino immutabilis. Quantum autem ad secunda praecepta, quae diximus esse quasi quasdam proprias conclusiones propinquas primis principiis, sic lex naturalis non immutatur quin ut in pluribus rectum sit semper quod lex naturalis habet. Potest tamen immutari in aliquo particulari, et in paucioribus, propter aliquas speciales causas impedientes observantiam talium praeceptorum."

4. *Summa Theologica* I-II, q. 100, a.8 ad 3.

5. Franz Scholz, "Durch ethische Grenzsituationen aufgeworfene Normenprobleme," *Theologisch-praktische Quartalschrift* 123 (1975):341-55.

6. John Mahoney, *The Making of Moral Theology* (Oxford: Clarendon Press, 1987), 80.

7. Charles E. Curran, "Public Dissent in the Church," *Origins* 16 (1986), 178-84.

8. Congregation for the Doctrine of the Faith (Vatican City: Vatican Polyglot Press, 1987), 26.

9. Kevin T. Kelly, *Life and Love* (London: Collins Liturgical Publications, 1987), 18.

10. John Paul II, *Familiaris Consortio*, AAS 74 (1982), n. 84. Cf. also *Familiaris Consortio* (Boston: St. Paul Editions, 1982).

11. Pius XI, *Quadragesimo Anno*, AAS 23 (1931), 190.

12. Pius XII, *Magnificate Dominum*, AAS 46 (1954), 671-73.

13. John XXIII, *Pacem in Terris*, AAS 55 (1963), 300-1.

14. John XXIII, *Mater et Magistra*, AAS 53 (1961), 457.

15. *The Documents of Vatican II*, ed. Walter M. Abbott, S.J. (New York: America Press, 1966), 199, footnote 2.

16. *Documents*, n. 43, p. 244.

17. *Documents*, n. 33, p. 232.

18. *The Challenge of Peace* (Washington, D.C.: U.S. Catholic Conference, 1983).

19. Cardinal Joseph Bernardin, "The Face of Poverty Today: A Challenge for the Church," in *Consistent Ethic of Life*, ed. Thomas G. Fuechtmann (Kansas City, Mo.: Sheed and Ward, 1988), 43.

20. John L.May, as cited in *South Bend Tribune*, 20 November 1987, A8.

21. Mahoney, loc. cit., 189.

22. Charles E. Curran, "The Changing Anthropological Bases of Catholic Social Teaching," *Thomist* 45 (1981):284-318.

23. *Documents*, n. 51, p. 256.

24. *Schema constitutionis pastoralis de ecclesia in mundo huius temporis: Expensio modorum partis secundae* (Vatican Press, 1965), 37-38.

25. F. Hürth, S.J., "La fécondation artificielle: Sa valeur morale et juridique," *Nouvelle revue théologique* 68 (1946):402-26, at 416.

26. Louis Janssens, "Artificial Insemination: Ethical Considerations," *Louvain Studies* 8 (1980): 3-29, at 24.

27. *Documents*, n. 44, p. 246.

28. *Documents*, n. 62, p. 270.

29. *Documents*, n. 43, p. 224.

30. "Dalla 'Rerum novarum' ad oggi," *Civiltà cattolica* 132 (1981):345-57.

31. *Documents*, n. 4, p. 349.

32. *Documents*, n. 16, p. 214.

33. Yves Congar, O.P., "A Brief History of the Forms of the Magisterium," in Charles E. Curran and Richard A. McCormick, S.J., *Readings in Moral Theology No. 3* (Ramsey, N.J.: Paulist, 1982).

34. John Paul II, *L'Osservatore Romano*, English edition, n. 27 (6 July 1987), 12-13.

35. Loc. cit., 327.

36. Avery Dulles, S.J., "The Theologian and the Magisterium," *Proceedings of the Catholic Theological Society of America* 31 (1976), 235-46, at 241-42.

37. Joseph Ratzinger, *Das neue Volk Gottes* (1970), 144, as cited in *Theology Digest* 34 (1987):45.

38. Josef Fuchs, S.J., provides an example of pluralism in earlier centuries. Cf. "Eheliche Liebe: Christlicher Pluralismus im 12. Jahrhundert," *Stimmen der Zeit* 203 (1985):803-17.

Chapter 9

Matters of Free Theological Debate

At a June, 1987 meeting of natural family planning experts, John Paul II stated that the Church's teaching against contraception is "clear" and "not . . . debatable." As he put it: "What is taught by the Church on contraception does not belong to material freely debatable among theologians."[1] This statement immediately calls to mind a similar statement of Pius XII in *Humani Generis*.

> But if the Supreme Pontiffs in their statements (*in actis suis*) deliberately state an opinion about a matter hitherto controverted, it is clear to all that matter, according to the mind and will of the same Pontiffs, can no longer be held to be a question of free debate among theologians.[2]

Avery Dulles, S.J., in discussing the functional specialties of the hierarchical magisterium, refers to this statement of Pius XII as pertaining to the judicial function of that magisterium. He notes:

> Others [than irreformable definitions] may be reformable decisions which nevertheless carry with them a certain presumption of truth and which may carry with them an implied command to terminate a theological debate. The position of Pius XII to this effect in *Humani generis* (DS 3885), even though not explicitly repeated by Vatican II, still seems to stand, especially in view of its reaffirmation by Paul VI.[3]

The "reaffirmation by Paul VI" is a reference to that pontiff's 1964 speech to the College of Cardinals.[4] The pope alluded to the ongoing debate on birth regulation and asserted that to that point he could not find sufficient reason for modifying the norms of Pius XII. He then added:

In a matter of such great gravity, it seems well that Catholics should wish to follow a single (*unica*) law, that which the Church authoritatively proposes. And it therefore seems opportune to recommend (*raccomandare*; ["enjoin"?]) that no one for the present presume to speak (*si arroghi di pronunciarsi*) in terms divergent from the prevailing norm.[5]

In this brief chapter I am not directly interested in discussion of birth regulation. Rather I am interested in exploring the meaning of statements such as "does not belong to material freely debatable among theologians" (John Paul II), "no one . . . presume to speak in terms divergent from the prevailing norm" (Paul VI), and "can no longer be held to be a question of free debate among theologians" (Pius XII). In the process of doing this, I shall liberally enlist the aid of colleagues in ecclesiology, notably Avery Dulles, S.J., and Yves Congar, O.P.

It seems fairly clear that John Paul II was using the concepts and language of Pius XII. Pius XII's assertion seems basically to be this: when the pope expresses his *sententia*, that gives the matter a doctrinal status it did not previously have. What was previously controverted, by the very fact of the expression of the papal *sententia* no longer is. The papal *sententia* has decided the matter. Given the atmosphere and ecclesiology of Pius' time, I believe that by the words "no longer be held to be a question of free debate among theologians" he meant to exclude any public disagreement with the papal position. He stated a factual situation (no longer a question of free debate) that he saw as the immediate inference of his ecclesiology: that any public disagreement with the papal position was unjustified. That was the way he conceived the ordinary noninfallible magisterium. It was simply decisive. "He who hears you hears me." Congar reflects this in his statement that the ordinary magisterium " in the light of an intense 'devotion to the pope', has been almost assimilated, in current opinion, to the prerogatives of the extraordinary magisterium."[6] For Pius XII, "according to the mind and will of the same Pontiffs" meant absolute obedience. It is another question whether the same words used in a different era should be understood as Pius understood them. Overall, however, the usage of Pius XII does seem to conform to Dulles' description of it as an *implied* command.

Where Paul VI's 1964 intervention is concerned, the same is not true. The command is *explicit*. Paul VI made two distinct moves. First, he passed judgment (his *sententia*) on the reasons adduced to that point to modify the norms of Pius XII on contraception. He found them wanting. As he worded it, "We say frankly that We do not so far see any adequate reason for considering the relevant norms of Pius XII superseded and therefore no longer obligatory."[7] The pope immediately added: "They should, therefore, be regarded as valid, at least as long as We do not consider Ourselves obliged in conscience to modify them." I have always regarded this as an authentic but noninfallible teaching (doctrinal) statement (*sententia*) about the persuasiveness of the arguments and analyses adduced to that point (1964) against the norms of Pius XII.

The pope immediately and explicitly added that it is "opportune to recommend that no one for the present presume to speak in terms divergent from the prevailing norm." This is the command-aspect of his intervention. But the question remains: *what* was he commanding? Was he "terminating a theological debate," to use Dulles' phrase? In other words, was he saying that all public theological debate of this matter should cease? I do not believe that this is a necessary understanding of Paul VI and I will offer my reasons below. What the mandate could be understood to be saying is this: *no one should present a contradictory view as if it were the Church's teaching or of equal authority with it.* Or again, what is practically the same, *no one should present his/her view as if the Church had not spoken officially on the matter.* "Freely debatable," then, should be understood as the type of debate conducted in a context where no official position has been stated. Conversely, when something is said to be "not a matter of free debate," this means only that an official position has been stated and must be reckoned with. It need not exclude public discussion or even dissent.

If that is a fair reading of Paul VI's 1964 statement—and I believe it is, for the reasons I adduce below—it seems also to be a legitimate restrictive reading of Pius XII's earlier "can no longer be held to be a question of free debate among theologians" and also of John Paul II's "does not belong to material freely debatable among theologians." For Dulles is correct, I believe, when he sees Paul VI's intervention as something of a "reaffirmation" of Pius XII. In that case, the reaffirmation can throw light on how we might also understand John Paul II, who uses words all but identical with those of Pius XII.

My reasons for believing that this is a defensible understanding of Paul VI, and therefore of John Paul II, are the following.

1. The moral teaching in question (birth regulation) is open to doctrinal development. Not only is this true of many concrete moral questions—as I think history shows—but it was the very premise of Paul VI's appointment of a commission to study the matter. Furthermore, in a press interview following his presentation of *Humanae Vitae*, Fernando Lambruschini was cited as noting that "the rule [against artificial birth control] is not unreformable. It is up to theologians to debate and expand all moral aspects involved."[8]

This very same point was made by Archbishop John R. Quinn in the 1980 Synod of Bishops. Noting that there was widespread dissent from *Humane Vitae* among "theologians and pastors whose learning, discretion and dedication to the Church are beyond doubt," Quinn called for a worldwide dialogue between the Holy See and the theologians on the meaning of this dissent.[9] How this could be done without "debate" is difficult to envisage. Furthermore, if such dialogue was appropriate *after Humanae Vitae*, one would think that it was all the more so *before*. Quinn also referred to "doctrinal development" in areas such as biblical studies and religious liberty, areas where development meant change.

2. Pope Paul VI himself admitted the legitimacy and even, I believe, the desirability of continuing debate on his authentic teaching. In a letter to the Congress of German Catholics (August 30, 1968), he stated: "May the lively debate aroused by our encyclical lead to a better knowledge of God's will."[10] If debate may lead "to a better knowledge of God's will," the pope would scarcely want to discourage it, even if this "better knowledge" is not necessarily to be understood as change. Once more, if this was true of *Humane Vitae*, it was all the more so the case with Paul VI's 1964 intervention which was much less authoritative. Since that time (1968), nothing that I know of has changed to lead one to believe that it is precisely absence of such debate that will provide us with a better knowledge of God's will.

3. The very health and credibility of the magisterium requires open exchange. Speaking precisely of sexual morality, Avery Dulles has noted:

> If they are to regain influence with now alienated intellectual Catholics, the bishops must not simply go by the book in condemning new ideas and their authors. They must sincerely and evidently examine the issues on their merits. Before rejecting any new doctrinal proposal, they must assure themselves that they have really heard and appreciated the reasons and motivations of those who favor the proposal.[11]

Clearly, if bishops are to "examine the issues on their merits" and "hear and appreciate the reasons"—as they must if the magisterium is to be credible—such merits and reasons must be available to them, the pro's and the con's. That is the definition of public debate. The termination of public discussion would by and large negate this possibility. Certainly John Paul II would not want his dictum understood in a way that brings the magisterium into disrepute.

4. During the Synod of 1980, any number of bishops rather interestingly noted that while *Humane Vitae* was certainly correct, "better reasons" had to be found to validate its conclusions. Furthermore, the Canadian bishops in a postsynodal report to their people, stated: "Many bishops recommended continuing research toward a new and fuller presentation of what is involved in this question."[12] "Better reasons" and "continuing reasearch" suppose public discussion, indeed the critique of past

and present "reasons," not excluding the determination of whether there are "better reasons" at all. But this is precisely public debate.

5. It is now widely admitted by ecclesiologists that Pius XII was working out of a neoscholastic notion of the magisterium. Yves Congar, O.P., has cited *Humani Generis*, and specifically the citation I have given above, as an example of this. Of the magisterium conceived in this neoscholastic way (with the ordinary papal magisterium demanding total obedience and the task of theologians said to be strictly in the service and under the control of the magisterium), Congar asserts: "Its pretensions seem excessive and unreal."[13] He continues:

> Today, theologians are going beyond the ecclesiastical work-category formulated for them by Pius XII and Paul VI; they are living according to a common standard of scholarly research.

Avery Dulles made the same point[14] in the paragraph I cited in chapter 8.

Since Pius XII's usage ("no longer be held to be a question of free debate among theologians") is rooted in a highly juridicized ecclesiology that most scholars have abandoned, since this ecclesiology had no realistic place for dissent, and since dissent is now viewed much more positively, continued use of Pius' language (as in John Paul II's "does not belong to material freely debatable among theologians") should be interpreted with this in mind. That is, "not freely debatable" should be understood to refer to the fact that there is an official position on the matter. It need not be understood to exclude all dissent from that position or debate about it.

In summary, then, Pius XII proposed that his *sententia* so decidedly changed the status of a disputed point that debate was no longer allowed (and by "debate," as noted, he meant public disagreement). It is precisely this notion of the ordinary papal magisterium that Dulles correctly says makes "insufficient allowance for distortion and possible error in the ordinary teaching of popes and bishops."

Karl Rahner[15] is adamant on this point raised by Dulles, as was noted in chapter 6. Certainly, Rahner's view was not the understanding of Pius XII. Nor is it likely the understanding of John Paul II. I am arguing in these reflections that it is a legitimate interpretation.

6. Vatican II took a remarkably different (from, for example, Pius XII) attitude toward the development of practical moral norms. Let me quickly pass in review points noted in chapter 2. The Council acknowledged the Church's reliance "on those who live in the world, are versed in different institutions and specialties."[16] It admitted that the Church guards the heritage of God's word "without always having at hand the solution to particular problems."[17] It urged lay people not to view their pastors as "always

such experts that to every problem which arises, however complicated, they can readily give . . . a concrete solution."[18] It urged lay people to take on "their own distinctive role." Finally, it acknowledged that "all the faithful, clerical and lay, possess a lawful freedom of inquiry and of thought, and the freedom to express their minds humbly and courageously about those matters in which they enjoy competence."[19]

Such statements suggest a qualification of the idea that a papal *sententia* settles matters so decisively that any public debate is outlawed—unless we are to rescind the above statements and the renewed ecclesiology that they nourish and suppose.

7. As I noted, Pius XII's usage suggests that the papal *sententia* gives a question a clarity and certainty it did not previously possess, so much so that there is an "implied command" no longer freely to debate it. Above I noted the ecclesiological difficulties with that view if it is understood to exclude all public debate. There are further difficulties with that assertion when we are dealing with matters said to be of natural law. Such matters are by definition available to human insight and reasoning. That means that their clarity and certainty attach to such processes, not primarily to papal assertion.

This is clear from the example of Paul VI. In an allocution to the Congress of the Italian Feminine Center, he stated:

> The magisterium of the Church cannot propose moral norms until it is certain of interpreting the will of God. And to reach this certainty the Church is not dispensed from research and from examining the many questions proposed for her consideration from every part of the world. This is at times a long and not an easy task.[20]

If, to reach (*raggiungere*) certainty, the Church is not dispensed from research, then clearly the results of this research bear on the achievement or maintenance of certainty. In other words, the pope was saying that he could not propose a moral norm until the matter was certain. It was not *his proposal* that made it certain. Rather, on his own terms, being certain was the condition of possibility of his proposal. Analogously, if the pope were going to issue a modification of traditional norms, such a modification would be plausible only on the supposition that it had already become clear *before his statement* that traditional formulations were inadequate. Any other view would involve us, it seems, in an unacceptably juridical and voluntaristic notion of the magisterium in the area of so-called "natural law morality."

In summary, I suggest here that there are significant reasons for understanding phrases such as "no longer freely debatable by theologians" in a very narrow sense as restricting not debate itself, but only those debates that proceed on the premise that they are *totally* free, that is, that no official position exists or has been stated. That may be understood to be the import of "free debate" (Pius XII) and "freely debatable" (John Paul II).[21]

The major objection to my interpretation of John Paul II's statement is this: if this is what the papal statement means, it scarcely needed saying. For everyone knows that there is an official position. Merely to state that is to reduce the pope's words to insignificance.

My response to this objection is threefold. First, I concede that it may be unlikely that this is what the pope meant. What I am arguing, however, is that it makes good ecclesiological sense and therefore, is morally permissible to *interpret* his statement as I have.

Second, knowing that there is an official position and knowing the theological implications of this are two different matters. Knowledge of the first can combine with idiosyncratic views or ignorance about the second. Thus, it can be useful to continue to point out the implications of "officialness."

Third, I do not believe that this interpretation "reduces the pope's words to insignificance." There are good reasons in our time to restate a moderate ecclesiology on authentic but noninfallible papal moral teaching—moderate in that it states the presumption of truth in such teaching. This is easily forgotten by many who have begun to dismiss such teaching *tout à fait*. On the other hand, such teaching is no less threatened when the presumption attaching to it is treated as something more and any public dissent is excluded in principle. Thus, ironically, the significance of the papal statement would be that it acts as a corrective to some magisterial maximalists.

Notes

1. *L'Osservatore Romano*, English edition, no. 27 (6 July, 1987), 12-13.
2. AAS 42 (1950), 561-78, at 568.
3. Avery Dulles, S.J., "The Two Magisteria: An Interim Reflection," *Proceedings of the Catholic Theological Society of America*, 35 (1980), 155-69, at 162.
4. AAS 56 (1964), 581-89, at 588-89.
5. Loc. cit., 588-89.
6. Yves Congar, O.P., "A Brief History of the Forms of the Magisterium and Its Relations with Scholars," in *Readings in Moral Theology* no. 3, ed. Charles E. Curran and Richard A. McCormick, S.J. (New York: Paulist, 1982), 325.
7. Cf. note 4.
8. Cited in William H. Shannon, *The Lively Debate: The Response to "Humanae Vitae"* (New York: Sheed and Ward, 1970), 114.
9. John R. Quinn, "'New Context' for Contraception Teaching," *Origins* 10 (1980), 263-67.
10. Cited on title page and cover of Shannon (cf. note 8).

11. Cf. note 3, at 168.

12. *Origins* 10 (1980), 329-30.

13. Cf. note 6, at 327.

14. Avery Dulles, S.J., "The Theologian and the Magisterium," *Proceedings of the Catholic Theological Society of America*, 31 (1976), 235-46, at 241-42. In this matter see also J. Robert Dionne, *The Papacy and the Church* (New York: Philosophical Library, 1987), especially 365-66.

15. Karl Rahner, "Theologie und Lehramt, "*Stimmen der Zeit* 198 (1980):363-75, at 374.

16. *Documents*, 246.

17. Ibid., 232.

18. Ibid., 244.

19. Ibid., 270.

20. AAS 58 (1966), 218-24, at 219.

21. This was the conclusion drawn by John J. Reed, S.J., in 1965. He wrote: "The expression 'quaestionem liberae inter theologos disceptationis jam haberi non posse' does not seem to mean that the question 'cannot be any longer considered open to discussion among theologians.' The idea would rather seem to be that it is not a matter in which both sides can be held and followed with equal freedom. This is quite a different concept, and I have tried to convey it, not very successfully, perhaps, in the phrase 'a matter of open debate'." "Natural Law, Theology and the Church," *Theological Studies* 26 (1965):40-64, at 57, footnote 30.

Chapter 10

Fundamental Freedom Revisited

It was noted in chapter 1 that the notion of fundamental or core freedom has settled pacifically into contemporary moral theology. It was also noted that this notion is under some recent challenges. In this chapter I shall attempt three things: (1) a brief review of the notion of fundamental freedom; (2) some pastoral implications of the notion; (3) recent misunderstandings and objections. My first two points will be preparatory for the third.

Fundamental Freedom

The notion of fundamental freedom entered systematic theological reflection largely through the writings of Karl Rahner. It would not be an exaggeration to say that his theological thought is quite simply "soaked" in the idea; for it is a key concept of his anthropology.

Letting Rahner speak for himself has its risks, the chief one being a nagging headache. It is no secret that Rahner often leaves the impression that he is speaking to himself in a kind of free flow of consciousness. Nonetheless, given the importance—theological and pastoral—of the notion of basic freedom, I will run the risks.

Rahner notes:

> Man's freedom and responsibility belong to the existentials of human existence. Since freedom is situated at the subjective pole of human existence and its experience, and not within what is categorically given, the essential nature of this freedom does not consist in a particular faculty of man alongside of others by means of which he can do or not do this or

that through arbitrary choices. It is only too easy to interpret our freedom this way, an interpretation based on a pseudo-empirical understanding of freedom. But in reality freedom is first of all the subject's being responsible for himself, so that freedom in its fundamental nature has to do with the subject as such and as a whole. In real freedom the subject always intends himself, understands and posits himself. Ultimately he does not do *something*, but does *himself*.[1]

For Rahner, then, freedom is transcendental, "not an object of experience nor merely the quality of an action, but a basic mode of being."[2] He immediately draws two conclusions from this. First, freedom, as the capacity to decide about oneself, does not stand behind the concrete physical, biological, historical dimension of the person, as if it were some unearthly power unrelated to historical life. That would be gnostic, dualistic. Rather it "actualizes itself" in and through the temporality that is our way of being. For this reason Rahner regards freedom as "much more nuanced, much more complex and much less unambiguous than the primitive, categorical conception of freedom as a capacity to do this or that arbitrarily."[3]

The second conclusion Rahner draws is that the actualization of this freedom "is not indeed an immediate, empirical, individual and categorically identifiable datum of our experience." It is "an element in the subject himself which the subject cannot make conscious and objectify directly in its own self."[4] Basic freedom is real in human experience, but is not "immediately and empirically observable in time and space." For this reason the "subject never has an absolute certainty about the subjective and therefore moral quality of these individual actions."[5]

The object, so to speak, of this core of transcendental freedom is God, absolute mystery, infinite horizon. Although we cannot know with certainty that a "yes" or "no" to God took place at a definite point in our lives, "we know that the entire life of a free subject is inevitably an answer to the question in which God offers himself to us as the source of transcendence."[6]

Thus, for Rahner there are two levels or dimensions to our concrete (categorical) actions, the level of categorical freedom and the level of core or transcendental freedom. He puts it as follows:

> Since in every act of freedom which is concerned on the categorical level with a quite definite object, a quite definite person, there is always present, as the condition of possibility for such an act, transcendence towards the absolute term and source of all of our intellectual and spiritual acts, and hence towards God, there can and must be present in every such act an unthematic "yes" or "no" to this God or original, transcendental experience. Subjectivity and freedom imply and entail that this freedom is

not only freedom with respect to the object of categorical experience within the absolute horizon of God, but it is also and in truth, although always in only a mediated way, a freedom which decides about God and with respect to God himself. In this sense we encounter God in a radical way everywhere as a question to our freedom, we encounter him unexpressed, unthematic, unobjectified and unspoken in all of the things of the world, and therefore and especially in our neighbor. This does not preclude the necessity of making this thematic. But this latter does not give us our original relationship to God in our freedom, but rather it makes thematic and objectifies the relationship of our freedom to God which is given with and in the original and essential being of the subject as such.[7]

Thus the very constitutive core of the human person is a capacity, a freedom to accept or not the divine self-communication we call grace. Rahner emphasizes over and over again that this self-disposition before the absolute mystery of God is not a categorical, thematic datum of human experience that is immediately and empirically observable. As Ronald Modras summarizes:

This renders freedom not only difficult to define but a mystery which, both as a reality and a concept, escapes reflection into the sphere of incomprehensibility, where we dwell with our divine mystery. God is unthematically but really present in every act of freedom, both as its supporting ground and ultimate orientation.[8]

In summary, then, transcendental freedom is at the heart of Rahner's anthropology. But because human beings are a unity of materiality and spirit, this transcendental freedom can only exist and be actualized in time and history, or in Rahner's words, "I always act into an objective world." This is a world of conditioning, restrictions, necessities. Our transcendental freedom is, as it were, impacted in and inseparable from the categorical or object choices that make up our lives. For this reason, the human person is "a many-layered being . . . constructed as it were in layers starting at an interior core and becoming more and more external."[9]

Of this notion of freedom, Modras accurately states:

Here we find the basis in Rahner's anthropology for distinguishing between ordinary free decisions and those which constitute a fundamental option. It is out of the inmost core of our beings that we make those basic decisions of transcendental freedom (fundamental options) which lead to or away from God. But because freedom extends formally to the whole person, free actions can arise from outside the inmost core which do not affect us as acts of transcendental freedom do.[10]

This, then, is the anthropology that stands behind the notion of fundamental option. A rich literature has developed around this anthropology.[11] Furthermore, it is all but taken for granted in most theological circles. This can be seen in its use by such authors as Josef Fuchs, Bernard Häring, George Lobo, Franz Böckle, Timothy O'Connell, Bruno Schüller and a host of others. Let Lobo's recent book be an example. Under the subtitle "The Fundamental Option," he writes:

> The personal ego, or the unity of the self, is more than the sum of individual acts and aims. There are intermittent expressions of the ego. While individual moral acts and aims are the object of moral knowledge and volition, the human person is also conscious of himself as a subject without necessarily reflecting on himself as an object. He can commit himself in freedom without realizing himself in action as an object.
>
> Hence, besides *freedom of choice* (*libertas arbitrii*), man has a *basic* or *transcendental freedom* which, in the words of Joseph Fuchs, "enables us not only to decide freely on particular acts and aims but also, by means of them, to determine ourselves totally as persons, and not merely in any particular area of behavior." This is moral freedom in the highest sense.[12]

Many contemporary authors explain both sin and conversion in terms of the fundamental option. In this sense they regard a negative fundamental option as "synonymous with mortal sin."[13]

As I read the literature, some of its descriptions of fundamental freedom in the moral-spiritual life could be systematized in the following way.

1. *Free.* It may seem ridiculous to speak of transcendental freedom as being free. The point being made, however, needs to be made. Since our reflex awareness of freedom is of *freedom of choice* (object choice), there is the danger that we would limit the notion of freedom to such awareness. When we say that fundamental freedom is free, we mean to underline the fact that our fundamental posture or orientation toward the ultimate good of human life is in our power, is our responsibility. Thus freedom is clearly an analogous notion, being realized in both object choices and self-disposition.

2. *Supernatural.* In the economy of salvation, self-disposition occurs under the influence of the grace of the Spirit. It is self-disposition under divine empowerment, our acceptance (or rejection) of God's enabling love. Of course, there is mystery here in the coexistence of divine empowerment and human freedom.

3. *Obscure.* A person acting in basic freedom is totally present to him/herself, not as object but as subject, not as perceived, but as self-aware, not as seen from the outside, but as experienced in the self. Transcendental

freedom is located at a level of consciousness which excludes adequate conceptual and propositional formulation, a level deeper than that of formulating consciousness. This accords well with several facts, as Fuchs points out.[14] For instance, St. Paul did not know whether he was worthy of love or hate. Or again, following Trent, theologians assert that we cannot have full certitude about the state of grace.

4. *Conscious*. Here again, we must be careful to avoid identifying consciousness with formulating consciousness. There is a form of self-awareness that does not lead to objective formulations.

5. *Variable as to time made*. That is, the capacity of self-disposition cannot be simply identified with the age of reason. It can occur at a time when the person is, at least in the obscure depths, in possession of his/her total self. This will vary depending on many factors such as personal growth, parental influence, formal education.

6. *Stable*. The experience of that freedom that defines our personal center has the characteristic of totality and definitiveness. Because of its dimensions and intensity (in order to achieve totality and definitiveness), such a use of human freedom excludes the possibility of a series of quickly repeated transitions between life and death.

Theologians who use this anthropology in their understanding of human moral activity, find it very compatible with the way Scripture portrays the moral life. For instance, there is a unity in the moral life found in the privileged position attributed to charity—as the epitome of the entire law, more elevated than all charisms, the bond of perfection, the root of other virtues. There is a similar unity in the depiction of sin as coming from the heart, as involving an *anomia* or hostility to God, as involving *hamartia* (singular) as the root of other transgressions.[15]

Some Pastoral Applications

Over the past twenty-five years, I have discussed the idea of core or fundamental freedom with numerous groups of priests and religious. I have formed several impressions of their reactions. First, they find the anthropology—especially in some of its pastoral applications which I will mention below—realistic and consoling, challenging and inspiring. It seems to coincide with their ideas of what is truly going on in their own lives and the lives of those they counsel. Second, they find the notion of core freedom elusive and puzzling, as they should. That is the very nature of core freedom. Concretely, there is the constant tendency—temptation is a better word—to conceive and speak of the self-disposition of transcendental freedom as another, even if more intense, *categorical act*. That is understandable simply because we are used to, comfortable with and pulled to reflex consciousness. Living with the mystery that is our openness to and embrace

176 / *Richard A. McCormick, S.J.*

of God's self-communication is unsettling, especially perhaps to those proud of their ability to control things, figure things out, devise and execute plans.

Third, if the use of fundamental freedom is not viewed as a categorical act, there is the tendency to *identify* this freedom with certain categorical acts. Thus I have heard some speak of marriage as "a fundamental option." While marriage involves a certain type of self-disposition, thematic and reflexly conscious at that, it may or may not involve the self-disposition of transcendental freedom. Unfortunately, even some theologians have written in such a way as to occasion this type of identification.

Having said that, let me turn to some of the pastoral implications of the anthropology described above. They are enormous and I can mention but a few here.

1. *Moral life as a growth process.* The notion of fundamental freedom obviously suggests that we conceive the moral life as a dynamic growth process, a gradual unfolding of our beings as Christians. The transformation of faith into love (charity-option) is what the Holy Spirit is operating within us. Seen from this perspective, the moral life is a progressive deepening, stabilizing, rendering more dominant and facile of our charity. It is strengthening the biblical *adherere Deo*. Fuchs has pointed out that the notion of the moral life as a growth process in Christlikeness avoids a kind of *objectivism* (an attitude which sees one's posture before God primarily in terms of the matter of acts) and *conformism* (the notion that external compliance constitutes morality).[16] As Lobo summarizes it:

> The idea of the fundamental option has very important implications for moral education. Such education should not consist merely in training people to perform good acts. Rather, it should concentrate on evoking the right basic response to the call of God and on strengthening such a response. Everything else should be seen in this context.[17]

2. *Conversion in the moral life.* A very rich literature has developed around the notion[18] and I can only refer to it here. Joyful conversion of the heart is, as Charles Curran notes, "the central moral message of Jesus."[19] Conversion, however, is an analogous term; for one converts from sin and sin is an analogous notion. Mortal sin is the prime analogue wherein we find realized most perfectly the elements of sin. Conversion from this condition realizes the notion of conversion most perfectly. Mortal sin is a serious moral act, involving one's fundamental liberty. The good option changes into a contrary fundamental intention or orientation.

By conversion this free self-actualization hostile to God is freely changed. This is a change of the *person*, and is achieved only by a free self-disposition of the person. "It involves one act of freedom as fundamental decision. Nevertheless, this fundamental decision is not wholly accessible to analytic reflection."[20]

What is often overlooked, however, is the notion of continual conversion. With the use of fundamental freedom, the whole person is converted *yet not wholly so*. This means that the growth process I referred to should be seen as a "continual conversion." Fuchs identifies three forms or dimensions of this: (1) a radical neoconversion when a person substantially deepens his/her option for Christ; (2) continuous verification of one's self-gift by the ongoing integration of the whole reality of our lives into the profound disposition of ourselves; (3) conversion from venial sin.[21]

Bernard Lonergan has beautifully described continual conversion in terms of the *effectiveness* of conversion. Let me cite him at length.

> Religious conversion is being grasped by ultimate concern. It is other-worldly falling in love. It is total and permanent self-surrender without conditions, qualifications, reservations. But it is such surrender, not as an act, by as a dynamic state that is prior to and principle of subsequent acts. It is revealed in retrospect as an undertow of existential consciousness, as a fated acceptance of a vocation to holiness, as perhaps an increasing simplicity and passivity in prayer. It is interpreted differently in the context of different religious traditions. For Christians it is God's love flooding our hearts through the Holy Spirit given to us. It is the gift of grace, and since the days of Augustine, a distinction has been drawn between operative and cooperative grace. Operative grace is the replacement of the heart of stone by a heart of flesh, a replacement beyond the horizon of the heart of stone. Cooperative grace is the heart of flesh becoming effective in good works through human freedom. Operative grace is religious conversion. Cooperative grace is the effectiveness of conversion, the gradual movement towards a full and complete transformation of the whole of one's living and feeling, one's thoughts, words, deeds and omissions.[22]

Lonergan's "gradual movement towards a full and complete transformation" includes all three forms of conversion mentioned by Fuchs.

3. The place of "matter" in moral acts. Traditionally, it was stated that among the requisites for mortal sin was "serious matter." We identified this with a whole host of things, right down to saying Mass without candles and omission of sections of the divine office.

With the notion of fundamental freedom as the heart of the moral act, "matter" (for a serious moral act, whether virtuous or sinful) is that concrete human choice which is *apt to occasion* a self-disposing response. It is what Enda McDonough refers to as a "critical response," one capable of changing a person's basic direction.[23] In yet other words, it is such a serious decision (destructively or constructively) that we must view it as the kind of choice that is capable of engaging core freedom. That is the meaning of the term "apt."

I add the term "occasion" to indicate that the concrete choice is not simply identical with self-disposition, even though this latter will occur only in such choices.

This understanding of "serious matter" is a slight move away from an earlier all too isolated and mechanistic understanding of the term. Furthermore, it relativizes the notion somewhat. That is, if people in general or people in a particular culture do not regard this or that action as particularly significant, such actions will hardly be a vehicle for a serious moral response. This has great significance for the pedagogy of morality. For instance, what is serious matter in the area of Church law (e.g., Mass attendance), sexual morality and other spheres of conduct must bear some relationship to what people perceive as serious. Otherwise, it has become a purely abstract concept with no relationship to human moral responses. One must wonder, for instance, about the meaning, even the accuracy of saying that every act of adolescent masturbation is serious matter.

There is meaning, of course, in such language. It underlines the objectivity of the morally right and wrong. But such objectivity can be pressed to the point of unreality and absurdity.

Let sexuality serve as an example. It is an accepted fact that our sexuality evolves through stages: infantile, latency, adolescent object relationships, more mature love relationships. Sexuality is not present as a univocal reality in the life of an individual. It develops. At various stages it is present in a way only analogous to mature sexuality.[24]

Now because sexuality in its mature form can be a medium of God's call or self-communication (call to the core of the person, serious matter), does it follow that this is true of sexuality in all its states? Is it not possible that just as nature (the person) grows, so does its ability to be the medium of a serious choice? Thus it would seem that a given dimension of nature (sexuality) can move through stages in its ability to elicit serious responses: an amoral reality, various stages of slight morality, grave morality. Is it not humanly wrong and pastorally dangerous to apply the adult model to those who are not adults?

The following citation from Karl Rahner and Herbert Vorgrimler strikes me as being utterly realistic.

> Each phase of life (childhood, youth, etc. and their different characteristics) has its own irreplaceable originality and hence its own role to play: to raise itself to the next phase and to integrate itself there as an abiding element. With this is set before us an eminently religious task, for the individual . . . as well as the educator, and above all for the theologian. The task is to work out the differences which the various phases of life pro-

duce in their existential relationship to Christian truths and to the individual moral goal-commandments . . . A failure to recognize such findings results in speaking to Christians in an unselective, undifferentiated and schematic way. This overburdens them and like ironbound legalism can end in a casting off of religion altogether. As long as deeper insight into these phases of life is lacking, a genuinely understood Christian patience can go a long way to help allow time for the development of the individual—even in the religious sphere.[25]

A good summary of what I have been proposing on the place of "matter" is provided by Franz Böckle.

The essence of sin, then, is turning away from God in unbelief. This turning away is realized and specified in individual human acts, each drawing its material from the manifold world of values where God is rejected in a wrongful turning to creatures. Moral theology concerns itself particularly with this "material." It orders and evaluates it and decides that this or that particular disordered turning to creatures contradicts the will of God and is apt to move man to radical existential decision against God. Whether the total decision is in fact made, we are generally unable to say for certain.[26]

4. *The distinction of sins.* With the wide acceptance of the notion of fundamental freedom into moral theology, theologians have accepted the idea that truly mortal sin is not as frequent a phenomenon as traditional presentations and practice would seem to assume. This should surprise no one. Even without the insights of contemporary psychiatry and psychology, St. Thomas wrote: "Although grace is lost by one act of mortal sin, it is not easily lost; for it is not easy for the possessor of grace to perform such an act because of a contrary inclination."[27]

Furthermore, nearly everyone would agree with Bernard Häring when he says that "I cannot conceive that a child of seven or eight can commit a mortal sin."[28] He extends this to preadolescents. Yet, as they mature, children and adolescents are capable of *some* moral activity. And we know, of course, that they do things that are seriously wrong.

Realizations such as this—and especially the type of freedom required for a truly mortal sin—have led many theologians to question the adequacy of the distinction venial-mortal sin. For the term "venial" suggests to many "not important," "not serious." Actually, so-called "venial" sins can contain greater or lesser degrees of freedom. Furthermore, they can often be concerned with very serious things. This has led some to suggest a threefold division: mortal, serious, venial. In the synod of 1983, several bishops proposed this.

Ladislas Orsy has put this simply and clearly.

Instead of the usual two categories that admitted only venial and mortal sins, we should broaden our horizon to three types of sin: venial, serious, and mortal. No need to change the definition of venial sin. Basically it is the refusal to grow. Serious sin would be the new category. Under it belong many acts that betray evil trends in the heart of man but do not necessarily bring about a radical break with God. They are like failings in a loving family. Mortal sins, on the other hand, are forceful options for evil; they are the conclusion of a process that leads away from God. They can be committed by adults only. Consider a tentative analogy from the New Testament. Peter's denial was serious, but not the conclusion of a deterioration, still less a cooly executed break with his Lord. It was a serious failure through weakness, but yet it remained in a loving context. Judas' betrayal was the completion of a long process of alienation from Jesus, manifested through a cooly executed plot, terminated by a brotherly kiss. To say that the sins of Peter and Judas are in the same category does not make sense.[29]

Orsy goes on to suggest that children need instruction about the possibility of serious faults that can occur within the family, "where there is love without exclusion from family life."

When I first heard the suggestion years ago of this tripartite division of sin, I did not think too much of it. Neither did John Paul II in *Reconciliation and Penance*. After noting that some synodal bishops proposed this division, he noted simply:

But it still remains true that the essential and decisive distinction is between sin which destroys charity, and sin which does not kill the supernatural life; there is no middle way between life and death.[30]

True enough. But perhaps not enough of the truth. There is also a very important difference between "everyday failings" and serious yet not mortally sinful faults. To continue to use "venial" to describe both—especially when venial is taken by the legalistic mind to mean "not important"—could be morally and spiritually misleading, even disastrous.

But we must be very careful and precise here. A tripartite distinction can be very misleading, too, especially when the distinction is said to apply to *sins*. Surely, John Paul II is correct when he says that "there is no middle way between life and death." There are *sins* that destroy charity and those that do not, even though those that do not can involve greater or lesser degrees of freedom, and more serious and less serious matter.

What the distinction aims above all to do is to point out that there can be greater or lesser violations *where the matter is concerned* depending on the context, persons involved etc. We might put it this way: enormous (e.g., homicide, adultery), serious but less than enormous, slight or everyday failings. But to make this a tripartite division of *sins* is misleading, even erroneous. Therefore, I would opt for the traditional twofold division (mortal, venial) while stressing that venial sin can vary in gravity, both as to matter and personal involvement.

5. The meaning of sacramental confession. The analysis of morality as rooted in a basic option which manifests itself in various particular acts helps in understanding the signifying character of confession, as Louis Monden has shown very clearly.[31] Confession and absolution are signs of a much more profound meeting between the sinner and the loving forgiveness of God.

Confession of sins is a sincere signifying of one's being a sinner before God. This sinner confesses a *sign* of what he has done morally: for that is all he/she can do. The full moral quality of the act is not known. Thus the sinner confesses more and often less that he confesses in words. In this context, species and number are important because they clarify a sign. (And, I would add parenthetically, new forms of penance are possible because new *signifying* is possible.) The priest's reception is a human meeting with this sinfulness *as signified*. As Monden rightly notes, both priest and penitent may be wrong in their assessment of confessed sins. But that is quite secondary, for God forgives not what has been confessed but what has been signified through confession.

There are many other questions and pastoral considerations that could be discussed here (e.g., the possibility of conversion or mortal sin in a single act, the relation of mortal sin to sin-unto-death, etc.). I shall not take them up since by and large they are discussed adequately in other literature and since I desire to present only enough here to make some recent misunderstandings and objections intelligible. That is why the chapter title states "Revisited."

Objections and Misunderstandings

When, on January 15, 1976, the Congregation for the Doctrine of the Faith released its "Declaration on Certain Questions concerning Sexual Ethics," I criticized its understanding of the fundamental option.[32] So did Charles Curran.[33] The Congregation describes the opinions of some theologians who see mortal sin only in a formal refusal directly opposed to God's call, and not in particular acts. Curran rightly wondered what theologians hold this position. He knew of none. Nor do I. The idea is a caricature. In other words, the theologians who collaborated in this document did not understand the anthropology of fundamental option. Especially, as Fuchs has recently pointed out, they did not grasp the true depth of the person which is envisaged in this teaching.[34]

Whether these same theological collaborators had a hand in John Paul II's *Reconciliation and Penance* will have to remain a speculative matter. What is not speculative is that the same misunderstanding that appeared in the Congregation's 1976 document reappeared in the apostolic exhortation of 1984. The document states:

> Likewise, care will have to be taken not to reduce mortal sin to an act of "fundamental option"—as is commonly said today—against God, intending thereby an explicit and formal contempt for God or neighbor. For mortal sin exists also when a person knowingly and willingly, for whatever reason, chooses something gravely disordered. In fact, such a choice already includes contempt for the divine law, a rejection of God's love for humanity and the whole of creation: the person turns away from God and loses charity. Thus the fundamental orientation can be radically changed by individual acts.[35]

Several things may be noted here in passing. First, no one who speaks of a fundamental option "intends thereby an explicit and formal contempt for God or neighbor." Such "explicit and formal contempt" (thematic) may or may not proceed from core freedom. But it is not what theologians mean by a fundamental option.

Second, we read that "mortal sin exists also when a person knowingly and willingly ... chooses something gravely disordered." What does "knowingly and willingly" mean? If it refers to *freedom of choice* only, that is one thing, and most theologians would deny the statement. For mortal sin is precisely synonymous with the use of *fundamental freedom*. The turning away from God that results in the loss of charity must be a *self*-disposition, not merely freedom of choice.

It is clear that manualist theology did not understand "full knowledge and full consent" as involving a use of fundamental freedom. It often referred to a "fully deliberate venial sin." If an action is "fully deliberate" (involving both freedom of choice and fundamental freedom), it is, *by definition*, not venial. Thus, strictly speaking, "a fully deliberate venial sin" is a contradiction in terms. It is not for *Reconciliation and Penance*; for it restricts "knowingly and willingly" to "something gravely disordered." That means that one could "knowingly and willingly" choose something not gravely disordered and not commit mortal sin. This is a clear indication that "knowingly and willingly" in *Reconciliation and Penance* does not encompass the depth of freedom understood by those who use the notion of fundamental option.

There is another interesting statement in the apostolic exhortation. It reads:

> Clearly there can occur situations which are very complex and obscure

from a psychological viewpoint, and which have an influence on the sinner's subjective culpability. But from a consideration of the psychological sphere one cannot proceed to the construction of a theological category, which is what the "fundamental option" precisely is, understanding it in such a way that it objectively changes or casts doubt upon the traditional concept of mortal sin.[36]

This is an extremely interesting and provocative statement. I am not at all sure that I understand it. But several things should be noted. First, it is not clear whether *Reconciliation and Penance* wants to deny the notion of fundamental option, or only some deviant understanding of it. I would think the latter, for the document accepts the notion at the very time it qualifies it, as did the Congregation for the Doctrine of the Faith in 1976. But, as I noted above, this qualification is built on a misunderstanding.

Second, there is the relation of a "theological category" (fundamental option) to the "psychological sphere." Surely, the exhortation does not want to deny the relevance of psychological data to theological categories. That would trivialize theology by consigning it to the world of the unreal. What, then, does the statement mean? It is not clear. The notion of transcendental freedom was not "constructed" from a "consideration of the psychological sphere," though it is quite compatible with what we know from modern psychology.[37] Rather, it developed out of consideration of the type of freedom that must be involved when acceptance or rejection of ultimacy, of *God* is being discussed.

Finally, there is reference to an understanding of fundamental option that "objectively changes or casts doubt upon the traditional concept of mortal sin." This gives rise to several questions. For instance, what if the "traditional concept of mortal sin" was excessively mechanized? Excessively objectified? Would there not be need, then, to "cast doubt upon" it? In such a case, is every change for the worse? Can there not be modifications that represent a deepening, an enrichment?

I want now to turn to two writers who have challenged the notion of fundamental freedom. The first is John Finnis. Let Finnis speak for himself.

> Some people imagine that one's moral life is structured by a fundamental option between, say, being reasonable (upright, just . . . etc.) and being unreasonable or selfish or one who refuses the opportunities open to him . . . But there seems to be no evidence that such fundamental options are made. What passes as evidence turns out to be questionably metaphorical: there is talk, for example, of "the depths of the soul, where a man is totally present to himself" and where he performs an act of "fundamental liberty" that is not a choice to do or abstain from doing anything in particular but is "rather the free determination of oneself with

regard to the totality of existence and its direction . . . a fundamental choice between love and selfishness."[38]

Finnis scoffs at this idea. "I can see no sense," he continues, "in talk of a self which (while not doing or considering doing anything in particular) is totally present to itself and which at the same time determines itself by a choice which is not a choice to *do* anything at all."[39]

Finnis' major problem with fundamental freedom is that "whenever we choose anything, we choose it because it seems to offer some good, some intelligible advantage or opportunity." "But," he continues, "what intelligible advantage could anyone see in being selfish rather than loving . . . *apart from the advantage offered by some particular objective, or some particular option for action by him?*" Rather he proposes that any serious and deliberate choice affecting a basic human good is a fundamental option.

Thus in six short paragraphs Finnis dismisses one of the major developments in theological anthropology. His sole references are to my "Notes on Moral Theology" (1967) and to the small book *The Future of Ethics and Moral Theology* (1968).[40] He shows no awareness of the enormous and enormously rich literature of the past twenty years or so.

Perhaps it is understandable, then, why he has misunderstood the notion of fundamental option. Finnis makes any number of mistakes, but two are key. First, he conceives of fundamental freedom being actualized apart from concrete choices ("which at the same time determines itself by a choice which is not a choice to *do* anything at all"). Of course, no one says that. Everyone insists that the self-disposition indicated by the term "fundamental freedom" can occur only in categorical behavior and choice. It is not some grand dramatic choice made in the solitary splendor of the isolated, inner self—with, as Finnis comes close to imagining, appropriate musical accompaniments. To present fundamental freedom as he does makes it unrecognizable to its proponents.

Finnis' second key mistake is simply to assume that human freedom is restricted to *freedom of choice* (object choice, to do this or that). He makes this explicit in any number of ways. For instance, his major objection against the notion of fundamental option is that all human choosing is of a good, "some intelligible advantage or opportunity." Of course, it is—if "human choosing" excludes *self*-disposition. Finnis makes object choice the standard and measure of freedom. He cannot imagine that freedom is an analogous concept, as is sin, as is conversion.

When Finnis provides his own understanding of a fundamental option, it is—sure enough—an *object choice* affecting a basic good. The notion of transcendence—implied in the fact that the self-disposition involved in sin or conversion is with regard to the all-holy, utterly mysterious and transcendent Other—simply disappears in Finnis' concept of "fundamental." The human person is, at it were, out on the table, capable of being examined and dissected. What cannot be seen and understood upon such examination does not exist. Or, as he puts it, "there seems to be no evidence that such fundamental options are made." For Finnis, the only allowable evidence is correspondence with object choice. Carl Jung once wrote: "It is an almost ridiculous prejudice to assume that existence can only be physical."[41] A paraphrase might say: "It is an almost ridiculous prejudice to assume that freedom can be reduced to freedom of choice."

In marked contrast to Finnis' breathtakingly superficial and misinformed treatment of fundamental option is that of Germain Grisez.[42] Grisez (or one of several of his collaborators) is thoroughly familiar with the literature and cites it abundantly. He has several problems with the notion of fundamental option or some explanations of it. The major problem is that current theories do not explain the difference between grave and light matter, "why some matters are likely to subvert a good fundamental option and others are not." As he words it:

> Current theories of fundamental option recognize the need for a principle to distinguish the morally more and less important, as the traditional distinction between grave and light matter has done. They propose fundamental option as this principle. In their view, fundamental option is a disposal of the whole self in reference to God or to morality as such. Hence, the principle proposed to distinguish the more and less important is equivalent to the first principle of morality or embodies it. Yet all deliberate sins are incompatible with the principle thus proposed—all are contrary to moral rectitude and to the perfect goodness of God. The implication is that the difference among immoral acts can only be one of degree, not of kind.[43]

Grisez lists other problems. He believes the notion of fundamental freedom is an unnecessary and unestablished postulate. Furthermore, Grisez locates the nobility of Christian life

> in cooperating consciously with Jesus in the redeeming work of God. Such cooperation depends upon awareness of one's basic commitment of living faith; which shapes one's personal vocation and thereby organizes one's whole life. *If, as many fundamental-option theories require, there were a mysterious and individualistic basic self-orientation, inaccessible to conscious awareness, Christians could hardly undertake consciously to shape their whole lives so as to fulfill their commitment of faith in Jesus.*[44]

Finally, Grisez argues that Trent's teaching about the duty to confess mortal sins would be misleading if the faithful, even after a diligent examination of conscience, could discover none. "This would be the case if a real mortal sin required change in a fundamental option in principle inaccessible to conscious reflection."[45]

As I read Grisez, he is not opposed to the notion of fundamental option as such. Indeed, he positively asserts it. "There is a fundamental option in Christian life, namely, the act of living faith."[46] What he opposes is the notion of fundamental option that explains it in terms of a fundamental freedom unavailable to reflex consciousness. And he opposes it especially for the reasons I have given. Therefore, I want to attempt a response to these objections.

1. The distinction between light and grave matter. It is Grisez's contention that the fundamental option as often presented (i.e., as involving transcendental freedom) needs but really cannot find a principle to distinguish light and grave matter. "They propose fundamental option as this principle."

Let me respond with a citation from St. Thomas. "God is not offended by us except in so far as we act against our own good."[47] Clearly and commonsensically, this "acting against our own good" can be slight or grave. Stealing five cents is different from stealing $100,000. The former does not disrupt human relations and human trust as would the latter. St. Thomas argues that when we make use of our members in a way not intended by nature (i.e., walking on our hands) "the good of man is not greatly injured."[48] Grisez himself refers to "acts which would be disruptive of any human community."[49] By implication there are also wrongful acts that are not disruptive of any human community. There are greater or lesser harms. I agree.

But we should not stop here. When one performs a wrongful act not disruptive of community, one generally does not *perceive* his whole being and orientation to be at stake. There is lacking the type of evaluative knowledge that would provoke fundamental freedom. I say "generally." There is the possibility—one unaccounted for in Grisez—that a religious or priest, for example, could coast along in a prayerless and selfish fashion without ever performing an act traditionally recognized as serious matter. Yet an individual could at some point recognize the pattern, see its direction and outcome, and consciously (in the depths of his person) ratify that direction. That could be mortally sinful.

In sum, recent theologians do not propose the fundamental option as the principle distinguishing light and grave matter, as Grisez seems to believe. That distinction is found in the objective nature of the "action against our own good," whether it is seriously disruptive of personal or communal good or not. Fundamental option enters to explain the existence and gravity of personal *sin*, which cannot simply be equated with the gravity of the matter.

2. The inaccessibility of fundamental choice to conscious awareness. This was Grisez's second objection. He argued that one could not consciously shape one's life in a Christlike way if fundamental freedom were "unavailable to conscious awareness."

The objection rests on a misunderstanding. Those who propose transcendental or core freedom as the basis of serious moral acts do not say that such freedom is "unavailable to conscious awareness."[50] They say it is not *completely* available to *conceptual* awareness. As Rahner puts it:

> For the freedom which finds realization in one individual life as a whole is not a mere sum of moral or immoral free actions, simply following one another in time. It involves one act of freedom as fundamental decision. Nevertheless, this fundamental decision is not *wholly* accessible to analytical reflection.[51]

Perhaps Fuchs is even clearer in affirming the conscious character of such a decision.

> Conversion evidently is the disposition of the whole person—a self-realization. This self-realization is to be achieved through an explicitly conceptualized act realizing some particular good action. Through this act on its deeper level, i.e., at the center of the person, conversion is achieved. Hence, once again, conversion is always on the level where a person is present to himself, where you cannot *fully* reflect on it. Consequently, in conversion *we are conscious that we are converting,* that we are now moving from sin to a love of God above all else. *I cannot love God without knowing it; as subject I am aware and conscious of it* but this love of God is not as an object of reflection. For full reflection is impossible.[52]

Far from being unconscious, this act (of conversion) is, in Rahner's words, "a resolute, radical and radically conscious . . . adoption of Christian life."[53] Indeed, in discussing pastoral care, Rahner insists that "a decision of this kind ought to be carried out as consciously and explicitly as possible."

3. Trent and the duty to confess mortal sins. Grisez believes Trent's mandate would be misleading if mortal sin required a change in a fundamental option "in principle inaccessible to conscious reflection." This objection is answered in the discussion of objection 2. But Fuchs explicitly notes that there can be "moral certitude" in one's assessment of one's fundamental option, through "signs of the disposition of the person not directly ascertainable," therefore "through conjecture," in the words of Thomas.[54]

It seems to me that the entire dynamic of the Spiritual Exercises of St. Ignatius Loyola is to discover one's deepest personal commitments (the movements of grace or the opposite) and to bring these to the greatest level of explicitness and consciousness.

I noted above that Grisez accepts the notion of fundamental option but his understanding of it has little resemblance to its presentation by other authors. He understands it as faith, "as a particular moral act of assent by free choice [that] can be located in conscious reflection."[55] It is a "choice to believe." In Grisez, it is clear that faith as fundamental option has two characteristics: (1) It is a *categorical* act, what Fuchs and others would call an act of "freedom of choice." (2) It is *not charity* or total self-disposition in that sense. It is an act of assent. To support this notion, Grisez presents the following as evidence.

> Not only do many converted as adults remember the precise moment when they made that choice, but many baptized as infants can recall a moment at which they freely committed themselves to their faith in rejecting a temptation to abandon it or freely recommitted themselves after having sinned directly against it.[56]

Such assertions falsely build on and suppose that acts of fundamental freedom are not available to conscious reflection in any way, and that therefore the remembrance of precise moments of conversion would be impossible. I say "falsely suppose" because theologians like Rahner and Fuchs do not say that fundamental freedom is simply unavailable to conscious reflection, as I noted above. Indeed, they are the very ones who want to make such moments as explicit and conscious as possible.

Grisez's presentation of the fundamental option (assent of faith) seems to me to be one-sidedly intellectualistic and separatist. By this latter term I mean that he distinguishes faith too decisively from hope and love. For most contemporary theologians, the response of faith enabled by grace is the *total self-commitment of the person.* It is not merely the kind of cognitive assent that Grisez's (Grisez is, we must remember, a philosopher) whole treatment supposes and emphasizes. Most theologians would endorse Tillich's notion that "faith as ultimate concern is an act of the total personality . . . It is not a movement of a special section or a special function of man's total being."[57] He goes on to point out that "in every act of faith there is a cognitive affirmation, not as the result of an independent process of inquiry but as an *inseparable element in a total act of acceptance and surrender.*" Thus, for Tillich, as well as many Catholic theologians, "love is an element of faith if faith is understood as ultimate concern. Faith implies love . . . "[58]

In summary, then, Grisez and his collaborators use the term "fundamental option" but the underlying anthropology that gave rise to the term has totally disappeared from their usage.

Notes

1. Karl Rahner, *Foundations of Christian Faith* (New York: Seabury, 1978), 93-94.

2. Ronald Modras, "The Implications of Rahner's Anthropology for Fundamental Moral Theology," *Horizons* 12 (1985): 70-90, at 74.

3. Rahner, loc. cit., 94.

4. Loc. cit., 96.

5. Loc. cit., 97.

6. Loc. cit., 101.

7. Loc. cit., 98-99.

8. Modras, loc. cit., 72.

9. Karl Rahner, *Theological Investigations,* III, 113.

10. Modras, loc. cit., 74.

11. An introduction to the literature may be found in the footnotes of Josef Fuchs' *Human Values and Christian Morality* (Dublin: Gill and Macmillan, 1970), 92-111.

12. George Lobo, S.J., *Guide to Christian Living* (Westminster: Christian Classics, 1984), 344.

13. Modras, loc. cit., 86.

14. Josef Fuchs, S.J., *General Moral Theology* (Rome: Gregorian University, 1963). This is my translation of Fuchs' *Theologia Moralis Generalis.*

15. Fuchs as in note 14, at 220.

16. Fuchs, loc. cit., 236.

17. Lobo, loc. cit., 348.

18. Cf. Walter E. Conn, *Conversion* (New York: Alba House, 1978).

19. Charles E. Curran, "Conversion: The Central Moral Message of Jesus," as in *Conversion,* 225-45.

20. Karl Rahner, "Conversion," as in *Conversion,* 203-11, at 204.

21. Josef Fuchs, S.J., "Sin and Conversion," as in *Conversion,* 247-62.

22. Bernard Lonergan, S.J., "Dimensions of Conversion," as in *Conversion,* 15-21. Cf. also Lonergan, *Method in Theology* (New York: Herder and Herder, 1972), 237-43.

23. Enda McDonagh, *Gift and Call* (Dublin: Gill and Macmillan, 1975), 64.

24. Cf. John W. Glaser, "Transition between Grace and Sin: Fresh Perspectives," *Theological Studies* 29 (1968): 260-74.

25. Karl Rahner and Herbert Vorgrimler, "Lebensphasen," in *Kleines theologisches Wörterbuch* (Freiburg, 1961), 220.

26. Franz Böckle, *Fundamental Concepts of Moral Theology* (New York: Paulist, 1968).

27. *De Veritate,* q. 27, a. 1, ad 9.

28. Bernard Häring, *Free and Faithful in Christ* (New York: Seabury, 1978), I, 194.

29. Ladislas Orsy, S.J., "The Sins of Those Little Ones," *America* 129 (1973): 438-41, at 440.

30. John Paul II, *Reconciliation and Penance* (Washington: United States Catholic Conference, 1984), 63.

31. Louis Monden, S.J., *Sin, Liberty and Law* (New York: Sheed & Ward, 1965), 44 ff.

32. Richard A. McCormick, S.J., "Sexual Ethics—An Opinion," *National Catholic Reporter,* 30 January, 1976.

33. Charles E. Curran, "Sexual Ethics: Reaction and Critique," *Linacre Quarterly* 43 (1976): 147-64. Benedict Ashley, O.P., reports that "some theologians" seem to believe that only a "direct act of hatred of God" constitutes mortal sin. Cf. "The Development of Doctrine about Sin, Conversion and the Following of Christ," in *Moral Theology Today* (St. Louis: Pope John XXIII Center, 1984), 52.

34. Josef Fuchs, S.J., *Christian Morality: The Word Becomes Flesh* (Washington: Georgetown University Press, 1987), 30.

35. Loc. cit., 63-64.

36. Loc. cit., 64.

37. "Compatible" is the strongest I would want to be here because, ultimately, we must agree with Paul Tillich that "the truth of faith cannot be confirmed by the latest physical or biological or psychological discoveries—as it cannot be denied by them" (*Dynamics of Faith* [New York: Harper & Row, 1957], 85).

38. John Finnis, *Fundamentals of Ethics* (Washington: Georgetown University Press, 1983), 142.

39. Loc. cit., 143.

40. Chicago: Argus, 1968.

41. C.G. Jung, *Psychology and Religion* (New Haven: Yale University Press, 1938), 11.

42. Germain Grisez, *The Way of the Lord Jesus* (Chicago: Franciscan Herald Press, 1983), vol. 1.

43. Loc. cit., 386.

44. The italics are his; so he apparently regards this as a key point.

45. Loc. cit., 389.

46. Loc. cit., 394.

47. *Summa contra gentiles* 3, 122.

48. Loc. cit. (note 47).

49. Loc. cit., 395.

50. This same mistake is made by Alberto Galli in "Una critica del Padre Fuchs ai documenti del magistero morale," *Sacra Doctrina* 30 (1985): 104-24, at 109. Galli equates "nonthematic" with "unconscious."

51. As in *Conversion,* 204, emphasis mine.

52. As in *Conversion,* 257, emphasis mine.

53. As in *Conversion,* 207.

54. I-II, 112, 5c.

55. Germain Grisez, "Moral Absolutes. A Critique of the Views of Joseph Fuchs," *Anthropos* 1 (1985): 155-201, at 164.

56. Loc. cit., 164.

57. As in note 37, at 4.

58. Ibid., 115.

Chapter 11

Theology in the Public Forum

The title of this chapter is admittedly somewhat imprecise. In a sense, for instance, there is no such thing as *theology* in the public forum. There are only theologians. But even the term "theologians" is sprawling. As soon as one begins reflecting on one's religious faith, theology begins. In this sense, Geraldine Ferraro's deliverances on abortion during the 1984 presidential campaign were a form of theology, at least in so far as Ferraro rooted her convictions in religious faith. So were those of Governor Mario Cuomo.

Whether or not Cuomo should have viewed his convictions about abortion as a religious matter is, of course, inseparable from the matter I want to discuss in this chapter. As a matter of fact, he did and in this sense he was doing theology. When he asked me to evaluate his now famous Notre Dame speech, I wrote to him in part as follows:

> There are only two minor points in your Notre Dame speech that I would like to question. The first touches the usage of the terms "religious beliefs," "religious values." I believe that the Church's position on abortion is not precisely a *religious* one, that is, one dependent on religious (i.e., revelation) sources. It is nourished and supported by religious sources, but is available to human insight and reasoning without such sources.[1]

I may be wrong in that judgment; but I think not. The many episcopal pastorals on abortion over the past twenty or so years talk this way and insist that abortion is not simply a "Catholic problem." That is why I wrote in 1974, summarizing papal and episcopal literature:

> The statements generally note that their teaching is not specifically

Catholic, though the Church has always upheld it and though it can be il-
lumined, enriched and strengthened by theological sources.[2]

More recently, Bishop James W. Malone, president of the National
Conference of Catholic Bishops, issued a statement noting that some
statements of the Catholic Conference are "a direct affirmation of the constant moral teaching of the Catholic Church."[3] He added:

> We seek, however, not only to address Catholics and others who share
> our moral convictions, but to make a religiously informed contribution to
> the public policy debate in our pluralistic society. When we oppose abor-
> tion in that forum, we do so because a fundamental human right is at
> stake—the right to life of the unborn child. When we oppose any such
> deterrence policies as would directly target civilian centers or inflict
> catastrophic damage, we do so because human values would be violated
> in such an attack. When we support civil rights at home and measure
> foreign policy by human rights criteria, we seek to do so in terms all peo-
> ple can grasp and support.[4]

Phrases such as "religiously informed," "fundamental human right,"
"in terms all people can grasp and support" bolster the point that we are not
dealing with a "specifically Catholic" matter, in terms of both concerns and
sources. That reveals the imprecise character of the terms "theology" and
"theologian" in this context. When one repeats "the constant moral teaching of the Catholic Church," one is *not necessarily* appealing to sources that
would make such teaching strictly and narrowly theological, in the sense of
"derived from religious beliefs." Teaching can be Catholic without the
sources of that teaching being exclusively Catholic or religious.

The term "public forum" is also somewhat indefinite. It can refer to
any forum open to public scrutiny and publicly accountable in some way or
other. It can also refer to those bodies that deliberate about and establish
public policy on a given matter. Furthermore, public policy can be policy
for any number of different groups: American Hospital Association, the
District of Columbia, American Fertility Society, Federal Government,
National Hospice Organization. I mention just these because I have been
involved in all of them at one time or another.

Given the vague and sprawling nature of the title to this chapter, I
want to narrow it for my purposes. By "theologian" I understand a professional theologian, and more specifically a Catholic one. That implies the
public acknowledgment of membership in a particular believing community. I want it also to imply openness to, even adherence to, that community's vision, ideals, values, ways of viewing the world and ways of form-
ing one's conscience. "Public forum" will refer here to bodies commissioned to draw up national policy (though the considerations I list will

apply to many other groups). I restrict "public forum" in this way because my experience has been concerned chiefly with such bodies. I testified before the National Commission for the Protection of Human Subjects (1974-1978) as well as The President's Commission for the Study of Ethical Problems in Medicine and Biomedical and Behavioral Research (1980-1983). I was a member of the Ethics Advisory Board of the then Department of Health, Education and Welfare under Joseph A. Califano, Jr., and Patricia Harris.

These national bodies were all concerned with bioethical issues. The list of such issues is almost endless: abortion, definition of death, genetic screening and therapy, treatment of newborns, experimentation on a variety of subjects (fetuses, children, prisoners), access to health care, etc. Two points. First, I shall limit my reflections to a single subject: in vitro fertilization with embryo transfer. This was an issue to which the Ethics Advisory Board devoted a great deal of time. It can function as a prism for other issues. Second, the following reflections will represent a personal statement, how one Catholic theologian perceived his role. The mischievous implication, of course, is a modest suggestion that this is the way it ought to be done. Let me disown that from the outset with the hope that this will be a descriptive account that will allow the issues to be lifted out for examination, and possibly even rebuttal.

As noted, I approach this matter as a Catholic moral theologian. That is not to say that this tradition is the sole proprietor of enlightening perspectives in bioethics, nor that it has not enjoyed its share of distorted perspectives. Nor is it to say that one is or ought to be a slave to papal formulations or conciliar documents. Nor is it to say that one is or ought to be constantly constrained to appeal to explicitly theological warrants for everything one says. Still less is it to suggest that all Catholics will or ought to agree with the analyses attempted or the conclusions drawn.

To say that I approach these questions as a Catholic moral theologian means to suggest above all three things: (1) Religious faith stamps one at a profound and not totally recoverable depth. (2) This stamping affects one's perspectives, analyses, judgments. (3) Analyses and judgments of such a kind are vitally important in our communal deliberation about morality in general and bioethics in particular.

Very few people would disagree with (1). Not all but many would accept (3). Number (2) is the controversial statement, especially in the claim that "stamping . . . influences one's . . . judgments." This statement conjures up a debate that has raged in Catholic circles for the past fifteen years. It is the debate between proponents of an autonomous ethic (e.g., Josef Fuchs, Bruno Schüller, Alfons Auer, Dietmar Mieth, Franz Böckle, Franz Furger, Wilhelm Korff, Charles Curran, Edward Schillebeeckx, J. M. Aubert and others) and proponents of a faith-ethic (*Glaubensethik*, e.g., B.

Häring, Konrad Hilpert, Joseph Ratzinger, Klaus Demmer, Gustav Ermecke, Bernard Stöckle, Johannes Gründel, Hans Urs von Balthasar).

Vincent MacNamara has dissected this debate in rich detail in *Faith and Ethics*.[5] I will not attempt to digest his work here. Unless I am mistaken, MacNamara comes out somewhere in the middle. Repeatedly, he opts for a specifically Christian ethic but the dispositions and judgments involved usually pertain to the more personal aspects of morality. He admits a "considerable" overlap of Christian and secular ethics, which means, of course, that the areas of overlap need not necessarily originate in Christian sources of faith.

At one point MacNamara writes:

> It will also be objected that, if background beliefs are allowed to influence judgment, there is no possibility of public policy: this is one of the fears of the autonomy school. But this is not necessarily so. Even if one can defend the claim for a specific Christian morality, the claim must not be overplayed. There is still considerable overlap between religious and secular ethics. Where there is difference due to different vision, it may, as we shall see, relate to the more personal, rather than to the more public, aspects of morality.[6]

Here MacNamara distinguishes personal and public aspects of morality and sees the religious-secular overlap in the public spheres. I am not sure what he means by this. Graft, for instance, pertains to the personal aspects of morality, but also to the public. So does in vitro fertilization. And so do a host of other actions.

In approaching the debate between autonomists and faith-ethicists—I have been associated with the autonomous school[7]—I believe the distinctions introduced first by Norbert Rigali are very helpful, much more so than the personal-public distinction.[8] MacNamara adverts to Rigali's distinctions but does not really bring them into play.

There are four levels at which the term "ethics" (as it is used in the question: does faith add to one's ethical perceptions?) can be understood where rightness or wrongness of conduct is concerned.

1. First, there is what we might call an *essential* ethic. By this term is meant those norms that are regarded as applicable to all persons, where one's behavior is but an instance of a general, essential moral norm. Here we could use as examples the rightness or wrongness of killing actions, of contracts, of promises and all those actions whose demands are rooted in the dignity of persons.

2. Second, there is an *existential* ethic. This refers to the choice of a good that the individual as individual should realize, the experience of an absolute ethical demand addressed to the individual. Obviously, at this level not all persons of good will can and do arrive at the same ethical

decisions in concrete matters. For instance, an individual might conclude that her/his own moral-spiritual life cannot grow and thrive in government work, hence that this work ought to be abandoned. Or, because of background, inclination, talent, etc. an individual might choose to concentrate time and energy on a particular issue rather than on others.

3. Third, there is *essential Christian* ethics. By this we refer to those ethical decisions a Christian must make precisely because she/he belongs to a community to which the non-Christian does not belong. These are moral demands made upon the Christian *as Christian*. For instance, to regard fellow workers as brothers and sisters in Christ (not just as autonomous, to-be-respected persons), to provide a Christian education for one's children, to belong to a particular worshiping community. These are important ethical decisions that emerge only within the context of a Christian community's understanding of itself in relation to other people. Thus, to the extent that Christianity is a church in the above sense and has preordained structures and symbols, to this extent there can be and must be a distinctively Christian ethic, an essential ethics of Christianity which adds to the ordinary essential ethics of persons as members of the universal human community, the ethics of persons as members of the Church-community.

4. Fourth, there is *existential Christian* ethics—those ethical decisions that the Christian *as individual* must make, e.g., the choice to concentrate on certain political issues not only because these seem best suited to one's talent, but above all because they seem more in accord with gospel perspectives; the choice to enter religious life, to embrace the priesthood.

If these distinctions are kept in mind, much of the cross-talk in this debate could be eliminated. At this point, I want to make five systematic points that represent my own perspective on the question. These points may seem to oversimplify the matter, and in some respects they may actually do so. Nonetheless they still strike me as worthwhile "points to consider."

First, those identified with the autonomous school of thought should be speaking above all about *essential* ethics. It is at this level that we should understand the position that has been quite traditional since the time of Aquinas. The Roman theologians F. Hürth and P. M. Abellan summarized it as follows: "All moral commands of the 'New Law' are also commands of the natural moral law. Christ did not add any single moral prescription of a positive kind to the natural moral law ... That holds also for the command of love ... The ethical demand to love God and one's neighbor for God's sake is a demand of the natural moral law."[9]

Such a statement must be properly understood as involving ethics in the first sense only, *essential* ethics. Thus the question could be worded as follows: does explicit Christian faith add to one's ethical (*essential* ethics) perceptions of obligations new content at the material or concrete level?

This is the more precise form of the question now agitating theologians under a different formulation: sc., is there a specifically Christian ethics? But this latter formulation I judge to be too vague and imprecise, and one that allows discussants to seem to disagree with each other, when in reality they are not addressing the same question.

More concretely, it should be readily granted that revelation and our personal faith do influence ethical decisions at the other three levels (existential, essential Christian, existential Christian). One's choice of issues, for example, and the dispositions she/he brings to these issues can be profoundly affected by one's personal appropriation of revealed truth, by one's prayer life, by one's immersion in the values of poverty, humility, compassion characteristic of the gospel. It is this level and these modalities that are highlighted in most literature when it refers to the "specifically Christian," "the style of life," "a special context."

Second, when the question of Christian specificity is aimed at and limited to the level of essential ethics, it is clear that this limitation does not reduce all of morality or the moral life to such questions. This accusation has been leveled at the autonomy school. Thus MacNamara writes of the autonomy school:

> In spite of the qualifications which it enters, its position amounts in essence to saying that the Christian can ignore everything that comes from Christian faith as he or she faces a moral question.[10]

I do not believe that theologians like Fuchs, Auer, Schüller, Mieth et al. are vulnerable to this accusation ("ignore everything that comes from Christian faith") if the various levels of ethics, as I have listed them, are considered.

Similarly, MacNamara at another point writes: "To reduce morality to the observance of norms or moral theology to the elaboration of norms is greatly to impoverish both."[11] I agree with that statement but I do not believe it is a telling objection against the autonomists if their position is understood as applying to the level of essential morality only. To identify such a level is not to say that it exhausts morality or even that it is the most important aspect of our moral lives.

The third observation is that the ethical questions that are the object of discussion in the public forum (as understood here) will pertain to the level of essential ethics. I can think of no exception here. One has but to review the types of questions discussed by the federal bodies mentioned above.

Fourth, at the level of essential ethics, I would think it remains appropriate to assert with Franz Böckle that there can be no mysterious ethical norms which are simply impervious to human insight. This refers to the inherent intelligibility of such norms. "Human insight" must be understood in its broadest sense. That broad sense would include three clarifications. First, it does not exclude the fact that the individual values that generate a norm can experience a special grounding and ratification in the sources of faith. Quite the contrary. Thus our *faith* that God loves each individual and calls each to salvation deepens our insight into the worth of the individual.

Second, I do not want to exclude the possibility that the insights of a faith-community can factually and historically be the medium of broader societal insight into and acceptance of a prescription at this level. That can happen and it still preserves the notion of the inherent intelligibility of the norm. (What also happens, conversely, is that a religious community can have its corporate eyes opened by a previous societal acceptance of a value the religious community failed to discern. I believe this happened to the Catholic Church with the notion of religious freedom.)

Finally, the broad sense of "human insight and reasoning" suggests that there are factors at work in moral convictions that are reasonable but not always reducible to the clear and distinct ideas that the term "human reason" can mistakenly suggest. When all these factors are combined, they suggest that the term "moral reasoning" is defined most aptly by negation: "reasonable" means not ultimately mysterious.

My fifth systematic point is a citation from Vatican II that lends powerful support to the point being made here. It concerns the autonomy of "earthly affairs."

> If by the autonomy of earthly affairs we mean that created things and societies themselves enjoy their own laws and values which must be gradually deciphered, put to use and regulated by men, then it is entirely right to demand that autonomy. Such is not merely required by modern man but harmonizes also with the will of the Creator. For by the very circumstances of their having been created, all things are endowed with their own stability, truth, goodness, proper laws and order. Man must respect these as he isolates them by the appropriate methods of the individual sciences and arts.[12]

This "autonomy of earthly affairs," their having their "proper laws and order" is the basis for distinguishing an *essentialist* level of ethics from other levels. It also leads to Bishop Malone's assertion that the bishops want to approach the ethical dimensions of contemporary problems "in terms all people can grasp and support."

With this as background, the precise question I want to raise is: how does a moral theologian (in the sense explained) play a role in the formation of public policy? There are probably many identifiable views on this question. Let me mention just a few I have heard.

1. Ethicists, especially religious ethicists, have no place in public policy. Public policy is the precipitate of the pragmatic art of balancing

competing secular interests. This balancing is only confused by ethics. Ethics is, in this sense, an abstract academic exercise.

2. Ethics has very little if anything to contribute to public policy. After all, ethics is concerned with values. There is an impenetrable and intractable pluralism on values and the meaning of the good life. The role of public policy is simply to guarantee the freedom of the individual to do his/her own thing, short, of course, of harming others. The introduction of ethics represents the intrusion of a value system on others, a kind of imposition. A view similar to this is seen in the *New York Times'* response to the Wade-Bolton abortion decisions of 1973. It stated: "Nothing in the Court's approach ought to give affront to persons who oppose all abortion for reasons of religion or individual conviction. They can stand as firmly as ever for those principles, provided they do not seek to impede the freedom of those with an opposite view."[13]

3. In a democracy, public policy is a majority determination, a workable consensus. It is crafted by *discovering* the value system of its constituents, not by *changing* their value systems. Since ethics is a normative discipline, one of its tasks is to identify what is wrong with various value systems. Thus it is unavoidably involved in changing value systems—a task which only complicates and pollutes public policy discussion.

4. There is a place for ethics in public policy, but its place is minimal and prophetic in character. Religious ethics is the ethics of a people, distilled from its story. This story (e.g., the Christian story) is necessarily circumscribed and not shared by all, or even a majority of, members of a religiously pluralistic society. In public policy discussions members of a religious (storied) tradition can only witness to their story, as they should. But they can hardly expect that in its particularism it would contribute substantially to public policy.

5. Public policy and sound morality are identified. If some action is morally wrong, a healthy community should reflect this in its public policy; for public policy has not only a penal dimension but a pedagogical one. In the mouths of the unsophisticated, this attitude frequently translates its outrage with the stark imperative, "There oughta be a law." In this perspective, ethicists not only contribute to public policy; they really are its principal drafters—especially if they agree with one's own moral convictions.

There are probably a number of other views on the relation of moral theology to public policy, and probably a whole spectrum of shadings of the ones suggested here. I disagree with all five of these postures as described here. Different as they are, these attitudes reveal two common denominators: a particular point of view about the nature of ethics, especially religious ethics; a particular point of view about the relation of morality to public policy. I find myself in disagreement with both of these denominators in the described positions. Before turning to in vitro fertilization, it is necessary to give the broad outlines of my own position, for it is that position that constituted the premise of my own participation in public policy discussions.

Morality and public policy. There is some relationship between morality and public policy. The statement that "you cannot and should not legislate morality" is a very dangerous half-truth. As Daniel Callahan has repeatedly observed, we do it all the time. Thus every civilized state has rules about homicide. The only question is : *what* morality ought we to legislate?

Thus I take it for obvious and granted that what is good public policy depends *to some extent* on morality. For example, if fetal life is to be regarded as disposable tissue (the moral evaluation), then clearly abortion ought not be on the penal code at all, except to protect against irresponsible and dangerous tissue-scrapers. If, however, fetal life is to be regarded as human life, then there is the *possibility* that taking such life should be on the penal code and prohibited.

I say "possibility" because morality and public policy are both *related* and *distinct*. In what sense are they related? As follows. Morality includes a concern for the moral rightness and wrongness of human conduct. Public policy has an inherently moral character due to its rootage in existential human ends or goods. The welfare of the community—the proper concern of law—cannot be unrelated to what is judged promotive or destructive to its individual members, to what is therefore morally right and wrong.

However, morality and public policy are distinct because public policy is concerned with the common good, the welfare of the community. Only when individual acts have ascertainable consequences on the maintenance and stability of society (welfare of the community) are they the proper concern of public policy.

What immoral or morally wrongful actions affect the welfare of the community in a way that demands legislation? The famous Wolfenden Report distinguished sin and crime, the private act and its public manifestation. (Parenthetically, the 1973 Wade-Bolton abortion decisions reflect this when they see abortion as a private matter, an exercise of privacy.) Nearly every commentator of my acquaintance views the Wolfenden distinction as inadequate.

Why? Briefly, because all actions that have ascertainable public consequences on the maintenance and stability of society are proper concerns of public policy—whether the actions are private or public, right or wrong, etc. Let duelling be an example. Duelling should not be on the penal code for the simple reason that its legal proscription is unnecessary. There is no need for such a policy. But were duelling a common way of settling disputes—as some have suggested it ought to be for all Texans!—then it ought to be on the penal code. Why? Because it erodes the public level of respect for life in a society, an ascertainable public consequence. The libertarian who defends duelling as a private matter has confused privacy with individualism, and become individualistic in the process. The fact that no person is an island means that even private actions have ripples on his/her shore.

If the private act-public manifestation distinction is an inadequate basis for deciding appropriate matters for public policy, what is the criterion? I believe it is what I shall call "feasibility." This refers to "that quality whereby a proposed course of action is not merely possible but practicable, adaptable, depending on the circumstances, cultural ways, attitudes, traditions of a people, etc. . . . Any proposal of social legislation which is not feasible in terms of the people who are to adopt it is simply not a plan that fits man's nature as concretely experienced."[14]

Another word for feasibility is "possibility." John Courtney Murray, S.J., once put it as follows:

> A moral condemnation regards only the evil itself, in itself. A legal ban on an evil must consider what St. Thomas calls its own "possiblity." That is, will the ban be obeyed, at least by the generality? Is it enforceable against the disobedient? Is it prudent to undertake the enforcement of this or that ban, in view of the possibility of harmful effects in other areas of social life? Is the instrumentality of coercive law a good means for the eradication of this or that social vice? And since a means is not a good means if it fails to work in most cases, what are the lessons of experience in this matter?[15]

It was this test to which Mario Cuomo appealed in his Notre Dame speech. He acknowledged that what is "ideally desirable isn't always feasible." He stated:

> But if the breadth, intensity and sincerity of opposition to church teaching shouldn't be allowed to shape our Catholic morality, it can't help but determine our ability—our realistic, political ability—to translate our Catholic morality into civil law, a law not for the believers who don't need it but for the disbelievers who reject it.[16]

It was on the basis of feasibility that Cuomo concluded:

> I believe that legal interdicting of abortion by either the federal government or the individual states is not a plausible possibility and even if it could be obtained, it wouldn't work. Given present attitudes it would be "Prohibition" revisited, legislating what couldn't be enforced and in the process creating a disrespect for law in general.[17]

One may disagree with Cuomo's political assessment of feasibility in our times. One cannot, however, disagree with his criterion. To legislate what is unfeasible, what would not work, makes political and, eventually, moral nonsense.

For the record, I agree with Cuomo's political judgment if it is restricted to a very prohibitive law, the type of absolute prohibition some pro-lifers seem single-mindedly bent on getting. For this reason I wrote to Governor Cuomo:

> I agree with you when you identify *feasibility* as a key in this question. You state that it is your judgment that a very prohibitive law just would not work in our present circumstances. I agree with that. But I also believe—and I am sure you would agree—that it is one of our tasks to try to change the circumstances so that (as you word it) the "ideally desirable" will become more feasible. That will happen only if we set a magnificent example through witness, a point you make very well. One form, but only one, of that witness is persuasion. Hence I have always felt that there is a middle ground between private conviction vs. public passivity: persuasion. However, at this point the forms of persuasion themselves become an issue. The types of things you are doing as governor speak eloquently for themselves, if only people would look.[18]

In summary, then, as a moral theologian I enter public policy discussion convinced of two things: (1) only those actions with ascertainable effects on the public welfare are apt matter for public policy; (2) public policy should ban only those activities whose legal proscription is feasible or possible as explained. These are my bridges between morality and public policy.

Ideally, it could be argued, where we are concerned with the rights of others, especially the most basic right (to life), the more easily should morality translate into law. And indeed it does, many times. But in some sense the easier the translation, the less necessary the law. In other words, if an easy translation from law to public policy represents the ideal, it also supposes it. *That* we do not always have, especially in an area such as in vitro technology where a central issue is evaluation of early (preimplanted) human life. I will return to this later.

Nature of religious ethics. Under this rubric I want to draw on and apply the considerations mentioned above, especially those that gather around the notion of essentialist ethics. Specifically, many persons regard moral theology—occurring as it does within and out of a religious tradition, a storied community—as inherently particularistic or sectarian. If that is the case and if a country is comprised of various distinct religious communities, it would seem that public policy discussion is stalemated in the standoff of conflicting particularistic stories. In this view, religious ethicians, far from contributing to disciplined public discourse, only complicate it and were better advised to withdraw.

I have no doubt that certain religious ethicists actually fuel this fire by an increasingly isolated sectarian manner of doing ethics. For instance, Stanley Hauerwas, notwithstanding the appropriately corrective aspects of his character-ethics, is judged to be highly sectarian.[19] When he testified before the Ethics Advisory Board in 1979, his remarks were viewed as something of a curiosity and were singularly unpersuasive. Hauerwas might respond that this is the way things ought to be, that when Christian ethics is taken seriously it will appear as folly to the Greeks, etc.

The Catholic tradition from which I come will have no part of such sectarianism. Let a few citations from Vatican II support this point. "Faith throws new light on everything, manifests God's design for man's total vocation, and thus directs the mind to solutions which are *fully human*."[20] Again:

> But only God, who created man to His own image and ransoms him from sin, provides a fully adequate answer to these questions. This He does through what He has revealed in Christ His Son, who became man. Whoever follows after Christ, the perfect man, *becomes himself more of a man*.[21]

The Catholic tradition, in dealing with concrete moral problems, has encapsulated the way faith "directs the mind to solutions" in the phrase "reason informed by faith." We see this reflected in Bishop Malone's phrase "a religiously informed contribution." "Reason informed by faith" is neither reason *replaced* by faith, nor reason *without* faith. It is reason shaped by faith and, in my judgment, this shaping takes the form of perspectives, themes, insights associated with the Christian story, that aid us to construe the world theologically.

Let a single example of such a theme suffice here. The fact that we are (in the Christian story) pilgrims, that Christ has overcome death and lives, that we will also live with Him, yields a general value judgment on the meaning and value of life as we now live it. It can be formulated as follows: life is a basic good but not an absolute one. It is basic because it is the necessary source and condition of every human activity and of all society. It is not absolute because there are higher goods for which life can be sacrificed. Thus in John (15:13): "There is no greater love than this: to lay down one's life for one's friends." Therefore laying down one's life cannot be contrary to the faith or story or meaning of human persons.

This value judgment (theme) has immediate relevance for care of the ill and dying. It issues in a basic attitude or policy: not all means must be used to preserve life. Thus in bioethics, the Catholic tradition has moved between two extremes: medico-moral optimism (which preserves life with all means, at any cost, no matter what its condition) and medico-moral pessimism (which actively kills when life becomes onerous, dysfunctional, boring). Merely technological judgments could fall prey to either of these two traps.

Thus far theology. It yields a value judgment and a general policy or attitude. It provides the framework for subsequent moral reasoning. It tells us that life is a gift with a purpose and destiny. At this point moral reasoning (reason informed by faith) must assume its proper responsibilities to answer questions such as: (1) What means ought to be used, what need not be? (2) What shall we call such means? (3) Who enjoys the prerogative and/or duty of decision making? (4) What is to be done with the now incompetent, the always incompetent? The sources of faith do not, in the Catholic Christian tradition, provide direct answer to these questions.

The influence of general themes (such as the one described) on biomedical ethics was rendered in the phrase "reason informed by faith." Practically, that means that such themes or perspectives do not immediately solve the moral rightfulness or wrongfulness of every individual action. That is the task of moral reason when faced with desperate conflict situations—but moral reason *so informed*. James Gustafson has something similar in mind when he refers to "theological themes" that form the basis of more concrete action guides. He refers to "points of reference to determine conduct."[22]

The question naturally arises: what about those who do not share the story, or even have a different story? If the theological contribution to medical ethics must be derived from a particularistic story, is not that contribution inherently isolating? Those who do not agree with the themes that can be disengaged from the Christian story need only say: "Sorry, I do not share your story." There the conversation stops. Public policy discussion is paralyzed in the irreconcilable standoff of competing stories and world views.

That would be a serious, perhaps insuperable problem if the themes I have disengaged from the Christian story were thought to be mysterious— that is, utterly impervious to human insight without the story. In the Catholic reading of the Christian story, that is not the case. The themes I have lifted out are thought to be inherently intelligible and recommendable—difficult as it might be practically for a sinful people to maintain a sure grasp on these perspectives, without the nourishing support of the story. Thus, for example, the Christian story is not the only cognitive source for the radical sociability of persons, for the immorality of infanticide and abortion, etc., even though historically these insights may be strongly attached to the story. In this epistemological sense, these insights are not specific to Christians. They can be and are shared by others.

Roger Shinn is very close to what I am attempting to formulate when he notes that the ethical awareness given to Christians in Christ "meets some similar intimations or signs of confirmation in wider human experience." Christians believe, as Shinn notes, that the Logos made flesh in Christ is the identical Logos through which the world was created. He concludes: "They (Christians) do not expect the Christian faith and insight to be confirmed by unanimous agreement of all people, even all decent and idealistic people. But they do expect the fundamental Christian motifs to have some persuasiveness in general experience."[23]

Since these insights can be shared by others, I would judge that the Christian warrants are confirmatory rather than originating. "Particular warrants" might be the most accurate and acceptable way of specifying the meaning of "reason informed by faith." If it is, it makes it possible for the Christians to share fully in discussion in the public forum without annexing non-Christians into a story not their own. I emphasize once again that I make these remarks about ethics at the essentialist level.

In summary, the Catholic tradition reasons about its story. In the process it hopes to and claims to disclose surprising and delightful insights about the human condition as such. These insights are not, therefore, eccentric refractions limited in application to a particular historical community. For instance, the sacredness of nascent life is not an insight that applies only to Catholic babies—as if it were wrong to abort Catholic babies, but perfectly all right to do so with Muslim, Protestant or Jewish babies. Quite the contrary. Reasoning about the Christian story makes a bolder claim. It claims to reveal the deeper dimensions of the universally human. Since Christian ethics is the objectification in Jesus Christ of what every person experiences of him/herself in his/her subjectivity, "it does not and cannot add to human ethical self-understanding as such any material content that is, in principle, 'strange' or 'foreign' to man as he exists and experiences himself in this world."[24] However, a person within the Christian community has access to a privileged articulation, in objective form, of this experience of subjectivity. Precisely because the resources of Scripture, dogma and Christian life (the "storied community") are the fullest available objectifications of the common human experience, "the articulation of man's image of his moral good that is possible within historical Christian communities remains privileged in its access to enlarged perspectives on man."[25]

That is a bold claim, and even an arrogant one unless it is clearly remembered that Christian communities have, more frequently than it is comforting to recall, botched the job. But it is a claim entertained by neither Jerusalem nor Athens—but one which offers hope of overcoming the partialities of either alternative.

In summary, then, two assumptions or presupposed positions provide the background for my entry into public discussions. One concerns the nature of concrete religious ethics (not impervious to insight and reasoning;

inherently intelligible and communicable). Another touches on the bridge between morality and public policy (feasibility test). It is against this background that I now turn in in vitro fertilization.

In 1977 the Department of Health, Education and Welfare received an application for support of in vitro fertilization. Current regulations of the HEW prohibit the support of such research until the Ethics Advisory Board has advised the Secretary as to its ethical acceptability. Hence, in 1978 Secretary Joseph Califano asked the EAB to review the procedure as to its "acceptability from an ethical standpoint."

In the process of our deliberations we discussed many aspects of the procedure (scientific, legal, social, ethical). From the ethical perspective some of the key concerns were: (1) the unnaturalness of the procedure, its artificiality; this was seen by some members of the public as "tampering with God's plan," "intruding into the mysterious life process," etc. (2) The status of the embryo in the preimplantation period (what many prefer to call the preembryo). It would be at this stage that zygote loss could occur and that prior (to clinical application) research would occur. (3) The safety (especially for the prospective child) of the procedure. (4) Potentially abusive extensions of the technology.

One of the most difficult problems we faced on the Ethics Advisory Board was that of the status of the embryo. In the early stages of the work of Steptoe and Edwards, there was considerable zygote loss in the attempt to achieve a "uterine fix." Steptoe estimated that they failed to achieve embryo transfer with about 200 fertilized ova before succeeding. Since that time it has become common practice to fertilize more than one ovum because success rates increase when several preembryos are transferred. Sometimes "spare" preembryos are frozen if not needed. And sometimes they are discarded. Furthermore, the physician-researchers on the EAB insisted that prior to clinical application (actual preembryo transfer), research is necessary. Without prior research, clinical application would be irresponsible. Is such research a manipulative violation of preembryonic integrity? Is it compatible with the type of respect everyone believes is due to the preembryo? This was probably the most difficult ethical problem we faced.

There are two facets to this problem that made it especially interesting and fascinating, not to say very delicate. First, there is a long Catholic tradition which regards human life as inviolate from *the moment of conception*. This formulation has been used frequently by popes, bishops and Roman congregations. Second, it is clear that the question of the status of the preimplanted embryo is an *evaluative* question, not a scientific one. Hence, official Catholic statements about the moment of conception must be seen as evaluative judgments. Whether they are sound evaluations will depend on the convergence of evidence.

One cannot, of course, *prove* evaluations one way or another. One can, however, assemble information that *leads to* or *suggests* an evaluation. I believe that there are significant phenomena in the preimplantation period that suggest a different evaluation of human life at this state from that made of an established pregnancy (spontaneous wastage, twinning, recombination of fertilized ova, hydatidiform mole, appearance [or not] of primary organizer, etc.). Therefore I do not believe that respect for nascent life makes the same demands at this stage that it does later. On this basis, I was able to approve—not without fear and trembling—preliminary research aimed at eventual safe embryo transfer. Furthermore, I was able to countenance the loss of embryos in attempted clinical application of in vitro fertilization.

However, I was aware that other conscientious persons would hold a different evaluation. Evaluations cannot be edicted. The Supreme Court in its Wade-Bolton decisions for all practical purposes *edicted* its own evaluation of nascent life as the morality and law of the land. The Ethics Advisory Board, while unanimously sharing the evaluation I describe above as my own, was aware of the fact that it could not simply *decide* an evaluation and make it public policy. That would be to repeat a mistake of the Supreme Court and to short-circuit the feasibility dimension of public policy.

Faced with this problem, the board, at my insistence (a minority report of one would otherwise have been made), inserted language in its report to reflect this problem. We insisted that the phrase "acceptable from an ethical standpoint" be understood as "ethically defensible but still legitimately controverted." We wanted to show that at the heart of the problem was an evaluation and that it was inappropriate for a board such as ours to declare the evaluative dispute finished. This leaves the matter inherently open—for reconsideration, for revision, etc. But it does provide a sufficient basis for departmental decision for the *present*.

I raise the matter of in vitro fertilization because it illustrates my first assumption about the matters of public policy discussion: they are not impervious to human insight. I raise it also because there is likely to be some confusion on this point. For instance, Dr. Donald Chalkley, formerly Director of Institutional Relations Branch, Division of Research Grants at the National Institutes of Health, was reported to me as having said (I quote loosely): "McCormick is good at public policy discussion because he leaves his personal religious convictions out of it." Much as I respect Dr. Chalkley, I must reject that interpretation of what I do—and more importantly, what it is appropriate to do. I definitely bring my ethical and religious convictions to public policy debate. However, these convictions are formed within a tradition that maintains that its more basic perspectival themes only inform reason and do not replace it. Furthermore, such themes are inherently intelligible and recommendable across religious and cultural traditions because they claim to illuminate the universally human. As Edward Schillebeeckx notes: "What speaks to us in Jesus is his being human, and thereby opening up to us the deepest possibilities from our own life, and *in this* God is expressed. The divine revelation as accomplished in Jesus directs us to the mystery of man."[26] Therefore such themes suggest that the task of the ethicist as public policy consultant is one of elucidation, invitation and persuasion (not enforcement). Moreover, even when reason informed by faith has grappled with concrete problems, there remains the task of determining at various times and in varying circumstances the feasibility of translating reasoned conclusions into public policy.

The issue of feasibility is raised by present discussions of in vitro technology. The ethics committee of the American Fertility Society (of which I was a member) drew up ethical policy on reproductive procedures (cf. chapter 19). I have personal ethical objections against the use of third parties in reproductive procedures (e.g. donor sperm, donor eggs, surrogate wombs, etc.). So did the Ethics Advisory Board. It stipulated that if transfer were to follow in vitro fertilization, "embryo transfer will be attempted only with gametes obtained from lawfully married couples."[27]

However, it is a well known fact that A.I.D. (donor insemination) has been widely practiced in this country (as well as elsewhere) for decades. Many people find no problem with it ethically if it is the only option for an otherwise infertile couple and if certain procedural safeguards are met. Indeed, I am a minority of one of the American Fertility Society's ethics committee. That suggests that legal or public policy proscription of donor semen in in vitro procedures is not feasible. It is not enforceable. Even if it were, there is not the will to enforce it since very many people have little problem with it.

In conclusion, then, I suggest that a Christian ethician working in the arena of public policy should be neither a sectarian nor a blind consensus-making accommodationist. Such an ethician should bring his/her convictions to the public table—even those nourished by religious faith—but also his/her sense of realism. For me, that realism means that my moral convictions are inherently intelligible. But it also means the willingness to acknowledge at some point that others may not think so.

Notes

1. Personal communication.

2. Richard A. McCormick, S.J., *Notes on Moral Theology 1965-1980* (Lanham: University Press of America, 1981), 491.

3. *Washington Post*, 19 August, 1984.

4. Loc. cit.

5. Vincent MacNamara, *Faith and Ethics* (Washington: Georgetown University Press, 1985).

6. Loc. cit., 143.

7. MacNamara, loc. cit. , 48.

8. Norbert J. Rigali, S.J., "On Christian Ethics," *Chicago Studies* 10 (1971):227-47.

9. F. Hürth, S.J., P.M. Abellan, S.J., *De principiis, de virtutibus et praeceptis* 1 (Rome: Gregorian University, 1948), 43.

10. MacNamara, loc. cit., 145.

11. Loc. cit., 131.

12. *Documents*, 223-34.

13. *New York Times*, 23 January, 1973.

14. P. Micallef, "Abortion and the Principle of Legislation," *Laval théologique et philosophique* 28 (1972):267-303, at 294.

15. J.C. Murray, S.J., *We Hold These Truths* (New York: Sheed & Ward, 1969), 166-67.

16. Mario Cuomo, "Religious Belief and Public Morality: A Catholic Governor's Perspective," *Notre Dame Journal of Law, Ethics and Public Policy* 1 (1984):13-31.

17. Loc. cit.

18. Pesonal communication.

19. Cf. James M. Gustafson, "A Response to Critics," *Journal of Religious Ethics*, 13 (1985):185-209.

20. *Documents*, 209.

21. *Documents*, 240.

22. James M. Gustafson, *The Contribution of Theology to Medical Ethics* (Milwaukee: Marquette University Press, 1975).

23. Roger Shinn, "Homosexuality: Christian Conviction and Inquiry," *The Same Sex*, ed. R. W. Weltge (Philadelphia: Pilgrim Press, 1969), 51.

24. J.F. Bresnahan, S.J., "Rahner's Christian Ethics," *America* 123 (1970):351-54.

25. Bresnahan, loc. cit.

26. Edward Schillebeeckx, *Christ: The Experience of Jesus as Lord* (New York: Crossroad, 1981), 76.

27. Ethics Advisory Board, "HEW Support of Research Involving Human In Vitro Fertilization and Embryo Transfer: Report and Conclusions," *Federal Register* 35033-58 (18 June 1979).

PART II

Practical and Pastoral Questions

Chapter 12

The Consistent Ethic of Life:
Is There a Historical Soft Underbelly?

I am very grateful to Cardinal Bernardin for having picked the "consistent ethic of life" as the theme around which he has developed so many of his rich presentations since the Gannon and Wade lectures. Cardinal Bernardin has made points that are, in my judgment, utterly essential if the moral vision that is the "consistent ethic of life" is to shape not only an ecclesial consensus, but public policy. For instance, he repeatedly grounds this ethic in the dignity of the human person. He sees it applicable to life-*enhancing* issues as well as life-*preserving* ones. He sees it as cutting across social, medical and sexual ethics. He sees the need to develop it in a way that is systematic but also analogical (covering issues that are different but having common characteristics). In this way he challenges all of us to rise above our one-eyed enthusiasms, to become multi-issue persons while always remembering that the issues are unavoidably interdependent.

My reflections in this chapter are subtitled "Is There a Historical Soft Underbelly?" By this title I mean in no way to undermine the validity of the moral vision captured in the phrase "the consistent ethic of life." I mean only to suggest that, if this vision is to become a true ecclesial and political leaven, it must face squarely factors that are likely to undermine or weaken it. It is precisely because I endorse the general thrust of the "consistent ethic" that I think it worthwhile lifting out in all honesty possible vulnerable points. Cardinal Bernardin certainly agrees; for he has repeatedly emphasized the desirability of vigorous but civil and charitable debate in this area.

I will develop these reflections under two headings: (1) global prescientific convictions; (2) the rule "no direct killing of the innocent."

1. Global Prescientific Convictions

This phrase is, as I noted in chapter 3, borrowed from Karl Rahner.[1] He used it to refer to the unexplained assumptions, mostly cultural in character, that shape our moral perceptions and analyses. He was discussing bad moral arguments and explaining how they often trace to such assumptions. Philip Rieff had something very similar in mind when he referred to "reasons" that form the "unwitting" part of a culture and give shape to its habits, customs, policies and procedures.[2]

I will mention six such "unwitting assumptions"—three with more remote historical roots, three more contemporary in origin—that can easily act as obstacles to the effectiveness of a consistent ethic of life.

1. *Biological giveness as normative.* It is clear that in Cardinal Bernardin's various presentations on the consistent ethics of life, the human person is absolutely central. This is as it should be. Vatican II similarly placed the human person front and center at the very outset of *Gaudium et Spes.* Further on in that document, it stated that "the moral aspect of any procedure . . . must be determined by objective standards which are based on the nature of the person and the person's acts."[3]

But such integral personalism was a conciliar achievement. It did not reflect the way decisive thinkers in the Catholic tradition proceeded. Furthermore, official teaching, notwithstanding the deliverances of Vatican II, still reproduces the basic anthropological assumptions of these decisive thinkers, as I shall try to indicate. That means that in some areas of practical moral instruction, the person is not really decisive. And if that is true, a "consistent ethic of life" rooted in the centrality of the person is somewhat undermined.

Let St. Thomas be the example here.[4] In his treatment of the content of natural law, Thomas pointed out that the order of our tendencies and the goods which are their objects determine the order of the precepts of the natural law. He identified three levels of natural tendencies and three corresponding goods: (1) The tendency to the good corresponding to the nature the person has in common with all beings (self-conservation). (2) The tendency to goods relating to the nature we share with animals. Here that pertains to the natural law which nature teaches to all animals (coitus and care of offspring). (3) The tendency to the good corresponding to the rational nature proper to human beings (knowledge of truth and social life).

All of these tendencies and goods relate to the natural law in the measure that they can be regulated by reason. Formally, natural law is the law of reason. But the content of natural law at the *generic* (no. 2) level is that which is natural, i.e., given in biological nature. The content of the natural law at the *specific* (no. 3) level is that which is proper to human beings as spiritual. At this specific level what is natural is what reason dictates to us. But at the generic level, the task of reason is to discern the demands of the natural order, that order inscribed by God in biological reality. At one level, we *recognize*. At another, we *invent* or discover.

When Thomas applies this to marriage, he sees marriage at two distinct levels: as founded on the *generic* natural law, as founded on the *specific* natural law. With regard to the former, the division of sexes is for procreation; the genital organs have as their proper finality procreation; woman is a helper to man via procreation. At the generic level, marriage is a good for the human race (*matrimonium officium naturae*).

Thus we can understand Thomas' notion of an *actus naturae*. Its demands are inscribed in biological function. Of the goods at this generic level, some pertain to the individual (eating), others to the species (coitus). Just as eating is sinless and good when done in the order and measure required for bodily health, so coitus is sinless and good on condition that it is performed in the manner required by procreation.

In summary, then, for Thomas sexual intercourse is an act of nature relating to the order common to man and animal. Its finality is inscribed by the Creator in its very biological function, and it is procreation. It follows, of course, that couples must pursue procreation and limit themselves to acts necessary to it. Any practice that impedes conception is a sin against nature because it vitiates an *act of nature*. It is clear, therefore, that the order of nature has a very foundational value in Thomas because of a notion of natural law at whose heart the biological function of an act receives the value of a first principle, and one that is absolute because inscribed by God.

As the subsequent centuries unfolded, there were serious modifications made in this notion of *actus naturae*. One thinks of the long (four centuries) controversy on the motive of pleasure, the acceptance of mutual love as a subjective motive (in some textbooks, by ca. 1850), the acceptance of "periodic continence." One can summarize the moments in this development as follows: (1) the couple must positively pursue procreation; (2) intercourse is licit if they do not positively exclude procreation; (3) intercourse is licit even though there is the intent to avoid procreation.[5]

Now enter *Casti Connubii*. It reproduces the Thomistic distinction between the *generic* and *specific* levels of natural law in different words, *strict* and *broad*.

> This mutual interior formation of the partners, this earnest desire of perfecting one another, can be said in a certain very true sense, as the Roman Catechism teaches, to be the primary cause and reason of marriage—if only marriage is taken not strictly as an institution for the proper procreation and rearing of children, but in a broader sense as a sharing, a community, a union of their whole life.[6]

The encyclical condemned contraception, but justified intercourse even when conception is not possible, "providing always that the intrinsic nature of that act is preserved and therefore its proper ordination to the primary end."[7] In summary, *Casti Connubii* reproduced the argumentation of earlier centuries elaborated on the notion of *actus naturae* without showing that the intervening modifications had seriously undermined that notion.

Then, of course, came the Council, with its emphasis on the centrality of the person and its adoption of the themes that had been developed since *Casti Connubii* (responsible parenthood and the personal notion of sexual intercourse—sc., an action whose intrinsic sense is to be an expression of love). This development we may characterize in states: *actus naturae, natura actus, actus personae.*[8]

Against this developmental background *Humanae Vitae* appeared in 1968. It rejected all contraception, appealing to the "inseparable connection, willed by God and unable to be broken by man on his own initiative, between the two meanings of the conjugal act: the unitive meaning and the procreative meaning."[9] The obvious and unavoidable implication of this analysis is that every act of sexual intimacy is somehow procreative.

Many have seen this notion of inseparability and its implication as a linear descendent—indeed, a prolongation—of the analysis of intercourse as an *actus naturae* with a single procreative purpose. They are confirmed in this by the repeated references in the encyclical (as well as in the subsequent document of John Paul II, *Familiaris Consortio*) to "natural laws of fecundity" (no. 11), "biological laws" (no. 10), "natural processes" (no. 16), "the human body and its natural endowments" (no. 17), as if these were normative.

In summary, then, while the basic values of marriage remain constant, the way in which they are explained and protected has gone through an evolutionary process. I agree with Joseph Selling when he notes that "the realization of the procreative end had become totally detached from the individual act of intercourse. Sexual relations were licit on the basis of their connection with expressing conjugal love alone. Consequently, a new set of norms was necessary to evaluate those relations."[10] Yet *Humanae Vitae* represents a continuation of the notion of *actus naturae*, with a decisive finality and significance located in biological facticity. How else explain the inseparability of the unitive and procreative *in every act* when the act is known to be infertile (because of age) or intended to be (as in natural family planning)? In another context, moral theologians John C. Ford, S.J. and Gerald Kelly, S.J. remarked:

> The marriage act has other natural and intrinsic ends in addition to procreation *which are separable* from actual procreation or any intention of actual procreation.[11]

Then came the March 1987 Instruction of the Congregation for the Doctrine of the Faith on reproductive technologies.[12] There are many excellent points in this instruction and they should not be overlooked. But when dealing with procedures between husband and wife (e.g., in vitro fertilization using their own gametes), the Instruction reproduces verbatim the words of *Humanae Vitae* on the inseparability of the unitive and procreative and rejects on this basis any procedure that is a replacement for sexual intercourse.

In detailing these points, I am in no way interested in provoking and continuing arguments about birth regulation. Most theologians have, in one way or another, rejected the perspectives of Franciscus Hürth, S.J.,[13] as St. Thomas *redevivus* or better, *continuatus*.

The rejection of these perspectives is expressed in a variety of ways. For instance, John Wright, S.J. states: "Immediate finality is always subordinate to the total finality of a reasonable human life."[14] The German theologian, Franz Scholz, states: "These natural ends are not the last word. They stand under the judgment of reason, as Thomas clearly emphasized."[15] Finally, English moralist Brendan Soane writes:

> Theologians seem to be generally agreed that the French hierarchy was right when it taught that the integrity of the marriage act is one value which can be balanced by others when couples decide what they should do.[16]

My purpose is not to rehearse such arguments. It is rather metaethical, and indeed with regard to two points: criterion and method. These two points are central in Cardinal Bernardin's presentation of a consistent ethic of life.

As for criterion, let the CDF's instruction on reproductive technologies be the example. It explicitly adopts, and repeatedly, the person as the key criterion in judging reproductive technologies—yet at a key point, when dealing with husband-wife artificial insemination and in vitro fertilization, it adopts as its key criterion the inseparability of the unitive-procreative as found in *Humanae Vitae*. In other words, it fails to *use and apply*, in its practical moral reasoning, the criterion it had explicitly endorsed.

Then there is method. In his stimulating book *An Inconsistent Ethic: Teachings of the American Catholic Bishops*, Kenneth R. Overberg, S.J., has amply documented the difference in approach of the bishops to social and so-called personal morality.[17] In the first instance, their teachings amply reflect the characteristics of sound moral reasoning: biblical, communal, dynamic, personal. Thus the teachings are empirically oriented, tentative, open to change, collaborative, etc.

By contrast, matters of personal morality are deductive, nontentative, authoritarian, noncollaborative, heavily reliant on past statements, etc. I have illustrated this in chapter 8 with a reference to the study in *Civiltà cattolica* that details the development of Catholic social teaching.

In summary, if, as Cardinal Bernardin rightly asserts, a consistent ethic of life cuts across social, medical and sexual ethics, that consistency is threatened—even undermined—when we have different criteria and different methods used in approaching these matters, a kind of double standard. As long as a double standard is perceived by large segments of the community to operate, consistency is gone. This is the first dimension of the soft underbelly that I fear.

2. Sexism. Cardinal Bernardin has rightly insisted that a consistent ethic of life is incompatible with racism or sexism. Yet here again we must deal with the remnants, at the very least, of a "global prescientific conviction"—that women are subordinate. Theology itself, as Jaroslav Pelikan points out, has had its role to play, providing justification for the inferiority of women in the twofold assertion that Eve was created after Adam and was the one responsible for bringing sin into the world.[18] Thus Joseph A. Grassi, after reviewing the New Testament evidence, concludes that "many statements about women are time-bound to the inferior economic, social and religious position of woman in the ancient world, as well as time-bound to an old theology that held this to be the result of woman's sin."[19]

Time-bound or not, sexism persisted in the Church for centuries. The record of this can be read in any number of sources. It is found in some of the great fathers and doctors of the Church. For instance, Thomas attributed the conception of woman to the indisposition of the reproductive materials or to adverse weather conditions. When writing of women and the sacrament of orders, Thomas states:

> Since, therefore, it is not possible in the female sex that any eminence of degree be signified, for a woman is in the state of subjection, she cannot receive the sacrament of orders.[20]

For centuries women were socially defined and limited by male definitions. Women who aspired to something unrelated to men and children were regarded as "masculine." And, of course, once a woman is defined in terms of sex-based stereotypes, the doors of political, economic, educational and ecclesiastical opportunity are closed one by one. Historically, then, we find no consistent ethic of life if such consistency has to include equality of women.

But the *Kinder-Kirche-Küche* syndrome has continued into the present and is still with us, perhaps in the Church more so than in Western social life in general. For two years the U.S. bishops' Committee on Women in Society and in the Church dialogued with representatives of the Women's Ordination Conference.[21] The NCCB representatives acknowledged sexist attitudes as pervasive among members of the Church and its leadership. They noted the discrepancy about the Church's teaching on women as applied in civil society and within the Church itself. The notion of "conplementarity" often practically translates into subordination of women. Finally, they admitted that patriarchy had "deeply and adversely influenced the Church in its attitude toward women as reflected in its laws, theology and ministry." It has now become common to speak of the "sin of sexism," so much so that the usage is found in a recent pastoral letter by Bishops Victor Balke and Raymond Lucker.[22]

To mention such a fact is to deplore it. My only point here is that Catholic history does not provide much support for a consistent ethic of life if that ethic is to include the full dignity of women. And to the extent that this history continues into the present, it constitutes a credibility barrier to that consistency. Pointedly, many women still feel that fetuses fare better, in official Church teaching and practice, than do women.

3. *Theological anthropomorphism.* This may seem a strange "global instinctive conviction" to introduce here. This is especially so since all notions of God are bound to be anthropomorphic to a greater or lesser extent. I have the "greater extent" in mind. In this context, by anthropomorphism I refer to the tendency to conceive God as another categorical actor in the world alongside other human actors. We are familiar with this phenomenon in a variety of ways in modern medicine. There are frequent examples of good people who refuse certain medical treatments for themselves or others on the grounds that "when God decides He will take me." There are also those who continue futile medical interventions to "give God a chance to perform a miracle." I mean in no way to belittle the genuine depth of religious faith and piety in such expressions and actions. I mean only to call attention to the fact that such notions contain two important implications: (1) that God is a direct actor on the human scene, like any other human agent; (2) that our own often anguishing decisional responsibilities can be postponed or transferred by such an approach.

Let Carlo Caffara be an example of this tendency.[23] Caffara attempts to provide theological backing to the *Hauptthese* of *Humanae Vitae*. The human person, he argues, cannot be a direct product of the biological procreative act, but must originate in God's creative intervention. Thus, in the procreative act God and the parents are cooperative. This cooperation supposes that the partners are open to procreation. From this perspective, contraceptive intervention contravenes the rights of God. Those who intervene in this way into God's active presence in the procreative act understand procreation as a merely human undertaking and prevent God "from being God."

Behind this analysis Josef Fuchs sees a concept of God as directly and immediately involved in human causality. According to this understanding of God, conflicts can indeed arise between the two causes at work (God, parents). But Fuchs argues that this notion of God's creative activity is inadequate. Instead, he suggests the analysis originally proposed by Rahner and now widely accepted. God, the transcendental ground of all created reality, is causally active only through created secondary causes. He is not causally active in the way Caffara's analysis supposes.

I introduce this subject here because there are numerous appeals in historical Catholic thought to God's permissions and authorizations where human life is concerned. Thus martyrs who rushed into the flames were often said to be acting by divine inspiration, or permission. More to the point, the direct taking of innocent human life was said to be morally wrong because of a "lack of divine authorization." The implications of this analysis are interesting and far-reaching, as I shall attempt to indicate below.

4. The dominance of independence in Western (especially American) thought.   Here I shall rely on and briefly summarize some remarks of Theodore Minnema. [24] Of June Spencer Churchill's death by suicide, the coroner stated: "She had cancer in all her bones and there was no cure . . . It would seem to me she died before she became totally dependent upon others . . . something she couldn't bear."

"Something she couldn't bear" is a good description of the attitude of many people toward dependence on others. Independence is felt and viewed as essential to human dignity. Dignity highlights the active virtues. There is a pronounced negativity that attaches to the passive virtues (meekness, humility, patience) in our cultural and personal consciousness. Active virtues arise directly from the moral agent whereas the passive virtues are reactions to what is outside the agent.

This personal repugnance to dependence has historical roots in our national self-image. We define ourselves nationally through the "Declaration of Independence" and live it out boisterously every July 4th.

Our abhorrence of dependence is only deepened even as we increasingly practice it, all the while *proclaiming* independence—for example, in matters of energy. Similar things are overtaking our individual social experience. We proclaim our independence, yet act more dependently all the time (sedation, drugs, acclaim from others).

This "unwitting" absolutization of independence has formidable effects on our moral consciousness and judgments, effects that can seriously affect a consistent ethic of life. In this sense, such a consistent ethic cries out for the incorporation of dependence as essential to our notion of human dignity. As a passive virtue, dependence refers to the ability to receive other persons and their achievements into our lives. That which is other than myself is freely accepted. Christians should know this down their pulses. Christ's dignity was manifested supremely in His dependence: "Not my will, but thine be done." The vulnerability of dependence can lead, as every lover knows, to the power of new life. The communal nature of life (cf. the body metaphor of 1 Cor 12) means that others become the completion of my incompletion.

In one specific area, the canonization of independence in our cultural consciousness means that "Death with Dignity" translates as follows: To die in *my way*, at *my time*, by *my hand*. Yet the Anglican Study Group was surely correct when it wrote:

> There is a movement of giving and receiving. At the beginning and at the end of life receiving predominates over and even excludes giving. But the value of human life does not depend only on its capacity to give. Love, *agape*, is the equal and unalterable regard for the value of other human beings independent of their particular characteristics. It extends especially to the helpless and hopeless, to those who have no value in their own eyes and seemingly none for society. Such neighbor-love is costly and sacrificial. It is easily destroyed. In the giver it demands unlimited caring, in the recipient absolute trust. The question must be asked whether the practice of voluntary euthanasia is consistent with the fostering of such care and trust.[25]

5. The interventionist mentality. By this I refer to the bias of a highly technologized culture to believe that interventionist manipulations are genuine (i.e., human) solutions to problems. Thus the solution to the problems of environmental pollution is more technology—the very source of the problem. We face the problem of the elderly by segregating them in leisure worlds where too often they have everything but what they really want, human companionship. We "solve" the problems of agricultural infestation with pesticides—only to learn later that they are carcinogens. We abort to make the problem go away. And on it goes.

I have always felt that a kind of ultimate symbol of this mentality is the judgment of Joseph Fletcher:

> Laboratory reproduction is radically human compared to conception by ordinary heterosexual intercourse. It is willed, chosen, purposed and controlled, and surely these are among the traits that distinguish *Homo sapiens* from others in the animal genus, from the primates down. Coital reproduction is, therefore, less human than laboratory reproduction . . .[26]

This is the ultimate in theology-by-incantation. The surest sign of its inhumanity is that the fun has gone out of things. But if it is a symbol—as I believe it is—then it stands as a sign of deeper cultural attitudes with historical roots in the Enlightenment. Daniel Callahan has adverted to something very similar when he contrasts the power-plasticity model of attitudes toward the world with the sacro-symbiotic model. That these attitudes will affect a consistent ethic of life is beyond question.[27]

6. Individualism. I can be brief here. This is an unexamined attitude that sees the precondition of the human and the moral as being left alone to do one's own thing. People are islands of self-conviction and self-direction. The good life—and eventually the morally right and wrong—is irreducibly pluralistic, because it is tied to individual preferences, which are precisely individual. Morality is eroded into the etiquette of "live and let live." Symbols of this dreary isolationism abound in our actions and language. "I didn't want to get involved" is the response of many onlookers as Kitty Genovese is stabbed to death in Central Park. "I am personally opposed but will not impose my views." "Who am I do judge?" Yes, even "you must follow your own conscience," as if its *formation* occurred in isolation. "He was just doing what he thought best." And on and on, until abortion itself is seen as a "private" matter. What is done in private or done from personal conviction is therefore a "private matter." *Individual* dignity can easily become an *individualism* that threatens the very dignity in which the claims originate.

These then are but six unexamined assumptions of which we must be aware and with which we must contend if a consistent ethic of life is to be more than a fancy phrase.

2. The Rule: "No Direct Killing of the Innocent"

First, let me recall the importance this rule plays in the Bernardin papers, especially the earlier ones. Cardinal Bernardin insists on the inner connection among life issues at the level of principle. Where war and abortion are concerned, Bernardin states that the connection "is based on the principle which prohibits the directly intended taking of innocent human life." This principle, he states, is "at the heart of Catholic teaching on abortion." It also "yields the most stringent, binding and radical conclusion of the pastoral letter [*The Challenge of Peace*]: That directly intended attack on civilian centers is always wrong." Bernardin insists that this principle cannot be successfully sustained on one count and simultaneously eroded elsewhere. "I contend the viability of the principle depends on the consistency of its application." Practically, I suppose that means that if one ever allows a direct abortion, one must entertain the possibility of allowing direct attacks on civilian populations in warfare.

If there is an inner connection between life issues—thus a consistent ethic of life—and if this connection is precisely the consistent application of the principle "no direct taking of innocent human life," then there are problems significant enough to merit the description "soft underbelly." The history of traditional Catholic reflection will point up these problems. I will gather this reflection under three titles: (1) "No direct killing of the innocent" as a principle. (2) The meaning and relevance of "direct." (3) The meaning of "innocent."

1. *"No direct killing of the innocent" as a principle.* I suggest here that the dictum is a concrete rule teleologically narrowed to its present form, rather than a principle. Where did such a qualified and circumscribed description come from? Why is only *direct* killing of an *innocent* person regarded as morally wrong? Why is this not true of *any* killing? The only answer seems to be that in some instances of conflict (e.g., self-defense, warfare) killing can represent the better protection of life itself. Obviously, such a conclusion roots in the weighing of the effects of two alternatives. It traces to a judgment about what would happen if some killing were not allowed.

Bernardin makes this very clear when he states the value that overcame the presumption against killing: "defending the innocent and protecting those values required for decent human existence" (war), "defending the society" (capital punishment). If these values were not at stake, the presumption against taking life would turn into an absolute rule against any intentional killing. Obviously, there is a weighing going on here.

If there is any doubt about this, a study by John R. Connery, S.J., will confirm the point.[29] Connery is at pains to establish in what sense Bernardin's "seamless garment" is truly seamless. A consistent ethic of life does not demand that we forgo all killing. Where self-defense (private or in war) is concerned, Connery sees the aggression as an instance of the presence of sin in the world. How do we cope with sin in these conflict situations? "If taking a life is the only effective means of doing this, however regrettable it may be, it will be acceptable." Connery repeatedly states the unacceptable alternatives: "The alternative would ordinarily be victory for sin and its gradual spread with increasing loss of life." Or again, forbidding self-defense or defense of one's dear ones in the name of a consistent ethic would "make sin automatically victorious. This kind of consistency would constitute a threat to innocent human lives." Briefly, Connery is comparing and weighing alternative outcomes.

Where capital punishment is concerned, Connery argues that the issue is not correctly framed as respecting the life of the criminal or not respecting it. "It is more a choice between the life of the criminal and the lives of possible future victims." Connery grants that there may be other forms of punishment "just as protective of human life." But the protection of human life and public order are the key issues. Connery shows himself a thorough-going teleologist with a twist, so to speak. And that twist is sin. Self-defense and capital punishment are "not just taking human life. They are a response to sin and by definition the only way of coping with sin and its effects. Without such a response, sin would triumph, and even worse, it would spread." What does it mean to say that "sin would spread"? Presumably, Connery refers to a multiplication of human violations, infractions, loss of life, etc.

For Connery, then, exceptions to the prohibition against killing leading to "no *direct* killing of the *innocent*" are the result of a weighing, a calculus. Now if such a calculus is necessarily implied in the sharpening of forbidden killing down to "*direct* killing of the *innocent*," then it seems that this sharpened category itself must be similarly tested—and by the very measure or criterion that shaped the narrowing in the first place (the better protection and service of life itself). In other words "no direct killing of the innocent" is a derivative application of a more formal principle. Such applications do not have the same stability, sweep and exceptionless character as more general principles.

Let me use Franz Scholz's study of St. Thomas to illustrate this point.[30] Scholz begins by noting several problem areas where earlier formulations are undergoing modification. For instance, the formulations of many manualists (e.g., Prummer, Noldin-Schmidt, Zalba, Ermecke) and of the magisterium (e.g., Pius XII) forbade direct abortion even to save the life of the mother. Now, however, we see statements similar to that of J. Stimpfle, Bishop of Augsburg: "He who performs an abortion, except to save the life of the mother, sins gravely and burdens his conscience with the killing of human life."[31]

Here we see a process of adjustment, according to Scholz, a shifting of marginal instances which, logically speaking, converts an exceptionless behavioral norm into a rule of thumb. Is such development justified? Scholz thinks so and cites St. Thomas as his authority.

For Thomas, the order of reason is the criterion of the morally right and wrong. It is reason that constitutes the natural moral law. Thomas distinguished two senses of the natural moral law, the strict (and proper) and the broader. In the strict and proper sense, it refers to those principles of practical reason that are intuitively clear (we must act according to reason, good is to be done and evil avoided, etc.) and to those conclusions that follow from them without discursive reflection. These are exceptionless principles because they correspond to the initial intention of the lawgiver or law. In the broader sense, there are derivative applications of these formal principles (e.g., "Thou shalt not directly kill an innocent human being"). Such concrete norms can suffer exceptions.

Thomas treats the matter when asking about the possibility of dispensations from the Decalogue. An exception is possible only when there is a difference between the original sense of the norm and its verbal formulation. Thomas seems to deny this possibility of "dispensation" in the corpus of the article, but his final word appears to be in the answer to the third objection, where the distinction between original sense and formulation appears.

Scholz takes the fifth Commandment as an example. The formulation of this prohibition forbids the taking of human life. Yet there are the instances of war and capital punishment. How do these make sense if the Decalogue is "beyond dispensation" (exceptionless)? For Thomas, the divine intention is aimed only at the unjust destruction of life ("occisio hominis . . . secundum quod habet rationem indebiti"). Thus the verbal formulation is not precise enough. As imprecise, it must be viewed as conditional, that is, applicable only to those cases in which the taking of human life contradicts the original divine intent. For this reason the formulated norm must be regarded as a rule of thumb where exceptions cannot be excluded.

On this basis, Thomas distinguishes the factual notion (*occisio*, killing) from the value notion (*homicidium*, murder). The only thing that is exceptionless is the sense of the norm that underlies the notion of murder. It is our responsibility to determine what actions fit this category, what do not— a determination that cannot be made a priori.

2. The meaning and relevance of "direct". Here I will but repeat what I have proposed elsewhere about the meaning and relevance of the notion of "direct."

First, the meaning. Traditional interpretations of the notion applied it to all cases of pregnancy-interruption except those where the interruption occurred as a result of a therapeutic procedure with a different description and purpose (e.g., cancerous uterus, ectopic pregnancy). The result of such an understanding was the prohibition of abortion even where the only alternative was the death of both fetus and mother, an understanding we find even in the *Declaration on Procured Abortion* of the Congregation for the Doctrine of the Faith.

Germain Grisez has argued that this is too narrow an understanding. He proposes the following. If the very same act (abortion) is indivisible in its behavioral process (the saving effect does not require a subsequent act), then he regards the abortion (even a craniotomy in earlier days) as indirect and justified.[32] The upshot of this is that the principle that Bernardin sees "at the heart of Catholic teaching on abortion" is not clear in one of its most relevant and urgent terms; for Grisez's understanding is certainly not that of popes and theologians who appealed to the rule.

Second, there is the relevance of the notion of "direct." When the Belgian bishops were discussing this matter, they adverted to the direct-indirect distinction but finally concluded: "The moral principle which ought to govern the intervention can be formulated as follows: since two lives are at stake, one will, while doing everything possible to save both, attempt to save one rather than allow two to perish." If that is the relevant principle—and I believe it is—then it is clear that the direct-indirect distinction is not functioning here—indeed, is redundant. What is functioning, in both Grisez's move and that of the Belgian hierarchy, is the common-sense assessment that we need not stand by and lose two lives (the fetus is doomed anyway) when by intervention one (the mother) can be saved. That constitutes the intervention as the only proportionate response in these tragic circumstances, whether it is direct or not.

The dictum "no *direct* killing of the innocent" implies, of course, the decisive moral character of the principle of double effect in this area. The very relevance of this principle has been challenged in a variety of ways for the past twenty years or so, most especially in the writings of theologians like Peter Knauer, Bruno Schüller, Louis Janssens, et al. If, of course, the rule of double effect turns out to be redundant, then clearly the consistent ethic of life is leaning on a precarious reed to the extent that it supposes this rule.

Let me give but a single example here, that again of Franz Scholz.[33] He approaches the moral relevance of the direct-indirect distinction through the study of two sets of notions: object-circumstances, essential effect and side effect. In the narrow sense of the word, found in the manual tradition, "circumstance" referred to an aspect of human action which was "extra substantiam existens" (Thomas). Thus there grew a gradual association of the notion of circumstances with that of accident. But as Scholz points out, some circumstances affect the very essence or substance of human action. This variability of circumstance is too easily overlooked when the idea is associated with "accident."

Scholz next turns to the notions of accidental and essential effects. Essential effects are those that proceed from the substance or essence of the action. Accidental effects are not produced by the substance but indicate that more than one cause is at work. Now when circumstances pertain to the very essence or object of the act, they cannot be said to produce side effects that are merely accidental. Thus the key question is: Which circumstances must in a given case be counted in the object itself, which remain accidental? This cannot be determined a priori; rather, reality itself is the test. Once we have determined this, we will know which actions are necessarily direct and which indirect.

To illustrate these rather fine speculative points (which he gives in considerable detail), Scholz cites three examples from the manual tradition. (1) An unarmed person meets a deadly enemy intent on killing him. The only escape is by horse and on a road occupied by a group of blind and crippled persons. He rides down the road, killing and maiming many people as he escapes. Traditional manuals argued that the presence of the cripples was accidental; thus there is question of a circumstance that remains external to the object; hence the deaths were side effects. (2) Innocent persons are present in a fortress attacked by the enemy. The attacker says he does not will their deaths, but only the cause (the explosion) and not the effect. (3) A person performs an act *minus rectum* (scandal) and foresees that another will thereby be given an occasion of sin.

Scholz asks: Are we concerned with side effects in these examples, which are patient of indirectness? To the first two he says no; to the third, yes. In the first case, e.g., some authors describe the act as "fleeing down the road on a horse." By what principle do they set the boundaries between object and circumstances? Excluding the blind and the crippled from the object contradicts reality. Scholz sees this as "preprogrammed object." One degrades what is essential to the action to a side effect, but at the cost of a mistaken reading of reality. The presence of the blind and crippled on the road is of such significance that it pertains to the very *object*. And if it does, it is a part of essential effects, not side effects. The escaper cannot say he only "permitted" the deaths. The deaths and injuries are means. "But the means, just as the ends, can only be directly intended." We would have a true side effect if, in the case described, the victims threw themselves at the last moment unavoidably into the path of the horse. In that case the rider could say: "I must permit what I cannot prevent."

As for the second case, the attacking general might say that he wishes only to kill combatants. But actually, the one natural effect of the bombing is destruction—of soldiers, civilians, beasts. His regret at the death of innocents means only that their deaths are not *propter se sed propter aliud* (for themselves but for another reason). Their deaths are a *conditio sine qua non*. But "he who is ready—under the call of the end—to realize the condition *sine qua non*, acts exactly as the one who chooses the appropriate means, scil., directly." Therefore, in these first two cases Scholz does not believe the deaths were indirect. Rather, they are a modified form of direct willing (scil., *secundum quid*, with regrets).

In the third case (scandal), we have a true side effect. He who seeks his goal by an *actio minus recta* (action less proper) does not cause the neighbor's sin. The operation of another cause is necessary for a true side effect. Therefore, the psychology of the will does not demand that the evil effect be willed either as a means or as a *conditio sine qua non*.

Since so many of the conflicts that were previously solved by the direct-indirect distinction really represent qualified forms of direct willing, Scholz moves to another model and espouses it: "direct, yes, but only for a proportionate reason." He sees this as not only more honest to reality but as advantageous. First, the direct confrontation of the will with the evil caused by it "ought to be to the benefit of a weighing of values" (*Guterabwägung*). Second, looking evil in the eye is healthy. It avoids development of an "exoneration mentality" associated with phrases such as "not directly willed," "only permitted." Finally, "the broken human condition with its tragic character appears more starkly. Unavoidably we become conscious of the fact that human beings not only cannot have, hold, and protect all goods simultaneously, but that they can be called, in the service of higher goods, to injure lesser premoral values, and that without any *animus nocendi*."

Here, then, is yet another theologian who argues that every human choice is the resolution of a conflict, that the direct-indirect distinction is only descriptive, and that when actions were legitimated as indirect permitting of evil, actually they were morally direct in most cases, even if in qualified form (*secundum quid*, with regrets: "I would not be prepared to do this unless I had to"). Hence Scholz is arguing that there is no morally significant difference between direct and indirect actions where nonmoral evils are concerned.

3. The meaning of "innocent". Over the centuries the term "innocent" has been used to limit the prohibition against killing to cases where no *material* injustice was involved. Thus the term left open the possibility of killing in cases of aggression (personal or national [war]) and capital punishment.

However, the term "innocent" may seem tighter than it actually is. There is historical reason to believe that it comprised those who had done nothing against the common good and therefore were *unwilling that their lives be taken*.[34]

That it comprised those who *consented to* or *even requested* lethal action against themselves is far from clear. This unclarity, if it is sustainable, means that in two of the most anguishing and controversial contemporary instances, the dictum may be being applied beyond the historical warrants that generated it. I refer to the cases of *voluntary* euthanasia of terminal patients and termination of pregnancy where the medical condition is incompatible with postnatal life—at least for more than an extremely brief period (e.g., anencephaly, Potter's Syndrome). In such situations, one thinks immediately of the axiom *consentienti non fit injuria* (no injustice is done to one who consents) and of the fact that termination of pregnancy is hardly an injury if postnatal life is impossible.

In other words, by conceptualizing permitted killings within the innocent and noninnocent categories (and meaning by this latter the presence of at least material injustice), the tradition by implication limits permitted killing to the *ratio* of injustice. Where such injustice is absent, the individual is "innocent" and taking such a life is injustice. But this overlooks the fact that there can be instances where there is "innocence" (no injustice), yet killing would involve no *injuria*. I am not arguing that killing in the two cases mentioned above is morally right. (That is another matter.) I am arguing only that the classical dictum, tied to the notion of justice as it is, may not be as all-encompassing and far-reaching as making it "bedrock" would suggest.

In summary, then, there are some serious lingering speculative problems with the apparently neat and airtight dictum "No direct killing of the innocent." I want to return to these in a moment.

Here a word about Cardinal Bernardin's earlier (the Seattle lecture) response to reflections similar to the above. His response is two-pronged. First, he refers to them as a "reduction of the prohibition against the intentional killing of the innocent to a status less than an absolute rule" and sees this as wrong.[35] A possible response, especially in light of the foregoing considerations, is: it is one thing to *reduce* a prohibition; it is quite another to *recognize* its possible theoretical limitations, all the while admitting its enormous pedagogical and political utility. If the reflections I have offered have any validity—and I believe they do—they have but a single effect: a reminder that concrete formulations are really derivative applications that do not exempt us from wrestling with marginal and truly exceptional cases. I have argued in chapter 8 that this was Thomas' understanding of derived rules.

The second prong of Cardinal Bernardin's response is that the just war theory's cutting edge is its capacity "to place a double restraint on the use of force" (principle of proportionality, principle of noncombatant immunity). But viewing "no direct killing of the innocent" as a teleologically developed derivative application means that "both principles would become proportional judgments." But that will "weaken the moral strength of the ethic of war."

For continued reflection, I propose the following. First, whether an understanding "weakens" the moral strength of the ethic of war is secondary for ethics. To view an analysis dominantly in terms of its power to prevent or curtail war is to subordinate its analytic validity to a high utilitarian purpose. The rule "no direct killing of the innocent" either admits exceptions or it does not. That is determined not by its greater or lesser power in achieving this or that desirable purpose, but by the warrants available to support it as all-inclusive and exceptionless.

Second, the fact that "no direct killing of the innocent" would be subject to proportional judgment does not mean, as Cardinal Bernardin states, that both principles (proportionality, noncombatant immunity) are the same. We may still maintain two distinct criteria, a "double restraint on the use of force," remembering only that one ("no direct killing of the innocent") is as exceptionless as we can show it to be.

That brings me to some further problematic points that still need attention. They all gather around the notion of "intending death." I will simply mention them here without going into any prolonged discussion. They constitute agenda for the future.

The philosophical unclarity of "intending death." I simply record here a puzzling disagreement among philosophers and theologians. There are those (e.g., Grisez, Ramsey) who argue that *any* morally permissible killing must be indirect. I take that to mean that it must be, in some sense, unintended. On the other hand, there are many theologians in the past who argued that *direct* killing in self-defense, capital punishment and war was permissible. That is, intending death in the action was seen as morally permissible. This means that the very moral relevance of "intending death" is unclear.

The direct intention of lesser (than death) harms, disvalues. There are many instances where theologians, both past and present, would permit direct (intentional) doing of harm. For instance, many (e.g., Gerald Kelly, S.J.) would understand the mutilation of life-saving surgery as directly done, but justifiably so. Many understand deception (falsehood) in a similar manner, as well as the taking of another's property. This suggests that the intention of death can be shown to be morally wrong only on the assumption that causing death is causing an *absolute* disvalue.

The wrongfulness of directly killing the innocent. Catholic tradition argued that intentional killing of the innocent was wrong because of a lack of divine authorization. To the point, Bruno Schüller, S.J.:

> Intentional killing of a human being, if considered only as such, allows of no definite moral appraisal. The executioner cannot dispatch a murderer without intending death as a result of his action. This intention does not impair the rightness of his action. Hence, if intentionally killing an innocent person is said to be invariably wrong, *the wrongness of the action cannot be derived from the intention of causing death, a nonmoral evil.* The proposition: "It is wrong intentionally to kill an innocent person" is a synthetic one. Tradition accounts for the wrongness of this action by the attempt to show that it is not authorized by God.[36]

Thus, if this is the case, then when tradition accepts killing in self-defense and capital punishment, it must see them as "authorized by God." But under examination (of the arguments), that means that certain human goods are otherwise unprotected, and left worse off. By inference, "unauthorized by God" means "unnecessary to such protection."

It is here that the anthropocentrism mentioned above becomes operative. If God's providence and causality in the world are conceived in a highly anthropocentric way, "divine authorization" is likely to be viewed in a highly positive, interventionist way. A less anthropocentric way would view such "authorization" (or its lack) in terms of the struggle of human *reason* as it attempts to serve basic human values in a conflicted world.

The weakness of the moral arguments. Attempts to show the absoluteness of "no direct killing of the innocent" reveal fundamental flaws. Let a recent attempt by Joseph M. Boyle, Jr. be an example here.[37] Boyle attempts to show that the difference between intending and permitting certain disvalues or evils constitutes the difference between good and bad persons. Here is the way he puts it:

In freely choosing to do something, a person determines himself or herself to be a certain kind of person. For example, those who choose, however reluctantly, to end the life an unborn baby by abortion make themselves killers, set themselves against life. But when the evil one brings about is a side effect only, one's self is not defined by the bringing about of the evil. For in this case one does not act for the sake of the evil but despite it; one does not set one's heart on it as one does when one resolves to do it in order to realize some ulterior state of affairs. Thus, in the case of indirect abortion, the child's death is not anything one seeks to realize but is reluctantly accepted and would be avoided if possible.

What is to be said of this? It could be reduced to the following syllogism: One who sets one's heart on evil (abortion) sets himself against life. But where one directly intends an abortion, one sets one's heart on evil. Therefore one who directly intends abortion sets oneself against life. Aside from the loose terminology ("set oneself against life," "set one's heart on evil"), it must be said that this involves a straightforward *petitio principii*. It asserts what is to be proven: that there is a fundamentally different moral attitude involved when abortion is directly intended (in the above sense) and where it is only permitted though fully foreseen.

Furthermore, how does one establish that those who choose to end the life of an unborn baby by abortion always "set themselves against life"? If abortion is the only life-saving, life-serving option available (as in the classical case: allow both to die vs. save the one [mother] that can be saved), one would think that the intervention is just the opposite of "setting oneself against life." Certainly, this is what the Belgian bishops implied when they said that "the moral principle which ought to govern the intervention can be formulated as follows: since two lives are at stake, one will, while doing everything possible to save both, attempt to save one rather than allow two to perish."

From a more positive perspective, Bruno Schüller, S.J., along with Franz Scholz, cited above, have argued that the identical moral attitudes of disapproval are revealed in life-saving abortions whether the effect is permitted or intended as a means: "I would not carry it out if it were possible to achieve the good effect without causing the bad one."[38] This is just about identical with Boyle's "reluctantly accepted and would be avoided if possible." As Schüller words it, "intending a nonmoral evil as a mere means and permitting a nonmoral evil, considered as attitudes of will, differ in degree, not in kind." Put differently, Boyle seems to me to have overlooked the possibility that something can be chosen *in se sed non propter se* (in itself but not for itself). When it is and there is a truly proportionate reason, how does one possibly establish the conclusion that one "sets oneself against life"? One sets oneself against life when one chooses an abortion *propter se*, or, if not *propter se*, then without a truly justifying reason. In either case, we may justifiably infer something resembling an attitude of approval, or Boyle's "setting oneself against life."

I believe it was a similar point that John Langan, S.J., had in mind when he critiqued John Finnis' notion of turning against a basic good as presented in *Natural Law and Natural Rights*. Langan wrote:

> One thing that is not clear in Finnis' approach is the connection between a basic value in its general form and its particular exemplifications. It is hard to see a reason why one should accord overriding importance to any particular instance of sociability or aesthetic experience or play or knowledge or why one should conclude that acting against a particular instance of any of these basic values entails disrespect for the value in general. Certainly the tradition did not draw such a conclusion even with regard to the taking of a particular life.[39]

The difficulty of establishing as absolute the prohibition of direct killing of the innocent is seen in the analysis of suicide. Many moralists, following the third argument of St. Thomas against suicide, argue that as creator, God alone is Lord over life and death. Human beings have only the right to the use of their lives (*dominium utile*), not a dominion over their lives (*dominium in substantiam*). Let me cite Schüller once more on this argument.

> As it stands this argument is no argument at all; it is only an analytic explanation of that which it is meant to establish. If one supposes that a man may not kill himself except in the case of a positive divine permission, it follows that man cannot have dominion over the substance of his life. For such dominion means precisely the power to decide whether an end should be placed to this life or not. Indeed, "not to be able to kill oneself" and "not to have dominion over the substance of one's life" are synonymous phrases. If we may say God alone is Lord over the life and death of a man, this is in the context merely an expression of that which is to be proved.[40]

In conclusion, then, I repeat my agreement with Cardinal Bernardin that, if we are to face successfully the many problems touching human life in our time, we must do so with a moral vision whose key ingredient is consistency. This means that the dignity of the human person must be supported in a variety of settings that cut across social, medical and sexual ethics.

The challenges we face come from two historical sources. The first source is a grouping of "global prescientific convictions" that dim our view of the centrality and dignity of the person and infect our deliberative processes. The second is the problematic character of translating the presumption against taking human life into viable derivative applications for practice. To the extent that these challenges are not acknowledged and squarely faced, the consistent ethic of life will be vulnerable to analytic attack. Briefly, it will retain a soft underbelly.

Notes

1. Karl Rahner, "Uber schlechte Argumentation in der Moral-theologie," in *In Libertatem Vocati Estis*, ed. H. Boelaars and R. Tremblay (Roma: M. Pisani, 1977), 245-57.

2. Philip Rief, *The Triumph of the Therapeutic: Uses of Faith after Freud* (New York: Harper & Row, 1966).

3. "The Church in the Modern World," *Documents of Vatican II*, ed. Walter Abbott, S.J. (New York: America Press, 1966), no. 51, p. 256.

4. For a more detailed analysis, cf. Louis Janssens, *Mariage et fécondité* (Paris: J. Duculot, 1967). *Summa theologica*, Ia IIae, q. 94, art. 2.

5. Janssens, loc. cit., 66-68.

6. AAS 22 (1930), 539-92, at 548.

7. Ibid., 561.

8. Joseph A. Selling, "Moral Teaching, Traditional Teaching and 'Humanae vitae'," *Louvain Studies* 7 (1978):24-44.

9. AAS 60 (1968), 488-89.

10. Cf. note 8.

11. John C. Ford, S.J., and Gerald Kelly, S.J., *Contemporary Moral Theology II: Marriage Questions* (Westminster: Newman, 1963), 405.

12. "Instruction on Respect for Human Life in its Origin and on the Dignity of Procreation" (Vatican City: Vatican Polyglot Press, 1987).

13. F. Hürth, S.J., "La Fécondation artificielle: Sa valeur morale et juridique," *Nouvelle revue théologique* 68 (1946):402-26, at 413.

14. John H. Wright, S.J., "An End to the Birth Control Controversy?" *America* 144 (1981):175-78.

15. Franz Scholz, "Innere, aber nicht absolute Abwegigkeit," *Theologie der Gergenwart* 24 (1981):163-72, at 170.

16. Cf. *Theological Studies* 43 (1982):73, footnote 13.

17. Kenneth R. Overberg, S.J., *An Inconsistent Ethic? Teachings of the American Catholic Bishops* (Lanham, Md.: University Press of America, 1980).

18. Jaroslav Pelikan, Jr., "Eve or Mary: A Test Case in the Development of Doctrine," *Christian Ministry* 2 (1971):21-22.

19. Joseph A. Grassi, "Women's Liberation: The New Testament Perspectives," *Living Light* 8 (1971):22-34.

20. Note 18, In IV Sent. dist. 25, q. 2, art. 1; also of S.T., Suppl., q. 39, art. 1.

21. For a report, cf. "The Future of Women in the Church," *Origins* 12 (1982), 1-9.

22. Victor Balke and Raymond Lucker, "Male and Female God Created Them," *Origins* 11 (1982), 333-38.

23. Cf. Josef Fuchs, S.J., "Das Gottesbild und die Moral innerweltlichen Handelns," *Stimmen der Zeit* 202 (1984):363-82 (chap. 3 of *Christian Morality: The Word Becomes Flesh* [Washington, D.C.: Georgetown University Press, 1987], 28-49).

24. Theodore Minnema, "Human Dignity and Human Dependence," *Calvin Theological Journal* 16 (no. 1, 1981):5-14.

25. *On Dying Well* (London: Church Information Office, Church House, Dean's Yard, SWIP 3NZ, 1975), 1-67, at 22.

26. Joseph Fletcher, "Ethical Aspects of Genetic Controls," *New England Journal of Medicine* 285 (1971), 776-83, at 781.

27. Daniel Callahan, "Living with the New Biology," *Center Magazine* 5 (1972):4-12.

28. *Origins* 13 (1983-84), 491-94.

29. John R. Connery, S.J., "A Seamless Garment in a Sinful World," *America* 151 (1984):5-8.

30. Franz Scholz, "Durch Ethische Grenzsituationen aufgeworfene Normenprobleme," *Theologisch-praktische Quartalschrift* 123 (1975):341-55.

31. From the *Kirchenzeitung für die Diozese Augsburg*, cited in Scholz, p. 342.

32. Germain Grisez, *Abortion: the Myths, the Realities, and the Arguments* (New York: Corpus, 1966).

33. Franz Scholz, "Objekt und Umstände, Wesenswirkungen und Nebeneffekte," in *Christlich glauben und handeln*, ed. Klaus Demmer and Bruno Schüller, S.J. (Dusseldorf: Patmos, 1977), 243-60.

34. Cf. Lisa Cahill, "A 'Natural Law' Reconsideration of Euthanasia," *Linacre Quarterly* 44 (1977):47-63. "In Thomas the adjective 'innocent' refers primarily to the man who is 'righteous' in the sense that he has *not forfeited* his right to life so that he may be deprived of it by lawful authority. To have lost one's innocence means to have injured the common good" (55). Cf. II-II, Q. 64, a. 2, 6.

35. Cf. chapter 8, note 19.

36. Bruno Schüller, S.J., "The Double Effect in Catholic Thought: A Reevaluation," in Richard A. McCormick, S.J., and Paul Ramsey, eds., *Doing Evil to Achieve Good* (Lanham, Md.: University Prss of America, 1985), 165-92, at 189.

37. Joseph M. Boyle, Jr., "The Principle of Double Effect: Good Actions Entangled in Evil," *Moral Theology Today* (St. Louis: Pope John XXIII Center, 1984):243-60.

38. Cf. note 36.

39. John Langan, S.J., in a review of Finnis in *International Philosophical Quarterly* 21 (1981):217 ff.

40. Bruno Schüller, S.J., "Zur Problemalik allgemein verbindlicher ethischer Grundsätze," *Theologie und Philosophie* 45 (1970):1-23.

Chapter 13

Divorce, Remarriage and the Sacraments

On November 27, 1985, at the Extraordinary Synod of Bishops, Archbishop Karl Berg (Salzburg, Austria) called for "more understanding" for divorced and remarried Catholics. He then suggested that "perhaps after a period of penance they might be re-admitted to the sacraments."[1] Archbishop Peter Seiichi Shirayanagi (Tokyo) stated that exclusion from the sacraments of the divorced and irregularly remarried "seemed an especially cruel measure." These people have not lost their faith and a way should be found "so that these people can fully participate in the life of the Church."[2]

A day later, November 28, Archbishop James Martin Hayes (Halifax, Nova Scotia) added his voice to those of the Austrian and Japanese prelates. Hayes said that "I feel a tremendous sympathy for persons in that situation, and I would certainly like to be able to reach out to them and come to their aid."[3] He then added at a press conference: "What I am asking for is that either the Synod or another group look at the theological principles involved there and see if the discipline we now have really interprets in the best way for the good of the persons concerned and especially the rights of the persons concerned."

These synodal interventions were not new. Similar suggestions had been made in the Synod of 1980. Archbishop Derek Worlock (Liverpool) asked: "Is this spirit of repentance and desire for sacramental strength to be forever frustrated?"[4] He noted that his own presynodal consultation would not accept the assertion that concession of the Eucharist to the irregularly remarried would scandalize Catholics and undermine the bond of marriage. At least fifteen of the 162 synodal fathers spoke to the question of finding a way to readmit Catholics in irregular second marriages to the sacraments. Archbishop Henri Legare (Grouard-McLennan, Alberta) went even further. The problem of the divorced-remarried, he said, cannot be faced merely at the pastoral level. The doctrine of marriage must be reexamined. It must be rethought "in a more existentialist and personalist framework" rather than out of an "essentialist philosophy."[5]

The response to such petitions is well known. It is contained in *Familiaris Consortio*, the apostolic exhortation of John Paul II that followed the 1980 synod. The pope, after insisting that the Church should make "untiring efforts to put at their disposal her means of salvation" and should "make sure that they do not consider themselves as separated from the Church," stated:

> However, the Church affirms her practice, which is based upon sacred scripture, of not admitting to eucharistic communion divorced persons who have remarried. They are unable to be admitted thereto from the fact that their state and condition of life objectively contradict that union of love between Christ and the Church which is signified and effected by the Eucharist. Besides this there is another special pastoral reason: If these people were admitted to the Eucharist the faithful would be led into error and confusion regarding the Church's teaching about the indissolubility of marriage.[6]

John Paul II then adverted to the situation of remarrieds who cannot separate. They must "take on themselves the duty to live in complete abstinence, that is, by abstinence from the acts proper to married couples."

In summary, then, the pope reaffirmed the practice of excluding the divorced-remarried from the Eucharist unless they live as brother and sister. He did this on two grounds, one theological, one pastoral. Theologically, the pope argued that there is a contradiction between the state of the divorced-remarried and the union of love between Christ and the Church that is signified in the Eucharist. In other words, their state does not fully symbolize or correspond to what the Eucharist represents and what they profess by receiving it. The effect of this state is that those who are in it can receive the sacrament of penance, "which would open the way to the eucharist" only if they are "sincerely ready to undertake a way of life that is no longer in contradiction to the indissolubility of marriage." The obvious implication of this is that they are in a state of sin. Otherwise, why could they not receive penance? The heart of this "state of sin" is the intention to have sexual intercourse. For once the couple determines to live in complete abstinence, the obstacle to penance (and the Eucharist) disappears.

Pastorally, the pope argued that any other policy would cause scandal by confusing people about the Church's teaching on the permanence of marriage.

An analysis virtually identical to that of the pope was made in 1978 by the International Theological Commission. It stated:

> From the incompatibility of the state of the divorced-remarried with the command and mystery of the risen Lord, there follows the impossibility for these Christians of receiving in the Eucharist the sign of unity with Christ.[7]

This analysis is far from unanimously shared. Indeed, over the past twenty years or so, there has developed a theological consensus that the divorced-remarried may, in individual instances and under certain conditions, receive the sacraments. One of those conditions is *not* that they abstain from sexual relations. An example would be the statement of a committee of the Catholic Theological Society of America published in 1972. After mentioning the traditional demand of a brother-sister relationship, the committee stated:

> It is the judgment of this committee that, whatever may have been its theological justification or benefits in the past, there is serious reason to modify this practice. From the many reasons we have already cited for questioning the validity of marriages that have broken down, and the powerlessness of any human community to judge so many of these cases with certainty, one can reasonably conclude that there are Catholics whose marital status in the eyes of God does not correspond to their legal status. Also, there are unions, e.g., where children are involved, where it may be morally wrong to terminate the relationship. Many will not understand how it will be possible for them to sustain this relationship without marital union. We do not think these people should be excluded from the sacraments or participation in the life of the church. If a couple decides after appropriate consultation, reflection and prayer that they are worthy to receive the sacraments, their judgment should be respected. If the consultation and the judgment that takes shape around it are to be responsible, they must center on the quality of the present union, its fidelity and stability, the state of conscience of the couple, the quality of their Catholic lives in other respects, their acceptance by the community, etc.
>
> Some might object that this solution would be a source of scandal. It would arise from the fact that these people are accepted into full participation in the life of the Church without any change in their present status. But we believe that if the reasons we have given are properly explained to the Catholic people, fear of scandal is unjustified. Moreover, when these couples are leading otherwise responsible and religious lives, their standing in the community is usually very good.[8]

In this chapter I want to respond to Archbishop Hayes' suggestion that we "look at the theological principles involved there and see if the discipline we have really interprets in the best way" the implications of the Church's teaching on indissolubility.

In order to clarify the exact question I want to discuss, I must say a word about both indissolubility and reception of the sacraments. By indissolubility I mean the doctrine *in itself* and its pastoral implications. The term "in itself" is used to distinguish the notion from any prevailing understanding of it at a particular time. In all matters doctrinal and moral we must always distinguish the substance of a teaching from its formulation at a particular point in history. That is a burden I wish the term "indissolubility in itself" to carry. Concretely, one particular understanding of indissolubility might join it inseparably with reception of the Eucharist by the divorced and force the conclusion that the two are but one issue. Another understanding might yield a different conclusion. To make the distinction between substance and formulation where indissolubility is concerned will, of course, clearly require an attempt on my part to state what I believe to be the substance of that teaching. That I hope to do, delicate and even arrogant as the attempt may appear.

As for reception of the Eucharist, I wish to understand a reception warranted by public teaching in the Church, a teaching stated in and controlled by public norms whereby at least some divorced-remarried persons can be allowed to receive the Eucharist. I put the matter this way, not because it is desirable or even tolerable that there be a policy of exceptions of equal valence with the demand of indissolubility, but because I do not wish the main emphasis to fall on internal forum solutions. Why? For two reasons. First, such pastoral solutions include the condition *secluso scandalo* and therefore when properly implemented should not, or at least need not, raise the indissolubility issue. Second, and more importantly, one instance of an internal forum solution is one where a conclusion of nullity of the first marriage is drawn on prudent and probable, but legally nondemonstrable or unacceptable grounds. If this is the case, the issue is not truly indissolubility itself as commonly understood, but the sufficiency of the legal structures whereby it is supported and adjudicated.

Within the confines of the above clarifications, the issue is the following: are those in a second canonically irregular marriage (and one that cannot be regularized and is not patient of an internal forum solution) necessarily to be excluded by policy from the reception of the Eucharist, the necessity being the demand of indissolubility? Or put differently, would the doctrine of indissolubility be intolerably undermined if the Church adopted a policy that allows some divorced-remarried to receive the Eucharist? Or again, can the Church maintain the doctrine of indissolubility and still administer the Eucharist to those whose life-status represents a violation of this teaching? Is not the indissolubility of marriage so fundamental to the gospel and the Church's proclamation of it that violation of indissolubility implies rejection of a substantial element of the gospel (and the faith) and therefore excludes one from celebration of the sacrament that is preeminently the celebration of unity in faith? The question can be worded in many ways, some more tendentious than others. My pleonasms here are simply an attempt to formulate the problem as it might be formulated by a variety of publics.

The answer given to this question *at the level of practice* varies. While this is to be regretted, it must not be the prime focus of concern here. For what is theologically enlightening is not only one's ultimate posture or conclusion, important as it may be, but how one got there. It is just as theologically (and canonically) irresponsible to be warm-hearted but wrong-headed as it is humanly irresponsible to be cold-hearted and right-headed. A healthy pastoral policy can exist only if a warm heart is guided by a right head, in this case one that does not betray the Lord's teaching.

My reflections on this matter will be grouped under three subheadings: (1) the negative response (that is, the position that holds that reception of the Eucharist and indissolubility are a single issue in the sense that the Church cannot allow the Eucharist to the divorced-remarried without fatally undermining her commitment to indissolubility); (2) the affirmative response; (3) personal reflections.

The Negative Response

To the best of my knowledge this position is not widely defined in recent theological writing but is found chiefly in the manualist tradition and episcopal statements. It is therefore what is properly known as "the official doctrine and policy."

First I shall state what I believe is the position itself, then the strongest arguments possible for it. A marriage that is sacramental and consummated is indissoluble by any human authority, be it the partners themselves (internal indissolubility) or any other authority (external indissolubility). In such a marriage, a bond comes into being that is dissolved only with the death of one of the partners. If the marriage factually breaks up and a partner to it remarries, his or her marriage is in violation of this existing bond. Such a partner, should he desire to remain in eucharistic communion with the Church, has but two options. Either he or she must abandon the second marriage, or if he or she cannot (because of obligations that have arisen within it), he or she must live as brother-sister. That is a brief, but, I believe, accurate summary of the official understanding of indissolubility and its pastoral concomitants. It was restated by John Paul II.

There are three major arguments used to support this official position on the Eucharist for the divorced-remarried: the state of sin, imperfect symbolization, scandal. A word about each.

The state of sin. It has been, and indeed still is, common teaching that one may not remain in the free proximate occasion of serious sin. If he does so, he may not be absolved "for the will to remain in the proximate occasion of sin constitutes a new grave sin."[9] Obviously, if the person's very determination indisposes him for the sacrament of penance, it also indisposes him for the Eucharist. This indisposition is acknowledged both in the treatise on the recipient of the sacraments and that covering the duty to deny the sacraments to the unworthy (*indigni*). They are described as those who are indisposed, "that is one who will receive a valid sacrament but not the grace of the sacrament."[10]

Applied to the divorced-remarried, this means that unless they are determined to forego sexual relations, they are in a permanent state of grave sin (a free proximate occasion of the grave sin of adultery). Their sexual relations are adulterous as long as the first spouse is still alive. Therefore, their remaining together without the determination to live as brother-sister is persistence in the free proximate occasion of adultery.

Imperfect symbolization. This argument was used recently by the bishops of the Ivory Coast. They first reject the full impact of the state-of-sin argument as follows: "actually God alone fathoms depths and hearts and knows the real spiritual condition of men. It would be, for priests and members of the community, an error and a sin against fraternal charity to consider those to whom church law forbids access to the sacraments as in a state of grave sin."[11]

Why, then, may the divorced-remarried not receive the sacraments? The bishops note that the sacraments have as one of their purposes "to build up the Body of Christ." Now in the Body of Christ, the divorced-remarried "cannot witness fully to the sanctity of the Church. It is because the sacraments are signs of the People of God for the world that those may not receive them who do not fulfill all the conditions required for being signs of the Church." Others might word the matter differently, but the substance of the argument is the witness or symbolization involved in sacramental participation. This seems to be the heart of the argument found in *Familiaris Consortio* as well as in the analysis of the International Theological Commission.

Obviously, this argument did not originate on the Ivory Coast. It is a concise statement of the rather traditional teaching on the obligation to administer the sacraments. Let me recall the highlights of that teaching. Moralists maintain that the "one who has the care of souls *ex officio* is obligated in justice to administer the sacraments to those under his care who reasonably request them."[12] This means that the faithful have a right to the Eucharist, a right reflected in the duty or office undertaken by the minister. This right is conditioned by the phrase "who reasonably request them" (*rationabiliter petentibus*). When, then, do persons "reasonably request" the sacraments? Genicot answers somewhat broadly: "This is to be judged by the laws of the Church and local customs." I think it can be said that apart from the laws of the Church and local customs, the reasonableness of this request is determined by a combination of the need of the recipient and the inconvenience to the minister.

However, at this point we must, by extrapolation, include among those who do not "reasonably request" the sacraments the so-called "unworthy" (those who would receive validly but not fruitfully). For if the minister ought to deny the sacraments to *indigni*, then clearly they do not request them reasonably. At this point, Josef Fuchs adds an extremely interesting sentence: "Equivalent to the unworthy are those who, though they are personally disposed for a fruitful sacramental reception, are however not to be admitted (to the sacraments) because of the common good of the Church and because of its concern for discipline and unity."[13]

In applying this to heretics and schismatics who are in good faith and personally well disposed, Fuchs notes: "The reason for the prohibition in this instance is different; it is that the sacraments are the greatest signs of ecclesial unity. Therefore, administration of the sacraments would easily promote indifferentism. And as a general rule (per se) unity in the sacraments supposes full unity in faith and discipline."[14]

If Fuch's reasoning were applied to the divorced-remarried, it would go as follows: since the sacraments are the greatest signs of ecclesial unity, their administration to the divorced-remarried would easily undermine that unity by undermining the permanence of marriage. For the permanence of marriage is indisputably a substantial element of the gospel. He who rejects such a substantial element rejects the Christ who demanded it. But since the Church must maintain unity in faith and discipline, she must not tolerate practices that undermine it. This is, in slightly different words, the argument used by the bishops of the Ivory Coast. And it is found widely in the manualist tradition. It is forcefully stated by Karl Lehmann as follows: "As regards admission to the eucharist anyone who publicly and permanently intends to persist in this state publicly contradicts the Lord's commandment by his adulterous life, while by taking part in the Lord's supper he would simultaneously make a profession of faith in Jesus Christ. This intolerable discrepancy publicly displayed contradicts the meaning of faith of the ecclesiastical community, and of the function of the sacraments as symbols effecting what they signify."[15] At this point Lehmann is stating the argument, not necessarily endorsing its every aspect or implication.

Scandal. This is but an explication of an argument already present in the second argument. But it is so important at the practical level that it deserves separate consideration. It would run as follows. If the divorced-remarried are allowed to receive the Eucharist, others will conclude that it is not wrong to remarry after divorce, that the Church is changing her teaching on indissolubility, that the Church is approving second marriages, etc. If this is the way the faithful would respond to a change in pastoral policy, then clearly we are dealing with a policy that would undermine the permanence of marriage by eroding the determination to permanence from the very beginning. Briefly, a policy that would constitute scandal in the theological sense.

The cumulative force of these three arguments is that indissolubility and reception of the Eucharist by the divorced and remarried are not separate or separable issues. A change in traditional pastoral policy will necessarily affect corrosively the teaching on indissolubility. For instance, if the second marriage (while the first spouse still lives) is *not* a "state of sin," then precisely what is wrong with entering this state? And if there is nothing wrong with entering this state, then what is left of the traditional notion of indissolubility? The same deductions could be drawn from the second and third arguments.

The Affirmative Response

Contemporary moral writing that adopts the position that the right to the Eucharist and indissolubility are separate issues usually proceeds in two steps. First, it shows the weakness of the arguments for the opposite position. Second, it attempts to show in a variety of ways that it would be for the overall good of the Church's mission of reconciliation and mercy were she to adopt a policy that allowed some divorced-remarried access to the sacraments. A word should be said about each to fill out the theological state of the question.

The state of sin. Clearly, there are some couples in a second marriage whose situation and personal awareness could be described as "the state of sin." But to say this of all second marriages that are canonically irregular labors under many telling, even fatal weaknesses. The following points are frequently made.

1. Some, even many couples are factually convinced that they are not living in sin, whatever may have been the sinfulness in the rupture of the first marriage and the entry into the second. The second union is stable, characterized by mutual respect and profound affection, and is often supported by deep Christian attitudes in all other spheres of life. To stigmatize this as a "state of sin" is to speak a language with little or no resonance in the couples' experience.

2. The state-of-sin argument identifies in the term "unworthy" the external state of irregularity with a subjective and personal sinful will. Of this facile identification Karl Lehmann says: "This seems to be one of the really problematic presuppositions of the traditional argument."[16]

3. In some instances the Church admits that it is humanly and Chris-

tianly better for the couple in the second marriage to remain together, deepen their Christian life, attend Mass, etc. This all supposes that they are living the life of grace and are not precisely in a state of sin. As a group of French moral theologians state it: "From the moment that the Church recognizes that the Christian divorced-remarrieds have the human and even Christian duty to live their second union, and not to ruin it or to attempt to revive the first marriage, she cannot impute sin to them or consider as a *state* of sin that which in other respects she considers their *state* of life and even as their obligatory *state*."[17]

4. The state-of-sin argument supposes the adequacy of the present tribunal system in determining the status of the first marriage and the freedom (or its absence) to enter the second marriage. It is canon lawyers themselves who have raised the most serious objections to this supposition. It further supposes a sufficiently well-developed theology of marriage to undergird any adjudicative system, a supposition denied widely within the theological community.

5. The official policy which sees the second marriage as a state of sin also sees this state of sin dissolved by a brother-sister relationship. But the notion of such a relationship has its own serious problems. First of all, there are the grave disorders that can arise for a couple and their children from an intimate life together without any sexual expression. *Gaudium et Spes* recognized this when it stated: "But where the intimacy of married life is broken off, it is not rare for its faithfulness to be imperiled and its quality of fruitfulness ruined. For there the upbringing of the children and the courage to accept new ones are both endangered" (no. 51). Second, there is an attitudinal contradiction in the brother-sister relationship. On the one hand, the Church views sexual intimacy as so essential to marriage that the marriage is not consummated without it (and is indeed dissoluble). On the other hand, this intimacy is denied to the divorced-remarried at the very time the Church urges them (at times) to remain together and deepen conjugal affection.[18]

6. The state-of-sin argument seems to suppose that the morality of sex relations depends solely on the recognition of the legal validity of the union. This is not compatible with canon 1161's express admission that even in invalid or irregular unions there can be a true marital intention. If such a marital intention were not present, the notion of a radical sanation (convalidation of marriage without renewal of consent retroactive to the moment the marriage was celebrated) would be empty and erroneous.

7. To view all irregular second marriages as involving a state of sin is to make the rupture of the first marriage an unforgivable sin. The Church does this with no other failures, even though the objective effects of the sins are irreparable (e.g., murder). An analogy may help enlighten what is the true state of sin in this matter. It is not the thief who repents who is in a

state of sin. It is the thief who intends to continue to thieve who is. His very mentality and outlook constitutes a state of sin. Similarly, it is not the divorced-remarried person as such who is in a state of sin; it is the divorced-remarried person who is unrepentant and intends to continue to allow his second union to go stale and to remarry. If we say anything else, we have made divorce and remarriage an unforgivable sin.

8. Finally, and quite tellingly, it is argued that if indissolubility is denied by reintegration of the divorced-remarried, it is because one concludes that no matter what the state of the second union, *the first still exists*. And thus the state of sin. There are two weaknesses to this conclusion. First, this means that indissolubility assures the existence of a reality with no other content, no other properties. This is an unacceptably essentialist notion of marriage and indissolubility. Second, this notion of indissolubility contradicts official pastoral practice. For this practice often and rightly attempts to promote the Christian life of the couple in the second union. The Church demands of the divorced-remarried a life of faith, attendance at Mass, the fulfillment of all familial obligations. This she does not do with bigamists as the term is popularly used. In other words, the Church acts as if the first marriage no longer existed.

In summary, then, the present official pastoral policy which sees the second union in which sexual intimacy occurs as a state of sin is, it is argued, impaled on contradictory attitudes. It both recognizes the marriage, but does not recognize it. It both recognizes the necessity and desirability of a Christian life for these Christians, but does not recognize it completely. The French moral theologians have summarized very trenchantly the difficulties in the state of sin approach.

> The single thing apropos of which one can speak of a personal actual sin, according to presently admitted pastoral practice, would be the practice by the partners of sexual union. This is why it is demanded of them that they abstain from the sacraments. But we have repeatedly underlined the paradoxical character of this demand. On the one hand, what notion of marriage and sexuality underlies the position of the Church that demands of Christians that they honor all the dimensions of their union with the exception of the sexual? On the other hand, what conception of the sacraments and of sexuality leads us to the notion that the sacraments would be compatible with the exercise of all the other dimensions of the conjugal union but that they would not be compatible with that of sexuality?[19]

This type of inconsistency is present in *Familiaris Consortio*. The document (no. 84) states that "the Church will therefore make untiring efforts to put at their [divorced-remarrieds] disposal her means of salvation." Clearly, among the most important "means of salvation" are penance and the Eucharist, the very means denied the divorced-remarried by the same document.

Imperfect symoblization and the Church's concern for unity in faith and discipline. The answer to this second argument is not the denial of the Church's concern for unity in faith and discipline. It is rather that the form this concern takes can and must vary, depending especially on one's assessment of two factors: the nature and purpose of the Church (and of the sacraments as actions of the Church), the cultural and theological perspectives on lack of full integration with the Church. In other words, the argument supposes that administration of the Eucharist to those who do not fulfill all the conditions for complete ecclesial integration will de facto undermine unity in faith and discipline, and thus undermine the common good of the Church. If that were true, the Church would have little choice in her pastoral response to the problem of the divorced-remarried. But whether it is true is highly questionable, so it is argued, and the determination of this revolves especially around the two factors just mentioned.

First, the nature and purpose of the Church. In the mind and words of the Second Vatican Council, the Church has a double finality which it expresses in its sacramental life: the unity of the Church (the only Body of Christ), the indispensable means of grace and salvation.[20] Just as the Church is both the sacrament of unity and the means of salvation, so her ministry has the twofold finality. As Ch. Robert has pointed out, neither of these finalities can be suppressed or forgotten. In concrete circumstances it is necessary to balance and compromise to do justice to both finalities. Concretely, the Church judges it appropriate at times to renounce the fullness of the conditions of integration which she imposes in principle in order to extend more widely the means of grace.

This she does, for example, when dealing with common worship. In the Decree on Ecumenism, the Council stated: "Such worship (common) depends chiefly on two principles: it should signify the unity of the Church; it should provide a sharing in the means of grace. The fact that it should signify unity generally rules out common worship. Yet the gaining of a needed grace sometimes commends it" (no. 8).

This dialectical balance was applied explicitly to common worship with the Eastern churches. In the *Decree on Eastern Catholic Churches* (no. 26), we read:

> Divine Law forbids any common worship (*communicatio in sacris*) which would damage the unity of the Church, or involve formal acceptance of falsehood or the danger of deviation in the faith, of scandal, or of indifferentism. At the same time pastoral experience clearly shows that with respect to our Eastern brethren there should and can be taken into consideration various circumstances affecting individuals, wherein the unity of the Church is not jeopardized nor are intolerable risks involved, but in

which salvation itself and the spiritual profit of souls are urgently at issue.

Hence, in view of the special circumstances of time, place, and personage, the Catholic Church has often adopted and now adopts a milder policy, offering to all the means of salvation and an example of charity among Christians through participation in the sacraments and in other sacred functions and objects.

Therefore, once the Church's double finality is acknowledged, there is nothing *in principle* that prevents sacramental reception by those who are incompletely integrated into the Church. If that is true of our separated brethren, is it not at least as true of those who are not separated but have encountered marital tragedy or failure?

Whether there is *in fact* (in our present circumstances) something that would prevent reception of the sacraments by the divorced-remarried is closely associated with our cultural and theological attitudes toward those who do not fulfill all the conditions for full integration in the Church. For example, whether granting the sacraments to heretics (in good faith) and schismatics will foster indifferentism and undermine unity in the faith, depends heavily on the prevailing attitudes toward heretics and schismatics. If the age is unecumenical and the atmosphere is one of religious distance and warfare between Protestants and Catholics—the Protestant being viewed dominantly in terms of what he/she does *not* share with Catholics—and if the atmosphere is one of suspicion, fear and rather low-grade apologetics, common sharing in the sacraments will more readily lead to practical indifferentism. If, however, our Protestant brethren are viewed as believing, good-faith separated *brothers and sisters* who share in most of our beliefs and with the Spirit's help and guidance are seen as struggling with us toward unity, then the atmosphere is such that common worship could not involve the same degree of danger of indifferentism. This the Council itself clearly concluded.

Something similar can be said of the divorced-remarried. What are the dominant notions or perspectives that lead to the conclusion that unity in faith and discipline would be threatened if some divorced-remarried could receive the sacraments? They are above all two: (1) the "state of sin" view of the second union; (2) the implication that the ability to receive the sacraments is tantamount to full legal good standing—scil., legal approbation of the second marriage with connotation of its validity before God—with the further connotation that marriage is dissoluble, a connotation at odds with the basic Catholic understanding of marriage.

However, if we have changed our perspectives on these two dominant notions, then the danger of undermining unity in faith and discipline by undermining marital permanence is profoundly lessened. Enough has been said about the "state of sin" to indicate that at least theologically the designation is, as a generalization, unsupportable.

The second notion needs attention here. The implication that the ability to receive the Eucharist is tantamount to full legal good standing or integration is an implication with roots in a widespread popular and highly legal mentality. That is, this is how many people think about the sacraments. They believe that going to communion is a sign to themselves and others that their marriage is accepted and approved by the Church. And obviously, they want this to be the case since their own peace of mind is closely connected with such acceptance and approval. In this sense, it is a popular mentality that makes of indissolubility and reception of the Eucharist a single, nonseparable issue.

However, with a fresh awareness in the postconciliar Church that we are a pilgrim Church, in need of sacramental sustenance not because of our sanctity and wholeness but precisely because we are weak, are sinners, are only more or less possessed by the faith we profess, are only more or less led by the charity that defines our being, we are well positioned to distinguish between sacramental nourishment at the Eucharistic table and full legal integration into the Church. Thus, though it can be admitted that the integration of the divorced-remarried into the Church is incomplete (as whose is not in one way or other?), still this incompleteness is, in a pilgrim Church, hardly reason for denial of the sacraments, sacraments of whose need and importance to the Christian life the Church herself has spoken so eloquently.

Briefly, a policy allowing some divorced-remarried to receive the sacraments would undermine unity in faith and discipline only if we (quite unrealistically and inconsistently) demanded full integration into the Church as a condition of sacramental life, and if we (quite legalistically) allowed participation in the sacraments to be viewed as the equivalent of complete integration or legal good standing. Since we need do neither—though some popular mind changing might be called for—the argument from imperfect symbolization is no insuperable obstacle to a change in pastoral policy.

Scandal. The third argument uniting inseparably indissolubility with sacramental reception was scandal. That is, people would conclude that, if the second union is a "state of sin" and the partners may receive the Eucharist, it is not wrong to remarry after divorce, that the Church is abandoning indissolubility, etc.

The answer given to this type of objection in the literature is simple, perhaps too simple. It is insisted that forgiving and reconciling need not and does not imply approval of what has gone before and even now come to be. Thus, the objection centers on the wrong thing. The precept of permanence is what the Church proclaims and what the couple must live. *That* is not affected by forgiving those who have failed, even sinfully, to live that command and find themselves in a position of irregularity as a result. Therefore, if the people are properly prepared for this change of approach by a careful explanation of its meaning, no scandal need occur. Recall again Archbishop Derek Worlock's statement cited earlier that his people would not be scandalized by a modified policy.

Once the weakness of the arguments uniting inseparably indissolubility and reception of the sacraments has been shown, the theologians who espouse the position of separability of issues develop other arguments to show why the Church ought to adopt a cautious policy of readmission to the sacraments. Some of the arguments are the following: (1) The need of the partners for sacramental sustenance. The faith of the individuals is imperiled without such sustenance. (2) Readmission to the sacraments better manifests the reconciling role of the Church in a sinful world and her message that it is always possible to begin anew. (3) An open juridically practicable policy avoids the confusion, abuses and disarray associated with the clandestinity of internal forum approaches. (4) The right to marry is a very fundamental right. Given the many doubts about the extent and meaning of Christ's injunction against divorce and remarriage, and of its practical consequences in the contemporary world, the Church ought to honor the fundamental character of this right by leaving the validity and dissolubility of the first marriage to God and put more emphasis on "the present dispositions and good consequences of those second-marriage Catholics who meet the four conditions I have described."[21]

This is the way the discussion has proceeded. It is fair to say that recent writing (at least of my acquaintance) favors a policy of *cautious* readmission of *some* divorced-remarried to the sacraments. In this sense, it constitutes a rather massive dissent from *Familiaris Consortio*. I say "cautious" because the literature lists in detail the conditions that ought to be observed. I say "some" because I know of no serious literature that proposes a kind of conditionless and indiscriminate "amnesty" for all divorced-remarried persons. In this sense, then, it is true to say that contemporary theological writing moves in the direction of answering the question posed at the beginning of this chapter as follows: indissolubility and the reception of the Eucharist are separate issues, at least in some cases. The reasons for this conclusion are, I believe, substantially the ones I have reported here.

There is one word in the above paragraph I would like to highlight. It is "policy" (as in "favors a policy of cautious readmission," etc.). In *Familiaris Consortio*, John Paul II referred (no. 84) to the exclusion of divorced-remarrieds from the Eucharist as "her [Church's] practice." It seems clear that he is speaking of a *public teaching* about the implications of indissolubility; for he refers to a "state and condition," a "way of life," that is an *objective* contradiction to the indissolubility of marriage. Such a teaching would not, it should be noted, exclude all internal forum solutions, even though it would restrict them to judgments about the validity of the first marriage.

At a key point, *Familiaris Consortio* states:

> Reconciliation in the sacrament of penance, which would open the way to the Eucharist, can only be granted to those who, repenting of having broken the sign of the covenant and of fidelity to Christ, are sincerely ready to undertake a way of life that is no longer in contradiction to the indissolubility of marriage.[22]

Much recent literature has pointed out that the ecclesial juridical status of a marriage cannot simply be identified with the real status of marriage before God. In other words, there will be some couples whose first marriage was invalid but who cannot establish this with the type of evidence required in the tribunal system of the Church. When parties to such a "marriage" remarry, it cannot be said of them that they have "broken the sign of the covenant and of fidelity to Christ" nor that their second marriage is "in contradiction to the indissolubility of marriage." In this sense, they are not indisposed for penance and the Eucharist. The "practice" reaffirmed by *Familiaris Consortio* does not, indeed cannot, exclude this possibility, unless it assumes the perfect adequacy of the tribunal system to determine the real status of the first marriage. Such an assumption is clearly unwarranted.

When, therefore, recent literature speaks of a "*policy of cautious* readmission of *some* divorced-remarried to the sacraments," it should not be read as referring to internal forum solutions of the kind mentioned. Rather it is discussing the consistency and persuasiveness of the type of analysis found in *Familiaris Consortio*. This analysis is directed toward those in a second marriage whose first marriage was clearly valid. The nature of the papal argument indicates this (i.e., indisposed for penance). It is this analysis which is appealed to to found a practice, i.e., a public policy. It is such a teaching and subsequent policy that is questioned in the theological literature.

Some might want to keep the papal teaching in place and "adapt" it in pastoral practice. But I believe this is not possible. For the very nature of John Paul II's analysis makes adaptation impossible. He has equivalently turned a prima facie duty (to refrain from the Eucharist) into an *actual and absolute one*.

Personal Reflections

This chapter began with the threat that it would conclude with some personal reflections. Let me now make good that threat. I believe that indissolubility and reception of the sacraments by the divorced-remarried are separable issues. That is, a practicable public policy of admission of some divorced-remarried persons to the sacraments need not constitute a challenge to the teaching on indissolubility of marriage, and thereby weaken the Church's unity in faith and discipline.

I use the words "separable" designedly. For at present, at the popular level and in the public mind, so to speak, they are possibly not separate issues. What does this mean? It means that for many decades, even centuries, the Church had interpreted the indissolubility of marriage in a particular way and drawn certain consequences from it with regard to pastoral policy. This has had the effect of inculcating a mentality in the faithful, a mentality that views indissolubility as open to but one pastoral policy where the divorced-remarried are concerned. Change the pastoral policy and you have changed or revoked the teaching. I may be wrong in this assessment of public attitudes, but if this is actually the popular understanding of things, then obviously a change in policy will indeed harm the common good of the Church by seeming to deny or weaken one of its substantial teachings. Therefore, some readjustment of perspectives is called for, first theologically, then at more popular levels, before indissolubility and reception of the sacraments by the divorced-remarried can become actually *separate* issues at the practical level.

What is this adjustment? In other words, what is the basic theological justification for saying that indissolubility and reception of the sacraments by divorced-remarried are separable issues? I believe it lies in the understanding of indissolubility. For many centuries marriage and its indissolubility were understood in highly "essentialist" terms, to use the wording of Archbishop Henri Legare. When a marriage was sacramental and consummated, a bond (*vinculum*) was said to come into existence which no human power, neither the pope (extrinsic indissolubility) nor the marriage partners themselves (intrinsic indissolubility), could untie. Thus, one form of pastoral accommodation for marital distress was "invalidation of the bond." Once indissolubility is conceived in this way, it seems to dictate inexorably certain practical conclusions—the "state of sin" being one of them.

But should indissolubility be conceived in this way? Or better, is this the only way indissolubility can be conceived if we are to to be true to the Lord's command? (Here I refer back to my suggestion that we talk of indissolubility in itself.) I think not. I would like to suggest that indissolubility ought to be thought of above all and primarily as an absolute moral precept, a *moral ought* inherent in the marriage union. Because marriage represents the most intimate union of man and woman and is inseparably tied to the procreation and education of children, it ought to be one and permanent. That is, from the very beginning there is a most serious obligation upon the couple to support and strengthen this marriage. They are absolutely obliged not to let the marriage fall apart and die. This is particularly binding on those who have made their marriage a sacrament to the world because they have undertaken a true ministry to the world: to mirror Christ's love for and fidelity to his Church. The moral ought of which I speak, in its imposing urgency, is rooted in faith in the redemption. With Christ's redeeming grace we know we can do what might appear to be impossible to sinful persons.

Indissolubility as a moral ought implies two things: (1) the couple must strengthen and support their union and not allow it to die; (2) when the relationship has fallen apart and separation occurs, they must resuscitate it. A too quick conclusion that the marriage is dead is itself a violation of this ought, just as a premature pronouncement of death in a heart donor is a violation of his life.

If indissolubility is thought of in this way, then when a marriage irretrievably breaks down it can be said that at least one of the partners (whether through weakness or sinfulness can be left, indeed must be left, to God's merciful understanding) has failed to live up to the precept of indissolubility. What ought not be has come to be. A serious disvalue, both personal and social, has occurred.

But when a marriage is truly dead, then it seems meaningless to speak of the moral ought of not letting the marriage die. If indissolubility is conceived in highly essentialist and juridical fashion, the unbreakable bond (*vinculum*) continues, and subsequent remarriage is in violation of this *vinculum*, is an objective state of sin, etc.

What I am suggesting, therefore, is that it may be quite possible to conceive of the permanence of marriage in a way compatible with Christ's command without viewing it in terms of a continuing moral and legal bond (*vinculum*). And if this *vinculum* is not present, then the basic reason preventing reception of the sacraments disappears. Another way of wording this would be the following: the indissolubility of sacramental and consummated marriage prevents the institutional possibility of another *sacramental* marriage, but not of another nonsacramental marriage. This seems to be the direction of the Church's pastoral practice when she advises some couples to stay together rather than break up the second union. But her recognition of this second union is incomplete and inconsistent, as noted. To circumvent this inconsistency the Church would have to abandon her teaching that every true marriage between the baptized is thereby a sacrament.

If this notion of indissolubility is viable, then it seems quite clear that indissolubility and reception of the sacraments by the divorced-remarried are separable issues. Is it a viable notion? John Donahue, S.J., believes that it is. Explicitly adverting to my suggestion, he writes:

The teaching of the historical Jesus is cast in the form of such a "moral ought", but it is not in the legal form of a declarative pronouncement about a bond which cannot be broken.[23]

Clearly, the Eastern Orthodox Church does not believe it has abandoned or compromised Jesus' teaching on marital permanence by its practice of *oikonomia*.[24] Behind such a pastoral practice there must be an understanding of indissolubility similar to the one I propose.

The understanding of indissolubility proposed here corresponds, I believe, to Archbishop Legare's plea for a more personalist and existentialist (in contrast to an essentialist) approach to the matter. If the indissolubility of marriage is understood as I have suggested—as a serious precept, and the bond as an obligation—then a readjustment of our theological and juridical concepts would occur. In impoverishing outline, it might build as follows.

1. Marriage is a "community of love," an "intimate partnership" (Vatican II). Inability to establish such a community is lack of capacity for marriage. Inability to achieve it is the death of marriage.

2. The capacity to establish this "community of love" plus the public determination to do so, generates the *bond* between two people, scil., the serious and absolute *obligation* to continue growing in the total "community of love." Thus: (a) this "intimate partnership is rooted in the conjugal covenant of irrevocable personal consent."[25] (b) "As a mutual gift of two persons, this intimate union, as well as the good of the children, imposes total fidelity on the spouses, and argues for an unbreakable oneness between them."[26] The capacity and the public determination (consent) *constitute* the *bond*. The spouses are *bonded* to each other. They *ought not* allow the bond to be broken and must do everything possible to protect it when it is imperiled.

3. Christ's absolute precept is merely an affirmation about the nature of marriage, of this particular perpetual covenant between men and women. It does not add "from outside" a characteristic not already there. It is marriage which is indissoluble, not a particular kind of marriage. If the Church can "dissolve" a marriage, this means and must mean that the *bond* was no longer there, the obligation rooted in the capacity. A *bond* is absent only when capacity is gone. Otherwise, *any* dissolution is an abuse. It is also an admission that the *bond* is not a metaphysical-juridical entity independent of the human reality.

4. Therefore, when the capacity to live in a "community of love" with a particular person is gone, is irretrievably lost, the *bond* is no longer there. For we should not speak of an obligation without a capacity. The bond remains only in so far as the capacity remains. The mere existence of a spouse is not a bond unless that existence carries with it the possibility of a "community of love."

5. Where there is no bond, a subsequent marriage cannot be a violation of that bond. A subsequent marriage can have a genuine human reality (not merely the "psychological relationship" admitted by the International Theological Commission)—though there may be good reasons why a divorced individual should remain unmarried. For instance, the individual would want to avoid undermining the permanence others are trying to lead. However, there may be reasons that lead an individual to a second marriage, e.g., the spiritual good of the individual. ("Let him accept this teaching who can" [Mt 19:12]. "Dissolution of the marriage *in favor of the faith*.") The Church may choose not to celebrate second marriages for pedagogical and other reasons.

The above five paragraphs contain an entire theology of marriage and a corresponding jurisprudence. In happy abandon I shall leave it to others to spell out the implications of such a theology and jurisprudence—indeed more basically, to pass on its merits. But the general lines of development do seem to me to be entailments of the idea of indissolubility as a precept.

Whatever the case, the Church must continually review its pastoral practices in the light of a new historical consciousness, as I noted in chapter 1. In doing so, it can derive guidance from biblical scholars. At this point recall the statement of Joseph Fitzmyer, S.J. cited in chapter 6.[27] Let me add to it a paragraph of Bruce Vawter.

> The Christian communities which have accepted divorce as a deplorable but an inevitable fact of life have taken some guidance admittedly from the New Testament exegesis, but far more they have taken their guidance from other indices to the realities of the human condition in their times, and this is perhaps partly as it should be. I speak here not particularly of the Protestant churches, for of no Christian community is this fact truer than of the Roman Catholic Church, which despite its reputation for an adamantine opposition to divorce in any form yet has asserted to itself more than any other Christian body the prerogative of dissolving—that is, divorcing—practically every conceivable bond of marriage save one; and that one, as it happens, which should be the chief focus of its pastoral concern, the sacramental marriage *ratum et consummatum*.[28]

One final remark to this admittedly tentative probe. If indissolubility and reception of the sacraments are not only *separable* issues, but are to be practically *separate*, then it is clear that the validity of the slightly de-juridicized notion of indissolubility I have proposed must not only be established in the academic community. It must be prepared for, understood, and accepted at the popular level. Otherwise, at the level where scandal and division ought not to be, it will continue to be and grow. As Charles Whelan noted: a modified pastoral practice "would require careful explanation to the membership of the Church of the reasons for the change in discipline. It must be abundantly clear that the purpose of the change is to show compassion and to do justice, not to introduce another form of divorce into the Church."[29]

"Abundantly clear." For if this is not the case, the Church will be seen, in adopting a more lenient policy on reception of the sacraments for divorced-remarrieds, to be adjusting not her partial and historically conditioned grasp of the consequences of indissolubility, but she will be seen as revoking the very notion of indissoluble marriage. That I think she cannot do, nor can she tolerate the conclusion by the faithful that this is what she is doing.

Notes

1. *New York Times*, 29 November, 1985.

2. Ibid.

3. Ibid.

4. Derek Worlock, "Marital Indissolubility and Pastoral Compassion," *Origins* 10 (1980), 273-75.

5. Henri Legare, "Current Situations: Value, Risk, Suffering," ibid., 280-82.

6. John Paul II, *Familiaris Consortio* (Washington: United States Catholic Conference, 1982), 83.

7. "Christological Theses on the Sacrament of Marriage," *Origins* 8 (1978), 200-04. These theses were composed by Gustave Martelet, S.J.

8. Cf. *America* 127 (172):258-60.

9. E. Genicot, S.J., *Institutiones Theologiae Moralis* II (Bruxelles: L'Edition Universelle, 1951), 17th ed., no. 357.

10. Genicot, loc. cit., no. 20.

11. *Documentation catholique* 69 (1972):739.

12. Genicot, loc. cit., no. 18.

13. Josef Fuchs,S.J., *De Sacramentis in Genere. De Baptismo. De Confirmatione* (Rome: Gregorian University, 1963), 50.

14. Fuchs, loc. cit., 51.

15. Karl Lehmann, "Indissolubility of Marriage and Pastoral Care of the Divorced Who Remarry," *Communio* 1 (1974):219-42, at 222-23.

16. Lehmann, loc. cit., 223.

17. "Le problème pastoral des Chrétiens divorcés et remariés," *Vie Spirituelle: Supplement* 109 (1974):124-54, at 146.

18. "Le problème . . . " loc. cit., 136.

19. Loc. cit., 145.

20. Ch. Robert,"Est-il encore opportun de priver des sacrements de la reconciliation et de l'eucharistie indistinctement tous les divorcés remariés?" *Revue de droit canonique* 24 (1974):152-76, at 169.

21. Charles Whelan, "Divorced Catholics: A Proposal," *America* 131 (1974): 363-65, at 365. It should be noted that similar proposals have been made by Joseph Ratzinger, Bernard Häring, Franz Böckle, Karl Hörmann, Johannes Gründel, Hans Rotter, Walter Kasper and many others in other countries. Cf. R. A.

McCormick S.J., *Notes on Moral Theology 1981-84* (Lanham: University Press of America, 1984), 101.

22. Loc. cit., no. 84.

23. John Donahue, S.J., "Divorce: New Testament Perspectives," *Month* 14 (1981):113-20.

24. Cf. Bernard Häring, "Pastorale Erwägungen zur Bischofssynode über Familie und Ehe," *Theologie der Gegenwart* 24 (1981):71-80.

25. *Documents*, 250.

26. *Documents*, 251.

27. Joseph Fitzmyer, S.J., "The Matthean Divorce Texts and Some New Palestinian Evidence," *Theological Studies* 37 (1976):197-226, at 224-25.

28. Bruce Vawter, "Divorce and the New Testament," *Catholic Biblical Quarterly* 39 (1977):542.

29. Loc. cit. 365.

Chapter 14

"A Clean Heart Create for Me, O God."
Impact Questions on the Artificial Heart

On May 24, 1985, there appeared in the *New York Times*, under the byline of Dr. Lawrence Altman, the following statement:

> [This is] probably the single most expensive medical procedure available . . . Yet in a report yesterday that would redirect national priorities on one of the boldest experiments in medical history, The Working Group called for a greatly expanded Federal research effort to develop a fully implantable, permanent heart.[1]

Altman was referring to a report of an advisory panel of The National Heart, Lung and Blood Institute of the National Institutes of Health. Albert R. Jonsen, a member of this panel (known as The Working Group on Mechanical Circulatory Support) disputes Altman's claim that the Working Group endorsed "a greatly expanded effort." It recommended, he states, only that the present effort continue.[2]

Whatever the case, there can be little doubt that the arrival of mechanical circulatory support (dating to December 2, 1982 and the implantation of an artificial heart in Dr. Barney Clark at the University of Utah) will function as a symbol of the way this country faces its health challenges in the next decade or so.

It is an easy prediction that we will relive the debate that surrounded dialysis for end-stage renal disease. Medicare began to operate in 1967. At that time kidney dialysis was provided by law for three groups: those eligible for veterans' benefits, Medicare beneficiaries aged sixty-five and over, beneficiaries of medicaid programs covering this expensive procedure. In

1972, Congress extended coverage for kidney dialysis to all who needed the treatment. Joseph Califano describes the discussions that preceded this congressional generosity.

> There was a spirited, sometimes angry, discussion around the conference table in my White House West Wing office. Some said it was immoral not to provide care to all who needed it. Others said even the Great Society at its peak could not provide every medical service to all who needed it. But this was a matter of life itself, another heatedly added, pointing out that just because of quirks in the law, some were eligible and others not; some had the money to pay for it, others did not. The discussion went on and on.[3]

Califano's brief cameo accurately identifies the two poles that also anchored the broader congressional discussion: life and money. Could the wealthiest nation in the world choose to withhold such a service from some citizens? Is it fair to let some people die when we have the means to give them added years of life? Obviously, such questions are important. But I have to wonder whether they should so dominate the policy discussion in the way they did. Many people have had long second thoughts about the end-stage renal disease program. Many of these thoughts are probably stimulated by the fat $2 billion bill that it costs. But I believe that there may be more behind such second thoughts than the financial factor.

Virtually every technological advance has its costs. Benefits come with burdens. Therefore, it is essential to an ethical analysis that all of the possible impacts of our interventions be identified. With that in mind, I will list areas of possible impact as we reflect on the future of the artificial heart, especially the permanent use of such a device.[4] It should be emphasized that I raise these as questions rather than assertions. Indeed, to stress this, each point will conclude with a question.

1. How we view life and death. How we preserve life manifests and reinforces what we think of life and death. In the Christian view, as I have stated already, life is a basic good, but not an absolute one. The Christian lives in faith that she/he is on a pilgrimage, that death is a transition not an end, that just as Christ conquered death and lives, so will we. We organize our lives around this belief.

Question: How will this faith be affected by the artificial heart? In a sense, such faith is affected by all medical interventions *in principle*. But the artificial heart might be in a category by itself.

2. How we evaluate people. In its 1972 study, the Artificial Heart Assessment Panel of the then National Heart and Lung Institute made repeated reference to a return to functionability as a possible benefit of the artificial heart. In a key paragraph it stated:

If the artificial heart works well, the demand for it may be so great that society will find itself hard pressed to supply the device to all who want it. Even assuming that an adequate supply would be forthcoming at some price so that rationing would not be necessitated by absolute scarcity, society might be unwilling to supply the device at public expense to all needful patients. Convicted criminals, drug addicts, and perhaps other persons viewed as non-contributing members of society might be seen as candidates for exclusion. But any such governmental process of rationing life on the basis of the value of individual members to society would take a heavy toll in public values.[5]

Question: Will the availability and use of this technology subtly affect our evaluation of human persons so that we increasingly perceive them in terms of functionability or value to society?

3. *How we evaluate other health care needs.* "Other health care needs" refers above all to preventive medicine and life style. The artificial heart is the "ultimate repair job." Short of such ultimate repair, we are societally deficient in attending to the causes of illness: High cholesterol, smoking, lack of exercise. Thomas Preston, chief of cardiology at the Pacific Medical Center (Seattle), notes:

> If the goal is to save lives, that can be done more quickly, more broadly and more surely by other means. Let us spend our resources instead on reducing our infant mortality rate, or treating hypertension in the inner cities, or taking care of the 25 million Americans who are without insurance or means of attaining adequate medical care.[6]

Joseph Califano makes the point I want to raise.

> Heart disease is America's number-one killer. Daily newspapers and television dramas give the impression that coronary bypass surgery, modern cardiopulmonary techniques, miracle hypertension pills, human heart transplants, and in the future, animal and artificial heart transplants are the way to battle heart disease. Right? Couldn't be more wrong.[7]

Question: Will the artificial heart blind us to more basic health care needs, comfort us in a comfortable life style that is radically unhealthy? Will it comfort the afflicted in their unspoken heterodoxy: "If it can be fixed, why worry about the breakdown"?

4. *How we evaluate other societal needs.* The allocation of our resources to various societal needs represents one of our major social problems. Roughly 11 percent of the GNP goes to health care. But there are other pressing needs: education, environment, housing, hunger, defense, etc.

Question: Will the introduction of this technology represent a factor that obscures or downplays other societal needs, some far more basic?

5. How we deal with our elderly population. The Artificial Heart Assessment panel noted:

> A particularly important societal impact of the artificial heart will appear in the form of an expanding elderly population. Persons who would have died young will live longer and may be substantially more productive in their older years than they would have been without the artificial heart. Moreover, elderly patients who are otherwise in good health should surely not be denied the right to an artificial heart—at public expense if that is the way things go. The result of enlarging the older population will be to exacerbate the problems which our society is already experiencing in trying to provide a meaningful existence for its senior citizens. Many older people who are in all respects, both physical and mental, the equal of many younger people are treated as if their ability to make any useful contribution to society had long since ended. For those who are less well off, the need to supply decent and dignified living conditions is also not being met. The costs and human challenges are very great already, but the artificial heart will add to both.[8]

Add to these considerations the fact that some cardiac disease is genetic in origin. The artificial heart might enable carriers of cardiac disease to reproduce, thus increasing prevalence of genetic heart disease. Thus the artificial heart may generate additional candidates for its use in future generations.

Question: Will the artificial heart promote or undermine our efforts to deal societally with our elderly population? While extending lives, will it also extend problems we have not yet solved?

6. How the patient views her/himself. There are any number of possible reactions and combinations of them that could structure the attitudes and reactions of recipients. There could be anxieties due to dependence on an external source of power. There could be preoccupation about being "dehumanized" by an artificial heart. There could be worries about finances that could lead to guilt feelings and intrafamilial tensions.

Question: What will be the overall quality of life available to patients with artificial hearts?

7. How the question of fairness is faced. I believe it is highly probable that the government will not pay for clinical practice involving artificial hearts. We simply cannot afford it. Therefore it will be available only to those who can afford it. Increasingly, this is seen as unacceptable in our egalitarian society.

It is this very unacceptability that leads others to a different view of public funding of clinic practice in this area. Thus Albert R. Jonsen writes:

> The possibility exists that a cry will be raised for federal subsidy of clinical implantation of artificial hearts. The sight of individuals doomed to die because they cannot afford an existing lifesaving treatment stimulates the demand for equality: in the face of death, the allocation of a lifesaving technology on the basis of an individual's ability to pay seems blatantly discriminatory.[9]

If public funds are allocated for clinical implantation of artificial hearts, there are likely to be other budgetary reallocations to accommodate this strain. As Jonsen notes, these reallocations are likely to be restrictions in already underfunded programs and this could have tragic effects on access to care. In this way, a new rescue technology ends up threatening the health of others.

Question: If the artificial heart becomes accepted clinical practice, how will its accessibility affect our notion of justice and fairness?

8. *How we evaluate euthanasia and suicide.* Presently, both mercy killing and suicide are rejected by our society even though there are powerful forces at work to legitimize both. For a variety of reasons we have experienced ethical confusion about the moral propriety of withholding or withdrawing respirators, nasal gastric tubes and gastrostomy tubes. Repeatedly, judges have stated that removal of such life-support systems would subject the removers to the homicide laws. This happened early on in the Quinlan case (New Jersey) and the Clarence Herbert case (California). It also happened in the case of Michael Brophy (Massachusetts). Behind such confusion—and I believe it is precisely that—there probably lies a single fact: The more we survive by machines and artificial life-sustainers, the more turning them off or withdrawing them looks like euthanasia or suicide.

Question: Will the obviously optional ethical character of the artificial heart further erode our rejection of mercy killing?

9. *How the direction of medicine is to be charted and by whom.* The type of health care we get can be determined in any number of ways, for instance, by the public or by independent medical investigators and their entrepreneurial backers. Since what kind of medicine we get and what we spend on it affects many other aspects of social life, these determinations pertain to the common good. I take that to mean that they should be governed by the public.

Question: Does the independent character of a program like that of Humana constitute a further step away from public scrutiny and control of the direction and priorities of medicine?

10. *How medicine perceives its role and implements it.* On everyone's admission, the health care system in the United States is in the midst of a major structural revolution. Whether it is merely a symptom or a cause, a key feature of this transition can be stated in terms of a move from a nonprofit service system to a business.

Question: If, *per impossibile*, news reportage of the artificial heart implant were prohibited by law, would Humana be involved in it? In other general terms, what is the impact of medicine's move to a business ethos on its self-concept, its practitioners, and its quality?

The ten questions I have raised may appear to some as answers looking for questions. I hope that they are not that. They were crafted out of the conviction that in dealing with the artificial heart we must consider more than life and money. Restriction of our deliberations to these twin factors could lead to a high-minded, warm-hearted but short-sighted humanitarianism. If I am correct, an adequate discussion of the artificial heart plunges us deeply into social ethics.

Notes

1. *New York Times*, 24 May 1985.

2. Albert R. Jonsen, "The Artificial Heart's Threat to Others," *Hastings Center Report* 16 (February 1986):9.

3. Joseph A. Califano, Jr., *America's Health Care Revolution* (New York: Random House, 1986), 146.

4. I say "permanent use" in contrast to a temporary assisting use.

5. Artificial Heart Assessment Panel, *The Totally Implantable Artificial Heart* (Bethesda, Md.: NIH, 1973), 74.

6. Thomas Preston, "Who Benefits from the Artificial Heart?" *Hastings Center Report* 15 (February 1985):7.

7. Califano, 187.

8. Cf. note 5, at 75.

9. Jonsen, 10.

Chapter 15

Genetic Technology and Our Common Future

Dr. LeRoy Walters of the Kennedy Institute of Ethics is chairman of a new Working Group on Human Gene Therapy, a subcommittee of the National Institutes of Health's Recombinant DNA Advisory Committee (RAC). On February 21, 1985, Dr. Walters received a letter from Sheldon Horowitz, M.D., of the Center for Health Sciences (University of Wisconsin-Madison). It reads in part as follows:

> I am now taking care of a 6-and-a-half-year-old child with adenosine deaminase (ADA) deficiency and severe combined immune deficiency who I feel should receive gene therapy as soon as possible. Enzyme replacement therapy, thymic factor and thymic transplant have been tried in this child without success. A bone marrow transplant could be tried in this girl. However, since there is no sibling who is identical, it would be a mismatched transplant. In this child, a mismatched bone marrow transplant would be very difficult since the minimal immunity she has would have to be "wiped out" with chemotherapy and radio-therapy prior to transplantation. Also, her chronic lung disease could be significantly worsened by the chemotherapy or radiotherapy. I think it is very likely that the transplant attempt would kill her. Both the parents and I feel that the known risks of bone marrow transplantation in this child (infection, graft versus host disease, lung toxicity, cancer) are greater than the potential risks of gene therapy. Her lung disease may become too severe if we continue to wait—I feel we have approximately 12 months to do something (Cited with permission).

Dr. Horowitz went on to urge the Walters subcommittee to approve clinical trials of gene therapy for certain life-theatening diseases even without previous trials in nonhuman primates.

As much as anything, this letter tells us where we are in the seemingly esoteric world of genetic engineering: right on the edge of clinical application. In a year or two, we are likely to see clinical trials of gene therapy for several diseases that have two characteristics: (1) they are extremely debilitating and often lethal; (2) they trace to a single defective gene. Take Lesch-Nyhan syndrome, for example. This is the devastating disease that afflicts some two hundred boys a year in the United States. It is characterized by profound mental retardation and self-mutilation. There is no known cure.

Something similar can be said of ADA-deficiency, even though it is much rarer, only about fifty cases reported worldwide.[1] As the Journal of the American Medical Association noted:

> These diseases are single-gene defects. Their appeal as candidates lies partly in the fact that the genes, which have all been cloned, code for a single enzyme or protein. Also, with the immune deficiency diseases, the expectation is that the defects in only a small number of primordial cells in the bone marrow . . . will need to be corrected for the therapy to be effective.[2]

As it now stands, gene therapy involves removal of bone marrow cells, then treatment of them with modified viruses in order to insert the new and normal gene, and finally replacement of the bone marrow cells back into the patient's body where the new gene would code properly for the deficient enzyme or protein. This is not the only therapeutic use of gene splicing, but it is, in a sense, the most delicate and sensational. Other uses would include production by DNA recombinant techniques of synthetic insulin. Or again, researchers at Genentech, a South San Francisco genetic engineering firm, have produced by gene splicing a natural human enzyme that acts as a clot-buster. When administered soon enough after a heart attack, it prevents potentially lethal damage to the patient's heart. This therapy, called tissue plasminogen activator (TPA) smashes blood clots without damaging the blood's coagulation machinery as other available therapies do. After approval by the FDA, during the fall of 1987, it is already in use in clinical practice. But gene therapy remains the centerpiece of gene splicing because of its enormous potential and its possible dangers.

Gene therapy is the end product of an interesting development. Where did it all begin? Quite simply, with Gregor Mendel, an Austrian monk, in 1866. Mendel studied meticulously the variations in pea plants and finally concluded that such variations were controlled by a single physical "factor" that we now call a gene. For instance, some seeds were round, some wrinkled. This variation meant that the factor for round seeds must differ from the factor for wrinkled. When the plants were crossed, the resulting hybrid would carry a factor from each. However, the offspring of a cross between wrinkled- and round-seeded peas always had round seeds. The wrinkled factor apparently was dormant. When the hybrids were crossed with each other, however, the wrinkled trait reappeared about one-fourth of the time. Thus Mendel argued that the trait for round seeds was "dominant," the trait for wrinkled "recessive," since wrinkled seeds would reappear only when the plant had two wrinkled factors, one from each parent.[3]

Such findings, though ignored for forty years, provide the basis for modern genetics. What Mendel called "factors" came to be known as genes at the beginning of the twentieth century. Some twenty years later, it was learned that genes are positioned on threadlike structures called chromosomes located in the nucleus of each cell. By exposing fruit-fly chromosomes to X-rays, scientists noted mutations that altered the physical traits of the next generation. But what was responsible for such mutations? In 1944, the basic stuff of these hereditary changes was identified as deoxyribonucleic acid (DNA) by O.T. Avery and colleagues at Rockefeller University.

The rest is history. In 1953, the famed double-helix structure of DNA was discovered by Francis H.C. Crick and James D. Watson. In 1970, two Johns Hopkins scientists discovered a kind of molecular scissors (called a restriction enzyme) to slice DNA molecules. In 1972, Stanford's Paul Berg combined the DNA from two viruses. Thus the name "recombinant DNA." In 1973, scientists from Stanford and the University of California inserted recombinant DNA into bacteria that reproduce or clone the foreign DNA. The *National Geographic* said of this achievement: "[With it] the age of genetic engineering begins."[4] The reason for that is simple: Bacteria modified with foreign genes operate like very efficient photocopying machines, churning out limitless copies of the gene. Robert F. Weaver of the University of Kansas has compared gene cloning to cutting a printed page in half, inserting a new paragraph in the middle, then photocopying the altered version over and and over to reproduce the new material.[5] Six years ago, bacteria were programmed to turn out human growth hormones, otherwise available at great cost and in small quantity. Insulin and interferon came next.

Genetic science is both immensely complicated and immensely simple. The simple part reads as follows: Genes control our biochemistry, and biochemistry controls our health. There are more than three thousand catalogued diseases traceable to a variation in a single gene. Pinpointing the culprit gene or its deficient protein is another question. Success has been achieved in only about 280 instances, but the implications are obvious. Baskin summarizes it neatly: "To relieve these and hundreds of other hereditary disorders, we must change the activity of our faulty genes—or send healthy foreign genes into the proper cells to do the work our own genes cannot handle."[6]

No one questions the enormous power that molecular genetics puts in human hands. Edward L. Tatum, in his 1958 Nobel Prize lecture, summed it up as follows: " . . . each and every biochemical reaction in a cell of any organism, from a bacterium to man, is theoretically alterable by genetic manipulation."[7] Such a realization, when combined with the cloning techniques developed in 1973, gave birth to some ghoulish scenarios that were utterly unrealistic, dangerously misleading and needlessly distracting. Journalists spent rainy afternoons conjuring up an NFL defensive line composed of the clones of former Minnesota Viking Alan Page. David Rorvik's *In His Image: The Cloning of Man* climbed to the best-seller list, and as nonfiction at that. The late André Hellegers, M.D., used to remark: "The book is really about a clown named Rorvik." Ira Levin's *The Boys from Brazil* (young Hitlers cloned from genes in the dictator's cells) was a best seller and a popular movie.

Such nonsense was not restricted to the pulp industry. In 1971, the prestigious *New England Journal of Medicine* published an essay by Joseph Fletcher, the ethicist, who cast his vote for the bioengineering of parahumans, "if the greatest good of the greatest number were served by it." He then unloaded one of the most remarkable sentences in the literature on genetics: "I suspect I would favor making and using man-machine hybrids rather than genetically designed people for dull, unrewarding or dangerous roles needed nonetheless for the community's welfare—perhaps the testing of suspected pollution areas or the investigation of threatening volcanoes or snow slides."[8] Such fanciful projections, ridiculous as they are, still linger in the public consciousness when the term "genetic engineering" is used.

It was the realization that genetic engineering, unlike other technologies, involves the creation of new life forms, that led the representatives of three major religious faiths (Dr. Claire Randall of the National Council of Churches, Rabbi Bernard Mandelbaum of the Synagogue Council of America and the Most Rev. Thomas C. Kelly, who at the same time was general secretary of the United States Catholic Conference) to send a letter to President Carter on June 20, 1980. The letter noted that the key questions raised by genetic engineering are moral and religious questions: "Who shall determine how human good is best served where new life forms are being engineered? Who shall control genetic experimentation and its results, which could have untold implications for human survival? Who will benefit and who will bear any adverse consequences, directly or indirectly?"[9] The letter urged that these and similar questions be addressed by a "broad spectrum of our society," not merely by the commercial or scientific communities, which too easily are interested parties.

If such questions are to be weighed carefully by a "broad spectrum of our society," then that broad spectrum must be sufficiently informed. This educational process would include at least two categories of information: (1) an elementary knowledge of the possible uses of genetic interventions; (2) a grasp of the issues at stake, issues that structure the development and refinement of the ethical judgments that would help shape public policy.

For several reasons, I do not underestimate the difficulty of this challenge. First, molecular genetics is a highly technical field with a language that may look like gibberish to most nonprofessionals. Genetic science and technology are studded with terms like restriction enzymes, nucleotides, antigens, monoclonal antibodies, plasmids, hybridomas, oncogenes, retroviruses, expression vectors and a host of other almost unpronounceable and mysterious neologisms. The head aches before the mind grasps.

Second, the field is a bit like a slippery pig. Just when you think you have it, you don't. Molecular genetics is progressing with astonishing rapidity. It is no exaggeration to say that nearly every day something new is learned, some advance is made. Books and articles on the state of the art published as recently as a year ago are likely to be obsolete in significant respects.

Finally, many people must shed the rhetorical shibboleths that often shape their approach to these problems. I refer to statements such as "We must not play God," "We must not tamper with nature," "We must not fall victim to the Frankenstein factor." In such statements, there lies buried the tidbit of truth. But, in general, these exhortations do not enlighten the analytic process. They promulgate conclusions or preferential options, sometimes even ideologies, usually drawn from shaky data and/or exaggerated fears.

In what follows I will offer a few suggestions that may begin to flesh out the two "catetgories of information" mentioned above.

Emphasis here will be on the use in human beings of DNA recombinant technology rather than on its agricultural and industrial uses. Gene therapy can be either somatic-cell therapy, germ-line cell therapy, enhancement genetic engineering, or eugenic genetic engineering.[10]

Somatic-cell therapy refers to the attempt to treat a discrete population of the patient's bodily cells other than germ (reproductive) cells in order to alter the functioning of a defective gene (or eventually replace it) and thus cure the disease at its root. It involves changes limited to the person being treated. Four steps are involved in this technology: (1) cloning the normal gene; (2) introducing the cloned gene in a stable fashion into appropriate target cells by means of a vector; (3) regulating the production of the gene product; (4) ensuring that no harm occurs to the host cells.[11]

At the present time, only the first step is technologically feasible. Yet there is pressure to allow therapeutic attempts even now, as Dr. Horowitz's letter indicates, because some single-gene diseases are presently incurable and fatal. W. French Anderson, Chief of the Laboratory of Molecular Hematology at the National Heart, Lung and Blood Institute of the National Institutes of Health, has argued that before gene therapies are attempted in human beings, three requirements should be verified in animal studies. It should be shown that (1) the new gene can be put into the correct target cells and will remain there long enough to be effective; (2) the new gene will be expressed in the cell at an appropriate level; (3) the new gene will not harm the cell, or by extension, the animal.[12] Some regard extensive prior animal runs as too conservative where devastating and lethal diseases are concerned. Whatever the case, all seem to agree that somatic-cell gene therapy, when technologically feasible, is nothing more than an extension of medical practice in an attempt to aid victims of currently intractable diseases. Given effectiveness and safety, there should be no insuperable ethical obstacles.

Germ-line cell (reproductive cells) therapy is a remarkably different thing. The altered gene would affect not only the individual, but that individual would pass the altered gene to his or her offspring. Such intervention, since it would affect the genetic inheritance of future generations, would involve "a significant departure from standard medical therapy."[13] Obviously, this kind of therapy involves ethical issues of much greater complexity and magnitude than somatic-cell intervention. For instance, what will be the effect of modifying a gene for future generations? Is the gene that is responsible for the present disease also responsible for beneficial effects , as is true of the gene that is responsible for sickle-cell anemia but seems also to resist malaria? In other words, do we know enough to take steps that will affect future generations? Whatever the answer to that question, the matter is largely academic because germ-line therapy is not now technologically feasible.[14]

Third, there is enhancement genetic engineering. This refers to the insertion of a gene or several genes to produce a characteristic desired by the individual, e.g., black hair, larger muscles, sharper memory. That is not therapy in any traditional sense; nor is it scientifically feasible at present. Furthermore, it raises two serious ethical concerns. First, the concept involves gene-insertion into a healthy human being with the possibility, even likelihood, that many nontargeted functions would be adversely affected. Second, such programming involves a subtle but very real change in our attitudes toward human persons. We can easily begin to evaluate them not for the *whole* that they are—unique refractions of the Creator, images of God— but for the *part* that we select. Such attitudes can powerfully nourish actions and practices that ought to be abhorrent to civilized people. Furthermore, the line between enhancement genetic engineering and eugenic engineering is fuzzy at best.

Finally, there is eugenic genetic engineering. This refers to the systematic preferential breeding of superior individuals (genotypes). It involves the attempt to intervene genetically to select for character traits, intelligence, various talents and mental and emotional characteristics. Scientifically, such proposals are sheer fancy because the traits in question are probably influenced by many unknown genetic factors. Furthermore, such genetic backgrounds interact with the environment in as yet very mysterious ways. Ethically, the matter is quite straightforward, and it is all bad. What characteristics are to be maximized to get a "better" human being? Is brighter necessarily better? Or, more pointedly, is white skin preferable to yellow or black? And who decides all of this? Questions like this point inevitably to the wisdom of C.S. Lewis's assertion: "The power of man to make himself what he pleases means, as we have seen, the power of some men to make other men what they please."[15] For these and other reasons, contemporary scientists rightly run from positive eugenics as if it were the plague.

If these are the potential uses of genetic technology in humans, there remain the issues at stake in such uses. I use that term (issues at stake) as a broad umbrella to include three concerns: (1) the criterion for judging genetic interventions; (2) the values involved; (3) the procedural method.

First the criterion. When dealing with the methods of responsible parenthood, Vatican II stated: "The moral aspect of any procedure . . . must be determined by objective standards which are based on the nature of the person and the person's acts." I have already discussed this personal criterion several times in this volume. Suffice it to note here that it suggests the questions we ought to be asking and the method necessary for discovering the answers. The central question always is: Will this or that intervention (or omission, exception, policy, law) promote or undermine human persons "integrally and adequately considered"? For instance, is the use of in vitro fertilization with embryo transfer in cases of sterility likely to support and promote human persons in their essential dimensions, or is it likely to undermine them? Pope John Paul II seemed to have this criterion in mind when, in speaking of genetic experiments, he referred to the fact that "they will contribute to the integral well-being of man."[16] The answer to such a question—if we take the criterion seriously—cannot be deduced from a metaphysical blueprint of the human person. It is necessarily inductive, involving experience and reflection upon it. Of course, there remain things that we have already learned from past experience (e.g., violence begets violence, adultery is harmful to those who engage in it); and there are things that so assault our sense of the sacred and the proper that no experience is necessary to expose their moral character (e.g., the Nazi medical experiments). Nonetheless, the principle remains: To judge the moral character of many human actions, experience of its impact on persons is essential.

This reflects St. Thomas's assertion that "we do not wrong God unless we wrong our own good."[17]

Second, the values involved. To decide whether certain actions or policies involve us in "wronging our own good," we must be clear on those dimensions of human persons that are brought into play by the possible uses of genetic technology. The following represent but a partial listing.

1. *The sacredness of human life.* Life is sacred because of its origin and destiny, because of the value God puts on it. Our grasp of this sacredness is marvelously deepened in Christ's costing love. Such sacredness demands reverential attitudes and practices from genetic science. Practically, that means that it must avoid undue risks, and especially discriminatory distribution of risks. As a study group of the National Council of Churches noted: "Throughout the process it [genetic technology] must protect the human and civil rights of all people, especially those least able to defend themselves."[18] The standard protection is, of course, the requirement of informed consent. There have been abuses in the past, especially where the poor and Third World populations are concerned, abuses that denied the sacredness of human life by forfeiting its basic equality.

2. *The interconnection of life systems.* There are many life systems in our ecological whole. Harm to any one will likely have a deleterious impact on others. In measuring the possible benefits of genetic interventions, it would be both foolish and morally wrong to sacrifice long-term well-being for immediate gain. Americans are a pragmatic, interventionist people. We succeed now and pay later. We eliminate the pests and learn only after that our pesticides are carcinogens. This we simply cannot afford where genetics is concerned. As Marshall Nirenberg, Nobel Prize winner of 1969, wrote: "When man becomes capable of instructing his own cells, he must refrain from doing so until he has sufficient wisdom to use this knowledge for the benefit of mankind."[19]

3. *Individuality and diversity.* Uniqueness and diversity (sexual, racial, ethnic, cultural) are treasured aspects of the human condition. Theologically viewed, we are images of God in our humanity, in its enchanting, irreplaceable uniqueness and differences. Diagnostic and eugenic interventions that would bypass, downplay or flatten these diversities and uniqueness should be viewed as temptations. We have a very mixed history in the United States regarding sterilization of the retarded and other "undesirables."

One thinks of the potential information explosion associated with increasing knowledge of the human genome. Who will have access to this information and how will it be used? As 1980 Nobel laureate Paul Berg put it:

I can see the potential for this information to intrude on personal freedoms. We can already see this in tests that can detect susceptibility to certain chemicals. Employers might not hire people who have risks associated with exposure to these substances. Insurers might charge high premiums to cover these people or not insure them at all. Conceivably, the government could use this information to mandate how and where we live.[20]

What Berg is rightly worried about is the collapse of the human person into knowledge about the person's genes. Interestingly and paradoxically, such reductionism could shatter our wonder at human individuality and diversity at the very time that elsewhere we are emphasizing it.

4. *Social responsibility and the priorities of research.* While genetic technology must respect the irreplaceable uniqueness and basic equality of the individual, both its purposes and processes must also take account of our essential sociality. Under this rubric, I mean to suggest the need for distributive justice both in the priorities of genetic research (allocation of resources) and the enjoyment of its benefits.

Take allocation of resources as an example. Such allocation reflects the values of a society. As Roger Shinn has put it:

Most countries of the world can afford little or nothing for elaborate genetic research. In this country, what resources should go into genetic therapies that may some day cure cancer as compared with correcting environmental causes of cancer that are operational right now? What resources should be assigned to research into the unknown as compared with correction of nutritional deficiencies for which answers are available now?[21]

Too few of our resources go to the most needy. Rather, as Shinn notes, the assignment of resources is proportioned "to the glamor of the project or the interests of groups who influence politics." In other words, it neglects the responsibilities inseparable from our sociality and interdependence.

Something similar must be said about the benefits of genetic innovation. They should be "generally available (not coercively) to all, regardless of geographic location, economic ability or racial lines" (The National Council of Churches study group cited above).

These are but four dimensions of the human person that are brought into play as we decide whether in the use of modern genetic technology we are "wronging our own good." It is reassuring to report that these value concerns are the object of meticulous attention in a recent report of the Working Group on Human Gene Therapy of the Recombinant DNA Advisory Committee of the National Institutes of Health.[22] Entitled "Points to Consider in the Design and Submission of Human Somatic-Cell Gene

Therapy Protocols," the document lists questions to be answered by anyone who wants NIH approval for gene therapy. In almost agonizing detail,
the "Points to Consider" asks about anticipated risks and benefits, research
design, various laboratory studies and clinical procedures, selection of subjects, informed consent, privacy and confidentiality.

Then the working group notes that the following issues will be considered in extending approval to any gene therapy proposal:

> 1. How strong is the evidence that the proposed somatic-cell gene therapy
> will not affect the reproductive cells of patients? 2. Is the proposed
> somatic-cell gene therapy an extension of existing methods of health care,
> or does it represent a distinct departure from present treatments of dis-
> ease? 3. Is it likely that somatic-cell therapy for human genetic disease
> will lead to a) germ-line therapy, b) the enhancement of human capabili-
> ties through genetic means, c) eugenic programs encouraged or even
> mandated by governments?

With such common-sense cautions in place to brake our uncritical enthusiasm, we are in good hands.

Third, the procedural method, the very process of our deliberations. In government, things tend to "get done" by a convoluted and compacted process involving political tradeoffs, compromises, power plays, constituency-
sensitive concessions, economic cost-benefit considerations and so on. I
note this not in cynicism, but because in many areas this is the way public
policy must be hammered out in a radically pluralistic society. But it should
not be the way here. The matter is too important to be left to the ordinary
political dynamic. I am in general confident, perhaps naïvely overconfident,
in the maturity of the scientific community to regulate itself. We saw a
splendid example of this in the (1974-75) moratorium scientists imposed on
their own DNA recombinant research. Their decision proved to be
healthily conservative.

Nonetheless, I judge it to be paramount that there be beyond NIH's excellent interdisciplinary working group some further *public* mechanism of
ongoing deliberation, assessment of progress and oversight in this area, not
least of all to keep the public informed. The judgments to be made, the controls to be set (if any), the finances to be allocated must be rooted in broad
human value judgments. These do not pertain to the exclusive expertise of
the scientific community. They necessarily involve all of us because it is a
common human future we are deliberating.

In the communal deliberation, the Church—and by this I mean the
believing community—has no mean responsibility. Vatican II stated:
"Faith throws a new light on everything, manifests God's design for man's
total vocation, and thus directs the mind to solutions which are fully
human."[23] The ultimate questions raised by genetic technology are

theological ("God's design for man's total vocation"). Who is the human person? What is her or his final destiny or future? What, therefore, is truly beneficial to the human person? The Church rightly believes that it has a perennial wisdom to contribute to such questions. But wisdom is not only a gift; it is above all a responsibility. Specifically, to absent itself from these discussions, to enter them ill-informed, to share in them from a posture of authoritative arrogance as if the Church were in prior possession of concrete answers—all such approaches would dim the "new light" and almost assuredly compromise "solutions which are fully human."

Notes

1. Barbara J. Culliton, "Gene Therapy: Research in Public," *Science* 227 (1985):493-96.

2. Kathryn Simmons, "Clinical Stage Draws Nearer in Ongoing Studies of Gene Therapy," *Journal of the American Medical Association* 253 (1985):13-15.

3. Yvonne Baskin, *The Gene Doctors* (New York: Wm. Morrow and Co., 1984), 30.

4. Robert F. Weaver, "Changing Life's Genetic Blueprint," *National Geographic* 166 (1984):832.

5. *National Geographic*, loc. cit., 820.

6. Loc. cit., 22.

7. Cited in Baskin, 34.

8. Joseph Fletcher, "Ethical Aspects of Genetic Controls," *New England Journal of Medicine* 285 (1971):776-83, at 779.

9. Cited in full in *Human Genetic Engineering* (Hearings before the Subcommittee on Investigations and Oversight of the Committee on Science and Technology, U.S. House of Representatives) no. 170 (1982), 130-31.

10. Cf. note 9, passim. These divisions are also found in *Splicing Life* (Washington: U.S. Government Printing Office, 1982). This is a report on genetic engineering by the President's Commission for the Study of Ethical Problems in Medicine and Biomedical and Behavioral Research.

11. *Splicing Life*, 42.

12. W. French Anderson as in note 9, 286.

13. *Splicing Life*, 46.

14. Barbara J. Culliton, "Congress Reports on Gene Therapy," *Science* 226 (1984):1404.

15. C.S. Lewis, *The Abolition of Man* (New York: Macmillan, 1947), 72.

16. *L'Osservatore Romano*, 24 October 1982.

17. *Summa Contra Gentiles* III, c. 122.

18. Panel on Bioethical Concerns, National Council of Churches of Christ—U.S.A., *Genetic Engineering: Social and Ethical Consequences* (New York: Pilgrim Press, 1984), 34.

19. Cf. *Human Genetic Engineering*, loc. cit., 303 and 305.

20. *Medical Science News*, November 1984.

21. *Human Genetic Engineering*, loc. cit., 305.

22. "Points to Consider in the Design and Submission of Human Somatic-Cell Gene Therapy Protocols," *Federal Register* 50 (no. 14, 1985), 2942-45.

23. *Documents*, 209.

Chapter 16

Sterilization: The Dilemma of Catholic Hospitals

In a report in *The Washington Post* (22 May, 1977), the Worldwatch Institute called sterilization "the contraceptive phenomenon of the 70's."[1] In one-third of all married couples in the United States trying to avoid conception, one or other partner has undergone sterilization. This trend has continued into the eighties. Sterilization now exceeds any other single preventive family planning measure. Bruce Stokes, author of the report, stated that the figures for the United States were based on a 1973 National Survey of Family Growth by the National Center for Health Statistics of the then Department of Health, Education and Welfare.

How do Catholics fit into these trends? Writing in *Family Planning Perspectives* (1977), Charles F. Westoff and Elise F. Jones (both of Princeton University, Office of Population Research) stated, on the basis of comparative figures for 1970 and 1975, that "within several years, even sterilization will probably be adopted by the same proportion of Catholics as non-Catholics. . . . "[2] After noting that three-fourths of the women surveyed are using some form of contraception (79.9 percent for non-Catholics and 76.4 percent for Catholics), they presented the following results on sterilization for 1975:

	Non-Catholic	Catholic
Wife sterilized	13.9	9.8
Husband sterilized	12.4	9.9

Dr. Conrad Taeuber and Dr. Jeanne Clare Ridley of Georgetown University have provided even more recent (1976) statistics similar to those of the Westhoff-Jones study. Using a computer tape file from the nationwide Family Growth Survey carried out under the direction of the National Center for Health Studies, the researchers note that "the conclusion that there has been a significant increase in the contraceptive use of sterilization since 1970 is clearly established, and there is little doubt that the rate for Catholic couples has increased more rapidly than the rate for couples identified as non-Catholic."[3] This conclusion supports the Westoff and Jones prediction that "sterilization . . . will probably be adopted in several years by the same proportion of Catholics as non-Catholics, judging from recent trends."

The Westoff-Jones prediction appears to be on target when evidence of another kind is assembled. For instance, in a 1986 letter to American bishops on the "Charles Curran affair," John F. Kippley, president of the Couple to Couple League and an advocate of natural family planning as the only morally acceptable form of birth regulation, noted that 95 percent of Catholic couples are using "unnatural, immoral methods."[4] Only 2-3 percent of nonpregnant newlyweds start their marriages with some form of natural family planning. Another indication is the Notre Dame Study of Parish Life entitled "Pastors and People: Viewpoints on Church Policies and Positions."[5] Opposition to *Humanae Vitae* was reported as very strong, especially among the better educated and those under fifty. Support for the encyclical was found only among pastors *as a group*, with large numbers dissenting.[6]

This trend presents a real dilemma for at least some, possibly very many Catholic hospitals. The problem is above all tubal ligation, the severing of the fallopian tubes to make meeting of sperm and ovum impossible. Vasectomy, male sterilization, is not necessarily a hospital procedure. There are repeated instances often involving so-called "medical indications," like renal or cardiac disease, when both the woman and the physician judge that another pregnancy would endanger the life or health of the mother or the fetus. They therefore judge that sterilization is the only solution and is in the overall best interests of the woman, her marriage, her family. Thus, in a survey of Catholic hospitals, published in the American Journal of Obstetrics and Gynecology, 20 percent (66 of 336 responding) permitted sterilizations for medical reasons.[7] This number would be higher had all hospitals responded and had some hospital personnel realized what constitutes a prohibited sterilization, as I note below. Forty-seven percent of the 270 not permitting sterilization reported that their medical staffs were interested in doing sterilizations. In my own discussions with Catholic physicians and health care providers throughout the country, I have found that heavy majorities believe that sterilization is at times a justifiable response to a critical medical problem.

I have also discovered a great disparity of practice and no little confusion. For instance, some hospital administrators assert that they follow the *Ethical and Religious Directives for Catholic Health Facilities* (1971) and therefore (!) allow sterilizations only for medical reasons. Others report that they tolerate only so-called indirect sterilizations, but further discussion reveals that they sometimes understand this as one "required by the health of the mother." Some assert that they "have no problem with sterilization," since they do not allow it at all, and yet a significant number of such responders preside over obstetrical services that are heavily underused, constitute severe financial burdens and whose very existence is threatened.

In the face of such diverging practices, the National Conference of Catholic Bishops issued a document (July 3, 1980) repeating traditional Catholic teaching on sterilization.[8] The document summarizes and applies, somewhat more rigidly at one point, the response of the Sacred Congregation for the Doctrine of the Faith given March 13, 1975.[9] It does this "since we note among Catholic health care facilities a certain confusion in the understanding and application of authentic Catholic teaching with regard to the morality of tubal ligation." It was this same "confusion" that led the NCCB to seek a clarification of the matter from the Congregation for the Doctrine of the Faith in 1974, a request that led to the 1975 response noted above. For instance, G. Emmett Carter, then bishop of London, Ontario, concluded in 1973 that there was enough theological support at that time to allow sterilization under certain specific conditions.[10] The same conclusion had been reached by other bishops. Quite a few have told me so personally. Indeed, the practice of a notable number of hospitals, the opinions of a significant number of bishops, theologians, physicians and administrators lead me to believe that what the NCCB document identifies as "confusion" is more likely straightforward disagreement with the absoluteness of the traditional formulation.

To dispel the confusion, the NCCB reasserted: (1) the objectively grave immorality of every direct (contraceptive in purpose) sterilization; (2) the invalidity of the use of the principle of totality to justify it; (3) that any material cooperation , which is said to be an "unlikely and extraordinary situation," is justified only by grave reasons extrinsic to the case, not by the medical reasons given for the sterilization. In other words, if pregnancy would threaten the life or health of the mother or risk a seriously defective child, that is insufficient reason for a Catholic hospital to tolerate the procedure.

The doctrine of the NCCB document and of the Congregation for the Doctrine of the Faith is not new, except perhaps that the NCCB doctrine seems stricter on material cooperation. Indeed, the overall teaching is utterly traditional. Some theologians argued that direct sterilization was condemned in Pius XI's *Casti Connubii* when it all inclusively stated that "any use whatsoever of matrimony exercised in such a way that the act is deliberately frustrated in its natural power to generate life is an offense against the law of God and nature."[11]

The Holy Office was asked "whether the direct sterilization of man or woman, whether perpetual or temporary, is licit." Its reply (24 February 1940): "In the negative; it is forbidden by the law of nature."[12] Pius XII made this very clear in his address to the Italian Society of Urologists (8 October 1953). He denied the application of the principle of totality (the principle allowing for the disposal or mutilation of a part of the body for the good of the whole person) to cases where the danger to the woman originated in pregnancy itself. As he put it:

> In this case the danger that the mother runs does not arise, either directly or indirectly, from the presence or the normal functioning of the tubes, not from their influence on the diseased organs—kidneys, lungs, heart. The danger appears only if voluntary sexual activity brings about a pregnancy that could threaten the aforesaid weak or diseased organs. The conditions that would allow the disposal of one part for the good of the whole by reason of the principle of totality are lacking. It is therefore not permitted to interfere with the healthy fallopian tubes.[13]

This same teaching was repeated very clearly in Paul VI's *Humanae Vitae*:

> Equally to be excluded, as the teaching authority of the church has frequently declared, is direct sterilization, whether perpetual or temporary, whether of the man or of the woman.[14]

The pontiff explicitly rejected the use of the principle of totality to directly sterilizing interventions.

It is no wonder, then, that the *Ethical and Religious Directives for Catholic Health Care Facilities* (1971) exclude direct sterilization. To have done anything else would have been to disagree with explicit papal teaching.

There have been several analyses of this absolute prohibition. For instance, some theologians like John C. Ford, S.J., and Gerald Kelly, S.J., argued in their *Contemporary Moral Theology II* that the "generative faculty . . . has a unique, inviolable character, because it is given to man principally for the good of the species rather than for his personal good."[15] Others varied this slightly by urging that direct sterilization is direct interference with the sources of life, and as such must be rejected, quite as vigorously as taking life itself. Again, in a commentary accompanying the NCCB document, it was argued by William E. May of the Catholic University that contraceptive sterilization involves us in "acting against" the power to give life. It deprives "a person of a good properly pertaining to him or her." To do that is "to do moral evil."

Let me give an example here. I know a prominent (non-Catholic) pediatric surgeon. He and his wife have eleven children. The last was slightly retarded, so the wife had a tubal ligation performed. The couple then adopted three more children, an Indian, a black and a retarded child. Anyone who argues that the tubal ligation involved this couple in "acting against" the power to give life or the "procreative good" is arguing from a mountain top that is thickly insulated from the real world by a coronal mist. If human actions must be tested by moral principles, it is no less true that moral formulations must be tested and purified by clinical complexity and the messiness and unpredictability of real life. I have the unavoidable impression that some more fundamentalistic Catholics are more concerned with defending past formulations than in critically testing them in new circumstances.

A significant number of theologians have therefore found these arguments insufficient to establish the absolute prohibition of direct sterilization. Such arguments either beg the question—by assuming what is to be established, that is, that sterilization is always a *moral* evil—or absolutize a biological aspect of the human person by equating the unequatable: human life and the sources of human life. Depriving a person of life is one thing; depriving oneself of the power to procreate is a remarkably different thing and ought not to be treated in an identical way ethically. For instance, the late Paul Ramsey, who agreed that we may never directly take human life because this involves us in "turning against the good of life," did not view sterilization as always involving our "acting against" the good of the power to procreate. Many would argue that in some cases the physiological condition of the mother has already negated or severely compromised procreation as a good in her case. To say anything else is to absolutize physical integrity.

In *Contemporary Moral Theology II*, Ford and Kelly wrote in 1963: "One cannot exaggerate the importance attached to the physical integrity of the act within papal documents and in Catholic theology generally."[16] Many theologians reject such an emphasis. Similarly, given Vatican II's rejection of the notion of procreation as a primary end, the argument that the generative faculty is given principally for the good of the species loses persuasiveness. Pope Paul VI stated in *Humanae Vitae*: "We believe that the men of our day are particularly capable of seizing the deeply reasonable and human character of this fundamental principle" (the inseparability of the unitive and procreative aspects of sexual union).[17] That has not happened, at least as a principle without exceptions or as applying to every act. G. Kelly wrote that the argument is to a great extent intuitive: "One either grasps it or one does not."[18] Very many theologians have not. Indeed, the appeal to intuition could easily be viewed as a reflection on the weakness of the arguments.

Thus, the so-called "Majority Report" of the Papal Commission on Population, the Family and Natality concluded: "Sterilization, since it is a drastic and irreversible intervention in a matter of great importance, is *generally* to be excluded as a means of responsibly avoiding conceptions."[19] This "generally" remains the conclusion of at least very many theologians today. Concretely, they assert that direct sterilization is not intrinsically evil. There are times when it can be justified. Walter J. Burghardt, S.J., a prominent theologian and editor of *Theological Studies*, spoke for many when he wrote in the *New York Times*: "Rome should not expect that every official document calls for the same degree of acceptance from every Catholic. A reaffirmation that Jesus really rose from the dead makes a legitimate demand for a single response. But do not question my faith or fidelity if I choke on the Congregation's arguments condemning all direct sterilization."[20]

In *Medical Ethics* the well-known moral theologian, Bernard Häring, put it as follows:

> Whenever the direct preoccupation is responsible care for the health of persons or for saving a marriage (which also affects the total health of all persons involved), sterilization can then receive its justification from valid medical reasons. If, therefore, a competent physician can determine, in full agreement with this patient, that in this particular situation a new pregnancy must be excluded now and forever because it would be thoroughly irresponsible, and if from a medical point of view sterilization is the best possible solution, it cannot be against the principle of medical ethics, nor is it against the "natural law" (*recta ratio*).[21]

I agree with that conclusion, as do many Catholic theologians. Such agreement is not a rejection of the Church's substantial concern where sterilization is involved. Nor is it a promotion of sterilization as some less careful, usually quite fundamentalist, commentators would have us believe. Sterilization, it can and should be argued, is not a neutral intervention, much less a desirable one. As drastic and often irreversible it has the character of a last resort, much as in its own domain violent self-defense, whether personal or national, is to be viewed as a last resort. That is why many theologians refer to sterilization as an *evil*, although premoral or non-moral until more is known of the circumstances in which it occurs. It is something to be avoided insofar as reasonably possible. But just as not every killing is murder, not every falsehood a lie, not every taking of another's property is theft, not every war is unjust, so not every sterilization is necessarily unchaste. Where evils are potentially associated with our conduct in conflict situations, the Catholic tradition has been by and large one of vigorous and reasoned control, not of absolute exclusion. Why not here too?

But where does that leave Catholic hospitals? In a genuine dilemma. On the one hand, the official teaching continues to state that sterilization for contraceptive purposes is *always* (inherently) wrong. On the other, this formulation is not accepted by a large segment of the theological community, and a significant number of the episcopal community.

There are three possible hospital policies. First, allow tubal ligation on an individual and carefully controlled basis, that is, for medical indications as an instance of the principle of totality. Second, allow sterilization as a form of material cooperation in the face of outside pressure to do so. Third, do no sterilizations at all.

There are problems in all three. If a hospital adopts the first policy, it is in dissent from official Church teaching and will often be in trouble with the local bishop. Furthermore, there is the difficult problem of establishing the criteria for line-drawing. How is it possible to draw the line at medical indications? Cannot economic and other factors threaten the stability of a marriage and family via pregnancy, as Pius XII conceded?

If the second policy is adopted, the hospital still is in trouble with the authorities, for the NCCB insists that toleration (material cooperation) of sterilization under the only circumstances allowable will be "an extraordinary and unlikely event." Many hospitals do not experience the pressures leading to sterilization as "extraordinary and unlikely."

If the third policy is adopted, the hospital will be in the position of denying to desperate women what is widely regarded as both good medicine and good morality. My concern here is not primarily the gradual abandonment of obstetrical-gynecological services, with possible threats to the very viability of the Catholic hospital, though that is increasingly a possibility and a tragic one. For Catholic hospitals to forfeit obstetrical-gynecological services in a culture where abortion is rampant and at a time when fetal therapy may well come into its own would be a regrettable dereliction. My own concern is above all the overall well-being of the patient and patients. If reputable theologians believe that direct sterilization cannot be absolutely excluded morally, then one has to question whether the hospital is pursuing the true overall good of the patient if it adopts a policy that is based on an absolutist moral position.

This is not to suggest that Catholic health care facilities ought to adopt a laissez-faire attitude or policy. Not at all. There are many reasons for being extremely cautious in this area. Sterilization has been and is being widely abused. As the *Washington Star* noted: "There is growing evidence that as many as two-thirds of the hospitals across the nation are ignoring them" (Federal Regulations on Sterilization).[22] Thousands of indigent women have been sterilized "in the best interests of society." In Maryland,

Virginia and the District of Columbia, 11,000 Medicaid patients were sterilized during the period 1975-1980. Joseph Califano told me, during his tenure as Secretary of the Department of Health, Education and Welfare (1977-79), that he was shocked to learn of the number of patients sterilized at government expense. Not only is there abuse, there is the fact that today's exceptions become tomorrow's rules or habitual practices. There is the fact that in a technologically oriented and comfort-conditioned culture many will seek sterilization where it is objectively unjustified. There is the genuine danger of coercion in many situations. And so on.

A stringent policy of control is assuredly called for, not least as a symbol to a society increasingly antinatalist. Reasons such as these lead me to believe that a Catholic hospital is justified in limiting its toleration to serious medical indications. It is only the absolutism of the present moral teaching and subsequent policy that is a cause for concern and is at the heart of the Catholic hospital's dilemma. What we have here is a confusion of policy with moral theology. There are many reasons for a cautious, even strict policy. But such a policy need not root in the highly dubious contention that every direct sterilization is morally wrong.

Behind this practical dilemma is, of course, the doctrinal problem. The Church is still divided, and deeply divided, on how it ought to formulate its genuine concerns in the area of birth regulation. But the division has hardened. Trenches have been dug deeper. True conversation has all but ceased. We exist in a stalemate. Those who endorse the official formulation are said to be "loyal," those who do not, "disloyal," "deviant," "unorthodox." Cardinal Joseph Ratzinger recently chastised such dissenters as captives to a "middle class" morality.[23] On these questions, consultation is increasingly limited and preprogrammed. A concrete symbol of this was the Synod of 1980. The Catholic health care facility is trapped in the intransigence of the moral question. I have heard this again and again from truly responsible health-care providers.

They state their concerns in terms of the couple at high risk for a congenitally defective child, of the woman whose life or life-span could be seriously threatened by a pregnancy, of the woman whose life-preserving medication would seriously affect any fetus's health. These are situations where a pregnancy would be, as Father Häring notes, "thoroughly irresponsible." Discovering whether natural family planning "works" means running an irresponsible risk. To demand that a couple forego sexual relations altogether is very often to threaten the marriage, as Vatican II noted when it said: "But where the intimacy of married life is broken off, it is not rare for its faithfulness to be imperiled and its quality of fruitfulness ruined."

This is the dilemma of Catholic hospitals as I experience it over and over again around the country. The problem is not going to go away. Indeed, it will only be exacerbated by a simple repetition of a traditional exceptionless formulation, as if the formulation were truer and truer the more often it is repeated. Perhaps that is why *Commonweal*, after high praise for the Vatican document on euthanasia, argued that the sterilization edict "promises to reduce rather than increase respect for traditional teaching." *Commonweal* continued: "It will create bureaucratic problems for Catholic hospitals, but for most Catholics it will only add to the church's unfortunate loss of credibility in all matters of sexual morals."[24]

What has happened, at least in not a few places, is that the dilemma has been taken underground. That is, at least some Catholic hospitals quietly and without publicity or fanfare allowed to happen what is officially prohibited. That is not a healthy situation, not least of all because it increasingly distances leaders in the Church from actual practice. That is a tragedy, particularly at a time when research and medical practice need the strong value-infusion that should be expected from Catholic leadership.

I have no solutions to this practical political problem. But I do have a suggestion: the conversation must continue. And the conversation ought to include all with a genuine competence and stake in the matter—bishops, physicians, married couples, theologians and others, much as the Birth Control Commission included these specialities. When a question is the object of a genuine dispute in the Church, the very worst thing to do is to close the conversation, decree a solution and select as consultants only those who will support it. This is what happened in the convention of moral theologians held in Rome in April 1986. Only those who adhered to a "Roman line" were invited. They were addressed by the pope and several cardinals in what can only be called a recrudescence of "court theology."[25] That is to abort the learning process in and of the Church. If the conversation is considered closed, if difficult problems are handled by mere repetition of traditional formulations, if finally Catholic hospitals go underground, I believe that the leadership of the American Church will be exposing itself to some painful and unnecessary self-inflicted wounds.

Regrettably, a "closing of the conversation" is precisely what has happened. In the remainder of this chapter I want to detail how this occurred as a kind of object lesson as to how it should not occur.

In 1978 the Sisters of Mercy of the Union, sponsors of the largest group of nonprofit hospitals in the country, began a study of the technological and ethical aspects of tubal ligation.[26] The study resulted in a recommendation to the General Administration of the Sisters of Mercy that tubal ligations be allowed when they are determined by patient and physician to be essential to the overall good of the patient. The General Administrative Team accepted this recommendation in principle. In a November 12, 1980, letter to their hospital administrators, the General Administrative Team reported the results of the study and indicated a desire to draw concerned persons into dialogue on the issue. They did not, as was inaccurately reported to the bishops of this country, mandate a policy.

Copies of the original study, the position statement of the General Administrative Team, and the letter to the hospitals somehow fell into the hands of officials in Rome and of the Committee on Doctrine of the NCCB. One thing led to another until finally a dialogue was initiated between a committee of five bishops (James Malone [chairman], Raphael M. Fliss, William H. Keeler, James D. Niedergeses, William B. Friend [Bishop Friend attended none of the meetings]) and six Sisters of Mercy (M. Theresa Kane, Emily George, Mary Ellen Quinn, Helen Marie Burns, Norita Cooney, M. Roch Rocklage). Both groups had theological consultants, Msgr. Richard Malone and John R. Connery, S.J., for the bishops, Margaret Farley and I for the Mercy sisters. Two meetings were held (September and December 1981). These were largely exploratory, get-acquainted-with-the-problem meetings. At the December meeting, it was decided that the next meeting (March 1982) would enter the substance of the problem. The sisters were to present a single-page position paper stating why they thought that not all tubal ligations were morally wrong. The episcopal committee was to do the same, showing why they were.

During the first week of March, Archbishop John Roach (President of the NCCB), just returned from Rome, informed Sister M. Theresa Kane that "after consultation with Church authorities in the United States," the Holy See had concluded that the dialogue had "not met with success" in convincing the sisters to accept the Church's teaching on tubal ligation. The dialogue was off. In its stead Rome had appointed a Committee of Verification (composed of three bishops, James Malone, William Keeler, Paul Waldschmidt). The purpose of this committee was to verify the Administrative Teams' answer to two questions: (1) Does it accept the teaching of the magisterium on tubal ligation? (2) Will it withdraw its circular letter (November 12) to its hospitals?

Parenthetically, I must add here how shocked I was at this turn of events. Just as the dialogue was to turn to the substantive issue, it was cancelled and replaced by jurisdictional muscle. I wrote to Bishop Malone protesting this. For reasons that are perhaps understandable—what response *could* Bishop Malone make?—I received no answer.

On May 11, 1982, the Administrative Team addressed their response to Pope John Paul II. The pertinent answers read as follows:

> 1. We receive the teaching of the Church on tubal ligation with respectful fidelity in accord with *Lumen gentium 25 (obsequium religiosum)*. We have personal disagreements as do others in the Church, including pastors and respectable theologians, with the formulation of the magisterium's teaching on sterilization. However, in light of present circumstances, we will not take an official public position contrary to this formulation.

2. We withdraw our letter of Nov. 12, 1980 and will notify the recipients of the letter of such withdrawal.

The letter concluded by urging "continued study and consultation within the Church on this issue."

This response was drafted with meticulous care. The Administrative Team was aware of the fact that the *obsequium religiosum* asserted by Vatican II does not exclude the possibility of dissent. They were also aware of the fact that, according to traditional theology, all the Church could demand of them in response to the teaching on tubal ligation was *obsequium religiosum*. Therefore the Administrative Team correctly concluded that they had an airtight response.

The Committee of Verification seemed quite pleased with the response. The Apostolic Delegate, Archbishop Pio Laghi, phoned Sister M. Theresa Kane on June 17 to inform her that the Holy See had accepted the Administrative Team's response. The archbishop told Kane that he wanted to meet personally with her to convey the good news. On June 24, Laghi met with Kane and Sister Emily George, reiterating the approval of the Holy See and expressly mentioning John Paul II, SCRIS and SCDF. The matter seemed quietly put to rest.

However, the sisters received a letter dated August 30, 1982 from Cardinal E. Pironio (Prefect of the Congregation for Religious and Secular Institutes). In part it stated: "In light of all the sentiments expressed in your letter of May 11, as well as your letter of withdrawal, dated May 17, 1982, your reply is not considered fully satisfactory and, indeed, your interpretation of the *obsequium religiosum* is judged incomplete." The sisters were told by Cardinal Pironio that a "subsequent response" would be coming from the congregation.

This subsequent response was a letter from Cardinal Pironio to Sister M. Theresa Kane dated November 21. The letter insisted that the religious submission of mind and will (*obsequium religiosum*) "calls for the Catholic not only not to take a public position contrary to the teaching of the Church but also to direct his or her efforts, by an act of the will, to a more profound personal study of the question which would ideally lead to a deeper understanding and eventually an intellectual acceptance of the teaching in question." The letter also requested the sisters to write another letter to their hospitals "clearly prohibiting the performing of tubal ligations in all the hospitals owned and/or operated by the Sisters of Mercy of the Union."

A letter dated July 6, 1983, was drafted by Sister Theresa Kane to the chief executive officers of the Mercy Sisters' hospitals and forwarded to Cardinal Pironio. It read as follows:

On November 21, 1982, the Sacred Congregation for Religious and

Secular Institutes (SCRIS) requested that we write you stating our reevaluation of tubal ligation and clearly prohibiting the performance of tubal ligations in Mercy hospitals owned and/or operated by the Sisters of Mercy of the Union.

As requested by SCRIS to reevaluate, we, the Mercy Administrative Team, have spent additional time in study and consultation on tubal ligation. In obedience to the magisterium we will take no public position on this matter contrary to Church teaching. As you face pastoral problems regarding tubal ligation, we ask that you continue to work in close collaboration with your local ordinary in implementing Church teaching.

The Congregation for Religious responded to this draft in a letter to Bishop James Malone dated August 22. The congregation insisted that the second and third sentences of paragraph 2 be changed to read as follows: "In obedience to the magisterium we will continue to study and reflect on Church teaching with a view to accepting it. We, therefore, direct that the performance of tubal ligations be prohibited in all hospitals owned and/or operated by the Sisters of Mercy of the Union." If any sister does not accept this, she is to specify the dissent in writing and with signature. Furthermore, Bishop Malone stated that "upon enquiry I have learned that the letter from the congregation is indeed a 'formal precept' to you." That was specified to mean that "no further compromises or word changes . . . will be entertained by the congregation."

The sisters recognized both the rock and the hard place. Failure to comply might, indeed assuredly would, lead to consequences that would compromise or nullify their important work in many other areas. Accordingly, on October 26, 1983, Sister M. Theresa Kane sent the required letter to the Mercy Hospital administrators. On January 16, 1984, Cardinal Pironio wrote Kane: "We are pleased that you and the sisters of the Administrative Team have accepted the decision of the Holy See and we pray that as you continue to study and reflect on the magisterium of the Church you will embrace it in its entirety."

Above I referred to these events as a "closing of the conversation" and as an "object lesson as to how it should not occur." I put the matter that way because of the heavy theological implications that invite explication. One such obvious implication is the powerlessness of women in the Church. This has been noted by others. I want to point out three others here.

First, in the exchanges over a two-year period, the substantive issue was never discussed. Indeed, at the very point (March 1982) in the dialogue where the substantive issue (Is direct sterilization intrinsically evil?) was to be discussed, Rome (SCRIS) intervened to terminate the dialogue and appoint the Committee of Verification on the grounds that "there is nothing to be gained by further dialogue on this issue."

Is there really nothing to be gained by further dialogue? That would be the case only if it were antecedently clear and certain that the magisterial formulation was absolutely and unquestionably accurate. Yet, how can one sustain this in light of the very widespread theological questioning of that clarity and certainty? I have discussed this matter with very many established theologians throughout Europe and the United States and can report that most would endorse the approach and analysis of Johannes Gründel,[27] which is all but identical with that of the Majority Report cited above. Surely this fact needs discussion, unless we are to exclude in principle the relevance of theological analysis. In my judgment that is exactly what has happened here.

The second theologically pertinent issue is the notion of *obsequium religiosum*. The Mercy Administrative Team had responded that "we receive the teaching of the Church on tubal ligation with respectful fidelity in accord with *Lumen gentium 25 (obsequium religiosum*)." The Congregation of Religious responded to this by saying that it was incomplete because a Catholic must also "direct his or her efforts ... to a more profound personal study of the question which would ideally lead to a deeper understanding and eventually an intellectual acceptance of the teaching in question."

This raises a host of interesting issues. First, the assumption seems to be that the members of the Administrative Team have not so "directed their efforts." But what is the evidence for that? Surely, it is not the simple fact of dissent. That would rule out dissent in principle and elevate the teaching to irreformable status—both theologically untenable. More positively, surely a group that has conducted a three-to-four-year study, consulting opposing theological viewpoints and a variety of competences, has satisfied the demands of *obsequium religiosum*. If not, what more is required? Is this "direct his or her efforts" a duty with no time limit? Does this go on forever with no discernible *terminus*?

Next, the congregation uses the word "ideally" of the outcome of such directed efforts. What if it does not turn out that way? Furthermore, what if a group such as the Administrative Team discovers that many competent and demonstrably loyal theologians throughout the world have had similar problems? Are these simply regrettable but ultimately irrelevant failures? If magisterial inaccuracy or error is possible and if dissent is the vehicle that reveals this, is there not a point at which obligations begin to return to and weigh upon the proponents of the disputed formulation? Specifically, must they not reexamine *their* position if it is truth and not juridical position that is our dominant concern? To say anything else is to discount the significance of personal reflection in the teaching-learning process of the Church. In other words, it is utterly to juridicize the search for truth.

Finally, the "Mercy Affair" seems to have all the characteristics of an "enforcement of morals." Bishop Christopher Butler, O.S.B., distinguishing between the irrevocable and provisional in Church teaching, states of the latter: "To require the same adhesion for doctrines that are indeed taught by officials with authority but to which the Church has not irrevocably committed itself is to abuse authority, and if this requirement is accompanied by threatened sanctions it is also to abuse the power of constraint."[28] I shall leave to readers the judgment whether these words fit this case. But if they do, their true theological importance should not be overlooked. One effect is to relieve bishops of their collegial task. An immediate implication of that relief is the undermining of authority in the Church. If the bishops cannot report the experience and reflection of the faithful, or if, when they do, it is brushed aside, then clearly the presumption of truth that ordinarily accompanies authentic magisterial teaching has been undermined. For that presumption roots—as I think history shows—not simply in the naked juridical claim that the Church has been commissioned to teach in the area of morals, but above all in the fact that in discharging this responsibility it has utilized its unparalleled means of overcoming the obstacles that threaten most individual human discernment. Those who treasure the magisterium as a privilege must view such a prospect, because of its generalizable implications, with profound sadness.

Notes

1. *Washington Post,* 22 May 1977, A3.
2. Charles E. Westoff and Elise F. Jones, "The Secularization of U.S. Birth Control Practices," *Family Planning Perspectives* 9 (no. 5, 1977), 203-07.
3. Personal communication.
4. The letter was provided to me by several bishops. It has not, to the best of my knowledge, been published.
5. *Origins* 15 (1986), 733-44. *America* 154 (1986):372.
6. *Origins* 15 (1986), 737. *Crux of the News,* 28 April, 1986.
7. John M. O'Lane, M.D., "Sterilization and Contraceptive Services in Catholic Hospitals," *American Journal of Obstetrics and Gynecology* 133 (no. 4, 1979):355-57.
8. "Statement on Tubal Ligation," National Conference of Catholic Bishops, *Origins* 10 (1980), 175.
9. *Documentum circa sterilizationem in nosocomiis catholicis,* translated in *Origins* 6 (1976), 33 and 35.
10. Cf. *Policy Manual* of St. Joseph's Hospital (London, Ontario), 1973, "Foreword."
11. AAS, 22 (1930), 560.
12. AAS, 32 (1940), 73.
13. AAS, 45 (1953), 674-75.
14. For the English version, cf. *The Birth Control Debate,* ed. Robert G. Hoyt (Kansas City, Mo.: *National Catholic Reporter,* 1968), 115-40, at 124.

15. John C. Ford, S.J., and Gerald Kelly, S.J., *Contemporary Moral Theology II: Marriage Questions* (Westminster: Newman, 1963), 319.

16. Ibid., 288.

17. Cf. note 14, p. 123.

18. Gerald Kelly, S.J., *Medico-Moral Problems* (St. Louis: Catholic Hospital Association, 1958), 158.

19. Cf. note 14, p. 93.

20. Walter J. Burghardt, S.J., "Rome and Rebellion," *New York Times*, 8 April 1980.

21. Bernard Häring, *Medical Ethics* (Notre Dame: Fides, 1973), 90.

22. *Washington Star*, 22 June 1980, 1.

23. *30 Giorni*, May 1986.

24. "Edges of Life I," *Commonweal* 107 (1 Aug. 1980):421.

25. *National Catholic Reporter*, 4 July 1986, 14. "Because it was planned as a celebration of moral theology loyal to the Church's teaching authority, Curran, McCormick and their friends were not invited to the party."

26. In what follows, the data and citations are taken from the notes compiled by the late Sister Emily George and are used with the permission of the authorities of the Sisters of Mercy of the Union.

27. Johannes Gründel, "Zur Problematik der operativen Sterilisation in Katholischen Krankenhäusern," *Stimmen der Zeit* 199 (1981):671-77.

28. B.C. Butler, "Authority and the Christian Conscience," *Clergy Review* 60 (1975):3-17.

Chapter 17

Homosexuality as a Moral and Pastoral Problem

In the sixties and seventies there was a great deal of ink spilled around this subject. The theological literature was, I would guess, a response to an emerging gay awareness and even militancy. Whatever the case, I approach this chapter with enormously mixed emotions. On the one hand, there is a powerful sense of the need to continue to examine this subject in order to provide a sound basis for moral principles and their pastoral applications. On the other hand, the atmosphere is hardly inviting and supportive. Charles Curran's recent difficulties with the Congregation for the Doctrine of the Faith (difficulties centered heavily on sexual ethics) are a stinging splash of cold water on any theologian who attempts, however tentatively and respectfully, to think new thoughts on this subject.[1] However, in the long run, a theologian who allows his/her agenda to be excessively influenced by ecclesiastical-political considerations is not acting in the best interests of the Church. There is nothing shameworthy in making a mistake. In a pilgrim church we all do. There is everything wrong in not risking it.

Two recent events stand as symbols of the importance and controversial nature of the homosexual question. The first is the "homosexual rights bill" of New York City. The bill forbids discrimination against homosexuals in jobs, housing and public accommodations. Prior to a vote on the bill by the City Council (March 20, 1986 the bill passed by a vote of 21-14), both Cardinal John O'Connor and Bishop Francis Mugavero opposed the bill, though Mugavero did not oppose an earlier version. On March 16 (1986), O'Connor condemned the bill from the pulpit at St. Patrick's Cathedral. "Divine law cannot be changed by Federal law, state law, county law or city law, even by the passage of legislation by the City Council."[2] The cardinal and the bishop apparently find the bill "exceedingly dangerous to our society."[3] According to the *New York Times*, the two prelates see this danger in "legal approval of homosexual conduct and activity"—a kind of equation of heterosexuality, homosexuality and bisexuality "from the standpoint of social desirability and acceptance." In brief, legal protection involves the sanctioning and sanctification of homosexuality.

Whether one agrees with this analysis or not—and I disagree—it does raise the question of the relation of moral conviction to public conduct, of morality and law in a way that supposes clarity about morality.

So did the second event I choose as a symbol. It is Civil Action No. 5863-80. This was the suit brought against Georgetown University by the Gay Rights Coalition of Georgetwn University Law Center. Two gay student organizations and twenty-three students sought "university recognition" and damages for violation of the District of Columbia's Human Rights Act of 1981. Plaintiffs lost their case in the trial court (Associate Judge Sylvia Bacon, D.C. Superior Court). The matter has now (1988) been settled. Georgetown University must provide certain services to the gay student organizations, yet it need not provide "official recognition" to such groups—a solomonic distinction (as I read it) that allows both sides to claim "victory."

In the trial court, I acted as an expert witness for the university on the moral theology of the Catholic Church. In this capacity, I stated repeatedly and at length, both during the pretrial deposition and the trial, that the heterosexual relationship of marriage was "normative" in Catholic teaching. That word means that *all ought to try* to conform their conduct (full genital expression of sexuality) to that norm. I further stated that an institution like Georgetown University could not adopt public policies that asserted or implied the equal normativity of an alternate life-style.[4]

When asked by counsel for the plaintiffs about those who, because of sexual orientation, could not achieve this norm, I stated that we would have to make "pastoral adaptations" for them. I was stunned that the matter was not pursued because what those adaptations might be seemed to be the heart of the question. Whatever the case, the Georgetown suit raises an issue similar to the New York "homosexual rights bill": the relation of morality to public conduct, this time, however, in a different sphere (university policy and action). No less than the New York incident, the Georgetown policy supposes clarity about the morality of homosexuality.

I believe that it is accurate to summarize authentic Catholic moral teaching by saying that the heterosexual relationship of permanent commitment (marriage) is normative. But that leaves open a number of key questions. What about those who, by orientation, cannot achieve this norm? Are there special norms for them? Is homosexual *behavior* (which obviously does not fulfill the norm) always morally wrong? How should we present the moral "ought" implicit in the term "normative" to those with no capacity to fulfill it? Do we modify it? What are the demands of Christian chastity for such people? If we must make pastoral adaptations, what form should these take and how should we speak of them?

Questions like these do not bear directly and immediately on civil rights (the New York bill) or university policy (the Georgetown case). These two cases involve relating morality to public policy of one kind or another. The questions I have raised touch on morality itself, how it is to be conceived and presented to the many who lack the capacity supposed in the norm.

This is the neurological issue, the one around which much recent writing is organized. In what follows I will: (1) review some recent theological analyses; (2) analyze some magisterial documents on this question; (3) lift out some key concepts as possible pointers toward a solution; (4) offer a modest proposal.

Recent Theological Approaches

Here no attempt will be made to be exhaustive. Rather I shall pick authors and pieces that represent different positions and show how they arrived at their positions.

1. John Harvey. Harvey has spent the better part of a theological lifetime reflecting on the problem of homosexuality.[5] His approach is utterly traditional, a term I use reportorially, not for the moment judgmentally. It accepts the analysis that the sexual faculty has a basic finality in procreation, so clearly so that every sexual act must be open to the possibility of procreation. When it is not, the sexual faculty has been misused. Thus, for Harvey, homosexual *acts* are objectively and gravely morally wrong. The *orientation* that leads to such acts is a different matter. It is not morally evil in itself and very often the individual is not responsible for such an orientation. Furthermore, responsibility for sexual acts may be reduced by a variety of circumstances that mitigate freedom.

In Harvey's approach, the homosexual is called to celibacy. That is the ultimate pastoral goal and Harvey is firmly convinced that, with God's grace, such a goal is achievable even though it may take time and patience. Whatever is deficient in this summary (and there may be points that are) Harvey can easily correct, as can Malloy, Cahill and Curran in what follows.

2. Edward Malloy. Malloy's reflections are explicitly intended as a response to certain "revisionists."[6] He contrasts the Christian way of life with the homosexual way and finds them incompatible. Where sexuality is concerned, the Christian way of life surrounds it with three virtues: chastity, love, faithfulness. Malloy summarizes it as follows:

> The Christian way of life inculcates three virtues in the realm of sexuality: chastity (disciplined determination of appropriate sexual behavior according to the degree of relatedness of the partners), love (intimate sharing of mutual concern according to the natural stages of attraction, passion, friendship and sacrificial service), and faithfulness to promise (patient perdurance in the voluntary exchange of reciprocal commitment according to the community based meaning of exclusivity and permanence).[7]

Malloy sees the homosexual way of life going in a different direction. At a pastoral level he believes that the celibate option should continue to be proposed as "the most consistent response to the Christian ethical judgment."[8] Here he is at one with Harvey. Yet he does concede that "homosexual couples, consciously committed to a permanent and exclusive relationship, offer the best hope for the preservation of Christian values by active homosexuals."[9] Thus for those incapable of celibacy, such a stable, committed relationship is "surely preferable" to other alternatives. In this conclusion, Malloy moves a step beyond Harvey.

3. Lisa Cahill. Cahill argues that any adequate account of homosexuality must correlate four reference points: Scripture, tradition, descriptive and normative accounts of experience.[10] These sources together point unavoidably toward a heterosexual norm for human sexuality, a norm that does not necessarily exclude exceptions.

Cahill insists that the proper focus of Christian ethics is character and moral values (honesty, love, service, fidelity, self-denial). By saying that the heterosexual within a permanent commitment is normative, Cahill means that material acts (sexual intercourse) of a heterosexual kind within marriage are *usually* conducive to and expressive of these moral values. But material acts are "good or evil precisely because of their relation to the former [moral values]."[11] In a broken world, fidelity to such values may be embodied in "less-than-ideal material decisions and acts." As she concludes:

> This amounts to a suggestion that while heterosexual marriage is the normative context for sexual acts for the Christian, it is possible to judge sexual acts in other contexts as *non-normative but objectively justifiable in the exceptional situation*, including that of the confirmed homosexual.[12]

Cahill notes that "another way to state my conclusion" is that homosexual acts are "evil" in that they are to be avoided generally.

"However, they are 'premoral' evils in that their sheer presence does not *necessarily* make the total act or relation of which they are a part 'morally' evil or sinful."[13] The total act is not morally evil "if there is sufficient reason in *this* case for causing 'premoral' or 'ontic' evil." As I read Cahill, she proposes a position very close to that of Philip Keane.

4. *Charles Curran*. Curran states that the "ideal meaning of human sexual relationships is in terms of male and female."[14] In this his position is substantially identical with Lisa Cahill's usage of "normative"; for he insists that those who can must strive for a heterosexual orientation. If, however, the homosexual orientation is irreversible, sexual acts in a context of a "loving relationship striving for permanency are objectively morally good."[15]

Curran's position is presented as a facet of a broader theology of compromise. On this account, Christians are justified in performing certain actions because of the presence of sin in the world, actions that would not be justified without such presence. Curran's "presence of sin in the world" is identical with Cahill's "brokenness." He differs from Cahill only in that Cahill explicitly ties the moral character or quality of acts to their embodiment and expression of moral values. Furthermore, Cahill sees "premoral evil" in homosexual acts, whereas Curran regards them as "morally good" without such a qualifier.

In these four examples, there is a certain progression involved. Using the traditional terminology of objective-subjective, we could say that Harvey would assert that homosexual acts are always objectively wrong though subjective responsibility may be diminished. Malloy would say the same but he must use some principle such as the lesser evil to regard as "surely preferable" a stable union where an individual is incapable of celibacy. Curran and Cahill would say that in certain cases homosexual acts are not objectively morally wrong, though Cahill recognizes in them the presence of premoral evil. Curran does not, at least explicitly.

These are but samples of some recent Catholic approaches to the issue of homosexuality. I have chosen these and not others (e.g., John McNeill's *The Church and the Homosexual*) because they profess to and do retain strong ties to the Catholic tradition. That is, they acknowledge and attempt to embody, each in its own way, the fundamental concerns and values of that tradition and the Church's proposal of it.

Episcopal and Magisterial Statements

A recent volume entitled *Homosexuality and the Magisterium* has collected various documents from the Vatican and U.S. bishops on homosexuality.[16] These documents cover the years 1975-1985. I shall use them to point out certain recurring themes or emphases in "official" presentations. I find four such themes.

1. *Importance of pastoral understanding and compassion.* This theme is dominant in the documents. The Congregation for the Doctrine of the Faith notes that "homosexuals must certainly be treated with understanding and sustained in the hope of overcoming their personal difficulties."[17] The American bishops in "To Live in Christ Jesus" insist that "the Christian community should provide them a special degree of pastoral understanding and care."[18] Bishop Francis Mugavero states his personal "concern and compassion for these men and women."[19] Archbishop John R. Roach notes that homosexuals "deserve a special degree of pastoral consideration from their churches."[20] Cardinal Humberto Medeiros asserts that "we are called to minister with pastoral love" to homosexuals and "to reach out in sacramental ministry to them."[21] Archbishop John Quinn refers to "a special degree of pastoral care and understanding."[22] Bishop Walter Sullivan underlines the "spiritual and pastoral assistance" the Church must provide.[23] Archbishop Raymond Hunthausen states that "we are called upon to provide the leadership, understanding and compassion that are so often missing in our society's approach to controversial issues such as this one."[24] Bishop Stanislas Brzana refers to a pastoral care "extended with understanding, care and sensitivity, but without permissiveness."[25] And so on.

The basis for this special "concern and compassion" in this literature is threefold. (1) Homosexual persons are our brothers and sisters in the Lord. (2) They have suffered from prejudices, misunderstanding and discrimination. (3) They have special challenges and needs.

2. *Complexity of the problem.* This is a recurring theme in nearly all the documents under review. Archbishop Quinn states that "homosexuality in itself is enormously complex in its origins, its psychological vectors, medical ramifications, societal norms and in the application of valid moral principles to individual cases."[26] In summary, it is "an issue of considerable complexity in all dimensions." Archbishop Rembert Weakland begins by noting that "I do not have all the answers in this highly complex issue."[27] He refers to it as a "complex moral issue." Bishop Walter Sullivan asserts that "few other issues . . . are as difficult and complex from every conceivable angle." Archbishop James Hickey regards the issue of homosexuality as "frequently misunderstood, enormously complex."[28] Archbishop Hunthausen calls it simply "a complex issue."[29] Archbishop Roach refers to it as a "complicated question."[30]

3. *Moral statements and analysis.* Here I want to lift out three points made in this literature. The first is the distinction between orientation and acts. Following the *Declaration on Certain Questions Concerning Sexual Ethics* and *To Live in Christ Jesus*, virtually every group or bishop who addresses the topic makes this distinction. Orientation, the American bishops note, is often "through no fault of their own." Others refer to it as simply a "fact" or "morally neutral." Interestingly, Bishop Mugavero, after stating that heterosexuality is normative, says that "any other orientation respects less adequately the full spectrum of human relationships."[31] The Washington State Catholic Conference sees homosexual orientation as "falling short of the norm of total integration implied in the two great commandments."[32] Though there is no personal guilt here, still "one is obliged to change an habitual orientation which falls short of the ideal insofar as one is able to do so." The Conference admits, however, that there is no known way of doing that.

The second notable point is the condemnation of homosexual acts. This is worded in various ways and since the wording is not without considerable significance I shall reproduce it in detail here. The Congregation for the Doctrine of the Faith says homosexual acts are "intrinsically disordered and can in no case be approved."[33] Therefore it concludes that "no pastoral method can be employed which would give moral justification to these acts on the grounds that they would be consonant with the condition of such people."[34]

To Live in Christ Jesus states simply that "homosexual activity . . . is morally wrong." Archbishop Roach uses only the word "wrong."[35] Cardinal Medeiros uses the term "objectively immoral."[36] Archbishop Quinn qualifies homosexual acts as "gravely evil and a disordered use of the sexual faculty."[37] Later, Quinn says "objectively immoral, a human disvalue, disordered." Archbishop Weakland refers to current Church teaching as "one [position] which I cannot sidestep."[38] He then refers to John Paul II's wording in his talk to the American bishops in Chicago. Cardinal Joseph Bernardin uses the term "morally wrong" for homosexual activity.[39] So does Archbishop John F. Whealon.[40] The Massachusetts bishops say "objectively wrong." Archbishop Hickey's phrase is "gravely evil."

Now let us turn to the analyses that are given for such judgments. I shall simply list them systematically.

"Declaration" of the CDF: " . . . acts which lack an essential and indispensable finality."[41]

Bishop Mugavero (of homosexual orientation): " . . . respects less adequately the full spectrum of human relationships."[42]

Archbishop Roach: "Homosexual behavior falls far short of this [sexual bond between husband and wife] sexual and personal ideal. It lacks both the complementarity which exists between masculine and feminine personalities and the possibility of the deepening that can come through sharing the joys and burdens of parenthood and family living."[43]

Cardinal Medeiros: "debase the human person."[44]

Archbishop Quinn: "Sexual intercourse is legitimate and morally good only between husband and wife."[45]

Washington State Catholic Conference: " . . . since it sees these acts as attaining their full significance only in the context of marriage."[46]

Bishop Brzana: "That homosexual acts are wrong is shown by natural law. God, the Creator of nature, established sexual attraction between men and women in order to invite them in marriage and allow them to express mutual love and to bring forth children. Thus human sex has unitive meaning and purpose and a procreative meaning and purpose. Homosexual acts are contrary to both."[47]

Archbishop Hickey: "a disordered use of the sexual faculty given us by God."[48]

Bishops of Massachusetts: "in as much as it falls short of the ultimate norm of Christian morality in the area of genital expression, i.e., a relationship between male and female within the marital union."[49]

Archbishop Whealon: "The Church teaches clearly that genital activity by God's plan is for the basic purpose of procreating the human race."[50]

4. The rights of homosexuals.   The fourth dominant theme of this magisterial literature concerns the rights of homosexual persons. Virtually every letter emphasizes this. For instance, Archbishop Roach states: "Like all persons they have a right to human respect, stable friendships, economic security and social equality. Social isolation, ridicule and economic deprivation of homosexual behavior is not compatible with basic social justice. Consequently, both religious and civic leaders must seek ways to assure homosexuals every human civil right which is their due as persons, without, however, neglecting the rights of the larger community."[51] Archbishop Quinn states that the "Church must continue to uphold the human dignity and the human rights of every person including homosexual persons."[52] Archbishop Hunthausen refers to the "Church's support of the civil rights of persons with a homosexual orientation."[53] Bishop Brzana notes: "Their rights should be honored despite their homosexuality."[54]

There is a twist, however, to all of this. As we have seen, Cardinal O'Connor and Bishop Mugavero opposed the New York City "homosexual rights bill." In 1984, the bishops of Massachusetts opposed a bill before the General Court of Massachusetts that sought to eliminate discrimination. They do so chiefly because such a bill would be viewed by many as "a step toward legal approval of the homosexual lifestyle."[55] They concluded: "Our failure to oppose this bill could give rise to the false impression that the Catholic Church accepts the homosexual lifestyle as a morally feasible option."

Similarly, Cardinal Bernardin, in a 1985 letter to the Illinois Gay and

Lesbian Task Force, distinguished defending civil rights and supporting specific legislation. His concern about specific legislation was its implications. "If it implies acceptance or approval of homosexual activity or advocacy of a lifestyle which encourages homosexual activity, we will have no choice as a Church but to oppose the legislation."[56]

I have tried to present the substance of this literature as completely and fairly as possible. A few personal reactions to it would not be out of place here. These reactions will be tentative in character, with the purpose of making a small contribution to the continuing discussion of this difficult and delicate subject.

1. I find somewhat disingenuous the cheek-by-jowl assertions of the profound complexity of the issue and of the utter clarity of the Church's moral teaching on homosexual acts. That teaching, of course, is that such acts are morally wrong and that homosexuals must live in a celibate life if they are to be chaste. If the matter is so complex, even "in the application of valid moral principles to individual cases" (Archbishop Quinn), where do we derive such clarity? Can we really have it both ways? It is hard to avoid the impression that we are being lulled by lip-service. The first place complexity should appear is in conclusions. Yet aside from Weakland, Sullivan, Hunthausen and Mugavero, there is very little indication of a sense of complexity.

2. *The Declaration on Certain Questions Concerning Sexual Ethics* and *To Live in Christ Jesus* are constantly referred to as representing "the teaching of the Church." What are the implications of that statement? Does it mean that any theological analysis or proposal that diverges from the formulations or conclusions of these documents is thereby invalidated? Is there no room for development beyond these documents? If they are simply the measure of acceptability of theological work, does this not endow them with a stability and permanence that we are rightly reluctant to give even more authoritative documents, and that is historically unsupportable? Is there legitimate place for dissent from these documents? What theological work really remains if "homosexual acts are intrinsically disordered and can in no case be approved"? (CDF)

I raise these questions because there are four remarkably different statements made about theological work in this area. The first is that of Archbishop James Hickey. In his 1984 letter he states: "Those who deny the teaching of the Church or equivocate by offering alternatives to official Church teaching must know that I am obliged by my duty as bishop to refuse both recognition and support."[57] Does anyone who offers "alternatives to official Church teaching" really "equivocate"? Is it not possible that such "alternatives" represent development rather than "equivocation"? Or is any development excluded in this area? If so, on what grounds? Even more radically, what constitutes a "denial" of Church teaching? Is there no room for the distinction between the substance and the formulation of this teaching, a distinction affirmed by John XXIII and Vatican II even for truths of the faith? What is the substance of the Church's teaching? What constitutes an "alternative" to this substance? Does not a bishop have some kind of duty to encourage or at least tolerate development of the Church's teaching? These are very legitimate theological questions. Unless I misread him, Archbishop Hickey presupposes a single answer to them.

The second statement is that of Cardinal Medeiros.[58] He acknowledges "the significant gift that theologians offer us in the Church." He then immediately adds: "Their probing work is always tentative until tested and refined in and by the Church. In pastoral practice we must adhere to the theological positions which have been officially incorporated into Church teaching."

Most theologians would, I think, agree with that statement. But they would squeeze it dry of the questions it raises. How is theological work "tested and refined"? Is it not by experience? Then by further theological exchange? If theological analyses that diverge, however slightly, from official formulations are to be rejected, how can theological work be "tested and refined"? Is this testing and refining done by mere comparison with official formulations? If testing and refining is to be done "in and by the Church," who counts as "the Church"? Is it only the Congregation for the Doctrine of the Faith ? Or the bishops who repeat its formulations? Are homosexuals included? Is testing and refining of some proposals permissible, but of others (e.g., Cahill and Curran) not? How do we establish the difference between the two? How and on what criteria are theological positions "officially incorporated into Church teaching"? What theological position of what theologians is incorporated into the "Declaration" of the Congregation? Was this position "tested and refined" before incorporation? How and by whom? Such questions are not arrogant assaults on authority. They are dead-serious attempts to insist that the Church be theologically (and publicly so) accountable, that it be as truly open to the Spirit as it professes to be.

The third statement is that of Archbishop Rembert Weakland. After admitting that "I do not have all the answers in this highly complex issue," Weakland states: "I look for more dialogue among the grass roots level, our pastoral ministers and academic people in all fields, so that all sides can contribute to a deeper understanding of this complex moral issue."[59]

It will come as no surprise that I find Weakland's statement outstanding. It conveys the sense of complexity that Weakland professes and takes it seriously. There is the inescapable sense in the document that there are no easy answers. Weakland admits frankly that "deeper understanding" is possible and desirable. Furthermore, if it is to occur, there must be dialogue involving "all sides." What this "deeper understanding" will lead to Weak-

land does not, indeed cannot, say. But he hints that the present understanding is incomplete; for he refers to the need "to work out the rightful
place of these people in Church life." What must be "worked out" is clearly
not presently available.

The final statement is that of Archbishop Raymond Hunthausen.
Asked if the "official position" of the Church is likely to change, Hunthausen responded that there are "credible theologians in the Church who
say it cannot; there are also credible theologians who believe that it can."[60]
In pursuing the matter, Hunthausen recalled that "certain aspects of the
Church's teaching on homosexuality have undergone development in recent years." As an example he adduced the distinction between orientation
and activity. "When one adds to this new developments in the human and
behavioral sciences, it is not difficult to understand why theologians are
continually in this kind of re-examination." Obviously, Hunthausen rightly
believes that if development has occurred already, further development can
continue to occur.

Like Weakland, Hunthausen notes that dialogue is occurring in the
Church and should continue. He explicitly states that "we need to be aware
of the lived experience of homosexual persons and their families." To the
collective body of knowledge and experience "we must bring openness of
mind, critical judgment and a profound sense of charity—as well as a great
deal of prayer."[61] This same emphasis was asserted by the document "A
Ministry to Lesbian and Gay Catholic Persons" (Archdiocese of Baltimore). It stated: "The Church must listen to gays and lesbians to learn
what they have to teach about the saving presence of Christ among us."[62] I
have the distinct impression that many churchmen are *speaking to*, rather
than *listening to* gays and lesbians.

Interestingly and prophetically, Hunthausen states: "I must say I
await with great interest the findings of our theologians and the ensuing
dialogue between them and the Church's magisterium." Clearly, Hunthausen believes that "the findings of our theologians" are relevant to any
further development of the Church's teaching. He must have had tongue at
least partially in cheek when he referred to the reactions of the magisterium
to such findings as an "ensuing dialogue." Would that it could be so!

In summary, then, I find the attitudinal distance (toward theology) between Weakland-Hunthausen-Mugavero and Hickey-Medeiros-Brzana-
Congregation for the Doctrine of the Faith to be immense.

3. The third point to be raised concerns the relationship between
orientation and acts. This distinction is a relatively recent arrival on the
Catholic scene. Charles Curran attributes it to the work of John Harvey.
Lisa Cahill sees its origin in contemporary scientific studies. Whatever the
case, it is recent in Catholic formulations, as Archbishop Hunthausen
notes. That is fact one.

Fact two is that official Catholic rejection of homosexual acts antedates by far knowledge of homosexuality as a not-chosen and most often irreversible orientation. That leads to the interesting and provocative question: does this knowledge have *no influence whatsoever* on the assessment of homosexual behavior (acts) at the objective level? One has to wonder if the distinction between orientation and acts, acknowledged now by all official documents and pastorals, has not remained abstract and unexamined in these documents with respect to its possible implications.

The Catholic Council for Church and Society (Netherlands) regards the relationship between orientation and behavior as "the heart of the matter in evaluating homosexuality."[63] If they are joined too closely, an easy and uncritical approval of homosexual behavior can occur. So can continued discrimination. If they are separated at too great a distance (with orientation accepted but behavior rejected), the orientation really means nothing in an objective evaluation. A dimension of reality is acknowledged but seems to remain essentially nonfunctional in critical reflection.

Archbishop Hickey adverts to the fact that objections have been raised about the Church's teaching in terms of new scientific discoveries, a different way of understanding Scripture, and the influence of ignorance, prejudice and social conditions on that teaching. His response is stunning: "The Church has taken into account all these objections and has given clear guidance regarding homosexuality."[64] How has the Church "taken into account all these objections?" Who is this "Church"? Has the gay and lesbian experience been listened to? Has pastoral and theological dialogue been encouraged? Or is it not the case that when theologians propose somewhat different analyses, their books lose the *imprimatur* (Philip Keane) or they lose their mission to teach as Catholic theologians (Charles Curran)?

Archbishop Hickey's first and chief reference is the "Declaration on Certain Questions Concerning Sexual Ethics." Can we say with a straight face, so to speak, that "the *Church* has taken into account ... " when we know that the declaration was mainly the work of three theologians (E. Lio, Pietro Palazzini, Jan Visser) whose perspectives were described by Bernard Häring as "not *the* preconciliar theology, but a very distinct preconciliar theology,"[65] the type rejected by Vatican II in its rejection of several preliminary drafts of "The Church in the Modern World"?

4. Several of the statements oppose specific civil rights legislation on the grounds that endorsing it might lead people to believe that the homosexual lifestyle was being endorsed. Is there not a better and available alternative to opposition? Is not such proposed legislation a fine opportunity to educate people? How long can we claim that we defend civil rights if we oppose every instance of specific legislation to secure such rights?

5. I want now to return to the wording of the rejection of homosexual behavior. The Congregation for the Doctrine of the Faith says such

behavior "can in no case be approved." That would seem to be simple and clear. Yet it leaves several questions. What does "approval" mean? Does one who acknowledges the presence of premoral evil in homosexual behavior simply "approve" it? Does one who sees homosexual behavior as falling short of the norm, as essentially "flawed," yet the best that can be hoped for in certain cases, "approve" it? Does one who states that in some cases such behavior might embody, in a broken world, the qualities of honesty, fidelity, commitment, "approve" it? Similar questions could be raised with the Congregation's term "moral justification." For instance, if one takes into account personal and social circumstances "in the application of valid moral principles to individual cases" (Archbishop John Quinn's usage), is one involved in "moral justification"? The terms used in the episcopal pastoral letters are "objectively immoral," "morally wrong," "objectively wrong," etc. Can we understand these terms as generalizations within "valid moral principles" but not always in their application? If application of "valid moral principles" must take into account personal circumstances and is very "complex" (Quinn), what does this say about the objective character of the acts to which such principles are applied? Or again, can an act be "intrinsically disordered" and still not be, because of personal circumstances, "morally wrong and presumably sinful" (Archbishop John Whealon's designation of not-open-to-procreation genital acts)? St. Thomas held this with regard to killing. Abstractly considered, he noted, it contained a "deformity" but it could be justified by circumstances.[66] If "intrinsic disorder" always translates into "morally wrong," what is so "complex" (Archbishop Quinn) about applying the norm to individual cases?

The Catholic Social Welfare Commission put my question in a different way.

> Of course, pastoral care does not consist simply in the rigid and automatic application of objective moral norms. It considers the individual in his actual situation, with all his strengths and weaknesses. The decision of conscience, determining what should be done and what avoided, can only be made after prudent consideration of the real situation as well as the moral norm.[67]

It seems clear that this document, under the notion of "application" of a moral norm and pastoral care, is not speaking merely about subjective guilt. It refers to a decision of conscience about "what should be done and what avoided."

The question I am raising can be put from the perspective of the analyses of the wrongfulness of homosexual acts. If one grants, with Archbishop Roach, that homsexual behavior lacks complementarity and procreative potential, and yet admits that in some instances it may be the only realistic option for an individual, is that "moral justification" and "approval"?

The answer to this question is crucial, not only to the meaning of the general understanding of moral norms and their application, but to the intraecclesial discussion. For if one's analysis is seen as "approving" or "morally justifying" actions that are "intrinsically disordered" (CDF), then one can easily be marginalized as "denying Church teaching."

6. Finally, it must be emphasized that the very manner of presenting the Church's teaching can be problematic. No one, of course, should argue that a moral judgment of homosexual behavior is itself a form of discrimination. In this respect, some advocates and activists burst the limits of common sense. However, there are ways of presenting the Church's teaching that contribute to prejudice. I find Cardinal Medeiros' usage ("debases the human person") in this category.

Above all, however, is what the Catholic Council for Church and Society calls a "too one-sided and exaggerated attention to sexual behavior."[68] Such overemphasis is not only unrealistic sexual reductionism (the reduction of the person to her/his private parts); it also tends to tie behavior and orientation so closely together that the latter suffers by association with the former. Thus fuel is added to the fire of prejudice. Firmness is not fixation. Negative overstatement and underlining gives the proclamation of compassion a hollow ring.

Key Concepts Pointing a Direction

Under this rubric I wish to list four points that can easily be overlooked when there is discussion of the "morality of homosexuality." Even such a phrase is misleading. There is no such thing as homosexuality. There are only persons with greater or lesser homosexual inclinations, experience, etc. That being said, the following points—all bearing on the term "morality"—seem important in developing a balanced position.

1. Specific and individual rectitude. The moral rightness and wrongness of our conduct has two distinguishable dimensions. One, which I call specific rectitude, refers to those characteristics independent of personal dispositions, attitudes, goals, circumstances. For instance, in traditional Christian theology, the married state is said to be required for the moral rectitude of sexual relations. Individual rectitude refers to the personal attitudes, actions, circumstances that qualify our conduct. For instance, for the *full* moral rectitude of sexual intimacy, there is required, beyond the married state, concern, respect, communication, tenderness, etc.

Many discussions of morality tend to overlook this and identify morality with specific rectitude alone. Such an exclusive emphasis leads to one-sidedness. For instance, the term "fornication" is occasionally used to designate all premarital intercourse. Such a usage overlooks aspects of human experience with enormously important moral implications. There are remarkable moral differences between casual sexual relations and those between persons engaged to be married. Exclusive emphasis on specific rectitude appears at times to be unreal precisely because it does not take account of all of reality.

2. Moral and pastoral levels. A moral statement is a normative statement of the morally right or wrong, of the humanly constructive or destructive. It embodies what is judged to be morally right or wrong and invites to it or to its avoidance. Thus "abortion is morally wrong" contains the implicit invitation or mandate to avoid this action in our personal lives and to create a world wherein it is no longer a tragic necessity. Such a moral statement says nothing about the personal weaknesses, background, and circumstances of those who must try to comply with it.

The pastoral level takes into account the personal circumstances, histories, strengths and weakness of individuals. It looks to the actual and the possible. Under "circumstances" two different kinds of considerations can be included. First, there are those that affect the very objective meaning of the action in question. Such circumstances are envisaged when we speak of the *application* of a moral norm. They can result in its qualification or even its suspension, depending on how completely formulated the norm is in the first place. Second, there are those circumstances that touch on individual strengths and weaknesses, on the degree of *responsibility* or *culpability* for nonobservance of the norm. I have the impression that these two kinds of circumstances are not always distinguished in the use of term "application" [of a moral norm]. Therefore, the terms "pastoral level" and "pastoral practice" sometimes confusedly include both.

Let me use the document of the Catholic Social Welfare Commission (English bishops) to illustrate my point. In dealing with the "pastoral care" of homophiles, it states at one point:

> There will frequently be a physical genital expression in such unions. Objectively, this is morally unacceptable. The question is: Are such persons necessarily culpable? That judgment cannot be made in the abstract but in the concrete circumstances in which the acts take place.[69]

Here "concrete circumstances" is concerned with circumstances that affect *culpability* only. For "objectively, this is morally unacceptable."

At another place the document states:

> The pastoral counselling of homophile persons cannot ignore the objec-

tive morality of homosexual genital acts, but it is important to interpret them, to understand the pattern of life in which they take place, to appreciate the personal meaning which these acts have for different people.[70]

Such considerations would seem to affect not just culpability but the very meaning of the actions in question. Therefore they really pertain more properly to the moral level. This impression is strengthened when the document states: "while objective norms are clear-cut the application of such norms may be complicated." It gives the following example:

A specially delicate situation arises when homosexual persons are convinced that, although they accept that homosexual acts in themselves cannot be justified, it is found impossible in practice to lead a celibate life. They might then claim that the choice remains between a stable union, in which there is a necessary and inevitable physical relationship and an obviously distasteful promiscuous way of life. Such persons argue that in their particular case the stability of the union outweighs the disorder of the homosexual acts which take place within it. They would argue that the goodness or badness of an act can only be judged morally in practice when consideration has been given to intention and circumstances.[71]

Clearly, the situation here is concerned chiefly with the "goodness or badness of an act," not primarily with culpability. And this is seen as an "application" of an objective norm. In summary, in one place "application" refers to subjective culpability. In another, it refers to the very rightness or wrongness of the act. And since both "applications" are seen as instances of "pastoral care," that term itself must include both.

This is very interesting. It must be recalled that the CDF states that "no pastoral method can be employed which would give moral justification to these [homosexual genital] acts on the grounds that they would be consonant with the condition of such people." Unless I badly misread the English document, it is claiming that it does not give "moral justification" for homosexual acts because it holds the *norm* that such acts are "morally unacceptable, objectively." When it "applies" this norm, it is moving clearly in the direction of moral justification for "specially delicate situations," for *individual instances*. Otherwise, why is the "application of such norms" so "complicated"? In saying this, I do not criticize it. I simply note it. The English document might escape the reach of the Congregation's stricture by arguing that it does, indeed, justify homosexual acts in its "application" of the norm, but not precisely "on the grounds that they should be consonant with the condition of such people." They might adduce other reasons, for example, "the stability of the union outweighs the disorder of the homosexual acts which take place within it."

I have no problem with that. Nor do I have a problem with understanding "application" of a norm in the two senses mentioned above (subjective culpability and the very meaning of the action). What I do have a problem with, however, is the implication that when we "apply" a norm to an individual case, we leave the realm of *objective* morality. We leave the realm of general statement, not the objective realm. Or better, we fit the general statement to individual circumstances and differences which pertain to the realm of *objective*, albeit individual morality.

At any rate, moral statements must be distinguished (though not separated) from pastoral adaptations. Under such adaptations I would include circumstances affecting both culpability (for what is clearly wrong) and the determination itself of wrongfulness at the personal level.

3. *Morality and acts.* This is close to but not identical with the first point. When the term "morality" is used, too often the attention is riveted on acts, especially external ones. Other dimensions are neglected. Morality is concerned with the meaning of our actions. Where sex is concerned, we have seen meaning and morality too exclusively in terms of acts. Human sexuality is our most basic capacity for relatedness and sexual expression is the language of relation. Thus it is the self relating in a constructive or destructive way. Sexual expression is so often an exploitative act, *self*-consoling, *self*-reassuring—a kind of outlet avenue for failure to adjust in other areas and to cope. That is why conversation with those with sexual problems is often about loneliness, frustration, inability to cope with setbacks. Growing sexually is not above all a biological matter. It is all about caring for others, respecting them, communicating with them. The sexually immature are so often the self-absorbed. One can avoid sexual violations and be profoundly sexually immature. Concentration on acts can easily miss what is the common task of all of us, the married, celibates, hetero- or homosexuals.

4. *Legality and morality.* The confusion of these two makes it difficult to discuss morality intelligently. There are still many people who believe that if certain actions are removed from the penal code, they are morally acceptable. Therefore they keep them on the penal code. The gay community has long suffered persecution for this reason. Measures supporting their basic rights are opposed because their lifestyle is rejected, or because such measures might appear to endorse their conduct or lifestyle.

A Modest Proposal

Before making such a proposal, I should state clearly my own moral position. I accept the heterosexual orientation and heterosexual genital expression as normative. By that I do not mean that all marriages or heterosexual unions are happy and fulfilling. Nor do I mean that all homosexual unions are unhappy and always destructive. Rather I mean that the covenanted friendship of marriage offers us the best opportunity to humanize our sexuality and our selves. Therefore we all *ought* (normative) to strive to structure our sexuality in this way.

It is a fair question to ask about the derivation of this moral position. I cannot "prove" this if by "proof" we understand the type of evidence associated with the hard sciences. Some try to work from sexual distinction. But sexual distinction is a fact. What human beings make of it is a different thing. This latter was modified throughout history but never, I judge, in such a way as to submerge the underlying human tendency to mate and procreate children. That has remained a basic value cross-culturally.

Others speak of the "biblical norm."[72] This is certainly accurate if we accept that notion in a quite general sense. That is, heterosexual genital expression seems to be taken for granted as normative in the biblical materials. That, of course, opens on and leaves unanswered a larger metaethical question: how do the biblical materials relate to our basic moral convictions? Do they originate or confirm them? I would opt for the latter although I think it legitimate shorthand to use the term "the biblical norm."

Some statements proposed as proofs are really descriptive. Let one from Eric Fromm be an example.

> The male-female polarity is also the basis for interpersonal creativity. This is obvious biologically in the fact that the union of sperm and ovum is the basis for the birth of a child. But in the purely psychic realm it is not different; in the love between man and woman, each of them is reborn.[73]

If I understand Fromm accurately, his analogy between the biological and psychic is saying that we grow and create psychically in the man-woman relationship. By implication we do not in homosexual relationships. Similar statements can be found elsewhere, for example, in Abel Jeanniere's *The Anthropology of Sex*. The affirmative statement might well be true without the implied negation following.

Even after one has introduced disclaimers, qualifiers and a hundred distinctions, I still believe that Bishop Francis Mugavero has it right when he states:

> The complexus of anthropological, psychological and theological reasoning in regard to human sexuality has contributed to the Church's teaching that heterosexuality is normative. All should strive for a sexual integration which respects that norm since any other orientation respects less adequately the full spectrum of human relationships.[74]

Having stated my agreement with Mugavero's formulation, I want immediately to identify myself with a statement made by Ralph Weltge.

> The bind I feel is not located in the Christian norm itself. Theologically I subscribe to that norm with conviction. For me the problem lies in how the norm is used in church and society, what is done by design or default to those who violate it. The homosexual bears pressures, indignities and injustices which demand relief. The question is how to take up his cause without either sacrificing the norm or sanctioning its use as a cover for persecution.[75]

To Mugavero's statement, a spontaneous question occurs: What if they have "striven for a sexual integration . . . " but failed? From Weltge's paragraph I lift out the question: How should the norm be used in the Church? These questions bring us to the heart of the moral-pastoral problem—and to my modest suggestion.

Twenty years ago, I taught a course on the moral-pastoral dimensions of homosexuality. I asked each student to respond to this question: How should the Church, as a community and in the person of the individual minister, respond to the gay phenomenon? The answer was to be one page in length because I remain convinced that if one is clear about what is to be said, one page will be enough. (At some point, of course, such a statement bucks the size of this volume.) I want to reproduce my own one-pager here because it constitutes the heart of my modest suggestion.

> I believe the formal position of the Church toward the gay community should coincide with a theologically sound and humanly healthy pastoral attitude. It might build as follows:
>
> 1. The power of sin in the world, even the redeemed world, remains virulent and manifests itself in oppressive and enslaving structures, both individual and social, that touch us all. Individually we are anxious, neurotic, physically ill, selfish, emotionally crippled, instinctively limited. Socially our structures prevent equality of opportunity, reinforce poverty and greed, discriminate. All these things isolate and divide us and inhibit our growth as loving persons.
>
> 2. Christ is the liberator supreme. He came to liberate us all by his graceful presence (life-death-resurrection) from the grip of sin and from its structural manifestations. This he did by offering to us the capacity to love after his example, and thus fulfill our potential as human beings. A lifetime work.
>
> 3. His followers, members of his body or people ("in Christ") are a continuation of his presence. Therefore they find the meaning of their lives in expanding the capacities of others to love—in liberating them from all that prevents love from growing and flowering in individuals. They bind every wound, shelter the sick, share possessions with the poor, educate the young, compassionate with the bereaved, protect the innocent, bring

therapy to the mentally ill—but above all work to change the structures that allow human vacua and deprivations to exist—and always with the intent to expand a person's capacity to love by loving that person in every concrete way possible. For we learn to love by being loved.

4. The power of sin will reveal itself in our sexuality, not only in exploitative, self-destructive *actions* and patterns of behavior, but also in the underlying personality *configurations* which are not totally of our own making. E.g., narcissism, impotence, deviation of instinct. The believing community, conscious of its own need, is there to liberate and heal wherever there is a human being in need. In doing this it is convinced that it is making Christ present and foreshadowing his coming Kingdom, even if stumblingly and imperfectly.

5. It has been and remains the Church's conviction (based on biblical, anthropological, philosophical evidence, her own experience and reflection) that the sexual expression of interpersonal love offers us the best chance for our growth and humanization—therefore for our maturation as loving persons in Christ's image—if it is structured within the man-woman relationship of covenanted (permanent and exclusive) friendship. Hence she invites all men and women to reach for this ideal in the interests of their own well-being. In her ministry, therefore, she attempts— in a spirit of reverence and respect for the individual—to prevent, remove, or attenuate any impediments that would make this impossible or more difficult, though this is not her prime pastoral concern.

6. If, however, an individual is incapable of structuring his sexual intimacy within such a relationship (is irreversibly homosexual), and is not called to celibacy for the Kingdom, the liberating presence and concern of the community will take a different form (for *nemo tenetur ad impossibile*). In this instance, both the Church and her ministers will be a liberating presence to the homosexual: (a) by inviting him to approximate the qualities of the covenanted man-woman relationship through fidelity and exclusiveness; (b) by aiding the individual to develop those healthy, outgoing attitudes and emotional responses that make this possible; (c) by extending the full sacramental and social supports of the Church to his striving; (d) by condemning and combatting all social, legal and ecclesial discrimination against and oppression of the homosexual.

I think it important to highlight several aspects of this admittedly tentative approach. First, it states that the Church "invites all men and women to reach for this ideal." This is intended to state the normative character (the *oughtness*) of the heterosexual, both orientation and acts, a point made by Mugavero, Curran, Cahill and many others.

Second, in no. 6, the situation of the "irreversible homosexual" is introduced. Two conditions are listed: (1) *If* the person is irreversibly homosexual and (2) *if* the person is not called to celibacy for the Kingdom. A word about each. It is generally admitted now—though all the literature admits that we have much to learn yet—that many persons with a homosexual orientation cannot, in spite of their best efforts, alter this. This is a factual matter; therefore I italicize *if*.

The second condition refers to the call to celibacy for the Kingdom. By that usage I refer to the situation where the attempt to lead a celibate life would prove destructive and disintegrating to the individual. That, of course, is an extremely difficult and delicate judgment, especially in times of cultural pansexualism. I have no idea of the number of people to whom it might apply.

One thing seems clear: both judgments (irreversibly homosexual, not called to celibacy) are the *responsibility of the individual before God*. If an individual concludes—even with the help of a pastoral counsellor—that she/he fulfills these conditions, the Church (remembering the difference between specific and individual rectitude, and the difference between the moral and the pastoral, this latter including application to individual persons) can understand this and *ought to respect such a decision made before God*. The Church does not "justify" such a decision for the simple reason that she cannot. It is the individual's responsibility. But the Church can respect it. It is at this point that a "pastoral of approximation" takes on significance (doing the best one can to achieve the normative).

At this point, two questions are unavoidable. First, does this solution differ from those proposed by Cahill and Curran? Materially, I think not. But it does make explicit—and that is why I call it "modest"—that the judgments involved are the individual's responsibility before God and that subsequent conduct is still guided by a "pastoral of approximation" (built on the distinction between specific and individual rectitude).

The second question is: does this approach "justify" homosexual behavior? This is the CDF's concern. But again, it must be recalled that the term "justify" is loose and ambiguous. If it is taken to mean "put on a par with heterosexual acts" or "give legitimacy to," it does not "justify" homosexual acts. It does not say that such acts are not flawed, not disordered. If it is taken to mean that homosexual acts, however incomplete, flawed and disordered, cannot in all situations be said to be morally wrong, it does "justify" them. But that is to say no more than that moral norms, however valid, are limited formulations. When they are applied, they encounter brokenness, complexity, and restricted options. That is why Archbishop John Quinn could say "homosexuality in itself is enormously complex . . . in the application of valid moral principles to individual cases." Moral principles do not themselves dissolve such complexity. Conscience must. The Church must acknowledge and respect that responsibility of conscience without trying to dictate its conclusions.

The modest probe that concludes this chapter would not be complete without reference to the CDF's "Letter to the Bishops of the Catholic Church on the Pastoral Care of Homosexual Persons."[76] The letter aroused a great deal of controversy. On the one hand, Gabriel Moran referred to it as "one of the most duplicitous documents in the modern era of the Catholic Church."[77] Benedict M. Ashley, O.P., by contrast, asserts that the document "tried to speak the healing truth."[78] Numerous commentators have scored what was seen to be the callous tone of the document, perhaps especially the following statement: "Even when the practice of homosexuality may seriously threaten the lives and well-being of a large number of people, its advocates remain undeterred and refuse to consider the magnitude of the risks involved" (no. 9).

What attracted most attention in the document was its statement that what it calls the homosexual "condition" (or "inclination") is itself "disordered." The CDF letter noted that its earlier treatment (December 29, 1975, "Declaration on Certain Questions Concerning Sexual Ethics") had distinguished "the homosexual condition or tendency and individual homosexual actions." Some had given this distinction an "overly benign interpretation," going so far as to call the condition "neutral, or even good." On the basis of this interpretation, some concluded that homosexual acts were not always morally wrong. For this reason the CDF goes out of its way (four times) to underline that the condition is disordered. As it words it:

> Although the particular inclination of the homosexual person is not a sin, it is a more or less strong tendency ordered toward an intrinsic moral evil; and thus the inclination itself must be seen as an objective disorder (no. 3).

At another point (no. 7), the letter refers to this disordered inclination as "essentially self-indulgent."

One of the major pastoral problems raised with this analysis originates with the December 29, 1975 Declaration (*Persona Humana*) cited above. At the very outset it states:

> The human person, present-day scientists maintain, is so profoundly affected by sexuality that it must be considered one of the principal formative influences on the life of a man or woman. In fact, sex is the source of the biological, psychological and spiritual characteristics which make a person male or female and which thus considerably influence each individual's progress towards maturity and membership of society.[79]

Now if "one of the principal formative influences" of the person is said to be "disordered," it seems quite clear that the individuals's dignity and self-esteem have been massively assaulted. No one welcomes "disorder" as a description of those biological, psychological and spiritual characteristics that make him/her a male/female person. For that means quite simply that the person is disordered. Further calls for compassion are cold comfort.

This is undoubtedly the most controversial aspect of the letter. It will continue to provoke scholarly commentary and reaction. Just a few tentative comments are in order here. All center around the notion of "disorder."

First, as Robert Nugent has observed, the CDF's letter invariably associates "tendency," "inclination," "orientation" with homogenital *acts*.[80] But, he continues, "sexual orientation is not fundamentally or even primarily a tendency toward *acts*, but a psychosexual attraction (erotic, emotional and affective) toward particular individual *persons*." Would the same designation ("disorder") be appropriate for this attraction toward persons? If so, why? I raise this question because it is precisely the morally wrongful character of the acts that leads the CDF to pronounce the orientation a disorder.

Second, what is the meaning of "disorder"? By linking orientation to acts, the CDF leaves the impression that it is a *moral* disorder of some kind. Yet obviously it does not and cannot mean this, for the letter states explicitly that the inclination is not a sin (by which I take it, generously, to mean "morally wrong.") If it were considered a *moral* disorder, the implication would be that it was freely chosen, which appears factually false in most cases.

What, then, does "disorder" mean when used to designate an orientation? A functional disability, like sterility, frigidity or impotence? This is the reading given by Benedict Ashley, O.P.[81] He refers to the orientation as a "disability," "such troubles." "Was not the term 'disorder'," he pointedly asks, "chosen precisely to indicate that the orientation is not 'immoral' but only a difficulty for the moral life?" If Ashley is correct, then one has to wonder why "disorder" was used at all. What is gained by so designating it? The term is precise enough in itself to invite extremely sinister interpretations, especially moral connotations. This question is all the more urgent since, in fact, the CDF uses "disorder" precisely because the inclination is to *immoral acts*. That makes it look much more like a *moral* disability.

Third, and more radically, does an "inclination" to an action that is morally wrong render the inclination "disordered"? Is there not a sense in which the vast majority of young people are "inclined to" sexual intercourse *before marriage*? When in love, they want (are "inclined to") sexual intimacy now. Yet it is clear that the CDF would view such intimacy as intrinsically evil. If the precise reason for referring to the homosexual orientation as "disorder" is that it inclines to immoral acts, then any inclination that does this in re immoral acts is also disordered. Is the sexual instinct (or appetite) therefore disordered? It "inclines to" masturbation in adolescence. Once again, then, the question returns: what is achieved by designating homosexual orientation a "disorder"? It strikes me as being totally unnecessary to the defense of traditional Catholic conclusions about homosexual acts.

One can say that homogenital acts always depart from the ideal or the normative. I would have little, indeed no, problem with that. But why not leave it at that? To work back from that tenet to the assertion that the orientation is disordered is neither necessary (to support of the tenet) nor pastorally helpful. Indeed, it makes any truly pastoral approach virtually impossible. I am afraid that it reveals—once again—that the CDF can hear only voices and formulations from the past, or is dominantly concerned with conclusions authoritatively formulated in the past. It is not difficult to call this "moralism." I hasten to say that this does not mean disagreement with the *substantial* concerns of the letter. But those concerns have been so poorly stated that the document will remain something of a museum piece. (One hates to be negative. But how do you get the CDF to realize this?)

But my main concern with the CDF's letter must be its relationship to the modest pastoral suggestion made above. After long study of the letter, I would conclude that it simply does not address the problem at the practical pastoral level in the terms used in my modest proposal.

Let me put this in a slightly different way. If the letter of the CDF meant to preempt the judgment about what is morally right or wrong (or at least tolerable) *for this individual in these circumstances*, it surpassed its competence. For I fully agree with Cardinal Ratzinger when he reported to the priests of his diocese (Munich) after the 1980 Synod:

> Wherefore the criterion of *Humanae Vitae*, clear as it is, is not inflexible, but open for differentiated judgments of ethically differentiated situations.[82]

If this is true of *Humanae Vitae*, which pronounced contraceptive acts intrinsically evil, it is no less true of the CDF's letter.

Notes

1. Cf. chapter 6 in this volume.
2. *New York Times*, 17 March 1986.
3. *New York Times*, 10 February 1986.
4. It was the judgment of all expert witnesses for Georgetown University that this is what the Gay Coalition was doing.
5. John F. Harvey, "Homosexuality," *New Catholic Encyclopedia* (New York: McGraw-Hill, 1967), vol. 7, 116-19. Cf. also "Contemporary Theological Views," in John R. Cavanagh, *Counseling the Homosexual* (Huntington: Our Sunday Visitor, 1977), 222-38.
6. Edward A. Malloy, C.S.C., *Homosexuality and the Christian Way of Life* (Lanham, Md.: Unviersity Press of America, 1981).
7. Loc. cit., 322.
8. Loc. cit., 360.
9. Loc. cit., 359.

10. Lisa Sowle Cahill, "Moral Methodology: A Case Study," *Chicago Studies* 19 (1980):171-87.

11. Loc. cit., 185.

12. Loc. cit., 186.

13. Loc. cit., 186.

14. Charles E. Curran, *Critical Consensus in Moral Theology* (Notre Dame, Ind.: University of Notre Dame Press, 1984), 93.

15. Loc. cit., 93.

16. *Homosexuality and the Magisterium*, ed. John Gallagher (Mt. Ranier, Md.: New Ways Ministry, 1986). Hereafter I shall abbreviate as HM.

17. HM, 7.

18. HM, 9.

19. HM, 8.

20. HM, 11.

21. HM, 15.

22. HM, 25.

23. HM, 43.

24. HM, 79.

25. HM, 93.

26. HM, 23.

27. HM, 34.

28. HM, 94.

29. HM, 83.

30. HM, 10.

31. HM, 8.

32. HM, 48.

33. HM, 7.

34. HM, 7.

35. HM, 10.

36. HM, 17.

37. HM, 25.

38. HM, 35.

39. HM, 103.

40. HM, 101.

41. HM, 7.

42. HM, 8.

43. HM, 10.

44. HM, 17.

45. HM, 31.

46. HM, 48.

47. HM, 91.

48. HM, 95.

49. HM, 97.

50. HM, 102.

51. HM, 10.

52. HM, 26.

53. HM, 80.

54. HM, 92.

55. HM, 98.

56. HM, 103-04.

57. HM, 96.

58. HM, 18.

59. HM, 34-35.

60. HM, 84.

61. HM, 86.

62. HM, 41.

63. *Homosexual People in Society* (Mt. Rainier, Md.: New Ways Ministry, 1980), 17.

64. HM, 94.

65. Bernard Häring, "Reflexionen zur Erklärung der Glaubenskongregation über einige Fragen der Sexualethik," *Theologisch-praktische Quartalschrift* 124 (1976):115-26.

66. *Quaestiones quodlibetales* 9, q. 7, a. 15.

67. *An Introduction to the Pastoral Care of Homosexual People* (Mt. Rainier, Md.: New Ways Ministry, 1981), 8.

68. HM, 18.

69. Cf. note 67 at 9.

70. Ibid., 8.

71. Ibid., 9.

72. Roger L. Shinn, "Homosexuality: Christian Conviction and Inquiry," in *The Same Sex*, ed. Ralph W. Weltge (Philadelphia: Pilgrim Press, 1969), 43-54.

73. Eric Fromm, *The Art of Loving* (New York: Harper & Row, 1956), 33-34.

74. HM, 8.

75. Ralph Weltge, "The Paradox of Man and Woman," in *The Same Sex*, 60.

76. Vatican City: Vatican Polyglot Press, 1986.

77. Gabriel Moran, "Gays: The Rome Way," *National Catholic Reporter*, 23 January 1986, p. 10.

78. Benedict M. Ashley, O.P., "Compassion and Sexual Orientation," in Jeannine Gramick and Pat Furey, eds., *The Vatican and Homosexuality* (New York: Crossroad, 1988), 109.

79. Congregation for the Doctrine of the Faith, "Declaration on Certain Questions Concerning Sexual Ethics," as in Austin Flannery, O.P., ed., *Vatican Council II: More Postconciliar Documents* (Northport, N.Y.: Costello Publ.Co., 1982), 486.

80. Robert Nugent, "Sexual Orientation in Vatican Thinking," in *The Vatican and Homosexuality*, 55.

81. Ashley, as in note 78 at 106 and 110, note 1. Further discussions of this matter as well as of the letter in general are found in Bruce Williams, O.P., "Homosexuality: The New Vatican Statement," *Theological Studies* 48 (1987):258-77 and Gerald D. Coleman, S.S., "The Vatican Statement on Homosexuality," *Theological Studies* 48 (1987):727-34.

82. Cited in Bernard Häring, "Pastorale Erwägungen zur Bischofssynode über Familie und Ehe," *Theologie der Gegenwart* 24 (1981):71-80.

Chapter 18

AIDS: The Shape of the Ethical Challenge

Californian Artie Wallace, 32, was diagnosed with AIDS (Acquired Immune Deficiency Syndrome) during July 1986. On August 3, 1987, his ex-wife fled with their nine-year-old son Shawn, who wanted to live with his father.[1] She feared their son would get AIDS and disapproved of Wallace's living with another man. This human tragedy—involving lawyers, judges and a private investigator—could easily be a symbol of the sufferings of thousands throughout the country. It has all the dimensions we have come to associate with AIDS: ignorance, fear, separation, loneliness, alienation, stigma, judgment, pain and death. It is not surprising, therefore, that the AIDS epidemic casts up ethical problems at virtually every stage of its relentless onslaught.

If we are to face these problems in a humanly compassionate and thoroughly Christian way, we must first be in control of some rudimentary facts. The moral obligations and policy decisions surrounding AIDS are synthetic. They are a synthesis or mixture of principles with empirical data. Obligations defined and decisions made without benefit of facts are likely to be nothing more than the promulgation of personal or cultural biases. Such method by incantation only intensifies the problem by wrapping it in moral confusion.

First, then, some facts. As of September 1976, the Centers for Disease Control (CDC) reported 42,354 diagnosed cases of AIDS in the United States. As I write, the number is well over 50,000. More than 25,000 have already died and the numbers change daily. The CDC estimates that 1.5 million are now infected with HIV (Human Immunodeficiency Virus). It projects that by 1991 270,000 will have AIDS, that 179,000 will have died from AIDS, and that in 1991 alone 54,000 will succumb to the dread disease.[2] I qualify these figures by "as I write." When this book appears, the figure could well have doubled.

The retrovirus responsible for AIDS infects and leads to the death of T helper cells, with resultant dysfunction of the immune system. It was originally referred to as "Human T-cell Lymphotrophic Virus Type III (TLV-III) and more cumbersomely as HLTV-III-LAV (lymphadenopathy-associated virus). Now most literature follows the usage of the International Committee on the Taxonomy of Viruses: "Human immunodeficiency virus" (HIV).

There are several technical and complicated ways of classifying the stages of HIV infection (whose diagnosis is referred to as "HIV positive," "antibody positive" and "seropositive"). They need not detain us here. For purposes of simplicity, I note the following:

—HIV positive or antibody positive: the individual's blood shows anti-bodies stimulated by the HIV virus, indicating exposure to HIV. The in-dividual is said to be "seropositive." A large proportion (perhaps between 30-50%) will develop full-blown AIDS but may remain asymptomatic for five to ten years.

—ARC (AIDS-related complex): this refers to a group of less severe symptoms such as chronic diarrhea, recurrent fevers, fatigue, weight loss, lymphadenopathy (persistent swelling of the lymph nodes). In May 1987, the CDC proposed dementia and emaciation as confirming AIDS, thus enlarging the number of those eligible for public health benefits.

—AIDS: this refers to the most severe clinical manifestation of the HIV infection. It includes opportunistic infections, and above all, the relative-ly rare *pneumocystis carinii* pneumonia and neoplasms such as Kaposi's sarcoma.

Figures for those with AIDS vary slightly (not substantially), depend-ing on the source. A representative breakdown is the following:

—73% in homosexual or bisexual men
—17% in IV drug users
—6% in those without a well-defined risk factor
—1% in children
—1.6% from prior blood transfusions
—1% in hemophiliacs
—1% in heterosexuals exposed to those in risk categories

From this it is clear that HIV infection is transmitted above all in three ways: (1) sexual contact (exchange of body fluids); (2) parenteral exposure (needle-sharing for drugs, blood transfusions); (3) perinatal exposure (transplacental and/or intrapartum transmission).

All HIV infected persons are potentially infectious, and probably so for life. At present there is no known cure for AIDS although various antiviral agents and immunomodulators are being developed. AIDS is quite simply fatal. AZT (azidothymidine) can prolong life and improve performance status; but it cannot cure.

These are some of the bare facts. It is clear that there are many ethical problems associated with the phenomenon of AIDS. For instance, is it ethical for a physician to refuse to treat an AIDS patient, for a nurse? What are the moral obligations of those who test seropositive? What are society's duties in the face of a killer epidemic like AIDS? Financially, legally? Is it permissible to inform a third party (e.g., a wife or prospective one) that her husband is HIV positive? May an employer dismiss an AIDS patient? May an insurance company refuse to insure a seropositive individual? May a hospital segregate AIDS patients? Is mandatory screening of all marriage-license applicants, hospital patients, surgical patients permissible? Do AIDS patients have a reduced claim on intensive care services? What are the obligations and cautions relevant to contact tracing for those who have been sexually promiscuous? Who has the right to information about a patient's diagnosis or a positive HIV result? How should Christians respond to such questions?

The list of problems and challenges is virtually endless. At some point further detailed listing becomes confusing and counterproductive. Here, therefore, I will list three general categories of ethical problems: the problem of attitude, the problem of prevention and containment, the problem of care.

The problem of attitude. Many people think of ethics as the solution to problems ("dilemma ethics"). Important as practical cases are, they are not all of ethics, nor its most important aspect. We are all vaguely aware that what we are becoming as persons is much more central to our moral selves than any isolated act or omission. In other words, we are aware of the importance of an ethic of character, an ethic of dispositions. Attitudes are central here.

Attitudes both reflect and reinforce our dispositions. They are so often the soil in which dispositions grow or wither. Furthermore, attitudes lead to actions. Attitudes, it should be noted, are our responsibility because to a large extent they are within our control. We can qualify, modify and change them. Therefore, our attitude toward AIDS is a basic ethical concern.

A recent Gallup poll showed Americans in increased numbers believe that AIDS victims should be treated with compassion (87%, up from 78% in July, 1987).[3] More in detail, 64% (up from 43%) deny an employer the right to dismiss an employee only because of AIDS. Only 54% (down from 80% in July) favored requiring AIDS victims to carry an identification card. Seventy-five percent deny landlords the right to evict because of AIDS and 65% would not be opposed to working alongside an AIDS victim.

Yet the popular biases hang tough, like, well, persistent viruses. Forty-three percent still hold that AIDS is a "divine punishment for moral decline." Families are still harassed; some school children are prevented from attending school. AIDS patients are dumped. The growing consciousness of AIDS has produced a backlash against the high risk groups seen as causing the problem. By five to three, Americans still want homosexual activity on the penal code.

The attitudinal problem is also lodged in sections of the medical community. Significant numbers of physicians in training in a New York hospital said they should be able to choose whether to treat AIDS patients and wished they could refuse.[4] One-third of 250 stated that they should have the choice and one-fourth would not treat, if given the choice. These results—not representative, I am convinced—are unsettling, particularly in light of the American Medical Association's recent determination (Council on Ethical and Judicial Affairs) that treatment refusal is unethical.[5]

Dentistry, too, has been touched by the attitudinal problem. According to a survey done in October 1986, four of five dentists would not treat AIDS patients. Many undoubtedly are afraid of losing patients because they would be known as "AIDS dentists." But Mathilde Krim, director of the American Foundation for AIDS Research, concludes: "Dentists suffer from the same delusions as the rest of the public—that you can catch AIDS easily."[6]

The heart of the attitudinal problem—and it is an ethical problem par excellence—is twofold. First, there is ignorance or misinformation about the transmission of AIDS. Unless this is corrected, what Krim calls "delusions" will persist, as well as the reactions and actions stemming from them. Second, there is the challenge of separating the medical problem and conditions from value judgments about the life style that may have caused it. ("Separation" does not mean elimination of one's moral convictions and judgments.) Unless this separation is achieved, compassion will be corrupted by latent condemnation, and will remain a pious but heartless veneer more comforting to the comforter than to the afflicted. This is all the more the case since the only known prevention of AIDS involves behavior modification. I do not underestimate the challenge of this separation, especially in a religious tradition long accustomed to distinguishing the "sin from the sinner." This is the very worst way to try to formulate the separation noted above. It verbally cements rather than separates, notwithstanding its validity in other contexts.

The separation of the medical condition and need from judgments about causative conduct is—somewhat paradoxically—even more complicated for the medical professional. That is because of the contemporary transformation of the medical profession, its deflation into a business occupation like any other. Within this commercialized conception of medicine, the notion of obligatory altruism gets flattened and eventually yields to the assertions of self-interest, as Edmund Pellegrino, director of the Kennedy Institute of Ethics, has pointed out.[7] And where self-interest controls, self-exemption from service can take that form of self-justification most easily at hand: "They brought it on themselves." The truth of that statement neither hides nor justifies medical distancing. Physicians have told me that some physician-refusal to treat AIDS patients, explicitly based on fear of exposure to HIV infection, masks value judgments on life style. Endorsing a differing, more service-oriented notion of medicine and the physician, Dr. Pellegrino states: "A medical need in itself constitutes a moral claim on those equipped to help." He was echoing what John Paul II stated in his speech to the Catholic Health Association (Phoenix, September 14, 1987), when he referred to "your moral obligation and social responsibility to help those who suffer" from AIDS and ARC and when he stated that "you are called to show the love and compassion of Christ and his Church."[8] Such love and compassion necessarily distinguishes and separates medical condition and need from value judgments about life style.

The responsibilities of the medical profession vis-à-vis AIDS can hardly be overstated. The profession, because of its undeniable achievements and special expertise, rightly enjoys great public esteem. That means its impact on public opinion is considerable. Specifically, it can expand or eviscerate public understanding and compassion by the posture it assumes.

The problem of containment and prevention. Everyone admits that, since transmission of HIV infection is heavily traceable to two sources (sexual conduct and IV drug use), education and behavior modification is the only known prevention of the disease. The form and content of this education involve moral issues, as the skirmish among some American bishops on the mention of condoms testifies.

On December 11, 1987 the Administrative Board of the National Conference of Catholic Bishops issued "The Many Faces of AIDS: A Gospel Response."[9] I want to discuss briefly a single aspect of that document, the educational.

Let me say straight off that I believe the document is a splendid piece of theological and pastoral composition.

The document combines the prophetic voice with the voice of compassion in a way that is contemporary yet traditional, right-headed yet warmhearted. The one section that has apparently occasioned the episcopal skirmish concerns the toleration of the presentation of information on condoms ("prophylactics"). The bishops have been accused by some writers (who shall remain mercifully anonymous) of "endorsing," "approving" and "promoting" the use of condoms. Such assertions reflect not the document, but a certain degree of dyslexia.

Is there a sound, indeed any, basis in the document for the episcopal controversy, and especially for criticisms leveled against "The Many Faces. . . . "? I think not. To substantiate that judgment requires a view of two points: what the document says, the criticisms made of it.

1. *What the document says.* Where the prevention of AIDS is concerned, "Many Faces . . . " stresses that everyone must be educated in a fully integrated understanding of human sexuality. "Any other solution will be merely short-term" and "ultimately ineffective." On this basis, the document explicitly opposes the approach to AIDS prevention called "safe sex." It further rejects sex education that reduces to the provision of "mere biological information."

It repeats over and over the conviction that the only true solution to the problem, both personal and social, is chaste behavior based on the type of value-oriented education in human sexuality that grounds the Church's teaching. Then at a key point, "The Many Faces . . . " acknowledges that not all will agree with the Catholic understanding of sexuality.

The document continues:

> We recognize that public educational programs addressed to a wide audience will reflect the fact that some people will not act as they can and should, that they will not refrain from the type of sexual or drug abuse behavior which can transmit AIDS. In such situations, educational efforts, if grounded in the broader moral vision outlined above, could include accurate information about prophylactic devices proposed by some medical experts as potential means of preventing AIDS. We are not promoting the use of prophylactics, but merely providing information that is part of the factual picture.[10]

The above was written with regard to education programs aimed at prevention of AIDS. The document then discusses educational programs for those already exposed to AIDS, and specifically the issue of public policy. It is in this context (public policy for those with HIV infections) that the document refers to the "teaching of classical theologians" on tolerating the lesser evil. Specifically, in addressing such policy, it sees the need to "balance the need for a full and authentic understanding of human sexuality in our society and the issues of the common good associated with the spread of the disease."

These are, I take it, the controversial areas. So what, in sum, have the bishops said in this section? Really, a single thing: *They have accepted public educational programs that include factual information about prophylactics*—but only after insisting that chastity and avoidance of drug use "are the only morally correct and medically sure ways to prevent the spread of AIDS" and that public programming "must clearly articulate the meaning of a truly authentic human sexuality." They do this with the realization that many people in our society will continue irresponsible behavior and threaten public health. It is for this reason that they are willing to accept programs that provide information whose implementation would contravene their own moral convictions.

The document explains this acceptance (footnote 7) with a reference to the rather traditional teaching on toleration of the lesser evil. What are the evils involved that the bishops tolerate, correctly in my view, in the interests of public health? They should be obvious. There is the danger that some programs will convert information into safe-sex advocacy in a way promotive of promiscuity. There is the danger that public health programs will not be "grounded in the broad moral vision" on which the bishops insist. There is the danger that acceptance will be interpreted as advocacy with a subsequent erosion of clarity about sexual morality in other areas. The bishops have gone many paragraphs out of their way to minimize and prevent such dangers. That is all one can ask of them.

2. The criticisms. The most detailed critique of the analytic structure of the document has been made by Archbishop J. Francis Stafford of Denver.[11] In these brief remarks, I cannot comment on the jurisdictional aspects of his critique. Stafford makes these objections.

The first is that the principle of toleration of the lesser evil, as enunciated by Aquinas, applies only to civil government, not to the Church. "It is *human government,* not the church, which may tolerate the lesser of two evils." I know of no persuasive reason to support this assertion. Thomas speaks of "human government" without qualification. Surely, church governance falls in this category. For centuries, those with jurisdictional authority in the Church (for example, bishops, religious superiors) have closed their eyes to (tolerated) certain violations, disruptions and abuses because to intervene would create even worse problems. John XXIII most recently articulated something very similar in his speech opening Vatican II.

> The Church has always opposed these errors. Frequently, she has condemned them with the greatest severity. Nowadays, however, the spouse of Christ prefers to make use of the medicine of mercy rather than that of severity. She considers that she meets the needs of the present day by demonstrating the validity of her teaching rather than by condemnation.[12]

Stafford next argues that by citing the reference to toleration of the lesser evil, the statement "appears to collapse the toleration of 'educational efforts (that) include accurate information about prophylactic devices' . . . into the toleration of evil." I am not at all sure what this means. But it is clear what Stafford thinks it means. "This reasoning makes the bishops participants in the promotion of a public policy which church teaching has consistently insisted is contrary to the dignity of the human person."

With all due respect, this appears to me to be a non sequitur. There are many things "contrary to the dignity of the human person," some more serious than others. Yes, it is a fair reading to say that homosexual acts, in Church teaching, are contrary to this dignity (though I think much more needs to be said before that statement can be applied with any measure of pastoral prudence).

It is also "contrary to the dignity of a human person"—and much more gravely so—to infect another, knowingly and carelessly, with a fatal disease. One would think that there is an obligation not to do that. When the only certain way of fulfilling this obligation (chastity) is quite probably not going to be adopted by very many, it is only realistic to recognize this.

This does not involve compromising Church teaching, nor does it involve the bishops as "participants in the promotion" of actions contrary to that teaching. It involves them only in saying that there are greater evils than the acknowledged evil of morally wrong sexual acts. There are morally wrong sexual acts that in addition bring illness and death to oneself or others.

Let us put it this way. For many decades, theologians have admitted that it is sometimes permissible to *counsel* the lesser evil. When a person is determined to commit an evil and cannot be reasonably prevented, it is permissible to urge that person to do the lesser evil. "Don't kill him, just blacken an eye." The reasoning behind this conclusion is not that eye-blackening is permissible and not morally wrong and may be indiscriminately approved. Rather, it is that in these circumstances (where it is the lesser of two evils and the agent is hell-bent on the greater), it is counseled precisely *sub specie boni*. I shall return to this point in chapter 22.

Equivalently, one is saying: If you are determined to be irresponsible, at least reduce the dimension of your irresponsibility. That is what *sub specie boni* means. According to our Catholic moral tradition, such counsel is not becoming a "participant in the promotion" of irresponsibility. Quite the contrary. And if that is true of positive counsel, I would think it is a fortiori true of acceptance of programs that provide information that can and might but need not be used in that way.

Finally, Stafford faults the document for failing to verify the question of fact necessary to the application of the principle of toleration of the lesser evil: that AIDS constitutes a danger so threatening that it justifies "toleration of error" (laws and social policies that promote prophylactic use).

I would have thought that a realistic knowledge of human (sexual) nature in combination with statistics of the Centers for Disease Control would have been sufficient to verify the question of fact. It is estimated that 1.5 million are seropositive. We know that many in the high-risk population will not accept the Church's sexual morality, will not be continent, will not cease dangerous activity. These facts have been established. The only question is one of numbers and geography.

Stafford's critique is by far the most detailed and thoughtful issued on "The Many Faces . . . " It is straightforwardly theological. As such, it invites a theological analysis. I find it theologically unpersuasive and quite vulnerable at the very points where it finds the episcopal document vulnerable.

I was in Washington, D.C., December 11 (1987) when the *Washington Post* initially carried the story of the release of the document. My early edition of the *Post* front-paged the story and continued it on page 12. The continuation headline said, "Bishops relax policy against birth control." I was stunned at this gaucherie because I had read the document and knew it had nothing to do with birth regulation.

By that I mean two things. First, where gays are concerned, contraception is not an issue. Second, when prophylactics are used to prevent HIV infection during heterosexual intimacy, such usage does not merit the name "contraception" if our intentions have anything to do with how we describe and assess our actions. I called the headline to the attention of my Catholic Health Association colleagues, all of whom, as hotel guests, had copies of the *Post*. In their copies, the headline had been changed. Obviously, even the *Post* headliners saw the point.

Perhaps it was this incident—and there may have been others like it—that initially led to some degree of public confusion, or the perception of it. At any rate, since that time, whatever public confusion there was has only been thickened by the hierarchical stirring that has occurred.

Impishly, I like to think such pluralism is not all that bad. If bishops can disagree on the meaning and application of moral principles—and remember, publicly and in the press—then surely a similar pluralism is not the greatest vice of the theological community in the Church. It tells the world in a very practical way that the substantials of the faith are one thing, that very specific moral rules and pastoral/political applications are something else. That is apparently a lesson we have yet to learn.

Education has brought about behavioral changes (e.g., reducing the number of partners) in a notable number of gay men. Yet, according to medical sociologist Karolyn Siegel, a substantial proportion (70%) continue to engage in risky sexual practices.[13] It is here that the attitude of HIV infected persons becomes itself an ethical issue. Carelessness easily becomes callousness. Technologically oriented Americans tend to finesse effort and restraint, and rest their hopes on medical magic bullets. That is, at least at the present time, illusory. Ronald Bayer, Carol Levine and Susan Wolfe are surely correct when they conclude:

> We believe that the greatest hope for stopping the spread of HIV infection

is in the voluntary cooperation of those at higher risk—their willingness to undergo testing and to alter their personal behavior and goals in the interest of the community. But we can expect this voluntary cooperation—in some cases, sacrifice—only if the legitimate interests of these groups and individuals in being protected from discrimination are heeded by legislators, professionals and the public.[14]

And that brings us to the matter of screening—the application of HIV antibody testing to populations. Screening proposals comprise one of the key ethical areas, one where there is continuing controversy. A symbol of this is the disagreement between Surgeon General C. Everett Koop and former Secretary of Education William J. Bennett. Bennett has proposed mandatory screening for hospital patients, couples seeking marriage licenses, prison inmates and immigrants. Koop counters: "Mandatory testing would not be good public health practice at this time."[15] A survey done by American Viewpoint, Inc., for the Hudson Institute indicates that 65% of Americans believe that mandatory testing is justified even if individuals have "to give up some of our civil liberties to help stop the spread of AIDS."[16]

How should we even begin to think about the morality of HIV screening? Such procedures involve not only public health, but also questions of individual liberty, privacy and confidentiality.

The potential for mischief, especially discrimination, in the balancing of these conflicting concerns is enormous. Vatican II rightly argued that the moral rightness or wrongness of human actions and policies must be measured by reference to the human person "integrally and adequately considered." That is broader than but certainly includes the commonly accepted philosophical principle of "respect for persons." Such respect parses almost effortlessly into concrete rules that protect fundamental aspects of human dignity and well-being: liberty, privacy and confidentiality.

The University of Virginia's James Childress, a knowledgeable and highly respected bioethicist, has pointed out that such rules are not absolute.[17] They do not bind at any cost, a nuance with which Catholic tradition would certainly agree. Rather, they are prima facie binding upon us. That is, they bind other things being equal. Departures from them demand justification. If we restrict liberty, intrude upon privacy or disclose the confidential, the burden of proof is on us that we may.

To justify departures from such person-protecting and dignity-promoting rules, Childress usefully proposed four conditions. (1) The policy infringing the rules will probably realize the goal of protecting public health, and its benefits will outweigh its costs and burdens. Thus two features: *effectiveness* and *proportionality*. (2) There is no feasible alternative. Infringing such rules should be a *last resort*. The bite of the rules is to direct us to seek alternative ways to protect the public health. (3) We must develop policies that *least infringe the rules*—specifically, that least restrict liberty, least intrude upon privacy, least disclose the confidential. (4) Finally, other *ancillary conditions* must at times be fulfilled. For instance, respect for persons would require that individuals be informed that they are being tested when donating blood. Moreover, screened individuals have a right to be informed of the test results. And everyone admits that pre- and posttesting counselling must be available.

On the basis of such general conditions, most ethical analysts believe that certain clarities have emerged. Thus nearly everyone agrees that universal mandatory screening is not morally justified. It violates conditions 1, 2, 3. It would not be effective in protecting public health because AIDS is not spread by casual contact. Its costs would be enormous and far outweigh any benefits. It would drive some high-risk persons (e.g., drug users) underground because their activity is illegal. Furthermore, other (educational) preventive alternatives are available.

Then there is the least-infringement condition. Present testing procedures, while highly accurate in the right hands, would yield both false positives and false negatives (this latter during the two-week to three-month "window period" when detectable viral antibodies are not generated). False positives could lead to all sorts of devastating assaults on human dignity—worry, suffering, isolation, discrimination. False negatives could provide a deceptive and ultimately cruel comfort. It must be recalled that the College of American Pathologists gave established negative samples to commercial laboratories. These laboratories reported 2% of the tests positive by the so-called Elisa test (enzyme-lined immunosorbent assay) and 5% positive by the Western blot test.[18] The Office of Technology Assessment has noted that of 100,000 low risk testees, eighty-nine would turn up positive with only ten true positives. In other words, eighty would be falsely labeled.

At the other end of the spectrum, no one questions the ethical propriety of testing where blood, semen and organ donations are involved. Not only are individuals free not to donate—and thus avoid possible infringements on liberty, privacy and confidentiality—but the public has an overriding interest in HIV-free donations not otherwise achievable except by testing.

Other populations fall somewhere between these two clarities. For instance, most analysts (I am both reporting and agreeing) view mandatory screening of all marriage license applicants as ethically unjustified *at present*. The likelihood of detecting a significant number of true positives is minimal in relation to the economic costs and the invasions of liberty, privacy and confidentiality. Those at risk for AIDS are not likely to be applying for marriage licenses.

General workplace screening is rejected on several grounds. Its usefulness for protecting others is not supported by clinical or epidemiologic evidence. Furthermore, the underlying reason for such screening is sometimes avoidance of the economic burden of health care benefits.

Screening of all hospital admissions is viewed as at present unjustifiable. The qualifier "at present" recurs repeatedly because conditions keep changing. This is the conclusion of the Special Ethics Committee of the American Hospital Association (to which I belong). Such screening is not done for hepatitis-B, which is far more infectious. Ordinary institutional precautions already in place for hepatitis-B are regarded as sufficient.

Screening of surgical patients and health care workers involved with open wounds (e.g., in emergency rooms) is somewhat more controversial. Reasons pro and con have been offered. But if standard infection control cautions are used, one has to wonder about the rationale for such screening, given the dangers associated with it.

The above examples deal with *mandatory* screening. No one objects, or should object to *voluntary* screening where adequate protections of confidentiality are assured and sound counselling is available.

The problem of care.[19] It is axiomatic—but often forgotten amid the tangled casuistry of plug-pulling, palliation decisions and proxy determination—that our major moral challenge in dealing with the dying is to reduce the human diminishments of the dying process and to maximize the values the patient treasured in life. Indeed, it is often only by attending to the latter that we achieve the former. Here the attitudinal problem can strike within the heart of care. It is possible that health care personnel and care providers do not share—may in fact disapprove of or even be revolted by—the values the patient treasures and around which he organized his life. The problem seems obvious. I am not implying that the problem of care is restricted to the dying. Far from it. Certainly, HIV-infected persons and those with ARC deserve care and there can be anguishing moral and pastoral problems involved in providing it. But the more intense problems surround the dying.

One need only profile an AIDS patient to realize this.[20] No one, of course, is a "typical" AIDS patient. But large numbers of those afflicted with AIDS will regularly reveal many of the following cluster of characteristics. Young; alienated from family; frightened (of isolation and abandonment, of pain and suffering, of dependency and loss of control); embarrassed and/or guilty; more or less alone; possibly angry; isolated further by societal attitudes, infection protection and a backlash of anger at their consumption of beds and resources; without financial resources; incompetent (toward the end).

One senses immediately the many faces of the ethical problem of care. First off, there is caretaker burnout. Physicians and nurses are trained to cure, and when they cannot, to comfort and care. When patients are young and otherwise healthy but are wasting away and there is no cure, when their care is increasingly demanding and sometimes demeaning, the pain of frustration can be deep, draining and depressing even to the point of compromising the ability to comfort and care.

Burnout is perhaps even hastened by the conflicted atmosphere in which care must be given. There is the conflict between need and available resources, between different philosophies of medicine among caregivers, between financed and financier, between values of family and patient, during incompetence between decisionmakers and their prerogatives (family or lover?), between revelation and dissimulation, between resignation and resuscitation, and eventually between hope and hopelessness.

There are few clear-cut answers to such problems and I shall make no attempt to drop them from the sky. At present there are but directional drifts. Everyone seems to admit the need of more coordinated local and grassroot efforts, more hospice-like and nonacute care facilities or at least settings, greater anticipation of decisional dilemmas and, of course, spiritual care that is shaped by acceptance.

This brief account of the shape of the ethical challenge of AIDS would be incomplete if it failed to mention an ethical dimension that is never mentioned but is ever present. It is no fundamentalism to assert that we know at least one thing Jesus would do in the present situation. Off his record he would accept, care and love—without reservation or qualification. In doing so, he would lay bare once again the chasm between his own selfless goodness and the hesitant, half-hearted, fearful, questioning, hedging, self-interested efforts of us, his followers. If that is not *the* moral problem of the AIDS epidemic, any others hardly merit the name.

Notes

1. *USA Today*, 8 December 1987.
2. For an excellent overview of the literature, cf. William C. Spohn, S.J., "The Moral Dimension of AIDS," *Theological Studies* 49 (1988):88-109.
3. *New York Times*, 22 November 1987.
4. *Chicago Tribune*, 5 June 1987.
5. *New York Times*, 13 November 1987.
6. *USA Today*, 14 November 1987.
7. Edmund Pellegrino, "Altruism, Self-Interest and Medical Ethics," *Journal of the American Medical Association* 258 (1987):1939-1940.
8. *Origins*, 17 (1987), 294.
9. The document appeared in many places, for example, in the *National Catholic Reporter*, 25 December 1987.
10. Cf. note 9, at 13.
11. Stafford's critique was attached to a letter addressed to the Most Rev. John L. May, president of the NCCB. The letter was dated December 17 and appeared in several diocesan weeklies.

12. *Documents*, 716.

13. Karolyn Siegel, "AIDS Prevention: Behavior Change in Gay Men." This is a paper distributed at a conference held in 1987 at Sloan-Kettering Cancer Center.

14. Donald Bayer, Carol Levine and Susan Wolf, "HIV Antibody Screening," *Journal of the American Medical Association* 256 (1986):1768-1774, at 1774.

15. *Newsweek*, 11 May 1987.

16. *South Bend Tribune*, 29 November 1987.

17. James Childress, "An Ethical Framework for Assessing Policies to Screen for Antibodies to HIV," *AIDS and Public Policy Journal* 2 (1987):28-31.

18. *New York Times*, 30 November 1987.

19. Robert Steinbrook, Bernard Lo, Jill Tirpack, James Dilley and Paul Volberding, "Ethical Dilemmas in Caring for Patients with the Acquired Immunodeficiency Syndrome," *Annals of Internal Medicine* 103 (1985):787-90.

20. David G. Ostrow and Terence C. Gayle, "Psychosocial and Ethical Issues of AIDS Health Care Programs," *Quality Review Bulletin*, August 1986, 284-94, at 288.

Chapter 19

Therapy or Tampering:
The Ethics of Reproductive Technology
and the Development of Doctrine

In this chapter I will consider five points: (1) the factual background, (2) standard in vitro fertilization, (3) third-party involvement, (4) the moral status of the pre-embryo, (5) the Instruction of the Congregation for the Doctrine of the Faith.

On September 8, 1986, the Ethics Committee of the American Fertility Society (AFS) released its report under the title *Ethical Considerations of the New Reproductive Technologies.*[1] The report is the result of eight arduous meetings beginning February 1-2, 1985. As a member of that committee, I would not qualify as its best critic. Yet if past experience with similar reports (e.g., the Ethics Advisory Board, 1979; the "Warnock Report," 1984; the "Waller Report," 1982–1984) is any indication, the AFS report will prove highly controversial. For instance, when the Ethics Advisory Board's final report was published in the *Federal Register* on June 18, 1979, it generated some 13,000 public comments, and they were overwhelmingly negative.[2] The Secretary of the then Department of Health, Education and Welfare received fifty letters, signed by twenty senators and seventy-three representatives. Most argued that *"in vitro* fertilization research was immoral and unethical, that the future implications were grave, that adequate guidelines to prevent abuses had not yet been developed, and that the rights of the embryo would be compromised."[3]

I have no doubt that the AFS report will continue to enjoy similar tender mercies. Even though time and clinical practice have taken the novelty and surprise out of in vitro fertilization, still there is an uneasy sense that a powerful technological dynamic is loose here, one with a capacity for considerable abuse. I doubt that the AFS report will allay such fears. Let me cite a single example. Chapter 15 of the report deals with "Artificial Insemination-Donor" (AID). After listing the indications for the procedure, it details some key reservations (e.g., possible psychological problems in the husband, wife, donor; risk of transmitting serious genetic disease; effect on child, etc.). The report then states: "Because of the general concern over the use of third party gametes, the use of A.I.D. remains controversial. However, the Committee finds the use of A.I.D. ethically acceptable." Some may see an act of the will in such leaps of logic. I did and wrote the following dissent.

> One member of the Committee argued that the use of third parties—whether by donor sperm, donor ovum, or surrogate womb—was ethically inappropriate. First, it seems violative of the marriage convenant wherein exclusive, non-transferable, inalienable rights to each other's person and generative acts are exchanged. Thus it fundamentally severs procreation from the marital union. Second, by premeditation—in contrast to adoption—it brings into the world a child with no bond of origin to one or both marital partners, thus blurring the child's genealogy and potentially compromising the child's self-identity. Third, once conceded the moral right to be inseminated by the sperm of another man, wives might easily conclude (and it would be difficult to reject their logic) that it is preferable to be inseminated in the natural way. Thus adulteries might be multiplied to the detriment of marriage. Fourth, the stud-farm mentality is supported with its subtle but unmistakable move toward eugenics. Fifth, the use of third parties tends to absolutize sterility as a disvalue and childbearing and rearing as a value, thus distorting—and potentially threatening—some basic human values: life, marriage, and the family.
>
> Taken cumulatively, such considerations suggest that the use of third parties to overcome sterility is not for the good of persons integrally and adequately considered. It involves risks to basic dimensions of our flourishing. Such risks to basic values outweigh, in a prudential calculus, individual procreative desires or needs. In summary: when calculus involves *individual* benefit versus *institutional* risk of harm, the latter should take precedence.[4]

This concern could be worded much more subtly and carefully, I am sure. For instance, one of my graduate students at the University of Notre Dame pointed out to me that if what I suggest about third parties is true, then the calculus does not really involve individual *benefit*. A genuine benefit should not involve institutional or social risk of harm. A putative one might. My point, however, is the types of concern raised by the new reproductive technologies. They touch on some very basic human values: marriage and the family, parenting, genealogy and self-identity of the child, human sexual intimacy and even the sanctity of life itself. It is perhaps understandable, then, why these discussions generate a heavy load of emotion and rhetoric about "playing God," "tampering with nature," "immoral means to good ends," "procreative privacy," etc. Such slogans do not analyze problems. They simply promulgate solutions that have been arrived at on other grounds.

Before raising some of the key ethical issues, I think it appropriate to supply a brief factual background.

On July 25, 1978 Louise Brown was born in Oldham, England, from in vitro fertilization (IVF). She was the first so-called "test-tube baby," the culmination of years of pioneering research by Patrick Steptoe and Robert Edwards. Since that time and as I write, some five thousand babies have entered this world via this procedure, most of them in Australia, England and the United States. The number changes almost daily.

IVF is relatively simple and straightforward. The ovaries are stimulated (by clomiphene citrate, human menopausal gonadotropin or combinations of these) to produce multiple eggs since pregnancy rates increase with transfer of more than one embryo. The eggs are ordinarily recovered by laparoscopy and follicle aspiration, though transvaginal retrieval (not involving general anesthesia) is increasingly used. They are then coincubated with sperm for around twelve to eighteen hours to allow fertilization to occur. After an additional forty-eight to seventy-two hours, the embryo (many scientists prefer the term "pre-embryo") is transferred to the uterine cavity by a catheter. If the procedure is successful, implantation in the uterus will occur in two to three days and a pregnancy will be detectable at about ten to fourteen days following transfer.[5]

Based on the experience of the past seven years, in vitro fertilization is both safe and relatively efficient. There is no known increased risk to parents or offspring and the success rate (depending on team-experience and technique) can approach that of the natural process (20-25% per cycle of treatment).

There are several reasons why couples might consider in vitro fertilization. The most common is tubal (fallopian) damage or destruction due to inflammatory disease. Other pelvic factors that have failed conventional therapy (e.g., pelvic endometriosis) could also be indications. The same could be said of simple unexplained or idiopathic infertility.

If the story ended here, there would be little cause for concern. Many ethicists and moral theologians (not all, as we shall see) have no problem with the procedure if the gametes (egg, sperm) come from husband and wife, and if the procedure is safe for mother and child-to-be. Indeed, LeRoy Walters (Kennedy Institute of Ethics) refers to the morality of in vitro fertilization as a "stagnant issue."[6] Nearly ten years ago (May 4, 1979) the Ethics Advisory Board reported to the Secretary of Health, Education and

Welfare that IVF is "acceptable from an ethical standpoint." The Board insisted that this was to be understood as "ethically defensible but still legitimately controverted" because it acknowledged genuine concerns about the moral status of the embryo and the potential long-range consequences as "among the most difficult that confronted the Board." The Board did not wish to wave the magic wand of its fiat at such concerns.

And this is where the story continues. Now that laboratory culture conditions for fertilization and continued development have been refined, clinicians are being confronted with requests for all kinds of variations of the basic technology: donor sperm, donor ova, donor embryo, surrogate mothers (with sperm and/or ova from donors), surrogate carriers, single women, lesbian couples, frozen sperm, frozen embryos etc. For instance, when the husband is sterile with irreversible azoospermia (dead or weakened sperm) or has some genetic disorder that would constitute an unacceptable risk to progeny, donor sperm is suggested. Or again, if the wife lacks ovaries because of surgical removal or suffers from ovarian failure, donor eggs are sought. If both partners are afflicted with one or more of the medical indications mentioned, they might look for a donated embryo.

The possibilities and variants are mind-boggling. As George Annas has pointed out, it is now possible for a child to be born with five distinct parents: a genetic father, a rearing father, a mother who provides the egg, the woman in whose womb the embryo gestates, the mother who rears the child.[7] Or again, an embryo could be frozen for a generation, then thawed and transferred to its now adult sister—thus becoming the daughter of its sister. Variations like this are not mere fantasies. The first case of a surrogate carrier (woman's egg fertilized in vitro by husband's sperm, then placed in another woman) was reported in 1985.[8] In another case, a lesbian was fertilized by donor sperm.[9] Clearly, the separation of genetic, gestating and rearing roles raises complex ethical and legal problems underlined by *Time's* question "which one gets the Mother's Day card?"[10] and by Red Foxx's throwaway aphorism "Mama's baby, Poppa's maybe."

Then there is the question of the embryo itself. International attention was focused on this issue when an American couple (Mr. and Mrs. Mario Rios) died in an airplane accident after leaving two frozen embryos in an Australian clinic. Are such embryos children, and in this case orphans? Or are they something less? To whom do they belong? What should be done with them? Should they be thawed and allowed to die, or should they be adopted? And more generally, is it ever permissible to experiment on spare embryos? Indeed, may they be produced precisely for this purpose?

Responses to questions like these are likely to be sharply divided. There have been any number of groups that have made reports or submissions (e.g., Medical Research Council [Great Britain], 1982; Royal College of Obstetricians and Gynecologists, 1983; Catholic Bishops of Victoria, 1982; British Medical Association, 1983; Catholic Bishops' Joint Committee on Bio-Ethical Issues, 1983; American Fertility Society, 1984). The two best known reports are British and Australian: the so-called "Warnock Report" named after chairperson Dame Mary Warnock ("Report of the Committee of Inquiry into Human Fertilisation and Embryology," 1984) and the "Waller Report" named after chairperson Louis Waller ("Interim Report," 1982; "Report on Donor Gametes in I.V.F.," 1983; "Report on the Disposition of Embryos Produced by In Vitro Fertilization," 1984).[11]

Both of these reports accept standard (between husband and wife) IVF, freezing of embryos, donation of oocytes, and donation of embryos in IVF. Both reject surrogate motherhood. Where research on the embryo is concerned, majorities of both the Warnock and Waller groups approved it in principle, the Waller Report specifying that only spare embryos are to be used. Both groups put a fourteen-day limit on such research because after this point there is present the "primitive streak" indicating developmental individuation. Prior to this point, the cell-mass (fertilized ovum—technically zygote) has a kind of totipotentiality. That is, it may divide (or be severed) and become twins. Two cell masses may recombine to become a single individual known as a chimera or mosaic. Indeed, animal studies indicate that individual blastomeres of the zygote can be removed without compromising future growth potential and can themselves become full-fledged individuals.

With this brief factual sketch, let me now turn to the moral issues. There are many moral issues that adhere to the new reproductive technologies. For instance, Clifford Grobstein and Michael Flower have listed the following aspects: the IVF process itself, freezing of embryo, marital status of patients, third-party involvement, embryo adoption, embryo research, fertilization across species boundaries, extended embryo culture, commercialization.[12] Obviously, I cannot discuss all of these.

Here I would like to review the issues from the perspective of recent Catholic formulations. There are three key issues that constantly surface and lie behind those mentioned above: (1) IVF itself; (2) third-party involvement; and (3) the moral status of the embryo.

1. Standard IVF. By "standard" I refer to the simple procedure minus any accompaniments or variations that might alter moral evaluation. Concretely, this means that sperm and ovum come from husband and wife and the pre-embryo is implanted in the uterus of the wife.

The analytic history in the Catholic community begins in 1897. On March 24 of that year, the Holy Office gave its response to the question "May artificial fecundation of a woman be done?" Its answer: "It is not permissible."[13]

Obviously, this is not a cut-through to clarity. Specifically, it remained unclear whether the artificiality of the procedure was being condemned or only the manner of obtaining semen (masturbation). Many authors (among them the American Gerald Kelly, S.J.) opted for this latter view and continued to defend artificial insemination if the semen could be licitly obtained.

It was against this background that Pius XII entered the picture. In 1949, in an address to the Fourth International Congress of Catholic Doctors, Pius XII stated: "The simple fact that the desired result is attained by this means does not justify the use of the means itself; nor is the desire to have a child—perfectly lawful as that is for married persons—sufficient to prove the licitness of artificial insemination to attain this end." He referred to "procreation of a new life according to the will and plan of the Creator" and concluded that artificial insemination by husband (AIH) "must be absolutely rejected."[14] This exclusion, to which Pius XII repeatedly returned, must be put into its proper context. Apparently, the congress which he addressed had factions that were supporting an *uncritical* use of AIH ("uncritical" meaning that they had glossed over too quickly the problem of obtaining semen).

Again, on October 29, 1951, in his famous address to the Italian Catholic Union of Midwives, the pope argued that AIH converts the home into a biological laboratory. He worded it as follows:

> In its natural structure, the conjugal act is a personal action, a simultaneous and immediate cooperation on the part of the husband and wife which by the very nature of the agents and the propriety of the act is the expression of the mutual gift which according to Holy Scripture brings about union "in one flesh only." This is something more than the union of two seeds which may be brought about even artificially without the natural action of husband and wife.[15]

On May 19, 1956 (Second World Congress on Fertility and Sterility), he spelled this out in even greater detail. After condeming contraception, he continued:

> And the Church has likewise rejected the opposite attitude which would pretend to separate, in generation, the biological activity from the personal relation of the married couple. The child is the fruit of the conjugal union when that union finds full expression by bringing into play the organic functions, the associated sensible emotions, and the spiritual and disinterested love which animates it. It is within the unity of this human activity that the biological prerequisites of generation should take place.[16]

In summary, then, Pius XII was insisting that the child (for the good of the child and the marriage) must be the fruit of the conjugal union. But it is the fruit of the *conjugal* union only when it is conceived *in a conjugal way,* that is, by sexual intercourse. Therefore, to be the fruit of the conjugal union the child must be conceived by sexual intercourse. But a child conceived by artificial insemination by husband is not conceived by sexual intercourse. *Ergo.* Pius XII, then, viewed the conjugal act as having a natural and God-given design which joins the procreative (life-giving) and unitive (love-making) dimensions. On this basis, he excluded both contraception and AIH. This approach would, of course, constitute a strong a fortiori argument against IVF. But Pius XII immediately added: "On the subject of the experiments in artificial human fecundation '*in vitro,*' let it suffice for us to observe that they must be rejected as immoral and absolutely illicit." That seems clearer than it really is. The basis of the rejection could be (most likely) the mere unnaturalness, or it could be that the pontiff saw this as experimental and dangerous tampering with embryonic life. Whatever the case, Pius XII would certainly have rejected IVF.

I believe it accurate to say that Pius XII, especially in his 1956 analysis, was foreshadowing the analysis of Paul VI in *Humanae Vitae.*[17] Paul VI asserted in that encyclical the inseparability, in the conjugal act, of the unitive and procreative dimensions of the act. This inseparability ("willed by God and not to be broken by men on their own inititative") was repeated in John Paul II's *Familiaris Consortio.*[18]

What are we to make of all of this in so far as it touches in vitro fertilization? At first blush, it might seem to commit the magisterium to a rejection of in vitro fertilization. But before that conclusion is drawn, several points should be weighed carefully.

First, there is the authoritative character of Pius XII's interventions. Pius was addressing a problem at the official level for the first time (the 1897 response of the Holy Office was interpreted by many as centering its rejection of artificial insemination on masturbation to obtain semen). Furthermore, his pronouncements are almost never cited by subsequent popes and by bishops around the world. In other words, the Church—to borrow from Ladislaus Orsy, S.J.—was in the inital stages of its reflection on this matter.[19] That being the case, it would be a disservice to attribute anything like a definitive character to Pius' conclusions.

This point is reflected in the attitude of two Roman theologians, consultors of the Congregation for the Doctrine of the Faith, and "teachers at prestigious Roman institutions in the very shadow of the Holy See."[20] They are Marcellino Zalba, S.J., and Jan Visser, C.S.S.R. Both have challenged Pius' condemnation of artificial insemination by husband. Zalba regards the papal analysis as too "physicist," leaning too heavily on the materiality of the act and not enough on its moral significance.[21] Visser ackowledges that we have come a long way from the days when a papal allocution would forever end a discussion. He believes that the argument of Pius XII retains its value as a general principle but doubts its absoluteness where insemination by husband is involved.[22]

The second point is the very meaning of the inseparability of the unitive and procreative. Some see this inseparability as excluding in vitro fertilization. Thus the Catholic Bishops of Victoria, in their submission (1983) to the Waller Committee stated: "In pursuit of the admirable end of helping an infertile couple to conceive and have their baby, I.V.F. intervenes in their supreme expression of mutual love. It separates 'baby-making' from 'lovemaking'."[23] Similarly, Carlo Caffarra, head of the Pontifical Institute for the Family, appeals to the inseparability of the unitive and procreative to reject IVF. "The moral problem is that procreation can no longer be said to be—and in fact is not—dependent upon the sexual act between two married people."[24] This is also the position taken by F. Giunchedi, G. Pesci, D. Tettamanzi and others.[25]

But the matter is simply not that clear. To the assertion that *Humanae Vitae* and *Familiaris Consortio* exclude procreation without the unitive act, William Daniel, S.J., notes:

> All we learn from this passage [of *Humanae Vitae*], however, is that *if the conjugal act is performed* it should have these qualities: it should not be falsified in either of its essential "significations." This does not necessarily imply that if there is to be procreation it should be by means of a unitive act.[26]

This very same point is made by G.B. Guzzetti.[27] He notes that the inseparability of the unitive and procreative is *of the conjugal act*. We may not extend or transfer this to an inseparability between the conjugal act itself and the generative process. In other words, the inseparability of the unitive and procreative in the conjugal act does not rule out generative acts outside of it. It must be remembered that Paul VI and John Paul II, in asserting the inseparability of the unitive and procreative, were directly concerned with rejecting contraception in marriage. Artificial reproductive procedures were not of immediate concern to them.

This is a technical, textual point, and in this sense Daniel is correct. What one says about the conjugal act does not necessarily apply when there is no question of the conjugal act. However, it seems clear that official formulations such as those of *Humanae Vitae* viewed the matter in more sweeping terms (the procreative process). Any lingering doubts about this were dissipated by the Congregation for the Doctrine of the Faith's 1987 "Instruction on Respect for Human Life in its Origin and on the Dignity of

Procreation." I adverted to this in chapter 8. The CDF sees in in vitro fertilization a separation of the unitive and procreative analogous to that found in contraception.

Other supportive arguments are marshalled against IVF. For instance, infertility is not a life-threatening disorder and IVF does not correct it, but only bypasses it. Use of a "therapeutic" modality for a condition that is not medically harmful and is not itself corrected, tends to medicalize more basic human problems. But this type of consideration is far too general to exclude IVF. If applied consistently, it would exclude many medical interventions, e.g., cardiac bypass surgery.

Or again, Carlo Caffarra has stated:

> *In vitro* fertilization . . . establishes between the one performing the fertilization and the one to be born a relationship of "production of an object." Herein lies the intrinsic illicitness: the person cannot be an object produced by human labour, but a subject willed by a personal act of love.[28]

A child, it is argued, should be begotten, not made. Anything else is literally a misconception. In other words, IVF is more tampering than genuine therapy.

Many other theologians reject this line of reasoning. They do not see IVF as "manufacture" of a "product." Fertilization *happens* when sperm and egg are brought together in a petri dish. The technician's "intervention is a condition for its happening: it is not a cause."[29] Furthermore, the attitudes of the parents and technicians can be every bit as reverential and respectful as they would be in the face of human life naturally conceived.

So where does this leave us? Prior to the CDF's "Instruction," matters seemed to be as follows. The pivotal consideration on IVF from the perspective of magisterial statements is the inseparability of the unitive and procreative dimensions of sexuality. (Obtaining sperm by masturbation does not present a formidable obstacle because many theologians regard this as a different human action from the type of masturbation rejected as ipsation or self-petting.) This inseparability can be understood in either of two ways, the narrow sense or the broad sense. A word about each.

The narrow sense. This refers to the inseparability of the unitive and procreative *in the conjugal act.* The sense is: if the conjugal act is performed, these dimensions may not be separated. This more narrow sense states nothing and implies nothing about artificial reproduction beyond the marital act. As William Daniel puts it: "It is about the way a couple present themselves to one another: that no inner contradiction be introduced into their bodily language."[30] This is all that the principle need mean as we find it in Paul VI (*Humanae Vitae*) and John Paul II (*Familiaris Consortio*). Understood in this way, the principle does not exclude in vitro fertilization. (I leave aside for the moment the validity of the principle, that is, whether blocking procreative potential via contraception involves introducing a contradiction into the bodily language of spouses. I think that it need not.)

The broad sense. This understands the inseparability of the unitive and procreative in such a way that procreation ought not occur in marriage except as the result of a sexual act. This represents an understanding of the principle that returns to the perspectives of Pius XII. On this reading, IVF would be excluded.

Many theologians do not see things in this way. As I noted in chapter 8, they argue that Pius XII was excessively influenced by the theology of F. Hürth, S.J., who explicitly stated that the moral law and the biological law coincide on these matters. They further argue that Vatican II shifted the criterion of judgment—away from faculties and their purposes to a strong emphasis on the centrality of the person. More in detail, they view IVF not as a substitution for sexual intimacy, but as a kind of prolongation of it, and therefore as not involving the total severance of the unitive and procreative. Not everything that is artificial is unnatural.[31]

I agree with this view. Indeed, I believe it has sufficient theological authority behind it to be regarded as what was traditionally referred to as "a solidly probable opinion." But the issue at stake should be clear. It is the meaning of the inseparability of the unitive and procreative. If this inseparability must be read *in the broad sense* in *Humanae Vitae* and *Familiaris Consortio*—as Caffarra and others argue—then clearly, both contraception and IVF must be excluded. If, however, inseparability can be understood differently, then IVF would not necessarily be excluded. Specifically, it might be sufficient if the *spheres* of the unitive and procreative are held together so that there is no procreation apart from marriage, and no full sexual intimacy apart from a context of responsibility for procreation, a question to which I adverted in chapter 8.

This matter is somewhat academic because it is possible to justify IVF without modifying the understanding of the inseparability of the unitive and procreative if this inseparability is read in the narrow sense—as applying only to the conjugal act *if it occurs*. In this way one could approve standard IVF without, for example, approving contraception. What is not possible, however, is to approve IVF and be consistent with Pius XII's understanding of things and with the Caffarra–Tettamanzi–Giunchedi reading of the inseparability of the unitive and procreative.

The departure from Pius XII means that IVF is at some point inextricably bound up with the notion of the development of doctrine. It is clear that many theologians—even some regarded as quite conservative, such as Zalba and Visser—have moved beyond the formulations of Pius XII. It is also clear that in doing so they must, in some way or another, modify the understanding of the inseparability of the unitive-procreative dimensions of sexual expression as Pius XII would have seen it and as Caffarra–Tettamanzi–Giunchedi see it. That raises the interesting question of the development of doctrine in moral theology. That such development has occurred in the past is unquestionable. For instance, Walter J. Burghardt, S.J., states the conviction of many when he asserts that "I am convinced that Vatican II's affirmation of religious freedom . . . is discontinuous with certain explicit elements within the Catholic tradition."[32] That such development can occur in the present ought to be unquestionable.

In the present instance we may well be confronted with a doctrinal development. If this is the case, such a development would probably have a recognizable structure. Using the emergence of *Dignitatis Humanae (Declaration on Religious Freedom)* as a vehicle, I would tentatively suggest attending to a three-step process: (a) the earlier formulation and the reasons and circumstances that explain it, (b) a change in the circumstances and reasons that supported the earlier formulations, (c) experience and reflection leading to an altered formulation.

Concretely, there were cultural and historical circumstances that led to Gregory XVI's *Mirari Vos* (which rejected religious liberty) and made it quite intelligible in those circumstances. But the circumstances had gradually changed by 1965 and "the American experience" had been reflected upon sufficiently to generate efforts at a new formulation of the Church's concerns.

This is only to admit that the Church's formulations of her moral convictions are historically conditioned. This should surprise no one, for even dogmas are historically conditioned. The Congregation for the Doctrine of the Faith acknowledged a fourfold historical conditioning. Statements of the faith are affected by the presuppositions, the concerns ("the intention of solving certain questions"), the thought categories ("the changeable conceptions of a given epoch"), and the available vocabulary of the times.[33]

Could an evaluation similar to the one that led to *Dignitatis Humanae* be occurring with regard to procreative technologies? One who defends that thesis could point at rather clearly identifiable circumstances that led Pius XII to reject all AIH. Specifically, as already noted, there was the influence of F. Hürth, S.J.[34]

In the nearly forty years since Hürth's influential essay, there has been a change in the basic categories of understanding surrounding the discussion. One such change was that the centuries-old primacy given to procreation over other meanings of sexual expression was, as John Mahoney, S.J., notes, "publicly and definitively abandoned" by Vatican II.[35] Another principal change is the criterion to be used in judging the rightfulness or wrongfulness of human conduct. Vatican II proposed as the criterion not "the intention of nature inscribed in the organs and their functions" but "the person integrally and adequately considered." Furthermore, to discover what is promotive or destructive of the person is not a deductive procedure.

This is not to blame Pius XII in any way. His achievement was magnificent. He was, after all and as it should be, dependent on his theologians. Similarly today, the pope must depend on theological advisors who, like all of us, are pilgrims and see only darkly. There are two points to emphasize in saying this. First, when teaching on doctrinal questions, the pope must be careful to prevent his circle of advisors narrowing so as to exclude legitimate currents of theological thought, as Rahner has repeatedly noted. Second, even with the broadest and best consultation, authoritative teaching will unavoidably be time and culture-conditioned. A certain form of ecclesiastical fundamentalism tends to forget this.

Is an evolution occurring with regard to the understanding of the unitive and procreative dimensions of sexuality? If Pius XII's conclusions are the measure, then it has already occurred, as much contemporary theological writing testifies. The really interesting and bound-to-be controversial question is: to what extent has the principle itself of the inseparability of the unitive and procreative been affected by this development? Will not the acceptance of IVF lead to a long second look at the inseparability principle as it is used to reject contraception? If a doctrinal development has indeed occurred since Pius XII, does it not very likely go deeper than the instantial acceptance of reproductive technologies?

Development usually involves both continuity and change. If doctrinal development is occurring, one might guess that the thread that yields both continuity and change is the notion of the inseparability of the unitive-procreative dimensions of sexuality. The continuity: the *general* validity of the insight. The change: a broadened understanding away from an act-analysis of this inseparability. This is certainly the understanding of any number of non-Catholic Christian groups, as was indicated in chapter 8. Whatever the case, the aforementioned inseparability principle must promote the person "integrally and adequately considered." When it becomes an obstacle to that promotion, it loses its (generally operative) normative force; for it is subject to and judged by the broader criterion.

In conclusion, then, from this perspective I see no insuperable theological obstacle to standard IVF. I will return to this below.

2. Third party involvement. Most often this will take the form of donor sperm. Sometimes it could involve donor eggs, donor embryos, donor wombs. Each has distinctive dimensions and problems that cannot be collapsed and overlooked. Yet all share a common denominator, even if in different ways: third party involvement. What is to be thought of that?

In 1949, Pius XII expressed himself unequivocally. "Artificial insemination in marriage, with the use of an active element from a third person, is equally immoral and as such is to be rejected summarily. Only marriage partners have mutual rights over their bodies for the procreation of new life, and these rights are exclusive, nontransferable and inalienable."[36] By this "active element from a third person" Pius meant donor insemination. But his argument would apply equally to donor eggs. Furthermore, he viewed such third party involvement as opposed to the good of the child because between the child and at least one rearing parent there is "no bond of origin, no moral and juridical bond of procreation."

By and large, theologians (even many non-Catholic ones) have supported Pius XII in his conclusion. Many of these are the very ones who parted company with him on AIH. Thus Karl Rahner argued that AID "fundamentally separates the marital union from the procreation of a new person."[37] Rahner also faults the anonymity of the donor, which represents a refusal of responsibility as father and an infringement of the rights of the child. It should be remembered that when Sweden passed legislation (1984) giving children conceived by AID the right (at eighteen years of age) to know the identity of their genetic fathers, donor insemination came to a virtual standstill. The same thing seems to be happening in parts of Australia. Obviously, donors want neither recognition nor responsibility.

Those who take a different point of view (and a few Catholic theologians have done so)[38] would argue that genetic lineage, while of value psychologically, legally and medically, does not have an absolute primacy. In some context, trade-offs to protect other values could be appropriate. Furthermore, they would argue that sexual exclusivity is not violated because there is no sexual activity.

There are two key issues here on which there is likely to continue to be strong disagreement: (1) Does third party involvement (via gametic donation or surrogate gestation) infringe on conjugal exclusivity? (2) Does having a jointly raised child justify such infringement? My own answer is yes to the first, no to the second. I hold these positions because I believe the notion of conjugal exclusivity should include the genetic, gestational and rearing dimensions of parenthood. Separating these dimensions (except through rescue, as in adoption) too easily contains a subtle diminishment of some aspect of the human person. Others, including very responsible persons, will see this matter quite differently, indeed would vigorously oppose these points of view. Given this situation, I believe that IVF with donor gametes (I do not include surrogacy here) is probably not feasible for prohibition by public policy. In addition to this, a legal ban might well be judged unconstitutional.

To insist that marital exclusivity ought to include the genetic, gestational and rearing components can be argued in at least two different ways. First, it might be argued that any relaxation in this exclusivity will be a source of harm to the marriage (and marriage in general) and to the prospective child. For instance, the use of donor semen means that there is a genetic asymmetry in the relationship of husband and wife to the child, with possible damaging psychological effects. If a surrogate mother is used, conflicts could arise that damage both the marriage and the surrogate.

William J. Winslade and Judith Wilson Ross recently raised some of the questions I have in mind.

> Is the child to know about the method of its birth? If so, how much information should the child have—only that which is deemed to be health-related data, or all of the other biological information about its heritage that most of us value? Whose interests, whose preferences, whose needs count here? Born into a society that is already fragmented by divorce and confused about alternative life styles, morals and sexual choices, the child may well have serious identity problems at a later time. Does such a possibility have to be seriously considered by those who want to undertake unusual reproductive methods?

The Winslade–Ross essay concludes:

> The interests and well-being of the baby-to-be-made seem to be the last issues considered, and sometimes (when physicians promise anonymity to the donor or parents require it of the surrogate) seem not to be considered at all.[39]

Another form of this first approach is the assertion that third party involvement separates procreation from marriage *in principle.* That opens the door, both by human proclivity and the logic of moral justification, to a litany of worrisome problems such as single-woman insemination and insemination of a lesbian couple. Furthermore, as I noted above, it might lead the wife of a sterile husband to conclude that the natural way (sexual intercourse) is less expensive and more convenient than donor in vitro fertilization or AID. Thus adultery would be fostered. The *Chicago Tribune* recently headlined a story as follows: "Unmarried, Pregnant and Proud of It." It went on to describe one mother as follows: "One night with a stranger gave _____ the baby she'd wanted for a year."[40] When sterility gets absolutized as a disvalue in our practices and thought patterns, strange things can happen.

An argument built on possible harmful consequences is one subject to empirical verification. It must be admitted in all honesty that the data is thin at best, often even conjectural. Fears of what might happen once marital exclusivity is relaxed are legitimate even if they do not always lead to clearly established absolute prohibitions. In the past I have argued that the risks and potential harms involved would support a safeside moral rule (procreation should be restricted to marriage) against the slide to abuse. This is a prudential calculus which gives greater weight to *institutional* risk of harm than to *individual* benefit, as I noted in my dissent statement cited above. I see no compelling reasons to modify this judgment.

A second form of argument is that third party involvement is itself violative of the marriage convenant independent of any potential damaging effects or benefits. This would appear to be the view of Pius XII. The view might be argued by appeal to Christ's union with the Church, or God's union with God's people. Such appeals root in the sources of faith and to that extent might not be shared by those of other faiths. For instance, the distinguished Paul Ramsey writes: "To put radically asunder what God joined together in parenthood when He made love procreative, to procreate from beyond the sphere of love . . . or to posit acts of sexual love beyond the sphere of responsible procreation (by definition, marriage) means a refusal of the image of God's creation in our own."[41] While many Christians might find this analysis quite persuasive, I do not believe it could be urged as a basis for public policy.

However, there is a simpler way of making this point. Many couples regard in vitro fertilization not as a *replacement* for their sexual intimacy, but as a kind of *continuation* or *extension* of it. On that view, third party presence (via egg or sperm) is presence of another in the intimacy itself, a thing that ought not to be.

3. The moral status of the embryo. The difficulty and delicacy of this issue may be highlighted by two references. Speaking to a distinguished group of scientists meeting in Rome in 1982, John Paul II stated: "I condemn, in the most explicit and formal way, experimental manipulations of the human embryo, since the human being, from conception to death, cannot be exploited for any purpose whatsoever."[42] On the other hand, the highly respected Karl Rahner came to a different conclusion. Admitting that the personhood of the embryo is highly doubtful, he stated: "It would be conceivable that, given a serious positive doubt about the human quality of the experimental material, the reasons in favor of experimenting might carry more weight, considered rationally, than the uncertain rights of a human being whose very existence is in doubt."[43] This is also the position of other reputable theologians.

Catholic formulations have for decades spoken of the human being "from the moment of conception." The underlying supposition is that from the moment (or process) of the union of sperm and ovum there is present a fully protectable human being. Yet this supposition has been seriously challenged by contemporary embryology, particularly the lack of developmental individuality in the early days after conception. Surely the pope is aware of these facts as Rahner was; yet he draws a different practical conclusion. It is possible to argue that the pontiff was drawing a kind of safeside rule against abuse. Such rules are as valid and persuasive as the dangers they envisage are unavoidable. In other words, if clear lines can be drawn that block this slide toward abuse, the rule is less persuasive.

Whatever the case, the difference between Rahner and John Paul II is reflected in the varying evaluations of the embryo found in the wider community. Some regard the embryo as a fully protectable humanity; others qualify that status. This latter was the position of the Ethics Advisory Board in 1979. It stated: "The human embryo is entitled to profound respect; but this respect does not necessarily encompass the full legal and moral rights attributed to persons."[44] The EAB went on to accept research that is designed to assess the safety and efficacy of clinical IVF.

Very similar approaches are to be found in the Warnock Report and the Waller Report. This should be of no little significance to the Church that holds that "in fidelity to conscience, Christians are joined with the rest of men in the search for the truth, and for the genuine solution to the numerous problems which arise in the life of individuals and from social relationships."[45]

What is at stake in our assessment of the moral status of the embryo? Several things. First, our attitude toward "spare" and/or defective embryos. May they simply be allowed to perish? Is even the possibility of such "spares" sufficient to interdict the entire undertaking? Second, our attitude toward cryopreservation of embryos. Embryos can be frozen and kept at the ready should an attempted transfer fail. Thus the need for a second or third invasive laparoscopy is prevented. Yet the thawing process is not all that benign. Some 30-40% of embryos do not survive it. Is that itself an abuse? Finally, there is experimentation. Researchers will undoubtedly want to divide embryos with a view to preimplantation genetic diagnosis. They may also eventually want to attempt gene repair in early embryos.

One thing should be clear: the status of the preimplanted embryo is an *evaluative* question, not a directly scientific one. One cannot, of course, prove evaluations one way or another. One can, however, assemble information that suggests or leads to an evaluation. I believe that there are significant phenomena in the preimplantation period that suggest a different evaluation of human life at this stage. Therefore, I do not believe that nascent life at this stage makes the same demands for protection that it does later. In this sense I agree with Rahner.

However, other conscientious persons will hold different evaluations. Evaluations ought not be decreed. The Supreme Court in its *Wade* and *Bolton* decisions for all practical purposes decreed its own evaluation of nascent life as the morality and law of the land. What, then, is to be done? I raise this question with regard to *public policy*; for I believe that the underlying moral question is as yet unsettled.

When there are no shared convictions about substantive outcomes, there is public wisdom in turning to procedures. Specifically, I believe that there should be a policy presumption against experimentation on embryos and exceptions to this should be allowed only after scrutiny and approval by an appropriate authority. In my judgment, the matter is of such importance that the body should be national in character.

At present, as I write, there is a policy stalemate. Congress imposed a moratorium on fetal research in 1974. In 1975, regulations were promulgated that required that fetal research and human in vitro fertilization research, in order to be federally funded, must be approved by an Ethics Advisory Board. The EAB reported to the Secretary of DHEW that in vitro fertilization with embryo transfer (and certain research necessary to it) is ethically acceptable. No Secretary of DHEW or HHS acted on this report, and the Ethics Advisory Board no longer exists. Hence there is a policy vacuum.

The American Fertility Society's *Ethical Considerations of the New Reproductive Technologies* moved into this vacuum. It should be studied very carefully and critically.

And that brings us finally to the CDF's Instruction. It was dated February 22, 1987, but was actually released somewhat later.[46] The Instruction is a rambling, repetitious document numbering forty pages. Much of its material, however, is excellent and will elicit agreement from a broad constituency. This is especially true of its first ten pages, where its anthropological assumptions are spelled out. It proposes a general criterion for the uses of science and technology: the integral good of the human person. This is a splendid beginning. The Instruction also acknowledges the constructive role science and medicine can play in aiding human persons. It cautions against a blanket rejection of newer technological possibilities on the grounds of mere artificiality and it expresses appropriate sympathy for the suffering of the infertile couple.

It is when the Instruction enters the realm of detailed applications that it is likely to encounter stormy weather. For instance, when it deals with the status of the pre-embryo, its conclusions are unambiguous. It refers to: "unconditioned respect"; "treated as a person from the moment of conception"; "rights as a person must be recognized." Finally, the CDF asks: "How could a human individual not be a human person?" The wording of the Instruction seems to me to vacillate between two assertions: the pre-embryo *must be treated as* a person; the pre-embryo *is* a person. These are remarkably different statements. It is, I believe, easier to defend the first assertion than the second.

More specifically, the Instruction fails to distinguish between *genetic* individualization and *developmental* individualization. The former is certainly present from the very earliest beginnings (a phrase I use instead of "moment of conception" since fertilization is now known to be a process, not a moment). The latter, however, is not. Developmental individualization is completed only when implantation has been completed, a period of time whose outside time-limits are around fourteen days.[47] Practically, then, to the CDF's question "How could a human individual not be a human person?" the proper answer is: by not being—yet—a human individual. The CDF states that it is "aware of the current debates concerning the beginning of human life, concerning the individuality of the human being." Yet it takes no account—other than genetic—of the phenomena that lead outstanding reproductive biologists such as Clifford Grobstein to deny developmental individualization to the pre-embryo. Charles Krauthammer summarized this as follows: "Where the report fails is in its refusal to draw lines, or rather in its insistence on drawing lines at such enormous protective distance from the hellish center that the exercise loses its power to persuade."[48]

The Instruction rejects third-party involvement in procreative technologies. My own agreement with such a rejection is clear from what I have written above.

What is likely to prove much more controversial is the rejection of the so-called "simple case"—artificial reproduction (AIH and in vitro fertilization) with the gametes of husband and wife. On my own reading, this rejection would have to apply also to GIFT (gamete intrafallopian transfer). Why? The Instruction states that artificial insemination cannot be justified within marriage "except for those cases in which the technical means is not a substitute for the conjugal act." In the GIFT procedure, technical means are clearly a "substitute for the conjugal act."

Four Catholic institutions (Nimegen, Lille, and the two Louvains) announced, shortly after the appearance of the Vatican's Instruction, that they would continue to provide in vitro fertilization with embryo transfer to otherwise infertile married couples (the "simple case"). That should be a tipoff about the persuasiveness of the position taken by the Congregation for the Doctrine of the Faith when it rejected any technology that replaces sexual intercourse for procreation.

I have discussed this "simple case" with physicians, moral theologians, healthcare personnel, married couples, and priests. Although my discussants are certainly not exhaustive, *no one* I spoke with accepts the Vatican's rejection of the "simple case." This informal consensus is underlined in the many committee reports from around the world. Such a consensus must give pause to those who maintain that the document is the Church's final word on this matter.

More to the point, such consensus forces our attention on the analysis that led the congregation to reject in vitro fertilization even when the gametes of husband and wife are used. What is that analysis? It is stated succinctly as follows: "The Church's teaching on marriage and human procreation affirms the 'inseparable connection, willed by God and unable to be broken by man on his own initiative, between the two meanings of the conjugal act: the unitive meaning and the procreative meaning'."[49]

The document goes on to point out that just as contraception separates the unitive and procreative dimensions of sexual expression, so also, in an analogous way, do technological interventions such as in vitro fertilization and artificial insemination by husband. The congregation's rejection of such procedures rests ultimately on the inseparability principle adduced by the document. Indeed, in a remarkable statement, the congregation notes that its rejection of in vitro fertilization between husband and wife "is strictly dependent on the principles just mentioned." In other words, if those "principles just mentioned" can be shown to reveal a weakness, the conclusion will have the same weakness; that is what "strict dependence" means. The statement is remarkable because in the past ecclesiastical documents have asserted that the conclusion's validity is not strictly dependent on the analyses given or available to support it.

It should not be overlooked that the congregation views the principle in question as applying both to contraception and to reproductive interventions. Thus, if that principle is modified, then the very analytical basis for the Church's rejection of contraception has been modified or rejected. In this sense, I believe that the document is more concerned with contraception than with reproductive technologies. If the Church's analysis of contraception were different than it is, the document would be substantially different.

What, then, is to be said of this inseparability principle? Other Christian groups have supported a similar principle, but they have interpreted it differently, as I noted earlier. They have asserted that the unitive and procreative dimensions should indeed be held together, that married love should be generously life giving, and that procreation should occur in the context of convenanted love. But they have viewed such inseparability as something to be realized in the *relationship, not in the individual act.*

Thus the document insists that the unitive and procreative be held together *in every act*—no contraception and, on the other hand, no in vitro fertilization. Others, asserting a similar inseparability, argue that the unitive and procreative should be held together *within the relationship;* or, in more practical terms, just as contraceptive intercourse can be life giving (as nourishing the couple's life giving relationship), so in vitro fertilization can be unitive (as strengthening the relational good, the bond between the couple).

Above, I referred to the "principles just mentioned." Really a single principle is in question here: the inseparability of the unitive and procreative dimensions *understood as applying to every act.* Modify that understanding and the conclusion does not follow.

What, then, is to be said of this understanding? I want to raise several points here to show why many theologians—to say nothing of others—have had and will continue to have serious problems with the official Catholic understanding of the inseparability of the unitive-procreative dimensions of sexuality (as expressed in the Instruction, *Humanae Vitae* and *Familiaris Consortio*).

First, there is the very notion of the procreative dimension of *every act* of sexual intercourse. The idea that in *every act* of sexual intercourse the unitive and procreative dimensions must be inseparable implies that every act of intercourse is in some sense procreative. What does it mean to attribute a procreative dimension to sexual union when it is known to be infertile (e.g., because of age)? It is simply and in every respect a nonprocreative act. What does it mean to attribute a procreative dimension to sexual union during periods (e.g., during natural family planning) when it is known to be and intended to be infertile? To maintain that such an action is "open to procreation" and maintains the inseparability of the unitive-procreative dimensions makes no sense. The action is unobstructed, to be sure. But to argue that it must (morally) be unobstructed is to attribute an overriding moral value to physical unobstructedness. That is why many theologians see in this analysis a form of "physicalism."

Some years ago, John C. Ford, S.J., and Gerald Kelly, S.J., wrote: "The marriage act has other natural and intrinsic ends in addition to procreation which are separable from actual procreation or any intention of actual procreation."[50]

If such separation of "other intrinsic ends" (the unitive) "from actual procreation or any intention" of it is achieved by nature itself in individual acts, in what sense is the act procreative? In what sense are the unitive and procreative held together in the individual act?

Second, I readily admit that the inseparability principle (as applied to every act) contains a germ of truth, but that germ is arguably a legitimate aesthetic or ecological (bodily integrity) concern. All artificial interventions, whether to promote or prevent conception, are a kind of "second best." They involve certain disvalues that, absent sterility or fertility, respectively, we would not entertain. In this sense, we can agree with the congregation that conception achieved through in vitro fertilization is "deprived of its proper perfection." Much the same can be said of the use of contraception. However, a procedure "deprived of its proper perfection" is not necessarily morally wrong in all cases—unless we elevate an aesthetic-ecological concern into an absolute moral imperative. It seems to me that insistence on the inseparability of the unitive and procreative in every act does precisely this.

Third, what is responsible for this elevation of an aesthetic-ecological concern into an absolute moral imperative? For centuries Catholic theological thought viewed procreation as the *only* legitimate meaning and purpose of sexual intercourse. The contemporary teaching that every act of intercourse must be open to procreation (thus no artificial contraception) is a linear descendant of that earlier view and of the inadequate biology on which it rested.[51]

Fourth, the congregation correctly notes that "the one conceived must be the fruit of his parent's love." No one would deny that. Indeed, that is precisely what many Christians mean when they say that the unitive and procreative must be held together *in the relationship*. But to move from that general premise to the conclusion that the child must be conceived through sexual intercourse involves a leap in logic whose implication is that sexual intercourse is the only loving act in marriage.

This gap is underlined in the congregation's attitude toward technology. It states: "The one conceived must be the fruit of his parent's love. He cannot be desired or conceived as the product of an intervention of medical or biological techniques."

Obviously, technology can be abused. And just as obviously, the form of this abuse is to make the prospective child a consumer item on a shopping list—"Give me blue eyes this time." But technology need not be so abused. Ultimately, then, the citation above involves a false opposition. Being a product of a medical intervention is not opposed to being "the fruit of his parent's love." If experience is our guide—and I think it clearly is not in the congregation's document—accepting medical interventions to overcome sterility between husband and wife is, or can be, precisely a concrete manifestation of their love. I have seen this repeatedly. In this sense, it is easy to understand why many physicians regard in vitro fertilization and embryo transfer not as a replacement for sexual intercourse, but as a help to it, a kind of extension or completion of it.

In summary, then, I find the congregation's analysis and reasoning on "the simple case" unpersuasive. So do many others. It is understandable, therefore, why several Catholic institutions have already indicated they intend to continue to perform in vitro fertilization for married couples. It is also understandable why individual couples and physicians might draw the same conclusion.

Finally, let me say that I find myself in agreement with French bioethicist Patrick Verspieren, S.J. He states:

> The techniques of artificial procreation thus contain an imperfection and undeniable risks; but this determination, by itself, allows only with difficulty the conclusion that any recourse to these procedures is immoral. The ultimate reasons that led the Congregation for the Doctrine of the Faith to pronounce every form of artificial procreation "illicit" are to be found elsewhere: in my opinion, in the arguments of authority and in the positions taken by the previous popes.[52]

In a sense, therefore, the CDF faces the future by looking backward, and in doing so it has to live with the assumptions that make "begotten, not made" an absolute moral imperative. In my judgment, that is not an easy theological life.

Notes

1. "Ethical Considerations of the New Reproductive Technologies," *Fertility and Sterility* 46 (1986), Supplement 1.

2. Susan Abramowitz, "A Stalemate on Test-Tube Baby Research," *Hastings Center Report* 14 (1984): 5.

3. Abramowitz, loc. cit., 5.

4. Cf. note 1, at 825.

5. For this basic information, cf. "Ethical Considerations" as in note 1.

6. LeRoy Walters, as in Abramowitz (cf. note 2), 6.

7. *Washington Post*, 14 April 1985.

8. *Philadelphia Inquirer*, 28 August 1985.

9. *Archives of Internal Medicine*, March 1985.

10. *Time*, 31 July 1978. Charles Krauthammer has summarized the issue at stake as synthetic children, synthetic families and synthetic sex (*New Republic*, 4 May 1987, 18).

11. Cf. LeRoy Walters, "Human in Vitro Fertilization: A Review of the Literature," *Hastings Center Report* 9 (1979): 23-43; also Walters, "Ethical Issues in Human in Vitro Fertilization and Embryo Transfer," in *Genetics and the Law III*, ed. Aubrey Milunsky and George J. Annas (New York: Plenum Publishing Co., 1985).

12. Clifford Grobstein and Michael Flower, "Current Ethical Issues in IVF," *Clinics in Obstetrics and Gynecology* 12 (1985): 877-91.

13. AAS 29 (1896-97), 704.

14. AAS 41 (1949), 559-60.

15. AAS 43 (1951), 835-54.

16. AAS 48 (1956), 467-74.

17. AAS 60 (1968), 488-89.

18. AAS 74 (1982), 119.

19. Ladislaus Orsy, S.J., "Reflections on the Text of a Canon," *America* 154 (1986): 396-99. For further confirmation of this, cf. G.B. Guzzetti, "Magistero della chiesa e fecundazione in vitro," *Scuola cattolica* 113 (1985): 284-99. Guzzetti is primarily concerned with responding to the rather expansive claims of Dionigi Tettamanzi, "Gli interventi del magistero della chiesa sulla fecondazione in vitro," *Scuola cattolica* 113 (1985): 67-113. See also Guzzetti, "Debolezza degli argomenti contro l'embryo-transfer," *Revista di teologia morale* 17 (1985): 71-79.

20. Guzzetti, "Magistero," 291.

21. M. Zalba, S.J., "Aspetti morali e giuridici circa l'inseminazione artificiale," *Palestra del clero* 58 (1979): 438 ff.

22. Jan Visser, C.S.S.R., "Problemi etici dell' embryo-transfer," in *Ricerca scientifica ed educazione permanente* 7-9 (1982-1983): 47 ff.

23. Catholic Bishops of Victoria (Australia), *Submission to the Committee to Examine in Vitro Fertilization*, unpublished document, 6 August 1982.

24. *Catholic Chronicle,* 16 November 1984. Caffarra has expressed himself frequently on this matter. Cf. *L'Osservatore Romano,* 4 July 1984, 5.

25. L. Leuzzi, "Il dibattito sull'inseminazione artificiale nella riflessione medico-morale in Italia nell'ultimo decennio," *Medicina e morale* 22 (1982): 343-71.

26. William Daniel, S.J., "In Vitro Fertilization: Two Problem Areas," *Australasian Catholic Record* 63 (1986): 21-31, at 31. Cf. also Daniel, "The Morality of in Vitro Fertilization," in *Moral Studies,* ed. Terence Kennedy, C.S.S.R. (Melbourne: Spectrum Publications, 1984), 47-71.

27. Guzzetti, "Debolezza" (cf. note 19), at 72-73.

28. Carlo Caffarra, *L'Osservatore Romano* (English edition), 30 July 1984. This interview was also published in *The Advocate* (Melbourne), 23 August 1984. For a response to this form of argumentation, cf. William Daniel, "In Vitro Fertilization: Two Problem Areas" (cf. note 26), 27 ff.

29. Daniel, loc. cit., 27.

30. Daniel, loc. cit., 31.

31. P. Verspieren, S.J., "L'Aventure de la fécondation in vitro," *Etudes* (November 1982): 479-92.

32. Walter J. Burghardt, S.J., in *Religious Freedom:* 1965 and 1975 (Mahwah, N.J.: Paulist, 1977), 72.

33. *Catholic Mind* 71 (October 1973): 58-60.

34. F. Hürth, S.J., "La fécondation artificielle: Sa valeur morale et juridique," *Nouvelle revue théologique* 68 (1946): 416.

35. John Mahoney, S.J., *Bioethics and Belief* (London: Sheed and Ward, 1984), 28.

36. AAS 41 (1949), 557-61. For an English version, cf. *Catholic Mind* 48 (1950): 250-53, at 252.

37. Karl Rahner, "The Problem of Genetic Manipulation," *Theological Investigations* 9 (New York: Herder and Herder, 1972), 225-52, at 246.

38. For example, Louis Janssens, "Artificial Insemination: Ethical Considerations," *Louvain Studies* 8 (1980): 3-29.

39. William J. Winslade and Judith Wilson Ross, *New York Times,* 21 February 1986, 27.

40. *Chicago Tribune,* 3 October 1985.

41. Paul Ramsey, *Fabricated Man* (New Haven: Yale University Press, 1970), 88-89.

42. *Origins* 12 (1982), 342.

43. Karl Rahner, S.J., "The Problem of Genetic Manipulation," *Theological Investigations,* as in note 37, 236.

44. *Federal Register* 35033-58, 18 June 1979.

45. *Documents,* no. 16, 214.

46. Congregation for the Doctrine of the Faith, "Instruction on Respect for Human Life in its Origin and on the Dignity of Procreation" (Vatican City: Vatican Polyglot Press, 1982).

47. A recent example of the fourteen-day rule is "Richtlinien zur Forschung an frühen menschlichen Embryonen," *Deutches Ärzteblatt–Ärztliche Mitteilungen* 50 (1985): 3757-64.

48. Charles Krauthammer, as in note 10.

49. "Instruction," 26.

50. John C. Ford, S.J., and Gerald Kelly, S.J., *Contemporary Moral Theology: Marriage Questions* (Westminster: Newman, 1963), 405.

51. Cf. Richard A. McCormick, S.J., "Begotten, Not Made," *Notre Dame Magazine* 15 (Autumn 1987): 22-25. Shortly before his death, the renowned Bernard Lonergan, S.J., noted of birth control: "The traditional views [on contraception] to my mind are based on Aristotelian biology and later stuff which is all wrong. They haven't got the facts straight. A conception is not intended by every act of insemination" (*Catholic New Times*, 14 October 1984, 15).

52. Patrick Verspieren, S.J., "Les fécondations artificielles. A propos de l'Instruction romaine sur le don de la vie'," *Etudes* 366 (May 1987): 615. For a critique of the recent literature on the Instruction, cf. Edward Vacek, *Theological Studies* 49 (1988): 110-31. See also the response of the Ethics Committee of the American Fertility Society in *Fertility and Sterility* 49 (no. 2, Supplement 1, 1988), 1S-7S.

Chapter 20

If I Had Ten Things to Share with Physicians

We all have fantasies about what we would say if we were granted one minute with the president of the United States or the pope. Most of us, I dare say, would propose to solve the problems of the world or the Church in a sentence or two. In the never-never land of dreams, both sentences and solutions flow freely. One can be both outrageous and uncontested. That is the risk of the genre.

But there are advantages as well. When we are locked into spatial or temporal limits, we are forced to pick and choose. Such enforced selectivity can generate an otherwise elusive clarity. With this hope and in this spirit I put to myself this question: If I could share ten things with physicians, what would they be?

Let me say upfront that my suggestions are not criticisms lobbed into the professional camp from outside. Physicians are far more capable than I of professional self-criticism. The points listed here are much more like invitations to more explicit ethical thinking by a profession so pressured and harried that some of its gravest concerns remain implicit and unexamined. Indeed, there is a sense of the term "professional ethics" that would render it as the explicitation of what is implicitly grasped.

My suggestions will be in the form of *don'ts*. This is not with the idea of casting ethics in negative tones. I want rather to underline the idea that their opposites are genuine temptations in our day.

1. ***Don't ignore the threat of depersonalization in modern medicine.*** There are three factors increasingly operative in health care delivery and in the way we perceive health care problems.

Technology. Everything from diagnosis through acute care to billing is done these days by computer. That is but a symbol of the massive presence of technology in modern medicine. In saying that, I mean in no way to knock technology. Technology quite simply makes possible the otherwise impossible. No one who has fought an uneven battle with kidney stones will take careless shots at the lithotriptor. No one who has been spared a stroke by carotid endoarterectomy will criticize the sonography and arteriograms that clinched the diagnosis. No one whose lesion was pinpointed by magnetic resonance imaging will belittle that wonderful technology.

Furthermore, high technology can actually facilitate human care. A recent ad from Dynamic Control was headlined: "We give you more time to care because you need less time to manage data."[1] The ad continued: "At Dynamic Control we understand the need in hospitals to make more time available to care for patients. That's why we've developed clinical as well as financial applications to integrate with our Hospital Patient Management System (HPMS). This gives your staff direct access to information the instant they need it. Your staff gets more time to care for patients because they need less time to manage patient information." Granted, this is a sales pitch. But the idea is nonetheless theoretically viable.

Even after technology has been given its due, it remains true that the price of efficiency can be a measure of depersonalization. This must give pause to a profession whose self-description is that of a healing ministry on a person-to-person level.

Cost containment. The cost of health care in the United States hovers around eleven percent of the GNP. It has become routine to encounter descriptive phrases such as "out of control" and "skyrocketing" to paint the picture. The factors contributing to the enormity of the health bill are well known: sophistication of services, higher wages, more personnel, inflation, cost pass-along systems, the malpractice system, unnecessary care, etc.

But there is a cost-containment revolution afoot. Diagnostic related groups (DRG) are a symbol of this. Joseph A. Califano, Jr., former Secretary of Health, Education, and Welfare (1977-79), puts it as follows:

> The spirited air of competition is for the first time swirling through the health industry. Fed up with years of waste, the big buyers of care— governments, corporations and unions—are demanding the facts, changing the way doctors, hospitals and other providers are used and paid, and reshaping financial incentives that have encouraged patients to seek unnecessary care. And a host of new health care providers is scrambling to get their business.[2]

Califano points out some interesting facts that form the background for new cost-containment efforts. Item. Some 20-25% of hospital admissions are unnecessary. Item. There are erratic geographical variations in medical practice. For instance, the rate of major cardiovascular surgery is twice as high in Des Moines as in Iowa City for patients with the same symptoms. Item. Patients of fee-for-service physicians are twice as likely to have bypass surgery as those in health maintenance organizations. Item. A small number of patients accounts for a disproportionately large proportion of health costs. For instance, more than 30% of Medicare's expenditures goes to patients with less than a year to live. In 1984, 3.4% of Chrysler's insured accounted for 43.5% of the company's health care payments.

Obviously, the new concern with cost containment will spawn many ethical problems. I will not attempt to detail them here since I am chiefly concerned with the emergence of the cost-containment factor itself and its impact on the depersonalization of health care.

Public entities. I use this term to refer to the increasing presence of legislation (e.g., Baby Doe rules), the courts and the legal profession in medical decision making. The symbols of this presence: legislated living wills, Wade–Bolton, Quinlan, Fox, Storar, Dinnerstein, Conroy, Brophy, Chad Green and a host of others.

It is my thesis that these three factors (technology, cost containment, public entities) can affect the very matrix of the healing profession. This matrix is constituted by the conviction that medical decision making best serves the interests of patients when it is located within the triad of patient-physician-family. (By "physician" here I mean to include all members of the health care team, e.g., nurses.) Decisions must be tailor-made to the individual patient. They are like a glove fitting an individual hand. They are personal decisions.

The three factors I have listed are impersonal factors. They can easily have the effect of preprogramming our treatment. And clearly this can result in depersonalized treatment, a subtle form of oppression of the weak and dependent by the powerful and healthy. This growing depersonalization of treatment has led George Caldwell, president of the Lutheran General Health Care System, to note that what goes on in hospitals too often is "fixing" and not "healing."[3] Whatever the case, the three factors I have mentioned touch every problem area of modern medicine by framing the questions and limiting the available answers. Simply being aware of this problem just might be half of its solution.

2. Don't think of ethics as a threat. I say "ethics" not "ethicists" because obviously some ethicists are a threat, just as some physicians are. But the ethicist is a threat precisely and only insofar as she/he is not doing ethics, but something else that masks under the name of ethics. Usually, that "something else" takes the form of intrusion and reinforces the old stereotypes protected and nourished by many physicians—that ethics is *something added to medical practice.* Thus we hear: "I am ethical. I don't need it."

When medical ethics is viewed as a threat, it is because it is judged to be what it is not: a set of rules or guidelines—often created outside of the profession—which physicians consult and to which they are asked to conform their conduct. If that is an inadequate account of medical ethics, a better description might run like this: the identification, analysis, assimilation and implementation of the value dimensions of medical practice.

In that description, the term "value dimensions" must be spelled out a bit. Medicine has been called the healing art. It is persons who are healed, and persons are multidimensional beings: physical, emotional, intellectual, spiritual, social. True healing must take account of all these dimensions. It is not mere body fixing. When someone is ill, it is the *person* who is ill.

It is this multidimensional aspect of the person that makes touch the classic symbol of human healing, and Mark, the classic locus. For touch is inter*personal* contact.

> There was a woman in the area who had been afflicted with a hemorrhage for a dozen years. She had received treatment at the hands of doctors of every sort and exhausted her savings in the process, yet she got no relief; on the contrary, she only grew worse. She had heard about Jesus and came up behind him in the crowd and put her hand to his cloak. "If I just touch his clothing," she thought, "I shall get well." Immediately her flow of blood dried up and the feeling that she was cured of her affliction ran through her whole body. Jesus was conscious at once that healing power had gone out from him. Wheeling about in the crowd, he began to ask, "Who touched my clothing?" His disciples said to him, "You can see how this crowd hems you in, yet you ask 'Who touched me?'" Despite this he kept looking around to see the woman who had done it. Fearful and beginning to tremble now as she realized what had happened, the woman came and fell in front of him and told him the whole truth. He said to her "Daughter, it is your faith that has cured you. Go in peace and be free of this illness."[4]

In this story touch is the vehicle and sign of the meeting of two persons. One can say with confidence that what happened here had physical, emotional, spiritual, intellectual and social dimensions. From this perspective, the challenge of contemporary medicine is to transform the sonograph, the scalpel, the MRI into a *human* touch. And from this perspective, failures in medical ethics are failures of dimension, the neglect of some dimension of the human patient. When we ask "What is wrong with betraying a confidence, with deceiving a patient, with failing to report incompetence, with oversedation?" our answer will always be in terms of a neglected dimension of the human person. With this in mind, medical ethics can be characterized as follows: being and acting in such a way that one responds to the person integrally and adequately.

In verbal shorthand, medical ethics is corrective vision, an opening of our eyes to easily missed dimensions of persons and the claims they make upon us in the medical context. Far from importing a set of extraneous rules-makers and rules that are "added to" the situation, medical ethics is seeing more accurately and deeply the dimensions and realities that are already there. That is a threat only to those who have collapsed all reality into their present ability to perceive it.

3. Don't look to ethics primarily for answers.   I do not mean to suggest that answers are not important. Mistaking what love demands is probably the next worse thing to not loving at all. Clearly, answers are important. But how one got there is more important. Not only does this now have carry-over value; it also reveals what the physician is seeing, his/her guiding values.

Let a concrete case exemplify my point.

This eighty-four-year-old man had essentially been hale and hearty until the onset of his acute illness. For many years he had been an active participant in the business community and had been involved in many charitable activities. On the day of admission to the hospital he fell down a few stairs, striking his head, but did not lose consciousness. However, within one or two hours he had evidences of increasing intracranial pressure and lapsed into a stupor. Upon admission to the hospital, it was found that he had classical findings of a subdural hematoma. Within twenty-four hours he had a craniotomy with evacuation of 150 cc's of blood. During and after surgery, he presented no major life-threatening complications. He did, however, have gastrointestinal bleeding, which was probably due to a stress ulcer. This responded to conservative therapy. He never had a return to normal consciousness. Upon vigorous stimulation he would appear to partially awaken and on some occasions would utter one or two words. At no time did he seem to voluntarily move his limbs on command. Approximately two months after admission, he had the usual findings of a gram negative septicemia. He did respond to antibiotics and temporary steroid medications. Throughout most of his hospitalization he did not require ventilatory assistance. His subsequent nursing care was very vigorous, but did not require special care, except that he was fed by nasal gastric tube. He repeatedly removed the tube. Approximately nine weeks after admission, further consultation was sought from an outstanding neurosurgeon from another community. It was the combined opinion of all consultants involved in the case that the patient had evidences of bilateral brain damage, especially in the base of the brain. It was felt that due to the duration of his illness and the lack of any evidence of improvement, especially during the last six weeks of his life, conservative management should be used. We wondered whether, under the circumstance, it was necessary to reinsert the feeding tube. How often?

It was a case such as this that was presented at grand rounds at Holy Cross Hospital on the outskirts of Washington, D.C. I offered some general principles and made several "clear case" applications. Several physicians approached me at the conclusion of the session to complain that "you have not answered the case." They looked disappointed and frustrated. I made two points with them. First, I could well understand their frustration, their desire for a clearcut "answer." In life-death decisions it is much more comfortable to have a rule (or a bioethicist) bear the burden of the decision.

Second, I insisted that there are no rules that would replace their prudence and exempt them from the anguishing task of wrestling with the untidy and unpredictable clinical realities of individual cases. Anyone who claims to have a rule that will cut through all the agonies of ambiguity and uncertainty is involved in deception. "Beware of ethicists bearing solutions." It is in this sense that I urge "Don't look to ethics primarily for answers."

Rules, it must be remembered, are conclusions or generalizations about the significance of our conduct. Thus, if certain actions promote and support the human person, they are prescribable. If they generally undermine persons, they are generally morally proscribed. If they always undermine human persons, they are always proscribed. In formulating "rules of practice," theologians and ethicists try to be as all-inclusive as possible. But the older (and hopefully wiser) they are, the more they realize that reality, in its incorrigible variation, outstrips their rule-making expertise. St. Thomas clearly recognized this when he noted that the more we are immersed in detailed reality, the more our principled statements meet exceptions.[5] The refusal at times of moral theologians to provide "answers" is anything but a copout. It is simply a recognition that it is inappropriate to attempt to usurp the prudence of the clinician.

4. Don't identify ethics with dilemma ethics.[6] Dilemma ethics is concerned with the moral rightness or wrongness of human actions. It attempts to analyze the moral fittingness or unfittingness of actions like abortion, experimentation on fetuses (or children or prisoners), withdrawal of life-supports, in vitro fertilization, access-to-health-care policies, etc. These are the neon problems of medicine. They get a great deal of ink and are talked to death on "Sixty Minutes," "The McNeil–Lehrer Report," and "Nightline." Furthermore, when freshly minted Ph.D.s offer courses in bioethics, they usually include a litany of such problems. Anthologies abound that present diverging views on such dilemmas. Little wonder that many physicians equate ethics with problem solving.

Problem solving is, of course, important. But no less important is what is happening to the problem-solver. I refer to that dimension of ethics known in the trade as "virtue ethics." Its concern is the moral formation of the medical practitioner. Thus it is much more formational than informational. This dimension of ethics is not taught from textbooks simply because it cannot be learned from them. It is an ethic of aspiration that one absorbs through one's pores by association with good and wise peers. Its dominant vocabulary is not surgical, biochemical, radiological, ventilatory, cardiological. It is concerned with notions such as honesty, loyalty, respect, caring, communication, patience, compassion. To think that the notion of "ethics" can do without these dimensions is to amputate the notion. It is to espouse a concept of ethics wherein the personal qualities and growth of the physician have no place, where ideals and beliefs have subordinate status, if any at all.

When "ethics" is collapsed into dilemma ethics, we are likely to see a strange and more or less tragic phenomenon: the split between the role and person. This refers to the alienation between the self and the societal role when an individual constantly presents himself to others in a role. The role develops but frequently enough the self does not. It remains anemic and immature. Thus we witness the disheartening phenomenon of a physician who is patient, caring, understanding, communicative in his professional ambience but seems incapable of such responses in his nonprofessional relationships. This splitting of the personality can, of course, afflict any of us. But I believe it is a particularly notable trap for professions that are pressure-packed and highly esteemed. In such circumstances the qualities that define the good person can easily be relegated to and exhausted in the role. It would be sad indeed if this happened in the name of ethics—a not improbable outcome when ethics is conceived of as merely dilemma ethics.

5. *Don't collapse patient good into medical good.* Both medical tradition—with its powerful Hippocratic emphasis on beneficence—and medical literature place the notion of a patient's "best interests" on center stage. Clinical decisions are shaped, controlled, modified and reversed in pursuit of such interests. We instinctively sense that something is wrong when these interests are subordinated or sacrificed to other concerns.

Notwithstanding the centrality and frequent usage of the notion of "best interests" of the patient, the depth and complexity of the concept is often unappreciated. Edmund Pellegrino, M.D., has noted that the concept has several components.[7] An ideal decision should attend to all of the components.

Medical good. This refers to the effects of medical intervention on the natural history of the disease being treated, to what can be achieved by the application of medical knowledge: cure, containment, prevention, amelioration, prolongation of life. This good can vary. For instance, the respirator could lead to complete recovery; or it could tide a patient over a crisis so that the underlying causes could be studied; or it could be used to discover whether the patient is terminal. Pellegrino notes that there is a tendency to equate medical good with the overall best interests of the patient. For example, if treatment of a defective newborn would result in a life "without meaningful relationships," the treatment is said to be not *medically* indicated. However, whether a life is worth living is not a medical decision nor is it measurable by medical means. Furthermore, when overall patient good is reduced to medical good, there is the tendency to conclude that what *can* be done *ought* to be done.

Patient preferences. The scientifically correct (medically good) decision must be placed within the context of a patient's life situation or value system. Thus to be good in this sense a decision must square with what the patient thinks worthwhile. Only the patient or the patient's proxy can make this determination. For instance, whether treatment that leaves one seriously disabled is tolerable in, mandated by, optional in a patient's value and/or religious perspectives must be decided by the patient.

The good of the human as human. This refers to the good proper to humans as humans. While this is philosophically debated (some opt for consciousness, others for rationality, capacity for art, etc.), one thing is not debated: unique to humans is the very capacity to make choices. Therefore, other things being equal—which they often are not— a treatment that preserves the capacity to choose is to be preferred to one that does not. In this sense, it is in the patient's best interests.

The good of last resort. This is the good that gathers all others, is their base and explanation. It gives life ultimate meaning. Many of us call this good God or Jesus Christ. Two things are to be noted about this good. First, it differs with different people. For instance, for some orthodox Jews every moment of life, regardless of condition or prognosis, is to be treasured as a near absolute value. It is at times very difficult to get such people off of respirators, even when they are in a persistent vegetative state. For the Christian—especially the Catholic Christian—physical existence has been relativized by the death-resurrection motif. The accumulation of minutes is not the criterion of "good dying" for the Christian. Thus, the Christian might be willing to say "enough" somewhat sooner than others when dealing with problems of life-prolongation. In summary, reasonable people may have differing theologies, different conceptions of the good of last resort.

The second point to note is that with the always incompetent patient (and this would include babies) it is this good that will undergird the judgment of best interests simply because the second and third components are irrelevant to the always incompetent. This complicates matters and means that a certain flexibilty must be allowed in determining best interests.

6. *Don't be socioeconomic referees.* It is no secret that American medicine is becoming thoroughly commercialized. In this process hospitals have come under enormous financial pressures. Stated in stark simplicity, two key goods (patient good, hospital good) can be competitive. When this happens, physicians can easily find their traditional role as patient advocate nudged aside by the new and unaccustomed role of fiscal gatekeeper for the institution, and more broadly for the health system.

A Symposium on Government and Corporate Influence on Patient/ Physician Relations, sponsored by the New York Academy of Medicine, discussed this problem.[8] Arnold S. Relman, M.D., editor of the *New England Journal of Medicine*, put the problem fairly and squarely:

> I see the current crisis as a crisis of my profession. I am discouraged by the slowness of my profession to see [what] its responsibilities are . . . Do physicans want to be hired hands working for . . . corporations, profit or not-for-profit? Or do physicians want to be independent professionals acting on behalf of their patients?

When physicians try to wear two hats, they obviously will be operating under conflicting pressures. Marianne J. Legato, M.D., symposium program chairwoman, summarized them neatly.

> Let me tell you what the doctor thinks now as he considers an admission for a 72-year-old patient with severe chest pain: "If I admit this patient, and he must stay more days than the allotted time for the diagnoses I put down in the chart, who will pay for the additional days? Will the patient? Will I?
>
> "Will I spend my time writing letters to justify to admit and keep the patient in the hospital until I judge him ready to go home?
>
> "Will I spend, as have my colleagues, days in court before a judge to argue the decision about whether days in hospital will be paid for by the third-party payer or by the patient? If I do admit the patient, will I be able to prove I utilized the time well? And that means will I be able to explain to a reviewing agency why a day went by when no test was performed . . . Never mind that the CAT scanner was inoperable that day?
>
> "Will I be able to construct a chart cannily enough to convince the reviewer that I am accurate, efficient and economically practical?"[9]

It is obvious in this scenario that purse tightening has had an influence on the physician-patient relationship. But that is not all. It will affect hospital-patient relationships and hospital-physician relationships. The most dramatic and controversial symptoms of the new forms of health care financing (and in particular the medicare prospective payment system with its 467 diagnostic related groups [DRG's]) are: (1) Patients are being discharged "quicker and sicker," frequently without community support. (2) Some people are turned away from private hospitals because they cannot pay and end up in public facilities in what has come to be known as the "dumping syndrome." The extent of the evolving problem becomes clear when it is known that some thirty-three million Americans cannot afford private insurance but are not quite poor enough to qualify for medicaid.

In making these comments, I do not mean to criticize the new frugality and streamlining in medical care. Nearly everyone concedes that belt tightening was and is called for. *U.S. News and World Report* summarized the situation accurately.

> It was a system that encouraged unnecessary tests and surgery—a gravy train for some unscrupulous doctors and a major drain on tax coffers. An estimated 30 percent of medical costs resulted from waste, duplication, fraud and abuse. Medicare was headed for bankruptcy. Meanwhile, corporate America realized that one reason it couldn't compete with foreign companies was that it was spending so much on health benefits for employees.[10]

My only point—and it is an eminently *ethical* concern—is that amid the ongoing revolution in health care it would be a sad day for all of us if physicians ceased to be patient advocates.

7. *Don't regard nurses as subordinate or pastoral care as peripheral.* I include this among my ten animadversions because I encounter complaints so frequently. It is obvious that hospital care is impossible without nurses. Nurses are quite simply the backbone of the hospital system. Physicians appear there. Nurses work there. But it remains true far too often that they *feel* unappreciated and undervalued, and at times abused.

Let the last—abuse—be an example. Nurses deeply resent the fact that it is they who must implement patient management decisions that they consider ill-advised, uncaring or even morally wrong. This is especially galling when they have no part in the decision-making process. "Slow codes" would be an example of this type of thing. Nurses argue, and correctly in my view, that in many instances they are more familiar with the patient, the patient's moods, illness, family, needs etc. than the attending physician. They want their knowledge and expertise acknowledged in the way decisions are made and implemented.

Whenever this matter comes up in a hospital setting, the response I frequently hear from physicians is: "There is one person who is ultimately responsible. I am the one that shoulders the blame. I am the one who has to pay exorbitant malpractice premiums. I go to court. The buck stops here, not at some aggregation of care-providers or some committee. Don't ask me to abrogate my responsibility."

I believe that misses the point so often made by nurses. They are not questioning the ultimate locus of decisional responsibility; they are protesting the *way* in which this responsibility is discharged. An analogy is in place here. When one bristles at the insulated procedural methods of some Roman congregations, one is not denying the doctrinal teaching competence of the pope. One is only insisting that this competence, if its product is to be credible and persuasive in the modern world, must be expressed in a way that respects the canons of accountability and the diversification of expertise explicitly acknowledged in principle by the Church.

Where pastoral care is concerned, perhaps the first thing that ought to be said about it is that it is not revenue producing. In the contemporary atmosphere, that could make it a threatened species. If it ever becomes an extinct species, hospital care would be leveled to body fixing and the medical profession diminished to technicians. If health-care givers are to treat the *whole person,* pastoral care is an essential dimension of the *treatment*. It is not something alongside of it, something to which the physician turns "when he can do no more."

An example here is instructive. John F. Kennedy Memorial Hospital (Atlantis, Florida) has, among its services, a Comprehensive Cancer Center. It boasts three medical oncology specialists, a PDQ Medline system to retrieve the most inclusive diagnosis and treament data, the latest and most sophisticated radiation oncology diagnostic and treatment equipment (dual energy linear accelerators with electron beams, an Odelft simulator, a computerized treatment planning system, etc.). In the midst of all this, in the smallest office in the complex, sat the person who was the heartbeat of the whole center. She was the oncology counsellor. It was in her tiny office that people with cancer, and often a very limited future, spoke of their fears, their follies, their families. It was here that hard realities were faced and tears were shed. It was here that past memories were sharpened as future expectations were foreshortened. It was here that human emotions ebbed and tided around the meaning of life and death, of suffering and pain, of belief and unbelief. Without this counsellor who listened and reached out, there would be no healing even though there was recovery. With her there was healing even though there was dying. That is what I mean when I say pastoral care is an essential dimension of *treatment.*

8. *Don't follow rules or regimens in pain management; follow the patient.* A few facts can set the stage for my central concern here.[11] In the United States there are more than thirty-six million arthritics. There are seventy million with wrenching back pain. Some twenty million persons suffer from migraines. Hundreds of thousands suffer from sciatica and gout. Cancer pain afflicts around 800,000 people. In a word, about one-third of the population of the United States have recurrent chronic pain. As

Time concludes: "It is the single most common reason for seeing a doctor. It is the No. 1 reason people take medication."[12]

The other side of the coin is that pain is poorly understood and poorly managed. Medical students receive very little education on it, probably because so little is understood in the first place. Pain research is neglected and underfunded. For instance, the National Cancer Institute spends only around one-fifth of 1% of its billion-dollar budget on pain research. A 1973 study by two psychiatrists at Montefiore Hospital (New York City) found that 75% of patients receiving narcotics for pain relief failed to be relieved. Dosages were 25% to 50% less than needed. As *Time* concludes: "The problem was largely due to ignorance: Most staff physicians simply overestimated the efficacy and duration of painkillers. They also overestimated the risks of narcotics, worrying excessively about the possibility of respiratory problems and addiction."[13]

My "don't" says "don't follow regimens; follow the patient." An example will illustrate the point. *The Miami Herald* carried the story of Dorothea Triest (of Menlo Park) following back surgery.[14] She was wracked with surging and receding waves of pain. There was an excruciating gap between the time she pressed the nurse-call buzzer and the actual injection of pain medication. The worst part of it all, said Triest, was that pain management was out of her hands. Back in the hospital in 1985 for a hip replacement, she was on PCA (patient controlled analgesia). PCA involves an intravenous line directly into the bloodstream. The patient depresses a button and the dose is released. For Triest, incipient relief took only twenty seconds, whereas it could take from one to ninety minutes when nurse-injected. As Triest remarked: "By doing it yourself, you feel somehow a little more in control of the pain. It's not something that's being done for you." Stanford's Dr. Paul White (anesthesia) concurred and noted that the device reduces the anxiety surrounding pain by putting patients in charge of their own medication.

This example of PCA opens on some general statements that flush out the notion of "follow the patient." These statements anchor in the conviction that pain is a somatopsychic experience. That is, it originates in a physical stimulus but is always modified by the mind. At the center of most pain is fear. With this in mind, "follow the patient" translates as follows.

(a) Trust the patient's assessment of her/his pain. In so far as possible, let the patient control pain medication personally after the physician and patient have worked out a pain control plan.

(b) Know the pharmacology of pain medication. Self-education may be required of physicians and one of its major themes must be the eradication of uninformed fear of addiction and respiratory depression. While physical dependency may occur (temporarily in most instances), psychological dependency (a craving for the psychic effects of the drug) will not.

(c) Respond to the total phenomenon of pain (spiritual and psychological), remembering that isolation adds to all suffering. Fear of abandoment is probably the greatest fear.

These suggestions may appear to be small gains. Experts—from whom I take them—tell me that this is not the case. If these experts are correct, "follow the patient" is not merely a medical injunction; it is at some point an ethical one.

9. Don't argue: "I will not impose my values on patients." There is a sense, of course, in which such a statement is correct. That sense is generated by patient autonomy, the right of the patient (self-determination) to accept or reject medical treatment. An older paternalism is now seen as one-sided. Seeking the patient's best interest without the patient's knowledge or against her/his wishes is another example of what I have called "failures of dimension." The recognition that the patient should be part of her own healing is not isolationist libertarianism. It is simply an acknowledgment that treatment is always treatment of a *person* with values and beliefs, and that it must take these into account if it is to remain humane and respectful of human dignity. Furthermore, far more than is noted in the bioethical literature, it points to the fact that the patient has responsibilities for his/her own healing.

Autonomy of the patient can, however, be overstated into a distortion. That overstatement translates as total accommodation to the patient's values. The physician attempts to become value-free as if he were to be conscripted simply to do the patient's wishes.

The physician is not a technological automaton. He or she must practice medicine within the confines of what he/she thinks is morally right or wrong. That inevitably means that there are certain things he will do and not do. That is *not* "imposing my values on the patient." It is simply insisting that the physician is a person, not a tool. I fear that the legitimate claims of patient autonomy can be so stated that the physician is diminished in the process. That danger is most seductive where a physician's dominant concern is income.

10. Don't see death as the ultimate enemy. The medical profession is committed to curing disease and preserving life. That we take for granted. But this commitment must be implemented within a healthy and realistic acknowledgment that we are mortal. The point seems so obvious as to be trivial. In a sense it is.

But living it out is not. The attempt to walk a balanced middle path between medico-moral optimism (which preserves life at any cost, with all means, regardless of diagnosis, prognosis, family history, patient preferences, etc.) and medico-moral pessimism (which takes life when it becomes onerous, boring, dysfunctional and "hopeless") is not easy, especially in a highly litigious atmosphere. Symptoms of this abound in the inflated statements we encounter on life-preservation. Let a few suffice here.[15] Worcester Hahnemann Hospital issued this policy directive. "No one, patient, family or physician, may consent to, direct or initiate the removal or withdrawal of care or treatment which may be considered in any way to be life sustaining to any patient, except as provided below." The "provision below" was that the patient be dead according to the so-called Harvard Criteria of Death and be declared so by the attending physician. In other words, no withdrawal of any life-sustaining technology unless the patient is dead!

Carol A. Smith, Assistant Attorney General of the State of Washington, gave this opinion (1977) regarding the law with respect to withdrawing or withholding life support from a dying patient: "Under the present law, an attempt to bring about death by the removal of a life sustaining mechanism would constitute homicide, first degree."

Such attitudes also pervade the medical profession. In testimony before the President's Commission for the Study of Ethical Problems in Medicine and Biomedical and Behavioral Research, Dr. Marshall Brummer, a pulmonary specialist, was asked: "Is it the duty of the physician to do everything for that patient until that patient is called to his or her reward?" The answer: "Yes."

Behind such assertions lies a kind of medical idolatry, the absolutization of physical existence. This idolatry takes concrete form in the conviction that the inability to cure or prevent death is medical failure. The disturbing corollary of this conviction is patient abandonment in terminal illness: "I can do no more. You have no further need of me." The implication, of course, is that the notion of treatment is exhausted by curing. Caring is, as it were, left to others—if there are others. Once again, a failure of dimension.

These ten "don'ts" must stand or fall on their own merits. If they have merits and stand, we shall all be better off if they are weighed and sifted. If they do not, no one is worse off—except perhaps their author, who once again must publicly own his moral-theological astigmatism.

Notes

1. *Health Progress* 66 (November 1985), back cover.

2. *New York Times,* 25 March 1986. Cf. also Califano, *America's Health Care Revolution, Who Lives? Who Dies? Who Pays?* (New York: Random House, 1986), as well as Eli Ginzberg, *American Medicine: The Power Shift* (Totowa, N.J.: Rowman and Allanheld, 1985).

3. George Caldwell, "Perspective: Hospitals and the Emergence of Bioethics," *Second Opinion* 1 (1986): 121.

4. Mark 5: 25-34.

5. *Summa Theologica,* I-II, q. 94, a. 5.

6. E. Pincoffs, "Quandary Ethics," *Mind* 80 (1971): 552-71.

7. E. Pellegrino and D. Thomasma, *For the Patient's Good* (forthcoming as I write).

8. *American Medical News,* 4 April 1986, 21. For a further discussion cf. Edmund D. Pellegrino, M.D., "Rationing Health Care: The Ethics of Medical Gatekeeping," in *Medical Ethics,* ed. John F. Monagle and David C. Thomasma (Rockville, Md.: Aspen Publishers, 1988), 261-70.

9. *American Medical News,* as in note 8.

10. *U.S. News and World Report* 100 (no. 14, 4 April 1986), 60.

11. *Time,* 11 June 1984, 59. For a recent report on undertreatment of pain, cf. *New York Times,* 31 December 1987.

12. *Time,* loc. cit., 59.

13. Loc. cit., 59.

14. *Miami Herald,* 26 September 1985.

15. For these examples, cf. John J. Paris, S.J., and Richard A. McCormick, S.J., "Living Will Legislation Reconsidered," *America* 145 (1981): 86-89.

Chapter 21

Nutrition-Hydration: The New Euthanasia?

Crista Nursing Center is a 271-bed nursing home in Seattle with a 35-bed nursing wing. In 1984-85 two families, after learning from the attending physician and two consulting doctors that death was imminent for their elderly dear ones, requested the removal of the nasal-gastric feeding tube. The patients had been diagnosed as being in a persistent vegetative state. Six of the twelve nurses in the nursing wing refused to act on the request. Nancy Farnam, one of the resisting nurses, stated: "They are trying to make us the executioners. And I don't like it."[1]

"Executioner" is a very loaded word. It conjures up the electric chair, the lethal dose, the guillotine. It obviously reflects Nurse Farnam's analysis of and feelings about what she was asked to do. Whether it reflects an accurate moral assessment of the withholding or withdrawing of artificial nutrition and hydration in some instances is another question. That question may seem to be trivial, at the far-flung fringes of ethical and theological concern in a world dallying with the temptation of nuclear self-destruction, one where thousands are wiped out by malnutrition, AIDS, illegal drugs and alcohol abuse, where millions never see the light of day due to abortion. Actually, I believe the question is a crucial one, not perhaps in itself as a bit of isolated casuistry, but for what it may symbolize and presage. For if the withdrawal of artificial nutrition-hydration is what some people (judges and theologians included) say it is—killing—then clearly we have lowered the barriers against extrauterine killing in a very ominous way. I say "ominous" because we will have accepted a principle whose constraints may be swayed by influences beyond our eventual control. It is this that Daniel Callahan has in mind when he locates the importance of this matter in the way we are in the future to understand the role of the physician. Is the tradition of always caring, even if nothing more can be done, to give way to one of neglect, or worse?[2]

During March 1986, the Council on Ethical and Judicial Affairs of the American Medical Association issued guidelines for the situation. The statement reads in part as follows:

> Even if death is not imminent but a patient's coma is beyond doubt irreversible and there are adequate safeguards to confirm the accuracy of the diagnosis and with the concurrence of those who have responsibility for the care of the patient, it is not unethical to discontinue all means of life-prolonging medical treatment.
>
> Life-prolonging medical treatment includes medication and artificially or technologically supplied respiration, nutrition or hydration. In treating a terminally ill or irreversibly comatose patient, the physician should determine whether the benefits of treatment outweigh its burdens. At all times, the dignity of the patient should be maintained.[3]

Under analysis, the AMA position is structured around three assertions: (1) The criterion for morally appropriate treatment is the burdens-benefits calculus. (2) It is at times ethical to withdraw all life-prolonging medical treatment from the irreversibly comatose. (3) Artificial nutrition and hydration are a form of such medical treatment. Implied in these statements is the judgment that for the permanently comatose the benefits of nutrition-hydration do not outweigh the burdens. The AMA statement leaves unstated or unclear whether it considers artificial nutrition-hydration as being of *no* benefit for such a patient, or of *some* benefit but a benefit outweighed by the burdens. As we shall see, this is a key analytic point.

The AMA statement was not the first of its kind to emanate from physicians. On July 17, 1985, at the height of the Paul Brophy case (see below), the Massachusetts Medical Society endorsed by voice vote the following resolution:

> The Massachusetts Medical Society recognizes the autonomy rights of terminally ill and/or vegetative individuals who have previously expressed their wishes to refuse treatment, including the use of intravenous fluids and gastrointestinal feeding by tube, and that implementation of these wishes by a physician does not in itself constitute unethical medical behavior provided that appropriate medical and family consultation is obtained.[4]

The reaction to the AMA ruling was predictable in light of the controversy that preceded it. Archbishop Philip M. Hannan (New Orleans) denounced it in his archdiocesan newspaper, *The Clarion Herald*. "The Church strongly condemns this position."[5] Hannan insisted that food and water are "ordinary means of preserving life and therefore obligatory." Similarly, the late John R. Connery, S.J. (Loyola University, Chicago) said the new guidelines would allow physicians to "determine treatment on the basis of the quality of life" and saw this as an instance of mercy killing by omission.[6] Below I will return to Hannan's allegation that "the Church strongly condemns this position" and to Connery's rejection of the quality of life ingredient in these decisions.

In order to get at the ethical issues, I will describe in reverse chronological order three of the most public and pivotal cases involving artificial nutrition-hydration.

Paul E. Brophy, Sr. Brophy was a married man with five children (ages eighteen to twenty-six at the time of the court case). On April 6, 1983, he underwent surgery for a cerebral aneurysm. He never regained consciousness. Postoperative diagnosis revealed a complete infarction (destruction of tissue secondary to lack of blood flow) of his left posterior cerebral artery and infarction of the right temporal lobe of the brain. At first he was maintained on a respirator, and somewhat later by tracheotomy. Nutrition was provided by a nasal-gastric feeding tube. On December 21, 1983 a tube gastrostomy was performed. This hole in the abdominal wall allowed the administration of nutrition and hydration directly into the stomach. Brophy was diagnosed as being in a persistent vegetative state.

During January 1985, Patricia Brophy, Brophy's wife and legal guardian, requested discontinuance of all life-sustaining treatment, including artificial nutrition and hydration. The medical staff at New England Sinai Hospital refused. So Patricia Brophy went to court February 6, 1985. Judge David H. Kopelman issued his judgment on October 21, 1985. He refused to allow removal of the gastrostomy tube.[7]

Kopelman's reasoning is interesting. He admitted that Brophy was in a persistent vegetative state and that on the basis of all evidence Brophy's own judgment "would be to decline the provision of food and water." Yet Kopelman rejected the request. In doing so, he explicitly relied on the testimony of ethicists John R. Connery, S.J., Patrick Derr and Arthur Dyck. Basically, Kopelman argued that artificial nutrition-hydration is not burdensome to Brophy and "that he does derive a benefit in that his life is sustained." He stated that Brophy is not terminally ill and that denial of food and water "will inevitably in each and every instance guarantee and cause the death of the patient." Kopelman sees such denial as "causing the preventable death of Brophy," that is, as killing him. The matter would be different were Brophy a dying patient. As Kopelman notes: "If Brophy were terminally ill or dying, and would, accordingly, derive no benefit from the noninvasive provision of food and water, it might, under those circumstances, be permissible to remove the feeding tube in accordance with his substituted judgment." But Brophy is not dying; he is simply permanently vegetative. He had clearly stated that he would not want to be kept alive in such a condition. Kopelman refused to honor this. Following Connery, he stated: "The proper focus should be on the quality of treatment furnished to Brophy, and not on the quality of Brophy's life. Otherwise, the Court is pronouncing judgment that Brophy's life is not worth preserving. The quality of life is an incorrect focus because there are no manageable criteria for making such a judgment."

I shall return to the Kopelman analysis below. Here I simply want to advert to the fact that it is in substantial disagreement with two previous court decisions to which I now turn.

Claire Conroy. Claire Conroy was an eighty-four-year-old nursing home resident. She suffered from irreversible physical and mental impairments, including arteriosclerotic heart disease, diabetes and hypertension. She could neither speak nor swallow and was fed by a nasogastric tube. Her movements were very limited though she could smile or moan in response to some stimuli. She was restricted to a semifetal position and lacked control of her excretory functions. Thomas C. Whittemore, Miss Conroy's nephew and guardian, requested that the nasogastric tube be removed from his awake but severely demented aunt. The application was opposed by Miss Conroy's guardian "ad litem" (for purposes of litigation).

At trial, two physicians testified that Miss Conroy would die of dehydration in about a week after removal of the nasogastric tube. They also concurred in the opinion that her death would be painful. One physician regarded the nasogastric feeding as optional medical treatment. Miss Conroy's own physician, however, believed that removal of the tube would be unacceptable medical practice. The trial court (Judge Reginald Stanton, February 2, 1983) decided to permit removal of the tube because Miss Conroy's life had become intolerably and permanently burdensome.

This decision was appealed by Miss Conroy's guardian ad litem, but she died while the appeal was pending. However, the appellate division considered the matter too important to be left unresolved. It reversed the trial court's judgment and stated that removal of the nasogastric tube would be tantamount to killing her. A guardian's decision, the court argued, may never be used to withhold nourishment from an incompetent patient. As the court worded it: "The trial judge authorized euthanasia [homicide] . . . If the trial judge's order had been enforced, Conroy would not have died as the result of an existing medical condition, but rather she would have died, and painfully so, as the result of a new and independent condition: dehydration and starvation. Thus she would have been actively killed by independent means."

Mr. Whittemore took the question to the New Jersey Supreme Court, the same court that had decided the Karen Quinlan case. The court released its decision January 17, 1985.[8] After acknowledging the right of a competent adult to decline medical treatment—a right embraced within the common-law right of self-determination—the court addressed the rights of the incompetent. It noted: "The right of an adult who, like Claire Conroy, was once competent, to determine the course of her medical treatment remains intact even when she is no longer able to assert that right or to appreciate its effectuation."

Clearly, a substitute decision-maker or proxy must be called upon to function at this point. May a proxy ever decide that life-sustaining treatment may be withheld or withdrawn from an incompetent but not comatose patient? The court responded in the affirmative and proposed three tests or standards corresponding to three different situations. First, there is the "subjective standard," under which life-sustaining treatment may be withheld or withdrawn "when it is *clear* that the particular patient would have refused the treatment under the circumstances involved" (emphasis added). This clear intent can be concluded from written directives (living will) or oral statements made to family, friends or health providers. It might also derive from a durable power of attorney or appointment of a proxy with authorization to make medical decisions on the patient's behalf.

Second, there is the "limited objective test." Life-sustaining treatment may be withheld or withdrawn from a patient like Claire Conroy when there is trustworthy evidence that the patient would have refused the treatment and the proxy is satisfied that the burdens of the patient's continued life with the treatment outweigh the benefits of that life for the patient.

Finally, there is the "pure objective test." Under this test the burdens of the patient's life with treatment should clearly and markedly outweigh the benefits the patient derives from life. Furthermore, the unavoidable and severe pain of the patient's life with treatment must be such that continued life-sustaining treatment would be inhumane.

In elaborating its decision, which was a reversal of the appellate division's judgment that cessation of artificial feeding was a killing act, the New Jersey Supreme Court made several interesting points. First, it stated that the record in the Conroy case did not satisfy the standards prescribed by the opinion. Second, it rejected several distinctions as analytically unhelpful in this case: the distinction between actively hastening death and passively allowing a person to die; the distinction between withholding and withdrawing; the distinction is "elusive" and "particularly nebulous" where withholding or withdrawing life-sustaining treatment is concerned. It stated: "In a case like that of Claire Conroy, for example, would a physician who discontinued nasogastric feeding be actively causing her death by removing her primary source of nutrients; or would he merely be omitting to continue the artificial form of treatment, thus passively allowing her medical condition, which includes her inability to swallow, to take its natural course?"

Third, the court stated clearly that artificial feeding by nasogastric tube or intravenous infusion is equivalent to artificial breathing by a respirator. In other words, it is a medical procedure and should be provided or withheld according to the criteria applicable to medical procedures.

Finally and very importantly, it stipulated a procedure to be followed in cases like that of Claire Conroy. The person (e.g., family member, guardian, physician) who believes that withholding or withdrawing life-sustaining treatment corresponds to the patient's wishes or would be in her/his best interests must notify an ombudsman. Those with contrary beliefs should do the same. The ombudsman is to treat every such notification of withholding or withdrawing as a possible abuse. Two physicians unaffiliated with the nursing home and with the attending physician must confirm the patient's medical condition and prognosis. I can remark parenthetically that I was repeatedly told by New Jersey officials in 1988 that these procedures have proved unworkable.

Clarence Herbert. Clarence Herbert underwent surgery for closure of an ileostomy at Kaiser Permanente Hospital, Harbor City, Calif. in 1981. Shortly after successful completion of the surgery, Herbert suffered cardiorespiratory arrest. He was revived and immediately placed on life-support equipment. Within the following three days it was determined that Mr. Herbert was in a deeply comatose state from which he was unlikely to recover. Tests performed by several physicians indicated that he had suffered severe brain damage, leaving him in a vegetative state that was likely to be permanent.

At that time Mr. Herbert's physicians, Dr. Robert Nejdl and Dr. Neil Barber, informed his family of his condition and the extremely poor prognosis. The family then drafted a written request to the hospital personnel, stating that they wanted "all machines taken off that are sustaining life." Dr. Nejdl and Dr. Barber complied and removed Mr. Herbert from the respirator. He continued to breathe. After two more days, the two physicians, after consulting with the family (though the record is a bit hazy here), ordered removal of the intravenous line and nasogastric tube that provided hydration and nourishment. Shortly therafter, Mr. Herbert died.

Dr. Nejdl and Dr. Barber were accused of murder by the Los Angeles district attorney. Los Angeles Municipal Judge Brian Crahan dismissed the case. It was reopened (May 5, 1983) by Superior Court Judge Robert A. Wenke on the grounds that the dismissal was erroneous.

Wenke made some truly remarkable statements. Item. "The law of the state does not allow anyone to shorten another's life unless the latter's condition is irreversible."[9] Item. "Murder is the shortening of life." Item. "The morality of the defendants' conduct, the purity of their motives, common practice in this type of situation, and the wishes of the decedent's family are all of no weight in the resolution of this motion. The answer lies in the law of the state."

The matter eventually reached the Court of Appeal. On October 12, 1983, Judge Lynn Compton exonerated Dr. Nejdl and Dr. Barber of any unlawful conduct. In the course of this opinion, the court made several interesting and important points.[10] First, Judge Compton noted that even though life-support devices are self-propelled, still each drop of IV fluid is "comparable to a manually administered injection or item of medication." Hence, disconnecting such devices is "comparable to withholding the manually administered injection." Second, the court viewed intravenous nourishment and fluid as "being the same as the use of the respirator." Third, medical nutrition and hydration resemble medical procedures rather than typical ways of providing nutrition and hydration. Hence they are to be evaluated in terms of their burdens and benefits. Finally, since the court viewed the physicians' actions as omissions rather than affirmative actions, the resolution of the case depends on whether there was a duty to continue to provide life-sustaining treatment. The court asserted that there is no such duty once the treatment is useless. And it was useless in Herbert's case because it merely sustained biological life with no realistic hope of a return to a cognitive, sapient state. Thus, continued use of life sustainers was "disproportionate."

The Conroy and Herbert cases have a key difference. Clarence Herbert was judged to be in a permanent vegetative state. Claire Conroy was not. She was incompetent but not comatose. Of those in a permanent vegetative state, the President's Commission for the Study of Ethical Problems in Medicine and Biomedical and Behavioral Research wrote:

> Most patients with permanent unconsciousness cannot be sustained for long without an array of increasingly artificial feeding interventions— nasogastric tubes, gastrostomy tubes, or intravenous nutrition. Since permanently unconscious patients will never be aware of nutrition, the only benefit to the patient of providing such increasingly burdensome interventions is sustaining the body to allow for a remote possibility of recovery. The sensitivities of the family and of care-giving professionals ought to determine whether such interventions are made.[11]

A footnote to this last sentence notes that it can be anticipated that courts will grant requests to withhold or withdraw further treatment, including IV drips, from such patients. And that is just what the court did in the Herbert case. But the New Jersey Supreme Court also did the same thing in principle in the Conroy case, and for some of the same reasons. That is, both courts regard feeding by IV lines and nasogastric tubes as basically medical procedures to be judged by a burdens-benefit calculus. Furthermore, both courts (to a lesser degree the New Jersey Supreme Court) allow "quality-of-life" components to function in determining the best interests of the patient. In both of these respects, the Conroy and Herbert courts disagreed sharply with the Brophy court. Indeed, they both represent reversals of lower courts that held that withholding or withdrawing nutrition-hydration from comatose and/or incompetent patients would constitute murder. I think it fair to say that these judicial disagreements reflect the state of ethical discussion that preceded them and still surrounds them.

Before unpacking some of the key issues, it would be useful to provide a quick sampling of the literature. One of the first shots in this discussion was fired by hospice nurse Joyce V. Zerwekh. She argued that it is not always more merciful to administer IV fluids to a dying patient. There are both beneficial and detrimental effects associated with dehydration and the judgment must be individualized.[12]

Since the Zerwekh study, the literature has piled up impressively. For instance, Kenneth Micetich, M.D., Patricia Steinecker, M.D., and ethicist David Thomasma (all of Stritch School of Medicine, Loyola University, Chicago) concurred that IV fluids may not be morally required under a threefold condition: (1) The patient must be dying. "Death will be imminent (within two weeks) no matter what intervention we may take." (2) The patient must be comatose. Comatose patients would experience no pain, thirst, etc. (3) The family must request that no further medical procedures be done in the face of impending death.[13]

James Childress of the University of Virginia and Joanne Lynn, M.D., of George Washington University carried the matter a step further.[14] They argued that there are cases, even though relatively few, when it is in the best interests of patients to be malnourished and dyhydrated. They listed three situations: (1) The procedures that would be required could be considered futile. (2) The improvement in nutritional and fluid balance, though achievable, could be of no benefit to the patient (e.g., persistent vegetative state). (3) There are cases where the burdens to be borne in receiving the treatment may outweigh the benefit. Terminal pulmonary edema, nausea and mental confusion may be more likely in some patients as a result of artificial hydration and nutrition.

Even more recently, a group of distinguished clinicians advocated the withholding of parenteral fluids and nutritional support from severely and irrevocably demented patients.[15] John J. Paris, S.J., who was involved in the three major cases discussed above, has consistently maintained that it is ethically permissible to withhold or withdraw nutrition-hydration from patients in a persistent vegetative state. Not only is this not contrary to Catholic teaching; it is, he argues, the traditional teaching.[16]

Another important voice in this discussion is that of James M. Gustafson. During the deliberations on the Brophy case, he wrote (May 22, 1985) to John Paris the following letter.

I appreciate your calling to inform me of the factual matters of the

Brophy case. My comprehension of it sets it in a class of cases of patients in a well diagnosed persistent vegetative state.

For patients in this class I find nothing morally inappropriate, and indeed would affirm that it is morally appropriate, to discontinue nutrition and fluids.

A second is that a persistent vegetative state is not a condition in which human beings have capacities for significant responsiveness; thus the qualities that distinguish human beings and are the basis of human valuing of, and respect for, persons no longer exist.

A Protestant theological precedent that backs my judgment can be found in the writings of Karl Barth, the greatest of twentieth century Protestant theologians. He wrote with reference to his own arguments against failure to treat, "Yet in this connexion the question also arises whether this kind of artificial prolongation of life does not amount to human arrogance in the opposite direction, whether the fulfillment of medical duty does not threaten to become fanaticism, reason folly, and the required assisting of human life a forbidden torturing of it. A case is at least conceivable in which a doctor might have to recoil from this pro-longation of life no less than from its arbitrary shortening." I argue that it is not *only* conceivable in this class of cases.[17]

Such voices have not gone unchallenged. Daniel Callahan (Hastings Center) agrees that it is morally licit to discontinue feeding in the circumstances noted by Lynn and Childress. Yet he is profoundly uneasy with that conclusion. The feeding of the hungry, whether they be poor or physically unable to feed themselves, is "the most fundamental of all human relationships."[18] It is, he argues, extremely dangerous to tamper with so central a moral emotion. There remains a deep-seated revulsion at stopping feeding, even under legitimate circumstances. As I read him, Mr. Callahan would respect that revulsion and continue feeding as "a tolerable price to pay to preserve—with ample margin to spare—one of the few moral emotions that could just as easily be called a necessary social instinct."

That was Callahan's initial reaction. Since then he has returned to the subject and has not abandoned his uneasiness, but has modified his conclusions.[19] When all is said and done, however, Callahan allows cessation of nutrition-hydration for those frail elderly who are "imminently dying" and for those who are "not dying but are irreversibly comatose, utterly vegetative." For this latter category, nutrition and hydration simply confer no benefit. "There is no meaningful life of any kind—it is a mere body only, not an embodied person. Thus there is nothing left that would deprive such a patient of something valuable."[20] The "line should be drawn here, a very firm and sharp line." Concretely, those frail elderly who are irreversibly demented must be fed and hydrated. We just do not know what goes on in their minds or what human capabilities remain. This fact, combined with the real potential for abuse, is Callahan's reason for drawing the line where he does. Callahan approaches the entire question with thoughtful wariness, not enthusiasm. I regard him as one of our most commonsensical and reliable resources on this matter.

Gilbert Meilander of Oberlin College would disagree with both of Callahan's categories of exception. He argues that the withdrawal of nourishment from permanently unconscious patients involves us in "aiming at their deaths."[21] This we should never do. Nor does their permanent comatose state mean that it is useless to feed them. In these cases, feeding remains care for the embodied person, and it is dualistic to think otherwise. Nor is the care "in any strict sense medical treatment." It treats no particular disease; rather "it gives what all need to live."

A physician (Mark Siegler) and an attorney (Alan J. Weisbard) are deeply troubled by the emerging literature justifying withholding or withdrawing of hydration and nutritional support.[22] They reject the idea that anyone (physicians, families, courts) can properly make such judgments for the incompetent. Therefore, they want to reverse the stream of this literature and offer several arguments to bolster this reversal. First, patients will be protected against diagnostic errors, inadequate treatment and unscrupulous (e.g., for financial reasons) care. Second, physicians will not be compelled to make ad hoc, quality-of-life judgments. Third, the medical profession will be protected against the gradual dilution of its dedication to the welfare of patients. Finally, society will benefit by rejecting this practice because it bears the seeds of unacceptable consequences (e.g., devaluation of the unproductive).

This is a sampling of the literature surrounding the issue of artificial nutrition-hydration. The discussion is far from finished and there can be little doubt that cases like these will continue to appear before the bench because they are, as Callahan observes, the gathering place for two important moral traditions: the general moral duty to feed the hungry and give drink to the thirsty and the duty to provide care and comfort even when nothing of medical value can be done.[23] With that in mind, in the remainder of this chapter I will examine what I believe to be the four central moral issues in this discussion.

1. The notion of a dying patient. Who should be said to be a dying patient? If a patient needs dialysis to survive, is that patient a dying or nondying patient? If one needs a respirator to survive and will die without it, is that person dying or not? If one needs a nasal gastric tube or gastrostomy for food intake, is that person dying or not? I am suggesting that the notion of "the dying patient" is somewhat ambiguous and sometimes related to the technology available. John Paris, S.J., refers to such technology as "halfway technology."[24] It can stave off death but is unable to restore health.

Let us look at the notion of "staving off death" a little more closely. There are certain functions absolutely essential to continued life. One thinks of heart and kidney function. One of "those functions" is eating and drinking. Increasingly, technology can take over and supply for these natural functions. Thus for the heart we have transplants and artificial hearts. For the kidneys we have transplants and dialysis. To circumvent natural eating and drinking, we have nasal gastric tubes and tube gastrostomy.

There are times when we judge that the use of these technologies is appropriate and called for. We *ought* to use them. There are other times when we judge otherwise, and, of course, the patient dies. In those cases where we judge it appropriate, I believe the appropriateness will trace to two features: (1) a return to relatively normal health: (2) ultimate independence from the technology. It is these two features that constitute the notion of "reasonable hope of benefit."[25] Thus if a person had to rely perpetually on dialysis or connection to an external cardiac power source, we begin to get into grey areas where we speak of optional treatment. Or where the person can be maintained, but in no way returned to anything approaching normal health, we also begin to view the treatment as inappropriate.

What I am provisionally suggesting here is that in some instances, the difference between a dying and nondying patient roots in a *value judgment* about whether we ought to use the available technology or not. This is the case, I believe, where artificial nutrition-hydration for the permanently vegetative patient is concerned.

The category "the dying patient" is often presented as if it were independently (of value judgments) and descriptively clear. Judge Kopelman, for instance, states explicitly that "Brophy is not terminally ill, nor has he reached the end of his normal span of years." Similarly, Daniel Callahan refers to those frail elderly "who are not dying but are irreversibly comatose, utterly vegetative."[26] They are "not dying" only if we judge that we *ought* to feed them artificially. And if we make that judgment independently of the two features mentioned above, are we not equivalently saying that anything that *can* be done *ought* to be done? William Schroeder is a dying patient—unless we give him an artificial heart. Paul Brophy is a dying patient—unless we give him a tube gastrostomy. Should we?

This is a key issue; for if a patient is said to be nondying, but dies as a result of nutrient-withdrawal, then that withdrawal appears to be positively causal, and the withdrawer a killer. This is Judge Kopelman's analysis in the Brophy case when he says: "It is ethically inappropriate to cause the preventable death of Brophy by the deliberate denial of food and water which can be provided to him in a noninvasive, nonintrusive manner which causes no pain and suffering." What Kopelman is unwittingly saying, it seems to me, is that Brophy is not a dying patient because we *ought* to give him food and water. We *ought* to do so because it can be done without "pain and suffering." On those grounds, should we not also give him a kidney transplant?

2. The nature of artificial nutrition-hydration. Is this most properly characterized as a medical procedure, as both the appeals court of California (Clarence Herbert case) and the New Jersey Supreme Court (Claire Conroy case), as well as much of the literature, contend? Or does it more closely resemble providing a person with a bowl of soup? Does the simple fact that artificial feeding "gives what all need to live"[27] imply that how it is given makes no difference in its description? Most of us would not know how to go about providing nutrition and hydration by nasogastric tube and IV lines. These procedures require skilled medical training. Does that not constitute them strictly medical procedures? This is an issue because normal feeding has profound symbolic importance in human relationships and societal structure. It is one thing to starve the hungry. We should be appalled at the idea. It is quite another to withhold or withdraw a medical procedure. That we do routinely, and justifiably.

Is artificial nutrition-hydration *medical treatment* or something else? Robert Barry, O.P., refers to "a growing consensus that nutrition and fluids are the means by which basic human needs are met and are not precisely medical treatments."[28] Where this "growing consensus" is located, who constitutes it, Barry does not tell us. By contrast, Daniel Callahan states: "A strong current of moral and medical thought has developed in the past few years holding that artificially provided food and water (through tubes rather than by mouth) is inherently no different from, say, the air artificially provided by a respirator. If the latter can licitly be stopped, then so should the former."[29] Where Barry sees a "growing consensus" in one direction, Callahan sees a "strong current of moral and medical thought" in the opposite direction. I shall not attempt to resolve this essentially factual matter here, except to refer to the Steinbrook and Lo study cited in note 16.

During October 1985 the Pontifical Academy of Sciences assembled a study group to discuss this question and others as well. The group distinguished "treatment" and "care."[30] By the former, the group understood "all those medical interventions available and appropriate in a specific area, whatever the complexity of the techniques involved." Care was taken to mean the "ordinary help due to sick patients, such as compassion and spiritual and affective support." With regard to those in an irreversible coma, the group concluded that "treatment is not required, but all care should be lavished on him, including feeding." Clearly, the group had to mean *artificial* feeding, for the patient is comatose. It gave no grounds for its conclusion that it must be "lavished."

More than anyone else Robert Barry, O.P., has attempted to provide those grounds. He argues that nutrition-hydration are not medical treatments. "Medical treatments *directly, proximately* and *immediately* aim at preventing clinically diagnosable conditions."[31] On the other hand, "nutrition and fluids meet the basic needs of organisms to function and grow, and they are not remedies of diseases in and of themselves." He continues: "The lack of resources which sustain the natural functions of an organism is not a pathological condition." In summary, Barry goes the *definitional* route. Medical treatments treat pathologies. But lack of nutritional resources is not pathology. Ergo. What Barry's definitions overlook is that the inability to receive nutritional support in the ordinary or usual way is indeed due to a pathology (e.g., brain damage) that must be circumvented by medical procedures (e.g., tube gastrostomy). The assumption of Barry's analysis is that the distinction between medical treatments and nonmedical procedures is to be made uniquely in terms of *what* is accomplished, and has nothing to do with *why* it is necessary, *how* it is accomplished or by *whom*. That is a huge assumption.

Indeed, at some point it flies in the face of common sense. Informally, as a test, I have asked any number of people not exposed to this discussion whether nasal gastric tube feeding and/or tube gastrostomy are medical treatments. Universally, the answer is yes.

What is going on here, I believe, is not a logical, deductive process that goes as follows: These are not medical procedures; therefore they are not controlled by the criteria we use for medical procedures. Rather, I believe that Barry and others—perhaps without realizing it—have decided *on other grounds* that nutrition-hydration should not be withdrawn from the permanently vegetative patient, and that *therefore* they should not be called medical treatments. I shall return to these "other grounds" below. Suffice it for the present to say that the cart is before the horse.

Whether artificial nutrition and hydration are medical procedures or not is often confused by the introduction of terms such as hunger and thirst. People can be denied artificial nutrition and hydration without experiencing hunger and thirst. Conversely, they can feel hunger and thirst without being malnourished or dehydrated. The usage "feed the hungry and thirsty" in this context tends to predispose us to regard artificial nutrition and hydration as something other than medical procedures.

3. The intention of death. When we withdraw nutrition and hydration from a permanently comatose patient, must we be said to be "aiming at death"?[32] The answer to this question will depend very closely on how we answer the first two. For example, if permanently comatose patients or profoundly incompetent ones are said to be dying patients (because their condition prevents normal ingestion of food, e.g., swallowing) and if artificial feeding by nasogastric tube is to be regarded as a medical procedure, then withdrawal of nutrients represents only omission of a medical procedure for a dying patient. This need not involve "aiming at death"; otherwise any such omission (e.g., of a respirator) would in principle involve this reprehensible intent.

On the other hand, if the patient is viewed as nondying, and artificial provision of nutrients is not a medical procedure but rather an instance of "normal, ordinary care," then omission of such nutrients could be more suspect.

Let me put it this way. Those who contend that withdrawing hydration and nutrition involves us in "aiming at death" or being involved in "the direct causal responsibility for death" (Siegler, Weisbard) must be consistent and apply their analysis to the competent patient. Is a competent patient who refuses a nasogastric tube or a gastrostomy guilty of suicide ("aiming at his own death")? Most of us would and should answer: "It all depends." If the patient can be tided over a transitory illness and returned to normal life, the treatment would surely be obligatory and refusal of it, other things being equal, would be suicidal. If, however, this is not the case and the artificial feeding is foreseeably permanent, the treatment would be morally optional. Being such, it would not necessarily involve a death-aim. It need involve only a thoroughly Christian assertion that there are values greater in life than living, that we all retain the right to decide how we shall live while dying.

On this matter, too, Judge Kopelman has confused the issue. He notes that removal of a respirator, termination of chemotherapy, removal of a patient from dialysis and denying cardiopulmonary resuscitation will not in every case guarantee and cause death. Therefore, because death is not inevitable, he concludes that nontreatment orders in such cases "are not written with the specific intent of terminating the patient's life."

Denying a patient food and water, however, "will inevitably in each and every instance guarantee and cause the death of the patient." Therefore, Kopelman finds that "the purpose of the guardian's request to terminate the provision of food and water is . . . to terminate his life." In other words, Kopelman ties intention to the certainty of the outcome. If death will certainly follow, the intention is to produce it.

Anyone familiar with the traditional casuistry of the double effect will see the fallaciousness of this reasoning. The quality of one's intention— whether, for example, it is said to be direct or indirect—never hinged on the *inevitability* of the foreseen effect. Otherwise one would never have treated an ectopic pregnancy on the grounds that death of the conceptus was indirect.

4. The burden-benefit calculus. Where medical procedures are in question, it is generally admitted that the criterion to be used is a burdens-benefits estimate. This was the criterion proposed by the Sacred Congregation for the Doctrine of Faith in its Declaration on Euthanasia and by the President's Commission. The question posed is: Will the burden of the treatment outweigh the benefits to the patient? The general answer: If the treatment is useless or futile, or if it imposes burdens that outweight the benefits, it may be omitted.

However, an ambiguity remains. What is to count as a burden, and correlatively as a benefit? If a patient's life can be prolonged, but only in a comatose state, is that a benefit to the patient? Or if treatment will preserve life, but only a pain-racked, incompetent life, is that a benefit?

The issue here is this: In weighing the burdens-benefits of a treatment, is it the burden of the treatment only (e.g., its pain, expense etc.) that is legitimately considered, or may we include in the assessment the burden of continued existence itself? In other words, may the quality of life preserved be a proper dimension of the calculus?

The President's Commission answered this last question in the affirmative when it defined the patient's best interest broadly to "take into account such factors as the relief of suffering, the preservation or restoration of functioning, and the quality as well as the extent of the life sustained."[33] Both the Herbert court and the Conroy court did the same. For instance, the Conroy court (New Jersey Supreme Court) acknowledged that "although we are condoning a restricted evaluation of the nature of a patient's life in terms of pain, suffering and possible enjoyment under the limited-objective and pure objective tests, we expressly decline to authorize decision-making based on assessments of the personal worth or social utility of anothers' life, or the value of that life to others."

It is here that we arrive at the true heart of this issue, the issue that is behind the other issues, what I referred to above as Barry's "other grounds" for assessing artificial nutrition-hydration as nonmedical interventions. It is the evaluation of life in a persistent vegetative state. Is such a life a value to the one in such a state? Is its preservation a benefit to the patient? Or is treatment really futile and useless because *that kind of life* is of no benefit to anyone? It is here that positions diverge and company parts. There are two sharply distinct positions.

Position One. We can refer to this as the "quality of treatment" position. It is that of Judge Kopelman, John Connery, Robert Barry and others. Kopelman, following Connery, stated: "The proper focus should be on the quality of treatment furnished to Brophy, and not on the quality of Brophy's life." He further insisted, once again following Connery, that "there are no manageable criteria for making such a [quality of life] judgment." Obviously, Kopelman had to say Brophy "does derive a benefit in that his life is sustained." At another place he accepts the idea that artificial nutrition-hydration "is useful in that it preserves his life and prevents his death."

But now let us hear John Connery.[34] In his testimony he had asserted that court focus should turn on the quality of the treatment, not the quality of Brophy's life. Two questions, he stated, help determine quality of treatment. (1) Is the treatment too much of a burden for the patient? (2) Is the treatment useful or beneficial to the patient? That is, does it sustain his life? Clearly, for Connery, it is beneficial if it sustains a merely vegetative existence. Connery is forced into this corner because he adamantly rejects *any* quality-of-life dimension to these decisions. Why? There are no "manageable criteria." I take that to mean that there is no way of preventing a slide on the slippery slope to abuse.

Robert Barry is in this same corner. Of Clarence Herbert, he states: "Provision of food and fluids would have been of nutritional value to him because they would have sustained his life."[35] At another place he notes (of Herbert) that food and fluids "could have achieved their fundamental purpose which was to sustain his bodily functions and support its natural defenses against diseases."[36] Any quality-of-life approach is too susceptible to biases and prejudices and "there is no rational way in which the 'quality of life' of individuals could be justly and certainly assessed."

At a conference on the Interface between Medicine and Religion (November 1985), Rabbi David Feldman, a celebrated Talmudic scholar, stated: "Even a vegetative state is still life,"[37] and it must be kept going. That is where Kopelman, Connery and Barry are. The question is: is it where they should be if they are true to their Catholic Christian tradition? I believe the answer to that question is "no."

Position Two. We can refer to this as the "quality of life" position. I associate this position with the Herbert court and the New Jersey Supreme Court. I would also associate this position with Daniel Callahan. Speaking of the "irreversibly comatose, utterly vegetative," he says that food and water can be stopped. Why? "Neither provides any genuine benefit: there is not meaningful life of any kind—it is a mere body only, not an embodied person."[38]

John Paris, S.J., is the person most prominently associated with this position. "Those who argue," he says, "that quality of life cannot be a consideration in the treatment decisions for such [persistent vegetative] patients are placing the maintenance of mere biological existence above all other considerations."[39] Paris maintains that a quality of life dimension has always been present in Catholic tradition. For instance, a patient with widely disseminated metastatic disease need not receive antibiotics for an intercurrent pneumonia. But, he argues, "absent the quality-of-life judgment, there could be no moral warrant for the withholding of such a simple, inexpensive and effective treatment for a life-threatening condition."

As for the Connery–Kopelman allegation that there are no "manageable criteria" for such a quality-of-life approach, both Callahan and Paris believe that there are: imminently dying and permanent vegetative state.

Dennis Brodeur is decidedly in the Callahan–Paris camp.[40] He rejects Connery's approach to the permanently vegetative patient. Artificial nutrition-hydration that "simply puts off death by maintaining physical existence with no hope of recovery . . . is useless and therefore not ethically obligatory." It is "vitalism" to think otherwise. Brodeur rejects a notion of quality of life that states that a certain arbitrarily defined level of functioning is required before a person's life is to be valued. But if it refers to the relationship between a person's biological condition and the ability to pursue life's goals, it is critical to good decision making. "In some circumstances, science's ability to respond helpfully to allow a person to pursue the goals of life is so limited that treatment may be useless."[41]

That is the way this key issue has been discussed. I agree with the Callahan–Paris–Brodeur approach. Indeed, the vast majority of people with whom I have discussed this question agree without hesitation that it is humanly "useless" and "futile" to provide nutrition-hydration to those in a persistent vegetative state.

At the outset of this chapter I noted that Archbishop Hannan stated of the AMA's position that "the Church strongly condemns this position." I believe that is straightforwardly wrong. Indeed, I believe that those who take such a position have departed from the substance of the Catholic tradition on this matter. That is quite possible if we allow ourselves to get lost in the "casuistry of means." It must be remembered that the abiding substance of the Church's teaching, its rock bottom so to speak, is not found in the ordinary means-extraordinary means terminology. It is found in a basic value judgment about the meaning of life and death, one that refuses to absolutize either. It is *that judgment* that we must carry with us as we face the medical decisions that technology casts up to us. Those who would count mere vegetative life a patient-benefit have, I believe, slipped their grasp on the heart of Catholic tradition in this matter.

Some continue to attempt to finesse this extremely difficult and delicate issue by conceptualizing decisions in terms of "ordinary" and "extraordinary" means. But it will not work. Such terms only disguise the quality-of-life component unavoidably present in some of these decisions. For this reason nearly every recent commentator would agree with the President's Commission when it stated: "The claim, then, that the treatment is extraordinary is more of an expression of the conclusion than a justification for it."

A final caution is in place here. The Claire Conroy case and the decision of the New Jersey Supreme Court may appear to be isolated instances. That is not the case. There are many thousands of nursing home residents like Claire Conroy. They are a terribly vulnerable population. They are elderly and often suffer from crippling disabilities. They often are without surviving relatives. Physicians play a more limited role in nursing homes than in hospitals, and patient advocacy is correspondingly less intense. Furthermore, as the New Jersey Supreme Court notes, nursing homes are often afflicted with industry-wide problems that make them a very troubled and troublesome component of the health care system. And all of this at the very time when there are economic and social pressures on health care delivery. Together these factors may make it extremely difficult to keep patients' best interests at the heart of these decisions. In other words, the potential for abuse is enormous.

We have moved from Quinlan (persistent vegetative state—removal of respirator) to Herbert (persistent vegetative state—removal of respirator, nasogastric tube and IV lines) to Conroy (incompetent but noncomatose—removal of nasogastric tube). The progression is obvious, and obviously dangerous, unless we draw lines based on clear criteria. If we do not, we will not long be confined within the limits set forth in cases like Conroy. Considerations such as this have led Daniel Callahan to conclude that the line should be drawn sharply at imminently dying patients and those in a persistent vegetative state. Presumably, therefore, he would reject the Conroy decision of the New Jersey Supreme Court.

I sympathize with his fears, but am not sure that we need to draw his conclusion *yet*. My doubts can be stated by a letter I received in 1985. It reads as follows.

> As far as I'm concerned the progression to withhold the nasogastric tube is not going fast enough. Nursing homes in New York have become concentration camps for torturing the elderly and not allowing them the right to die with dignity.
>
> I have been a geriatric nurse for fifteen years. I remember when people died with dignity, just gave up the fight to live and gently, painlessly slipped away. That was when a human being was treated like one and every decision was based on the individual case by the people who knew and cared for them twenty-four hours a day. Now the law has become the forerunner of the administration's decision to intubate every patient who does not eat.
>
> What is often overlooked is that most of these patients have their hands tied to the sides of the bed so they cannot pull out the tube. This is where the torture comes in.
>
> In the case of Mrs.____, 93 years old and senile, but physically alert, we have a woman who stopped eating and the tube was ordered, not because the doctor wanted it but because the administration forced the doctor to order it. When the tube was inserted, Mrs.____ fought it tooth and nail with the most awful expression of fear. She was then tied to the bed so she couldn't remove it. She had a constant look of discomfort and futility. It's really a wonderful way of breaking a person's spirit if she has any left at that point. It is very effective for that purpose.

How long is the patient tied? Months, even years! No such decision to insert a feeding tube should be made without consultation involving the doctor, the patient, nurse, and relatives. Yet I have seen the administration inform relatives to take their mother out of the nursing home "unless you allow us to put a tube in."[42]

I cite this letter to indicate that technology can help us or hurt us, individually and societally, and in ways that are awesome in their implications. The recent technological revolution in methods of hydration and nutritional maintenance is a case in point. This revolution challenges us to rediscover, if that is necessary, our substantial concerns in changing times and circumstances.

Notes

1. *Seattle Times,* 14 April 1985.

2. Daniel Callahan, "Feeding the Dying Elderly," *Generations* (Winter 1985): 15-17. Cf. also Callahan, "On Feeding the Dying," *Hastings Center Report* 13 (1983), 22.

3. *Current Opinions* (of the Council on Ethical and Judicial Affairs of the American Medical Association—1986), 9-10. Ronald E. Cranford, M.D., has pointed out the misleading character of the AMA's statement when it refers to "irreversible coma." This is not the same as a "persistent vegetative state." Cf. "The Persistent Vegetative State: The Medical Reality (Getting the Facts Straight)," *Hastings Center Report* 18 (1988), 27 ff.

4. Resolution of the Massachusetts Medical Society, 17 July 1985. This is reported in *The Boston Globe,* 23 May 1985.

5. Cited in *National Catholic Register,* 6 April 1986.

6. Ibid.

7. Brophy v. New England Sinai Hospital, Inc., Massachusetts Probate County Court, Norfolk Division, 21 October 1985 (No. 85E0009-G1).

8. In re Conroy, 486 A 2d 1209 (N.J., 1985).

9. Superior Court of the State of California, No. A 025586, 5 May 1983. Cf. also *Los Angeles Times,* 6 May 1983.

10. Robert Nejdl and Neil Barber v. Superior Court of the State of California for the County of Los Angeles, 2 Civil No. 69351 (Superior Court No. A 025586).

11. *Decisions to Forego Life-Sustaining Treatment* (Washington: Government Printing Office, 1983), 190.

12. Joyce V. Zerwekh, "The Dehydration Question," *Nursing 83* (13 January 1983): 47-51.

13. K. Micetich, P. Steinecker, D. Thomasma, "Are Intravenous Fluids Morally Required for a Dying Patient?" *Archives of Internal Medicine* 143 (1983): 975-78.

14. James Childress and Joanne Lynn, "Must Patients Always Be Given Food and Water?" *Hastings Center Report* 13 (1983), 17-21.

15. S.H. Wanzer, S.J. Adelstein, R.E. Cranford, et al., "The Physician's Responsibility toward Hopelessly Ill Patients," *New England Journal of Medicine* 310 (1984): 955-59. I have been advised that this is not the meaning of the article but is a misinterpretation due to an injudicious paragraph-placement.

16. John J. Paris, S.J., "Withholding or Withdrawing Nutrition and Fluids: What Are the Real Issues?" *Health Progress* 66 (December 1985): 22 ff. Cf. also John J. Paris, S.J. and Richard A. McCormick, S.J., "The Catholic Tradition on the Use of Nutrition and Fluids," *America* 156 (1987): 356-61. That the position we espoused in this article is becoming something of a consensus position is clear from Robert Steinbrook, M.D., and Bernard Lo, M.D., "Artificial Feeding—Solid Ground, Not a Slippery Slope," *New England Journal of Medicine* 318 (1988): 286-90.

17. Personal communication to John Paris, cited with permission.

18. Daniel Callahan, "On Feeding the Dying," *Hastings Center Report* 13 (1983), 22.

19. Callahan as in *Generations* (cf. note 2).

20. Callahan as in *Generations*, 17.

21. Gilbert Meilander, "Against the Stream," *Hastings Center Report* 14 (1984), 11-13.

22. M. Siegler and A. Weisbard, "Against the Emerging Stream: Should Fluids and Nutritional Support be Discontinued?" *Archives of Internal Medicine* 145 (1985): 129-31.

23. Callahan as in note 20, at 16.

24. Paris as in note 16, at 25.

25. Bishops of the Federal Republic of Germany, "Das Lebensrecht des Menschen und die Euthanasie," *Herder Korrespondenz* 29 (1975): 335-37.

26. Callahan as in *Generations*, 17.

27. Meilander as in note 21.

28. Robert Barry, O.P., "The Ethics of Providing Life-Sustaining Nutrition and Fluids to Incompetent Patients," *Journal of Family and Culture* 1 (no. 2, 1985): 23-37, at 34.

29. Callahan as in *Generations*, 15.

30. *L'Osservatore Romano*, English edition, 11 November 1985, 10.

31. As in note 28, at 27.

32. Meilander as in note 21.

33. As in note 11, at 135.

34. Connery's testimony is given in Judge Kopelman's decision as in note 7. His further systematic reflections are found in "Quality of Life," *Linacre Quarterly* 53 (1986): 26-33. Cf. also John R. Connery, S.J., "The Clarence Herbert Case: Was Withdrawal of Treatment Justified?" *Health Progress* 65 (February 1984): 32-35.

35. Barry as in note 28, at 32.

36. Loc. cit., 32-33.

37. *Miami Herald*, 15 November 1985.

38. Callahan as in *Generations*, 17.

39. John J. Paris, S.J., "Critical Life Issues," *Health Progress* 66 (December 1985): 23.

40. Dennis Brodeur, "Feeding Policy Protects Patients' Rights, Decisions," *Health Progress* 66 (June 1985): 38-43.

41. Loc. cit., 41.

42. Personal communication.

Chapter 22

The Physician and Teenage Sexuality

A few facts should set the stage for the question I want to raise in this chapter. Every year in the United States, more than a million teenagers become pregnant.[1] Of this number, 30,000 are under fifteen years of age. The United States leads nearly all developed countries in pregnancies in the age group fifteen to nineteen. Around 45% of the pregnancies end in abortion. Of those that end in childbirth, more than half are illegitimate, and that figure is considerably higher in many areas.

Behind such figures we will find what will surprise no one: a change in attitudes toward sexual conduct, unwed motherhood etc. Fully 20% of fifteen-year-old girls admit to having had sexual intercourse. The figure climbs to around 45% for seventeen-year-olds. Of teenagers who are sexually active, only around 30% use some form of contraception and many of those who do are poorly informed about methodology. Of the abortions now performed in the United States, nearly 30% are performed on teenagers.

From figures such as these we can draw two easy conclusions: (1) There is an enormous problem. (2) This problem is not going away and is not likely to do so in the immediate future. I say "problem" because teenage pregnancies are associated with all sorts of problems: abortion, high divorce rates, financial dependence, school dropoutage, attempted suicide, underprivileged and uncared-for children, increased medical risk. It is widely agreed that the overall consequences of adolescent child-bearing are adverse.

There are many aspects of this phenomenon that could be addressed in a useful way. In this chapter I want to relate it rather narrowly to the physician's possible role in facing it. I say "narrowly" because I want to raise a single practical question: should or may the physician ever give contraceptive information (or, for that matter, natural family planning information), and indeed, contraceptive devices to so-called "sexually active" teenagers?

The question may appear somewhat quaint. After all, in a poll done by Yankelovich, Skelly and White, Inc., for *Time* magazine, 78% of Americans answered yes to the question: "Do you favor sex education in the schools, including information about birth control?"[2] Furthermore, in some places on-campus health clinics that offer contraceptive information and dispense contraceptives have been established. So, what is so problematic about an individual physician, in the privacy of her/his office, prescribing a contraceptive on an individual basis?

I raise this question for two reasons, both methodological in nature. First, it concerns the always thorny problem of cooperation in evil and as such it may be useful in lifting out the structural approach to such problems. Second, it may throw light on the physician's role insofar as this role demands of a physician that he/she practice medicine in accord with the dictates of conscience.

To the question as put, I suspect that there would be two spontaneous but opposite answers. The first would say: "Why *yes*, of course. This is the best and apparently the only way to prevent teenage pregnancy and its terrible consequences." This is especially the case if the spontaneous responder abhors abortion.

There are two sorts of data that tend to indicate that at least very many would respond in this way. One is the Yankelovich poll cited above. Seventeen years ago (1972), a Gallup poll yielded similar results. It revealed that 75% of the American people believed that "birth control information, services and counselling should be made available to unmarried teenagers who are sexually active."[3] Second, "numerous national physician and health organizations have endorsed the physician's right to exercise his medical judgment, free of legal barriers, in the provision of contraceptive care for the best interests of his minor patients."[4] Included are: AMA, American College of Obstetricians and Gynecologists, American Academy of Pediatrics, American Health Association and others.

The second spontaneous answer to the question raised is a firm and final "no." Provision of such information and services encourages, is a contribution to further sexual license, and a betrayal of the physician's responsibility for the *overall health* of his patient. After all, it would be argued, the physician is not just an animated tool responding to those desires and demands. She, too, has a conscience, and her conduct must reflect that.

The Utah Supreme Court seems to support this approach. A trial court had ruled that the requirement of parental consent for contraceptive services to girls older that fourteen and boys over sixteen was a violation of the minor's constitutional right to privacy. The Utah Supreme Court overturned that ruling and argued that "the giving of information or contraceptive paraphernalia to a minor child so as to avoid pregnancy from unlawful sexual relations would certainly tend to make a child of immature judgment more likely to commit the crime of fornication and to become infected with venereal disease, to say nothing of the morals of the situation."[5] The U.S. Supreme Court declined to review the case.

These two opposing views are represented at other levels. For instance, syndicated columnist Ellen Goodman has several times expressed the view that the only thing adults can do for teenagers is help them avoid pregnancy. Eunice Kennedy Shriver sees this as a one-eyed, technologically narrow and ultimately self-defeating approach. She wrote: "I find such statements shocking and demeaning—to parents because they are dismissed as failures; to teenagers because it implies they are without values, or if sexual values are held, they are nothing more than raw pleasure principles."[6] Vera Almon, writing in *America*, agrees: "Children are starving for the kind of counseling that advocates self-control and discipline."[7] So does Dr. Richard V. Lee of Yale University School of Medicine. Speaking specifically to physicians he states:

> The idea of virginity to prevent disease and to control population seems to be something physicians may ignore when teaching about sex or counseling their young patients.[8]

He then added:

> We boast to our young people about our great breakthroughs in preventing pregnancy and treating venereal disease, disregarding the most reliable and specific, the least expensive and toxic, preventative of both gestational and venereal distress—the ancient, honorable and even healthy state of virginity.

This matter broke into the press recently when the then Education Secretary William J. Bennett, in an address to the Education Writers Association, criticized school-based birth control clinics as an "abdication of moral authority." He granted that such clinics might prevent some births, but added: The question is: "what does it encourage, what behaviors does it foster?"[9]

David Andrews, executive vice president of the Planned Parenthood Federation, scoffed at Bennett's view as "moralistic" and said it "goes back to the old argument that ignorance is better."[10]

Here we see concerned people with profoundly different approaches. One can be styled the "get at the causes" approach; the other, the "prevent the consequences" approach. I suspect that since physicians deal so often with the tragic consequences of teenage sexual activity, they will show a marked tendency to the latter approach in their attitudes and practice. Whatever the case, I want to list briefly the elements I think ought to play a role in developing sound physician practice in this area. In order, I will say a word about: (1) premarital intercourse; (2) the role of the physician: (3) the relationship of teenagers to parents and physicians where health care is concerned; (4) pastoral versus moral positions: (5) counseling the lesser evil. Then on the basis of these five considerations, I will attempt to make a statement that could serve as the general basis for a physician's thinking and practice in this area.

1. Premarital intercourse.   The first issue that must be discussed is premarital intercourse. (Some sexually active teenagers are, of course, married. The problems they present to the physician are different and much less intense than those of the nonmarried. So I omit the married teenager from this discussion.) It is the moral character of premarital intercourse that is my concern here. Concretely, if the physician believes that premartial intercourse is not a moral issue in itself—as long as pregnancy is avoided—then there is not much of a moral problem in his aiding the couple in avoiding pregnancy. If, however, he believes that such intimacy is ethically inappropriate conduct whether pregnancy is involved or not, then there is much more of a problem. For provision of contraceptive devices then is a form of cooperation—aiding and abetting—*in a morally wrongful action.* Furthermore, many past moral theologians would view it as formal cooperation, that is, one *necessarily* involving approval of the wrongful action. (I believe that there is room for doubt on this point, as I shall indicate below.) At any rate, the basic moral question is: what is the meaning and purpose of sexual expression?

My own answer to that question, put in impoverishing summary, would be outlined as follows. Sexual intimacy is an expression or sign (a language) of a special kind of relationship. The relationship is one with two closely intertwined and inseparable aspects. It is *total,* sc., the persons are given unreservedly to each other, have taken permanent and public responsibility for each other, have undertaken the risk of shared lives. Second, the relationship is *procreative* in character, sc., is fundamentally related to the procreation and education of children. These two characteristics form the basis of Vatican II's analysis of human sexuality.[11]

Sexual communion is the expression or sign of this relationship. By that I mean it is the existence of the relationship which gives full human meaning to genital sex acts. As Peter Bertocci puts it: "Sexual intercourse is as meaningful as the shared values of the couple."[12] Kalt and Wilkins state it this way: "Their promise to belong to each other always makes it possible for sexual intercourse to mean total giving and total receiving . . . It is the totality of married life that makes intercourse meaningful, and not vice versa."[13] Monogamous marriage is, I realize, in trouble. It needs serious criticism and reshaping. But I would argue, with my tradition—and against all kinds of contemporary nay-sayers—that it is still the best chance we have to humanize our sexuality, because it is the best chance to develop friendship.

All this means that sexual expression, to have *full* human meaning, to be nourishing and promotive of our personhood, to avoid being trivialized, is not just the present moment. It is both affirmation and promise. As language it celebrates the past and guarantees the future. It is the past and future compressed into the present. It is this past and future which offers us present quality. It is the friendship of the past and future which surrounds sex with loyalty, constancy, fidelity and allows it to speak a fully human language. Sex and eros are fleeting, fickle, and frustrative unless they are supported by *philia,* friendship—the friendship of a permanent covenant.

This is descriptive language and *proves* nothing. But it represents my own moral conviction that if sexual intimacy is to remain a truly viable and nourishing language, it must be the language of covenanted friendship (marriage). When it departs from this relationship, it departs from the very goals and values that best protect it. That means that intercourse that is genuinely *premarital* is always missing something—or in normative terms, is morally wrong, is to be avoided.

The significance of this for our present discussion is this: if that is a reasonable account of the meaning and morality of sexual intimacy, then clearly we ought not encourage, or do things that encourage, premarital sexual intimacy. Contrarily, our efforts and our conduct—while avoiding the moralism of unadorned do's and dont's—will be shaped to invite youngsters to grow to share this evaluation of sexual relations. That will be true of parents, educators, counsellors, physicians and all who impinge on the formation of the young. And it will be an important component in attempting to determine physician policy where sexuality is concerned.

2. *The role of the physician.* How the physician conceives his or her role will have profound effects on how he or she responds to different and challenging situations. There are two possible extremes here. The first is that the physician is an animated tool, a technologist to the body and desires of people, and totally without formative counselling and other responsibilities. At the other extreme is the notion of the physician as priest, *in loco parentis,* charged with responsibility for all aspects of the patient's well being, and empowered to be the arbiter of all decisions, even those involving acceptance or rejection of life-preserving treatment. Through the expansion of the notions of health and disease, contemporary medicine is increasingly treating the desires and demands of people in a move toward a discomfortless society. One can understand then how physicians could easily be tempted in two extreme directions in their role definitions: to be mere technologists to the desires of people in a kind of abandonment of the patient, to influence and manipulate and control those desires in a kind of total takeover of the patient.

If the physician is neither an animated tool (mere technologist) nor an all-responsible parent, what is he/she? A little bit of everything. That puts him somewhere between these extremes for two reasons. First it is so because we are the souls of our bodies and the bodies of our souls. That means that the physician treats the person and in doing so is at least indirectly and implicitly involved in all aspects of life that touch personal well-being. It is the person who is born, lives, gets sick, is depressed, misbehaves, overeats, becomes alcoholic, breaks a leg, dies. These happenings are not independent of life-styles, value-preferences, family relations, states of conscience. A physician's ministering to the person means somehow or other touching or being involved with all of these aspects of the person. That is why the physician's role is somewhat kaleidoscopic. Inevitably at times he is advising, consoling, fathering, ordering, teaching. And because of that he cannot act as if his actions and prescriptions are merely technical. Whether he wishes it or not, the physician in his practice is a value communicator or teacher.

The second reason is that the physician is herself a person. By that I mean to suggest that the physician, while she is the servant of the patient (not the master), is not the slave to the patient's demands, or even others' desires or demands. As a professional *person* she is a member of society and as such is responsible also to (1) the public (her competence and conduct must inspire confidence); (2) to the profession (her actions must promote the integrity of the profession); (3) to herself (her actions must be compatible with her convictions, otherwise she tears herself apart). That is, she must practice her profession according to her conscience, to her well-informed judgment about what is right and wrong. That does not mean that she imposes her values on the patient, as I have already noted. It means minimally that (1) she cannot pretend that her actions, decisions, advice are value-free; (2) she may not allow the patient to impose his/her values on her.

This is an extremely difficult and delicate role to play, to walk a balanced middle path. Some never succeed. They become mere technologists for the desires or demands of patients (or society) or they become moralists. All I am trying to say here is that the physician does teach in his healing and ministering role and he teaches as a person with a conscience, and this must be taken into account in determining physician-policy with regard to teenage sexuality. Put negatively, if the physician were a *mere* tool or technician, there would be no problem. Nor would there be a problem (for him/

her) if he/she were *mere* moralist. He would simply refuse all contraceptive services to all unmarried persons.

3. The relationship of teenagers to parents and physicians where health care is concerned. Traditionally, teenagers (that is, minors) have been regarded in law as incompetent to consent for their own medical care. Therefore parental consent was required and a physician treating a minor without parental consent faced the risk of liability.

In our time, however, a loosening has occurred. With the reduction of majority from twenty-one to eighteen, there has been increasing recognition of maturity in teenagers. States have endorsed the "mature minor doctrine" by which a minor who is sufficiently mature to understand the nature and consequences of a medical treatment proposed for her/his benefit may effectively consent to it. Some states have enacted specific legislation affirming the right of individuals younger than eighteen to consent to medical care in general, or to pregnancy-related services, including contraception. The legal right of an eighteen-year-old unmarried woman to consent to contraceptive services is established. In many states even young people under eighteen have the right to obtain contraceptive services.

I am not interested in pursuing the legal status at great length. I introduce it to make several points of importance concerning a physician's policy in this regard.

(a) With the increasing recognition of the unmarried minor's rights to contraceptive services, it is important that we understand that right. It is a right to *pursue* (not to be impeded, interfered with) contraceptive services and, as far as the physician is concerned, a right to provide such services without penalty. It is above all a right qualifying and restricting the need for parental consent. (The Reagan administration attempted to control the access of teenagers to contraception via the so-called "squeal rule." This rule required that federally funded clinics notify parents within ten days that contraceptives had been prescribed. The squeal rule did not survive the courts.) The right of the teenager is not a right to *demand* contraceptive services from any particular physician, a kind of right of entitlement whereby the physician is liable for not providing such services. Unless we understand this distinction, we may conclude erroneously that such laws solve the policy question for the individual physician.

(b) Enactment of laws enabling teenagers to have access to contraceptive services does not preempt the moral question of whether it is right or wrong to provide such services for individual teenagers. It simply removes legal obstacles to such a determination. Pragmatic Americans often confuse (by identifying) legality with morality. That is, if something is made legal by removal from the penal code, they tend to think it is thereby morally right, as I have noted in chapter 17.

(c) Legislative provision of access (via the physician) to contraceptive services for minors without parental consent does not mean that all parents should or will approve of a physician's providing such services to their children. More people approve birth control education than would approve health programs that give contraceptive services to teenage girls who request them.

Whether one agrees with their reasons or not, one can understand why parents might object to this. It *seems* to promote permissiveness; it *seems* to infringe on parental educational prerogatives and responsibilities, etc. (I say "seems" to promote permissiveness because most data indicate that sexual activity among teenagers is not affected by the nonavailability of contraceptives. As Allen J. Wilcox noted more than ten years ago: "Little relationship seems to exist between the availability of birth control and sexual activity. In fact, most sexual relationships between adolescents develop without benefit of regular contraceptive use."[14] This is true today and the reason for it has become even clearer. Teenage pregnancy is very often a socioeconomic problem. Poverty is often accompanied by a sense of fatalism, deprivation, boredom. Pregnancy gives status, a sense of being someone. Many poor young girls *want* to have babies.)

Clearly, a physician runs certain risks for himself and the profession if his policies incur the wrath of parents. This is especially true where the physician's policy is indiscriminate—that is, where the physician dispenses almost mechanically contraceptive services to any teenager who requests them or where he positively suggests this even where the teenager does not so request.

4. Pastoral procedure and moral statements. To develop a sound policy on teenage sexuality, it is important to understand the difference between moral statements and pastoral procedures or accommodations. I have discussed this above; but it bears repetition here. A moral statement (as I shall understand it here for our purpose) is a statement of the rightness or wrongness of human actions. It is a statement embodying the good and inviting to its realization. In this sense it is normative, that is, we all *ought* to try to make our conduct a reflection of the values incorporated in such statements or principles.

Let me give an example from an admittedly controversial area—abortion. It has been a Christian conviction—variously expressed—that it is wrong to kill nascent human life except when the only alternative is greater loss of life (mother and child). In other words, it is morally objectionable to sacrifice fetal life except to save the mother's life. I do not want to debate this statement here. I give it simply as an example of a moral statement.

A pastoral statement or approach is not simply identifiable with a moral statement. It takes into account the personal biography, strength, weaknesses, circumstances, education, etc. of the individual. Or again, it is the responsibility of an individual to assimilate and appropriate the values incorporated into moral statements. Sometimes an individual is simply incapable of doing this—whether the reason be personal suffering, education, home life, intractable emotional revulsion or simple judgmental error.

When this happens, the moral counsellor (or parent, or physician or anyone whose role involves teaching, whether direct or implied) can reach a point when it is fruitless to insist on or invite to a course of action that he knows to be fully right. Not being able to change matters or alter perspectives, we try to wrest from a tragic situation the maximum of good—or what is the same, we minimize the evils that we cannot change or prevent. I mention this difference between a *moral* statement and a *pastoral* procedure to underline the idea that certain pastoral responses (accommodating to the individual's circumstances) need not imply abandonment of or compromise with one's moral convictions. It simply represents a realistic acceptance of the individual where that individual is—however regretfully or even wrongly.

An example will help. Let us suppose I accept the indissolubility of Catholic marriage and understand by this the moral impossibility of a second marriage after the first has broken up and is beyond salvage. If, notwithstanding this conviction, a divorced Catholic came to me for help— *determined* to enter a second union, one which I would judge to be morally wrong, and there was nothing I could do to dissuade the individual from this course of action—it would not be abandonment of my principles or a compromise thereof if at some point I urged the individual at least to take those steps and build those precautions that would help promote the stability of the second union. Equivalently, I would be saying: if you are determined on this course of action—with which I disagree—and I cannot dissuade you, I want to accept you where you are and help you to make of this situation the best we can. The key word here is: the person is *determined* to perform a particular action. If the person is not so determined, then my advice or aid takes on the character of suasion. This will have obvious application where provision of contraceptive services to teenagers is concerned.

One form of the distinction between moral statements and pastoral procedures is the matter of counseling the lesser evil. I want to say a word about that—a word that will fill out what is given only initially here.

5. Counselling the lesser evil. One who provides, and all the more so one who *suggests*, the use of contraceptive devices, seems *to some extent or other* to approve of them and encourage them, to counsel their use. Is that morally proper? The question can be argued as follows: If we disapprove of premarital relations (particularly among teenagers, and most particularly among very young teenagers), is one not approving and encouraging the very thing one disapproved by providing services that make such conduct easier, risk-free? In technical ethical language, this would seem to be *formal* cooperation in wrongdoing, a form of cooperation that involves approval of the wrong and hence is seen as morally wrong itself. Phyllis Schlafly summarizes this by insisting that there is no way of telling youngsters about contraception "without implicitly telling them that sex is O.K. You've put your Good Housekeeping seal on it."[15]

I do not wish to enter a long technical discussion here. I will only detail the conclusion of a long historical discussion in moral literature.[16] It is this: it is *sometimes* permissible to counsel the lesser evil. For instance, if one is about to steal $1000 and I cannot otherwise prevent the theft, I could urge him to take only $100. Or again, if one is determined to murder someone and I am powerless to stop him, I could persuade him to get drunk instead. Ethicists defend this because the object of the counsel is not evil but good— that is, the lesser evil precisely *as lesser.* Two conditions are always given to justify this: (a) the person counselled is determined to and prepared for the commission of the greater evil; (b) there is no other way of preventing the greater evil.

Let me apply this to the physician and the teenager. First, I think we can agree that intercourse without pregnancy following is a lesser evil than intercourse with pregnancy ensuing. I speak, of course, of the unmarried teenager. Second, given our cultural atmosphere and the situation of some youngsters, it is clear that some teenagers are going to be sexually active with or without contraceptives. In this sense, they are detemined to the commission of wrongdoing. (I already mentioned the fact that lack of contraceptives does not affect teenage sexual activity significantly.) Third, there certainly could be cases where the physician (and anyone else) is powerless to deter such activity.

To me that means that there are times when provision of contraceptive services is tantamount to counselling the lesser evil, and could be ethically permissible. Equivalently, the physician is saying: if you must be irresponsible, at least diminish the effects of your irresponsibility by not bringing a child into the world in disastrous circumstances. If the physician is careful to make this clear by his attitudes, actions, and words, then I do not see that provision of contraceptives to an unmarried teenager *necessarily* involves or expresses his approval of conduct he judges to be morally wrong.

These are the basic considerations that will go into the building of a physician's policy in this matter. There may be others but these are essential. I will now shake and mix the ingredients to see how they come out. I realize that there may be disagreements on several of these ingredients— especially the morality of premarital intimacy and the role of the physician.

Therefore I cannot conclude to what every physician ought to do (though I would like to). I can only suggest what I would do were I the physician, and then let others reflect on this to see whether it makes sense to them.

Were I a physician, I believe my policy would be the following:

(1) Avoid giving contraceptive services
(2) unless the unmarried teenager is going to remain sexually active
(3) and there is no reasonable way that I can alter that situation.

A word about each statement.

(1) *Avoid giving contraceptive services.* There are many reasons for this. (a) I believe that something is always lacking in premarital sexual relations, the more so the younger and more unstable the relationship. That is, I believe it is morally wrong and conduct to be avoided. (b) Provision of contraceptive services unavoidably aids and abets the teenager—is a form of cooperation. (c) In doing so, it risks teaching the youngster and confirming him/her in conduct I judge to be personally and socially irresponsible. (d) In doing this, it is all too easy to undermine the integrity of the medical profession. (e) In spite of the laws making access to contraceptive services legal without parental consent, there are certainly very many parents who would resent this—a resentment that only deepens the problems of the physician and his profession.

The thrust of this statement ("avoid giving contraceptive services") is that I would not easily accede to requests of the teenager for such services. There are just too many strong objections to doing so.

(2) *Unless the unmarried teenager is going to remain sexually active.* I say "unless." That means my policy would be a *general* one, not an absolute one. It means that there are times when I believe the provision of such services is justifiable. (Some physicians might conclude that they will *never* get involved in this, that the teenager can always go to someone else. There is much to recommend this attitude and I will not criticize it or argue that it is untenable. All I want to say is that I do not see this as the only justifiable conclusion for all cases. In other words, while the physician is not *obliged* to provide such services, he *may* justify doing so ethically at times.)

The specific ground or warrant here is that the teenager is judged to be one who is going to remain sexually active regardless of efforts to the contrary. This is a judgment not always easy to make. To make it with a fair degree of assurance means that the physician will have to get to know the person and the person's circumstances. If I were to provide contraceptive services without such knowledge, I would feel myself irresponsible—indeed, I would judge that I was involved in a type of cooperation calculated to confirm the individual in irresponsible conduct. I would be compounding a bad situation.

(3) *And there is no reasonable way that I can alter that situation.* My own understanding of the physician's role, especially with regard to teenagers, is that far more than he may like it, the physician is physician-teacher-parent-protector in some situations. We must not forget that these young people are children. Furthermore, they are often poor, deprived, uneducated and frequently enough family-less children without supervision of any kind, all but living their lives in the streets, exposed to and formed by the ethic that prevails there. Desires to help such children encounter enormous obstacles. To think otherwise would be unrealistic and a failure in physician responsibility. To me that means that the physician—again, like it or not—is in a value-communicator role. He is not just a technician responding to desires or demands. Therefore he should do all *reasonably* possible to communicate solid values.

The word "reasonably" is crucial. Where the line is to be drawn depends on a host of circumstances I cannot detail here: circumstances of the patient (age, family, education, past history), circumstances of the physician (personality, acquaintance with patient, relation with family, hospital connections, etc.). What I am suggesting is that there is a line beyond which physician attempts would be counterproductive. Probably only prudence and common sense can draw this line.

After this point has been reached, I myself would, as a physician, feel it necessary to state that I do not approve or condone premarital intimacy in giving contraceptive services. I would make it clear to the person that I am doing this with great reluctance and sadness, and only because of the tragedies so often inseparable from teenage, unmarried pregnancies. Furthermore, I would feel irresponsible if provision of such services were more than a relatively rare exception.

Ultimate justification for this approach is rooted in the notion that provision of contraceptive services *need not* involve encouragement and approval of premarital relationships and especially promiscuity. If such provision becomes routine, I believe it does involve encouragement and approval. But within the conditions as stated, it need not when it occurs as a rare exception. It can be encouragement of the lesser evil in circumstances where human prudence tells me that there is no other way to avoid the greater evil, or risk thereof.

In conclusion, two final glosses should be stated. First, the analysis presented in this chapter does not stand or fall with the Church's teaching on contraception. The pivotal moral issue is premarital sex. Concretely, one could accept the analysis presented here even if he/she regarded contraception as morally wrong. Similarly, one could reject my analysis even if he/she disagreed with *Humanae Vitae*.

Second, the analysis presented here does not and cannot take account of all local and personal circumstances. It is quite possible that such circumstances would lead to a different conclusion in individual cases. That suggests that physicians must constantly reexamine their policies in light of changing circumstances.

This chapter has been about a case. The case turned on teenage sexuality. It could have been organized around a hundred different subjects in medicine. That means that its most important aspect is that of vehicle—a vehicle for inviting medical professionals to ask themselves in a very personal way who they are as professionals, what is the end and purpose of medicine, what are the virtues of the medical professional. These are, I believe, the key moral questions to be put to and weighed by medical professionals.

Even more generally, and more importantly, such questions point to the shift in moral emphasis and pedagogy mentioned in chapter 1, a shift that highlights values and life-styles. As such, they constitute a general challenge to all of us to put the right questions to ourselves as we try to live out the ideals of the Lord in our lives. These questions are not the types that have clean-cut answers. Rather they leave us in a peaceful and serene state of discomfort and with an abiding sense of incompleteness. The mature Christian should and does have many answers. One he/she does not have concerns the answer-giver. That is the way it should be.

Notes

1. These and the following figures are from *Time,* 9 December 1985.

2. *Time,* loc. cit.

3. Loc. cit.

4. Loc. cit.

5. Eve W. Paul, "Pregnancy, Teenagers and the Law, 1974," *Family Planning Perspectives* (Summer 1974): 145.

6. *Washington Star,* 3 July 1977.

7. Vera Almon, "Sexual Liberation, V.D. and Our Children," *America* 137 (1977): 171.

8. *National Observer,* 20 January 1973.

9. *Washington Post,* 12 April 1986.

10. *Washington Post,* loc. cit.

11. *Documents,* 252-56.

12. Peter Bertocci, *The Human Venture in Sex, Love and Marriage* (New York: Association Press, 1949). Cf. also *Sex, Love and the Person* (New York: Sheed & Ward, 1967).

13. William J. Kalt and Ronald J. Wilkins, *Man and Woman* (Chicago: Regnery, 1967), 25, 27.

14. Allen J. Wilcox, "The Pediatrician and the Prevention of Adolescent Pregnancy," *Clinical Pediatrics* 14 (1975): 226-31.

15. *Time,* loc. cit., 89.

16. The various positions may be found in the so-called "manuals" of moral theology authored by the likes of Noldin, Genicot, Merkelbach, et al.

INDEX